An Assembly Language Introduction to Computer Architecture

An Assembly Language Introduction to Computer Architecture

Using the Intel Pentium

KAREN MILLER
University of Wisconsin, Madison

New York • Oxford
OXFORD UNIVERSITY PRESS
1999

Oxford University Press

Oxford New York

Athens Auckland Bangkok Bogotá Buenos Aires Calcutta
Cape Town Chennai Dar es Salaam Delhi Florence Hong Kong Istanbul
Karachi Kuala Lumpur Madrid Melbourne Mexico City Mumbai
Nairobi Paris São Paulo Singapore Taipei Tokyo Toronto Warsaw

and associated companies in
Berlin Ibadan

Published by Oxford University Press, Inc.
198 Madison Avenue, New York, New York, 10016
http://www.oup-usa.org

Library of Congress Cataloging-in-Publication Data

Miller, Karen, 1962–
An assembly language introduction to computer architecture : using
the Intel pentium / Karen Miller.
p. cm.
Includes index.
ISBN 0–19–512376–X (cloth)
1. Computer architecture. 2. Assembler language (Computer program
language) I. Title
QA76.9.A73M55 1999
004.2'2—dc21 98—27757
CIP

Editor's Note: This text is based on *A Programmer's View of* Computer Architecture: With Assembly Language Examples from the *MIPS RISC Architecture* by James Goodman and Karen Miller. The first edition was published in 1993 © Saunders College Publishing and subsequently transferred to Oxford University Press. All material herein and any changes to the original Work are the result of work initiated by the Publisher and Karen Miller.

Printing (last digit): 9 8 7 6 5 4 3 2 1

Printed in the United States of America
on acid-free paper

CONTENTS

PREFACE

Why teach assembly language programming? Twenty years ago, the answer to this question was easy: "Real programmers do it in assembly." A decade ago, the answer to this question was still easy: Compilers are not efficient, and if you want the ultimate performance, you have to do it in assembly. Today, that statement is arguably no longer true. Compilers are capable of generating extremely high-quality code, and the best can generate more efficient code than a human. A human often can duplicate the efficiency only by using the same tedious algorithms that the compiler uses. So why teach assembly language? Does it even belong in the undergraduate curriculum?

The answer is definitely yes, but for reasons that were hardly recognized a decade ago. As the software and user interface become more complex, the hardware becomes increasingly obscured by the abstractions built on top of it. Students must know where the software stops and the hardware begins. What are the capabilities of the hardware? What does the software build on? These questions are fundamental to understanding computer architecture and computer science. All students should have a good intuitive model of the hardware. This is important for those investigating computability as well as those selecting algorithms. Proficiency in programming at this level is not so important; understanding the capabilities of the machine at this level is critical.

OBJECTIVES AND COVERAGE

This text is intended to introduce the basic concepts of assembly language programming as a means of introducing computer architecture. The reader should have completed an introductory course involving programming in a high-level language. Typically, this text is used for the second or third course a student might take in a computer science or computer engineering curriculum. This text covers the material of a four-credit, semester-long course. It can be used for a shorter course with the omission of some material.

This text utilizes a proven top-down approach to the material. An abstract (registerless) assembly language is introduced first. This approach capitalizes on the students' previous knowledge, programming in a high-level language. In the traditional, bottom-up approach to teaching assembly language, the student uses little previous learning, starting from scratch with bits, bytes, fields, and formats. Many concepts must be taught before anything can be covered in depth: number representation, memory organization, the instruction cycle, addressing modes, exception handling, and so forth. The top-down approach, in contrast to the bottom-up approach, has the student building on previous knowledge. Students can write code from the beginning. Complicated examples can be introduced immediately, and the topics can be introduced one at a time, in a comfortable order. The concept of registers, for example, is not introduced until Chapter 9. Thus the urgency to present many of the topics of this material is eliminated, and the important topics can be introduced sequentially, in a carefully chosen order. This top-down approach is superior with respect to student learning. It facilitates understanding the motivation behind computer architecture design, and it allows students to see how the topic they are reading about fits into the big picture.

SUGGESTIONS FOR TEACHING

This textbook is written with both the student and the instructor in mind. Each chapter has a summary and a set of practice problems. These problems are suitable for independent student practice. The problems are also suitable for instructor use as homework and programming projects.

Central to an assembly language programming course is the programming. The book itself has been written to be nearly independent of a specific software tool. Writing and testing programs is a matter of having a computer of the right architecture, an assembler, a linker, and some sort of debugger. The abstract assembly language, called SASM, is implemented by a set of macros. These macros are currently available and provided for use with Microsoft's assembler. An easy-to-use environment for programming and debugging is Microsoft's Visual C++ tools. It gives a simple I/O interface, and provides all the features that any programmer could want. It supports single stepping through code, and also shows all register values at the touch of a button. The instructor's manual for this text describes the details for the use of these tools. Note that with the tools, students can write and debug assembly language programs without fear of crashing machines.

A web site for this text is located at

`http://www.cs.wisc.edu/~smoler/x86text.html`

The web site will maintain a list of text errata, lecture notes to go with the text, and macros to use with programming tools, along with other useful items.

There is quite a bit of variability in the amount of material that is taught in an assembly language course. This text contains more material than can be covered in many courses. Additionally, the emphasis placed on various topics varies tremendously from instructor to instructor. Many treat the subjects of number systems and data representation as review, allowing very little course time to be spent on them. Some would rather skip the subject of floating point arithmetic entirely in an assembly language course. The chapter on floating point arithmetic is correctly placed in a logical order, directly following the chapter on integer arithmetic. The floating point arithmetic chapter is written in such a way that it may be covered out of order, or it may be skipped. The remainder of the text does not build upon or depend upon the floating point arithmetic material. The final three chapters in the text attempt to provide some insight into more advanced topics, those not covered by traditional assembly language courses. The point of the chapters is to interest the student in exploring the more advanced topics within the field of computer architecture. Again, courses lacking the time to cover these chapters may omit them.

A CHAPTER-BY-CHAPTER OUTLINE

This text contains 17 chapters. The first 14 chapters are central to understanding all aspects of assembly language. The last three cover some basics of subjects relevant to computer architecture. There are also sections of the early chapters that present more advanced topics. A chapter-by-chapter description of the text follows, outlining the material covered in each chapter.

1. **Background and Introduction**. The introductory chapter presents an overview of where assembly language fits into computer science. The concept of **levels of abstraction** is used to drive the discussion. A brief history of computer development and Intel's architectural family of processors is included.
2. **Computer Basics**. The chapter concentrates on illuminating those very basic concepts such as what the various components of a computer system are, and how memory works. A discussion on the instruction fetch and execute cycle as it applies to the assembly language programmer's model of a computer is included. A simple model of a computer is given to drive the discussion of what happens when. Performance is discussed.
3. **SASM—Simple Abstract Language**. Since readers of the text are presumed to understand a high-level language before tackling assembly language programming, this chapter presents a simple assembly language that bridges the gap between high-level languages and the intricate details of an architecture. This allows readers to begin programming in an assembly language at once while the language hides the details of the architecture. High-level language code is written in C.
4. **Number Systems**. Binary, octal, and hexadecimal are introduced by way of a discussion of the requirements for number systems in general. Noninteger systems (floating point) are presented, along with a discussion of accuracy and precision.
5. **Data Representation**. This chapter addresses the constraints imposed in representing data in fixed-size memory cells. The integer representations of unsigned, sign magnitude, one's and two's complement, and biased integers are detailed in an architecturally independent manner. A floating point section and a character section contain discussions and examples of standard representations.
6. **Arithmetic and Logical Operations**. The chapter title is descriptive of this chapter's contents. The arithmetic operations of addition, subtraction, multiplication, and division are described for the various integer representations. Logical operations and shift/rotate operations are also discussed.
7. **Floating Point Arithmetic**. Although this chapter only skims the surface of material relating to floating point arithmetic, it does provide a solid introduction to the IEEE Floating Point Standard operations of addition, subtraction, and multiplication. Division is not thoroughly covered. Rounding algorithms and the importance of standards are briefly covered.

8. **Data Structures**. The data structures arrays, stacks, and queues are discussed in their relation to assembly language programming. Implementation of operations on the data structures in assembly language is presented.
9. **Using Registers for Efficiency**. Registers form the necessary link between the simple assembly language and the Pentium architecture. One-, two-, and three-address architectures are introduced to motivate the use of registers and addressing modes.
10. **The Pentium Architecture**. The details of a substantive subset of the Pentium instruction set are presented along with examples. Addressing modes and memory models are also discussed.
11. **Procedures**. The general topic of procedure implementation in assembly language is covered in the chapter. Topics include: setup, calls and returns from procedures, saving return addresses, preservation of register values, usage of stack frames, and parameter passing.
12. **The Assembly Process**. Assembly language to machine code translation is covered in sufficient detail such that a student should be able to hand generate machine code. Code relocation, linking, and loading are discussed as an advanced topic.
13. **Input and Output**. This chapter is intended to give a broad introduction to I/O, particularly as seen by the programmer. It contains descriptions of devices, and it covers the concepts of memory mapped I/O and DMA.
14. **Interrupts and Exception Handling**. This chapter introduces the difficult concept of exception handling. The discussion centers on alternatives for both hardware and software implementations.
15. **Features for Architectural Performance**. Once the basic material (Chapters 1–14) has been covered, advanced subjects relating to improving performance of architectures and implementations can be discussed. The topics of memory hierarchies (caching) and pipelining are covered.
16. **Architecture in Perspective**. A discussion is presented of some of the driving forces behind the field of computer architecture, plus the details of other architectures such as Cray 1, MIPS RISC, Motorola 68000 family, and other more modern architectures. This chapter aims at providing some perspective on the history of computer architecture design, keeping an eye on where the field is headed.
17. **Memory Management and Virtual Memory**. This chapter contains both the motivation and the architectural features needed to support virtual memory. The basics of real and virtual addressing, paging, segmentation, and design tradeoffs are discussed.

ACKNOWLEDGMENTS

I have been fortunate to have the help of many people in producing this version of the text. My thanks go to:

James Goodman for coauthoring the original text, *A Programmer's View of Computer Architecture,* with me. This current text found its genesis in that earlier work. **Perry Kivolowitz** for helping to get me started using the tools to do what I wanted, when no one else seemed to be able to. **Rodney Rushing** at Microsoft for giving me technical support to make the tools work. **Ariel Tamches** for setting me straight on SPARC details. **Andy Glew** for developing my understanding of Intel's exception-handling mechanism. **Mark D. Hill** for discussing coverage of topics in the text. **Jim Smith** for reading chapters and providing technical details. The comments were, as always, right on target and of enormous help. **Bart Miller** for providing encouragement at every stage of this project, advice on many issues, and most of all for writing a chapter on virtual memory.

CHAPTER 1

BACKGROUND AND INTRODUCTION

The area of study referred to as computer science can be thought of as the study of the many pieces of computer science. Compilers are the crucial programs that allow programmers to write high-level language programs when the computers those programs execute on do not execute high-level language programs. Artificial intelligence studies various ways to make computers think and make intelligent choices. The area of computer architecture deals with the interface between the computer's software and its hardware. This text is about that interface. It is about what the hardware must be able to do in order to make the software possible, and what the software looks like at this interface.

Over the course of years, both hardware and software have become increasingly complex. To deal with the complexity of design and use, computer scientists have found it useful to create abstractions. An **abstraction** is a simplified picture of the relevant information, including those aspects that are important for the question at hand, but excluding extraneous detail. The designer can then focus on a single important aspect of the problem without becoming bogged down in many details that are irrelevant to the problem being addressed. Often it is possible to introduce new concepts to capture the essence of an idea without having to remember the details. Such an abstraction is said to be a **model**.

This chapter is about abstractions and how they apply to computer architecture.

1.1 LEVELS OF ABSTRACTION

People frequently use abstractions in everyday life. These abstractions constitute a hierarchy that orders the abstraction. A map is a commonly used abstraction. Near the most abstract or highest level of abstraction might be a map of one of our planet's continents. Such a map will often show the boundaries between countries, large cities, and large bodies of water. Alternatively, a map may show the largest of physical features, such as mountain ranges, deserts, lakes, and rivers.

A road map is a commonly used abstraction. It contains limited information about certain roads, such as connecting roads, the towns they pass through, and the size of each road. It also leaves out a lot of detail. Curves are often not shown, nor are hills. Sometimes local roads are not shown at all. A map captures the notion of a route, often better than the road itself. On a map, a route is a continuous line, often designated by a number, suggesting the way a traveler might go from one place to another. A person planning a trip makes plans by selecting a route that creates a continuous line from the point of origin to destination. In reality, a route is another abstraction, just a collection of streets, roads, and highways that connect together, with some street signs placed at strategic points to help travelers find their way. (Signs are also abstractions.) Often there are other ways that are just as good, or even better, but the map may not show them at all.

An abstract model allows details to be ignored while capturing the essence of a problem. Different models are appropriate for different problems. A biking map of a city highlights different aspects from one intended to be used by motorists, and a hand-drawn map showing how to get to a person's house has little resemblance to the road map one might use if only the street address were known. The model allows one to reason within the constraints of the abstraction, and to make decisions and obtain results that are useful after the model is discarded. Associated with the model are a set of **primitives**, or elementary operations that can be applied. These primitives can be characterized in ways that reflect cost and function in terms appropriate for the abstraction. For example, a map may have numbers indicating distances between points. The numbers can be used to compute the distance necessary to travel from one place to another. There are two different primitives for determining distance: (1) Measure the distance with a ruler and use the scaling factor or chart to determine the straight-line distance between the points, and (2) add up the distance indicators on the map along the route. The primitive used depends on what question is being asked. Both primitives provide the capability to determine distances without traveling from one point to the other to measure them.

Figure 1.1 shows a simplified road map containing four towns. Measuring the distance between Middleton and Seaside with a ruler gives 1 kilometer. This is the straight-line distance between the two towns. The distance that an automobile would travel to get

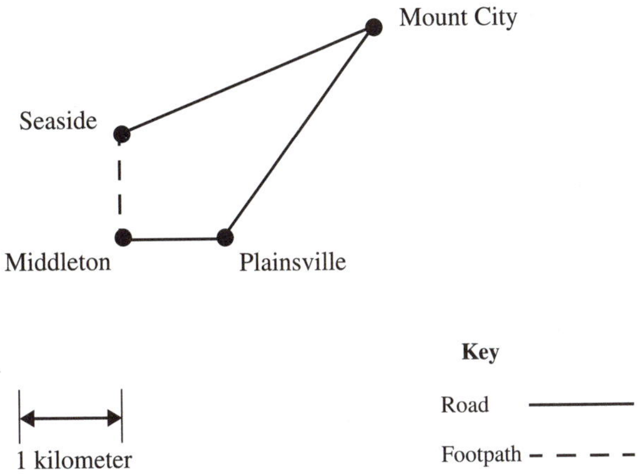

Figure 1.1 Sample road map with distances.

between the two towns can be calculated by summing the distance indicators, 1 + 2 + 2 = 5 kilometers. Assuming the map is to scale, a pedestrian seeking to minimize walking distance would be better off to measure the distance with a ruler.

Abstractions are often built on top of other abstractions. A highway map often includes more detailed maps of cities. The traveler to a large city, nevertheless, will probably require a still more detailed map to navigate within the city. While the highway map may show a city as a single point, its detailed map will show only the major streets, and a street map of the city will show all the streets. Each level of abstraction is appropriate in its place.

Another example of the use of abstractions is the basketball coach who uses a diagram with Xs and Os to explain a play. The fact that the Xs and Os are humans having arms and legs is irrelevant. The color of their clothes is also irrelevant. The abstraction of the diagram captures the relevant information of the starting position of the various players along with the direction that they should move in order to execute the play. It tells how many players are on each team, but it does not relate irrelevant details such as the current score or the number of people watching the game.

Computer-Related Abstractions

One of the more important contributions of computer science to date is a better understanding of complexity. The use of abstractions is one of the keys to understanding. A computer system is extremely complex, consisting of millions of components. Some programs written for computers are candidates for the most complex problems humans deal with. Modern computers are so complex that one person cannot hope to remember the interactions among all their parts. A series of abstract models has been developed to help with this problem, and to help in predicting how a computer might behave in a given situation. While far from perfect, these models help enormously in both the design and use of computers. The models are **hierarchical**. Higher, more abstract models are built upon lower-level, more detailed models. The lowest-level models are simple in that they consist of only a few types of components and primitives, and they are typically small because they capture only a tiny part of the computer. Higher levels in the hierarchy build on these primitive models, providing abstractions such as programming languages and applications like spreadsheets and word processors.

The use of levels of abstraction in software design allows the programmer to focus on a critical set of problems without having to deal with irrelevant details. For example, a procedure or function allows the programmer to create an operation of arbitrary complexity. The procedure is invoked with a minimal amount of information: those aspects that can vary from one invocation to another. The actions taken by the procedure are not specified, but rather understood to be primitives, and in fact, the lower-level details of how the procedure accomplishes its function are often intentionally hidden. One procedure may invoke another procedure, which may in turn invoke yet another, and at each level the function is defined, but the implementation of the function is obscured.

Shielding the implementation details of a procedure makes possible many implementations. The procedure may be a program written in the same language as the program that called it, or it might be a program written in a different language, or it might be a command directly executed by a piece of hardware. The point is that the programmer does not need to be concerned with the details of the procedure and does not know, or even care, how it is implemented. Thinking of a program as a procedure allows the construction of more complex programs that can specify increasingly sophisticated actions without having to specify how the actions are accomplished.

This layered approach is carried on at many different levels, making possible high-level languages that accomplish complicated operations while communicating with the user through a simple dialogue or by pointing at and clicking on icons with the use of a mouse. Low-level languages are also possible. Their operations are very simple but efficient and are used primarily to build up more complicated operations that can be used in a higher-level language.

1.2 FROM PROGRAM TO EXECUTION

At the lowest, most detailed portion of a computer's hardware design are its transistors. Transistors are essentially simple electrical switches. They are designed to produce one of two values. These two values are often referred to as ON and OFF or as 1 and 0. The circuitry of a computer passes around these 1s and 0s, sometimes storing them and doing logical operations on them at other times. In creating a computer design with the transistors, an abstraction is provided. The computer hardware offers a small, fixed number of operations or **instructions** that it can perform. While each instruction may be simple, collectively the instructions define the total capabilities of the computer. The instruction set defines a programming language, and therefore provides the interface between the hardware of the computer and the software that can be written for the computer. This interface is known as a **computer architecture**. The programming language provided by the architecture is called **machine language**.

A programmer wants to write programs in a high-level language such as C++, C, Fortran, or Pascal. These languages provide a clean, abstract way of representing data structures and implementing algorithms. They are far removed from the language offered by a modern computer architecture. It is important to note that any programming language can be used to define a computer architecture. It would be possible to build a computer that directly executes C++ statements. Computers such as this do not exist for two reasons.

```
55
8b ec
83 ec 08
53
56
57
c7 45 fc 01 00
c7 45 f8 00 00
83 7d fc 14
0f 8f 12 00 00 00
8b 45 fc
0f af 45 fc
01 45 f8
ff 45 fc
e9 e4 ff ff ff
```

Figure 1.2 Sample machine language code from the Pentium architecture.

First, the code executed by this computer must consist only of C++ statements. Programs written in other programming languages could not be directly executed by such a machine. They would need to be translated to C++ before execution, and this would require a program to do the translation. The second reason for not implementing a computer to execute a high-level language directly is more compelling. A high-performance architecture comes about, in part, by designing an instruction set that can be implemented to execute quickly. The kinds of operations that can be executed quickly are simple ones. An example of a simple instruction is one that adds two integer values together. A high-performance architecture could not be built to execute directly the complex operations that C++, or any high-level language, defines.

So, the language that the programmer wants to use is far removed from the machine language offered by the computer. Machine language code for a small portion of a program on a Pentium architecture is given in Figure 1.2. The machine code is part of an executable program. It contains several instructions. Given that the machine language is given with 1s and 0s, a logical first step toward making it easier to read is to combine the 1s and 0s into fewer digits. The digits in the figure are hexadecimal digits. A next step is to identify instructions by separating them. The figure has already done this step as well, placing the encoding for each instruction on a separate line. There are fields within each instruction that identify what the instruction does and the variables involved. The machine code from Figure 1.2 can have these substitutions made, and the resulting code is given in Figure 1.3. This more human-readable language is **assembly language**. Programmers do not write machine language programs. Instead, they utilize an **assembler**, a program that translates from assembly language to machine language. Every computer system provides an assembler; so programmers may write assembly language code instead of machine code. Traditionally, there was always a one-to-one correspondence between assembly language instructions and machine language instructions. With the sophistication of software tools, many assembly languages now contain instructions that the hardware is not capable of executing. These instructions can be assembled into machine language using one or

```
push ebp
mov ebp, esp
sub ebp, 8
push ebx
push esi
push edi
mov dword ptr _counter$[ebp], 1
mov dword ptr _squares$[ebp], 0
cmp dword ptr _counter$[ebp], 20
jg $L112
mov eax, dword ptr _counter$[ebp]
imul eax, dword ptr _counter$[ebp]
add dword ptr _squares$[ebp], eax
inc dword ptr _counter$[ebp]
jmp $L111
```

Figure 1.3 Assembly language of a portion of a program.

more machine language instructions. The language accepted by the assembler can be more abstract than the instruction set offered by the architecture.

Assembly language code is still much too detailed for programmers to be able to generate quickly. Because of the abstractions in high-level languages, programmers can write large, sophisticated programs easily. A common software tool used to translate a high-level language program into assembly language is a **compiler**. A different compiler is needed for each high-level language used by a programmer on a machine.

The result of these software tools used for translation is that the programmer can write programs in a high-level language, and the computer can execute machine language programs. Both the programmer and the computer can work in their most efficient way. Figure 1.4 diagrams this translation process. The programmer writes a program in a high-level language. To do this, the programmer uses an application such as an editor to enter the program. The program is stored in a file, and is then used as input to a compiler. The compiler generates an assembly language version of the program. The assembly language version of the program is used as input to an assembler, and the assembler produces a machine language version of the program as output. Once the program is placed in memory, it can be executed.

This text focuses on introducing computer architecture, as described by an instruction set. The abstract assembly language, SASM, is detailed in Chapter 3, making it possible to write assembly language programs before the details of one computer architecture (the Intel Pentium architecture) are described. SASM is structured as an assembly language, but it contains some features that are more appropriate to a high-level language. SASM is designed to bridge the gap between a high-level language and an assembly language, in this case, Pentium assembly language. A program written in SASM is translated to Pen-

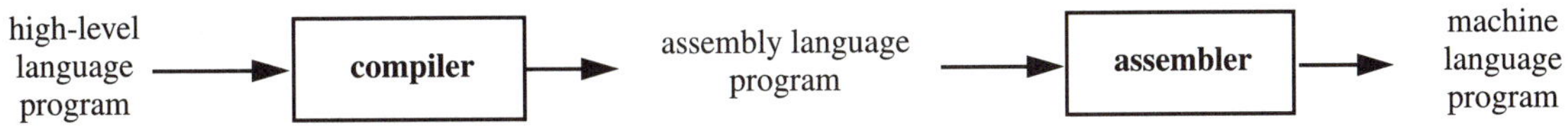

Figure 1.4 Translation from high-level language to machine language.

tium assembly language, and then the Pentium assembly language is assembled to machine language for execution. In this way, the intricate details of the Pentium architecture are hidden by introducing an abstraction.

1.3 A BRIEF HISTORY OF COMPUTER DEVELOPMENT

The history of computer development is one that has been driven by the available technology. This technology can be categorized into software and hardware. Before the software could be considered, the hardware had to be available. Therefore, the earliest computers placed all emphasis on working hardware. The software (programs to be run) was secondary, since it required less time and effort in comparison to the design and implementation of the hardware.

The very first computers were designed using electromechanical switches. These switches were large. The computers designed from them were more like automated adding machines than today's computers because of their usability. A program written for these earliest machines was entered into the computer by placing a set of relays into appropriate places. The program was then executed. To execute a new program, the relays would need to be unplugged and placed again for the new program.

With the technological advance of the vacuum tube, faster computers could be designed. Vacuum tubes can be used as switches, and are much faster devices than electromechanical switches. The hardware technology still required tremendous effort, leaving little to no effort in the area of software design.

A revolution in thinking came with the notion of storing a program in memory. Before this, a program was entered into a computer just before it was run. If a program is placed in memory, it can be executed several times, and the effort of entering the program into the computer is reduced to entering it once. All modern computers use this **stored program** concept.

In these early computers, memory space was extremely limited. The cathode ray tube (called a Williams tube in this usage), used in the late 1940s, provided 1 Kbits of storage. Mercury delay lines were also used for memory during the same time period, but suffered from the difficulty that access to the memory was not random. Core memory was a major invention in the field of computer design. It appeared in the 1950s. Because core memory was smaller (per bit), it allowed computer designers to include a much larger main memory.

Another (and perhaps the most) major hardware innovation came with the invention of transistors. They are easily used as switches, and they are much more reliable than vacuum tubes. Computers manufactured from discrete transistor technology required less space and power than previous computers. The space required for a computer went from a very large room down to a very small room. This allowed computer architects to try out new ideas (using the space freed by the use of smaller circuitry). With these machines, software technology also blossomed. High-level languages and compilers became like their modern-day versions. The operating systems for these new machines were also transformed from the basic batch processing system that executed programs one at a time in a queued order to programs that gave the user the ability to interact directly with the operating system.

There was also a trend toward designing computer architectures that implemented high-level language abstractions. Hardware can be built to do anything that software can do, and the hardware can do it much faster than software can. Taken to an extreme, adding too much to the duties of the hardware can have an adverse effect on the speed of execution of all hardware on a computer. It was also the case that the compiler technology of that period could not efficiently utilize the more abstract instructions offered.

The final chapter in technological innovations brings us to the present. The ability to place more than one transistor on a single integrated circuit fueled a race to place as many transistors on an integrated circuit as possible. The more the better to a computer architect, who can always find productive uses for more circuitry. As technology gained the ability to place approximately 10,000 transistors on a single integrated circuit, the single-chip processor was born.

1.4 THE INTEL iAPX ARCHITECTURE

This text presents the details of the Intel iAPX architecture by concentrating on the Pentium processor. Intel entered the race to put an entire processor on a single integrated circuit. The very earliest single-chip processors were not useful by themselves as processors. They did mostly arithmetic manipulation on 4-bit pieces of data. It took several of these processors working together to act as a useful general-purpose computer.

The Pentium architecture evolved from the 8086 architecture introduced in 1978 as a 16-bit architecture, implemented on a single integrated circuit. Since then, each new processor within the family of architectures has maintained backward compatibility with its predecessors. Backward compatibility means that each new member of the architectural family can execute the code of the earlier processors. At the same time, each newer processor has expanded the features of the architecture, making it more usable and modern as technologies have advanced. Figure 1.5 lists some of the processors within the architectural family. Each subsequent processor within the family runs faster than previous processors. Each also added a few additional instructions to the instruction set.

The 8086 contained some interesting architectural features. Of these, perhaps the most notable is its segmented address space. A segmented address space is an alternative method of addressing that implies part of a location. This feature has propagated itself through all subsequent members of the architectural family. One of the architectural additions to the 486 is the availability of a flat address space. This method of addressing specifies explicitly all locations. The programmer is given the choice of using the segmented addressing or flat addressing. This addition brings addressing within programs written for the more recent entries in the architectural family to the method utilized by most processors.

The size of data processed in the processors before the 386 was 16 bits. This is a relatively small amount of data for a processor to work with. As technology allowed, the architecture expanded to facilitate 32-bit data sizes.

Name	Year of Introduction	Notes
8086	1978	
8088	1979	Used in the IBM PC.
80186		
80286	1982	Virtual memory supported.
80386	1985	Expanded to handle 32-bit data.
80486	1989	Flat address space supported.
Pentium	1993	Floating point hardware on chip.
Pentium Pro	1995	
Pentium II	1997	Enhancements to handle video, audio, and graphics data more efficiently.

Figure 1.5 Intel family architectures.

SUMMARY

Abstractions allow large problems to be broken into smaller pieces. Each of these pieces can then be broken down again and worked on independently. Computer hardware and software design follows this approach.

A computer's architecture is defined by its instruction set. The instruction set defines a programming language. Modern architectures provide a machine language that is very fast to execute, but the detailed nature of machine language makes it a poor programming language for programmers. To ease the job of programmers, high-level languages are designed. High-level language programs are compiled and then assembled to produce a machine language version of a program.

Advances in technology have driven computer architecture design.

PROBLEMS

1. What are the primitives of a highway map? Assume that the map is one that shows large highways and the towns and cities they connect.

2. What are the primitives of an assembly language abstraction?

3. What are the primitives of a high-level language?

4. Why do computer manufacturers provide an assembly language specification when what the computers execute is machine code?

5. What is the difference between a compiler and an assembler?

6. A computer can be designed to execute a high-level language directly. Why not design this type of computer?

7. Does a compiler need to be written in assembly language? If so, why? If not, how is a machine language version of the compiler generated?

8. Can an assembler be written in a high-level language? Explain.

CHAPTER 2

COMPUTER BASICS

The interface between a computer's hardware and its software is its **architecture**. The architecture is described by what the computer's instructions do, and how they are specified. Understanding how it all works requires knowledge of the structure of a computer and its assembly language. This chapter presents these basics, starting with the hardware organization and ending with a discussion of computer system performance.

2.1 THE PIECES AND PARTS

A **program** consists of a collection of variables, a set of instructions that act upon those variables, and the rules describing the order in which the instructions are executed. A program is executed by a **processor** or **central processing unit (CPU)**. The processor contains the

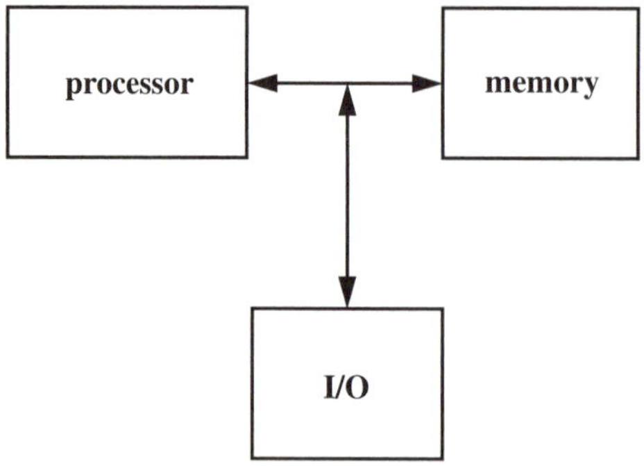

Figure 2.1 A simple computer system.

hardware needed to execute programs. Programs are stored in a memory. This main memory and input and output devices (I/O) are generally separate pieces of hardware. A simple diagram of these logically separate components of a computer system is given in Figure 2.1. The physical organization of the computer system may place one or more of these components into the same box.

When a program is run, the processor reads **instructions** from the memory and executes them. The instructions specify ways that variables are manipulated and stored in the computer's memory.

A high-level programming language such as C permits the statement

```
A = B + C;
```

which means to add the value of variable `B` to the value of variable `C` and assign the result to variable `A`. An architecture might have the same capability in its assembly language instruction

```
add A, B, C
```

which means exactly the same thing. For an instruction, the **mnemonic**, `add`, stands for an **operation code** or **opcode**, and the variables are the instruction's **operands**. These different parts of an assembly language instruction will be represented by different fields within the machine code for this instruction.

Involved in modifying the variables of a program are two of the major components in a computer: the processor and the main memory. The processor is responsible for executing the instructions and determining how the memory is to be modified.

Aside from handling input and output, a processor must perform two types of operations. It must evaluate arithmetic and logical functions to determine values to assign to variables, and it must determine the order of execution of the instructions in a program. In assembly language, these instructions are categorized as **arithmetic** or **logical** instructions and **control** instructions. Arithmetic and logical instructions evaluate variables and assign new values to variables. Control instructions test or compare values of variables and make decisions about what instruction is to be executed next.

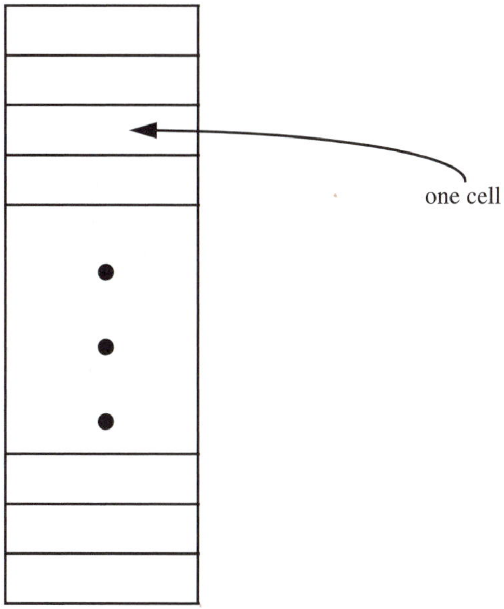

Figure 2.2 Diagram of main memory.

2.2 MEMORY OPERATION

The main memory of a computer is a place to store data and programs. The memory has a fixed, but very large, number of memory locations as diagrammed in Figure 2.2. At each of these locations is a **cell**, a piece of memory large enough to store a particular type of data. Three cells might be used to store variables `A`, `B`, and `C`. The hardware does not attach these names to the cells, but the software does. The name is called a **label**, and the label identifies a location in memory.

The processor interacts with memory in three ways. First, the processor will need to fetch instructions. Second, it needs to be able to load the value of a variable. Third, it needs to be able to store the value of a variable. The memory is capable of only two operations. A **read** is the operation required by either a load or a fetch operation. A **write** is the operation of placing the value of a variable in memory. An **address** accompanies all memory operations. An address is a label indicating the memory location to be accessed. When the processor needs to interact with memory, it initiates the memory operation, and it indicates whether it wants to perform a read or a write. If the operation is a read, then the processor must supply the address of the memory cell involved. The memory responds by supplying the value of the specified cell. If the operation is a write, the processor must not only provide the address of the memory cell, but also the value to be placed in the cell. The value is accepted by the memory and remembered as the contents at the specified address.

The flow of data required for a **memory access** is given in Figure 2.3.

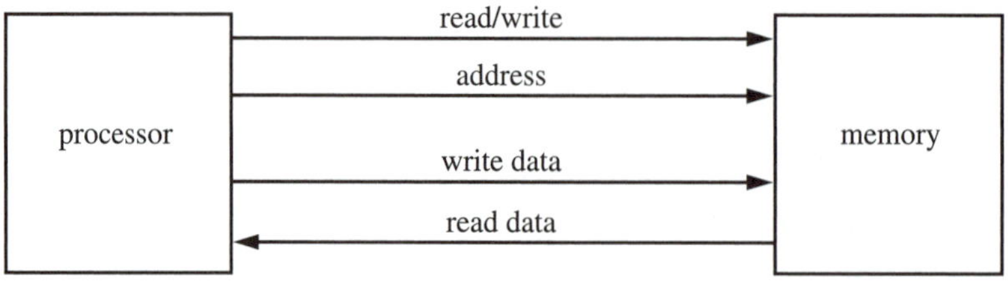

Figure 2.3 Flow of information in a memory access.

2.3 THE INSTRUCTION FETCH AND EXECUTE CYCLE

The processor in a computer simply fetches and executes one instruction after another until the hardware is forced to stop by some external means (like turning off the power). An instruction fetch requires the address of the instruction. Within the processor is a variable that always contains the address of the next instruction to be fetched. It is called the **program counter** or **PC**. The value in the PC is maintained by the processor. Intel calls this variable the **instruction pointer** or **IP**.

Consider the steps necessary for the fetch and execution of an instruction. The instruction is contained within a program that is stored in memory. In order to execute the instruction, the processor must first fetch the instruction. The operating system sets the value of the PC to the address of the instruction to be fetched. The processor begins by supplying the contents of the PC (the address of the instruction desired) to the memory and initiating a read operation. The memory receives the address and responds by supplying the instruction to the processor. For this example, assume the assembly language for the instruction fetched is

```
add A, B, C
```

The processor decodes the machine code for this instruction by identifying the opcode and the operands within the machine instruction. The processor determines that this is an `add` instruction. The operation required is that the variables specified by the second and third operands be added. It is presumed that the processor keeps a copy of the instruction. The machine language for the `add` instruction must contain addresses of variables `A`, `B`, and `C`. The variables to be added are in memory; so the processor loads them. The processor supplies the address of variable `B`, as taken from the copy of the machine language instruction, and initiates a memory access to read the variable. Memory responds by supplying the value of the variable. The processor then supplies the address of variable `C` and initiates a read. Memory responds by supplying the value of the variable. Once the processor has acquired both `B` and `C`, it adds the two operands together. The result is to be stored in memory at the location specified by the label `A`. The processor supplies both the address and the result, and initiates a write operation. The memory writes the given result at the correct location.

The execution of the `add` instruction has been completed, and the processor is now ready to fetch its next instruction. The PC is defined such that it contains the address of the next instruction to be fetched. Between the time that the first instruction is fetched and the time that the next instruction should be fetched, the processor must modify the PC such that it is again pointing to the next instruction to be fetched. This modification of the PC is implied by the model of program execution assumed by a programmer. The programmer assumes that statements (instructions) get executed in the order given within the code. Statements (instructions) written sequentially are expected to be executed sequentially. The hardware must explicitly implement the modification of the PC to meet the programmer's assumption.

Control instructions provide a way for program code to explicitly modify the PC. An assembly language example of a control instruction might be

```
br forloop
```

The assembly language for this instruction contains an mnemonic, `br`, and it contains a single operand. The operand is given as a label, `forloop`. The implied operation of this instruction is to modify the PC so that it contains the address given to the label `forloop`. This type of instruction is an **unconditional branch** or an **unconditional jump**. It is also common for assembly languages to include **conditional branch** or **conditional jump** instructions. The conditional branch or jump instructions only explicitly modify the PC if a variable contains a specified value.

An example of the fetch and execution of a conditional branch instruction might be the assembly language instruction

```
beq x, y, endif
```

This conditional branch instruction has a mnemonic and three operands. The mnemonic, `beq`, stands for branch if equal. The implied operation for this instruction is to check if the contents of variables `x` and `y` are equal. If the two variables do contain the same value, then the branch is taken. In this case, the address given by the label `endif` is placed in the PC. If variables `x` and `y` are not equal, then the branch is not taken. The PC is not explicitly changed, and the address of the next instruction to be fetched will be the next instruction within the program. When the machine code for this instruction is fetched, the processor keeps a copy of the instruction, and it decodes the instruction. The processor determines that this is an instruction that explicitly modifies the PC if the value of the two variables are the same. If this is the case, the address given to the label `endif` is placed into the PC, and the instruction at that address will be the next fetched. In the case where the two variables `x` and `y` are not the same, the PC is modified (as with arithmetic and logical instructions) to contain the address of the next instruction in the program.

An alternative method for implementing conditional control instructions in some computer architectures does not use the comparison of variables to decide whether or not to take a branch or jump. Instead, an implied variable checked is called a **condition code**. It is a special variable contained within the processor (like the PC) that is set based on the result of a previous calculation. The condition codes are really a set of variables all kept together. What information they give about a previous result varies from machine to machine, but virtually all machines that have condition codes will have one that identifies if a result was zero, and another that identifies if a result was negative. As an operation for an arithmetic or logical instruction is completed, the result is checked, and the condition codes are set appropriately. A conditional control instruction then uses the condition codes to make a decision on whether or not to take a branch or jump. An example of such an instruction might be the assembly language instruction

```
bz loop_top
```

where the mnemonic, `bz`, stands for branch if zero. The condition code bit set if a result was zero is checked. If the condition code bit indicates that a result was zero, then the branch is taken. The address given to label `loop_top` is placed in the PC. If the condition code bit indicates that a result was not zero, then the branch is not taken. The PC is not explicitly changed, and the address of the next instruction to be fetched will be the next instruction within the program.

For both arithmetic or logical and control instructions, the processor simply fetches and executes instructions continually. The series of steps that it repeats is the instruction **fetch and execute cycle**. The steps in this cycle are given in Figure 2.4. For arithmetic and logical instructions, the steps are the same as detailed. For control instructions, these steps are also followed. The fetch of a control instruction is no different than the fetch of any other instruction. After the instruction fetch, the program counter is updated to contain the instruction following the fetched instruction. The machine code for the instruction is decoded to reveal that it is a control instruction. As the fourth step in the cycle, the operands are loaded from memory. The operands of a control instruction may be variables to compare, if the architecture is defined this way. For an architecture that uses condition codes, there may be no operands to load. There will also be one operand containing information about the target address of the control instruction. There are two operations involved in the fifth step of the instruction fetch and execute cycle. The first operation is a comparison, either of variables or of condition codes, to use as a basis for a conditional branch or jump decision. The second operation in a control instruction is usually to calculate a target address. The sixth step in the instruction fetch and execute cycle is conditional. It is based on the result of the comparison operation. If the branch or jump is to be taken, then the PC is overwritten with the calculated target address. If the branch or jump is not to be taken, then nothing occurs during this step.

The modification of the PC is placed as the second step in the instruction fetch and execute cycle. As it is defined (the PC always contains the address of the next instruction to be fetched), the PC update step must be placed after the instruction fetch step, but could occur at any point before the fetch of the next instruction. It is convenient to place it directly after the instruction fetch step. For noncontrol instructions, the PC is not explicitly changed. Its value can be modified independent of other variables. If they were not independent, then the steps

1. Instruction fetch
2. Update program counter
3. Decode instruction
4. Load operands
5. Do the operation
6. Store results

Figure 2.4 Steps in the instruction fetch and execute cycle.

would need to done **sequentially**. Sequential execution finishes each step before it starts the next step. In most implementations, this independence allows the PC update step to be completed in **parallel** with the other steps in the instruction fetch and execute cycle. Parallel execution allows more than one step to be executed at the same time. The ability to complete the steps in parallel improves the performance of an implementation.

A code fragment used to show the instruction fetch and execute cycle in action is given in Figure 2.5. An assembly language defines a computer architecture; so this code fragment implies many assumptions about a processor that could execute this fragment. The first instruction within the code fragment will be fetched when the PC contains the address of this instruction. After the machine code for this instruction is fetched from memory, the PC is updated. Then the fields within the instruction are decoded, allowing the processor to determine that this is a `move` instruction. The assumed operation of this `move` instruction is to copy the value given by the second operand into the location given by the first operand. The second operand is a constant, and it is assumed that this constant will be encoded within the machine code for this `move` instruction. Therefore, the fourth step within the instruction fetch and execute cycle will be to get the value of the constant from the instruction itself. This is the equivalent of loading an operand for this instruction. The operation involved as the fifth step within the instruction fetch and execute cycle does nothing for this `move` instruction. The final step is to place the value of the constant into memory at the location given by the first operand. The location is given by the label `i`. The processor stores the value by generating a write operation. The fetch and execute cycle for this move instruction is completed, but the processor does not stop. It repeats the steps of the instruction fetch and execute cycle for the next instruction.

The PC will contain the address for the machine code of the second `move` instruction within the code fragment. The processor generates a read operation, giving memory the address within the PC. The remainder of the fetch and execute cycle is much the same for this second `move` instruction as it was for the first `move` instruction. The processor updates the PC to point to the third instruction. After decoding the machine code, it then gets the constant 51 from the machine code for the `move` instruction. As the final step within the instruction fetch and execute cycle for this instruction, the processor writes the value 51 to the variable `limit`, located in memory.

The fetch and execute cycle continues with the third instruction, fetching, updating the PC, decoding the machine code to determine that the instruction is again a `move` instruction. It gets the constant zero from the instruction and writes this value to memory at the location given by the first operand, `sum`.

The fetch and execute cycle continues for the fourth instruction, first fetching the machine code at the address given by the contents of the PC. The PC is then updated. The processor decodes the machine code to reveal that this fourth instruction is an `add` instruction. The

```
        move      i, 1
        move      limit, 51
        move      sum, 0
loop:   add       sum, sum, i
        add       i, i, 1
        bne       i, limit, loop
```

Figure 2.5 Assembly language code fragment.

implied operation of this add instruction is to add the variables given by the second and third operands, placing the result of the addition at the location given by the first operand. After the decode step, the processor generates two memory operations to load the variables, sum and i. Once the variables have been loaded, the addition operation is done. As the last step in the instruction fetch and execute cycle (for this instruction), the processor generates a write operation to memory, writing the result of the addition to the variable sum.

Again, the fetch and execute cycle continues, this time fetching the fifth instruction within the program fragment. After the PC is updated, the instruction is decoded to reveal that it is an add instruction. Like the move instruction, the constant given by the third operand is assumed to be encoded within the instruction. The processor generates only one memory operation to load the value of variable i. The other variable is taken from the instruction itself. Then comes the addition of the two operands. The processor generates a write operation to the location given by variable i to write the result of the addition.

The fetch and execute cycle continues, fetching the sixth instruction within the program fragment. After the PC is updated, the instruction is decoded to reveal that it is the conditional branch instruction, bne. The branch will be taken, explicitly placing the address given by the label loop if a comparison of the first two operands determines that they do not have the same value. The two operands, i and limit, are loaded. The comparison is done, and a branch decision is made by the processor. If the variables i and limit do not contain the same value, then the address given by the third operand is placed into the PC as the last step within the instruction fetch and execute cycle. If the variables i and limit do contain the same value, then nothing is done as the last step within the fetch and execute cycle. As a result of this instruction, for this code fragment, the branch will be taken, since i = 2 and limit = 51 the first time the bne instruction is fetched and executed.

The next instruction to be fetched is the add instruction at label loop. It is followed by the second add instruction, and then by the bne instruction. The branch is again taken the second time through this code, since i = 3 and limit = 51. These three instructions will be fetched and executed 50 times. The last time through the loop, i becomes 51, and comparison within the bne instruction determines that the values are the same. The branch is not taken, and the fetch and execute cycle will continue by fetching the instruction following the bne in the program. That instruction is not shown in the code fragment.

2.4 PERFORMANCE

Central to the field of computer architecture is understanding how fast a computer system operates. This concept is related with the term **performance**. There is no single value that can completely state the performance of a computer system. Contributing to the performance are many factors.

Processors are implemented with digital designs that run based on a clock. The clock's speed is often given in **megahertz**, the number of times the clock cycles (or pulses or ticks) per second. Each of the steps within the instruction fetch and execute cycle will likely be implemented to take an integral and fixed number of clock cycles to complete. Knowing the clock speed alone says little about the performance of the computer, since the fetch and execution of a single instruction may take many clock cycles to complete. What makes clock speed even less a predictor of performance is that different instructions may take different numbers of clock cycles to complete. For example, and addition instruction may take a different number of clock cycles to complete than a conditional control instruction.

Making predictions of performance even worse is that the same instruction may take different numbers of clock cycles to complete at different points in time. This is because current architectures are implemented with a hierarchical memory system. A hierarchical memory design decreases the **average memory access time** (**AMAT**) so that (on average) programs take less time to finish. In reality, each memory access takes a fixed amount of time (an integral number of clock cycles) to complete. An instruction may take many clock cycles to fetch one time, but may take few clock cycles to fetch another time.

A program written in a high-level language must be compiled and assembled before it can be executed. The level of sophistication placed into compilers has risen. The compiler has choices about which code sequence to use in the implementation of a high-level language code segment. These choices often involve levels of code optimization that the compiler can perform. A higher level of optimization usually requires more time for compilation, but the compiled program executes in less time. The same program can be compiled with different levels of optimization to produce assembly language code that results in different execution times.

The speed of I/O devices is integral to the performance of a computer system. The speed of devices is independent of the speed of the processor. Many devices process data at speeds considerably slower than the processor could handle. The effect of this is that a program may need to wait for input or output to complete before it can continue its execution. This affects the speed of the executing program.

Yet another factor involved in the performance of a computer system is the overhead of its **operating system** (**OS**). The operating system is itself a program. While the operating system is running, other programs are not. It controls the execution of all other programs, as well as the memory and the I/O devices. The operating system essentially juggles all the programs, implementing a policy to decide which program will be executed at which time.

Given all these various factors contributing to the performance of a computer system, it is difficult to identify a single performance figure that corresponds to a computer's overall performance. The best measures of performance execute real programs under realistic conditions (compiler, OS, I/O devices) and measure **latency**. Latency is the time something takes from start to finish. The level of compiler optimizations, the operating system, the memory system, and the I/O devices are specified and fixed for the measurement.

A number sometimes given as a performance figure for a processor is its **MIPS**. MIPS stands for millions of instructions executed per second. To illustrate this performance figure, consider an imaginary computer architecture that has only three instructions in its instruction set, called A, B, and C. If each instruction takes the same amount of time to execute, then MIPS is given by

$$\text{MIPS} = \frac{\text{total number of instructions executed}}{\text{total time to execute (in seconds)} \times 10^6}$$

For a processor where each instruction always takes the same amount of time to execute, this is a reasonable performance statistic. However, if instruction execution times vary, then so will the MIPS performance statistic. Figure 2.6 illustrates this. The figure shows

A Instruction Latency	% of A Instructions in Program	B Instruction Latency	% of B Instructions in Program	C Instruction Latency	% of C Instructions in Program	MIPS
1 nsec	50%	2 nsec	40%	3 nsec	10%	630
2 nsec	50%	1 nsec	40%	3 nsec	10%	590
3 nsec	50%	2 nsec	40%	1 nsec	10%	420

Figure 2.6 MIPS statistic for variable instructions' execution time.

A Instruction Latency	% of A Instructions in Program	B Instruction Latency	% of B Instructions in Program	C Instruction Latency	% of C Instructions in Program	MIPS
1 nsec	50%	2 nsec	40%	3 nsec	10%	630
1 nsec	40%	2 nsec	40%	3 nsec	30%	480
1 nsec	30%	2 nsec	50%	3 nsec	20%	530

Figure 2.7 MIPS statistics for varying mixes of instruction types.

that for an imaginary mix of instructions within a program, when the latency of the instructions change, so will the MIPS performance figure.

A similar difficulty with this measure of performance can be seen if instruction latency is held constant while the percentage of each instruction within a program changes. This would illustrate the case where the MIPS performance statistic is calculated for different programs. Figure 2.7 demonstrates this point.

Possibly the worst attribute of the MIPS performance statistic is that it cannot be used to compare the performance of one computer system to another computer system. The instruction set offered by one architecture will be different from the instruction set offered by another architecture. The amount of work accomplished by an instruction varies from architecture to architecture. It may take several instructions on one architecture to accomplish what one instruction does on another architecture.

A much better way to compare the performance of two computer systems is to run a program on each, and compare the latency of program execution. The one that takes the least time has higher performance (for that program). A program or set of programs executed for purposes of performance measurement is a **benchmark**. Over time, many benchmarks have been proposed and used. A benchmark will exercise some portions of a computer's abilities. It may heavily use the integer arithmetic portion of hardware, or the floating point hardware, or it may do little other than to test how fast memory accesses can be completed. Different computers will likely do better or worse on these benchmarks depending on their design. These synthetic benchmarks are often very short programs that test performance in a specific area. The difficulty with these synthetic benchmarks is that they may not predict the performance of a computer system if its normal workload does not utilize the same portions of the computer's capabilities as the benchmark.

Different from comparing one computer system to another is the comparison of the execution time of a single program that has been optimized. **Speedup** is a ratio comparing performance before and after program enhancement:

$$\text{speedup} = \frac{\text{execution time before optimization}}{\text{execution time after optimization}}$$

Note that a speedup of less than 1 implies that the program is not sped up, but rather it is slower than before. A speedup of 2 says that the optimized version of the program executes in half the time it took before optimization. This performance figure can be used to help guide efforts in program optimization. Suppose an assembly language program that executes 1000 instructions is being optimized. A programmer finds a way to eliminate one instruction from the initialization code within the program. Presuming all instructions take the same time to execute, then the speedup of this optimization is

$$\frac{1000 \times 1 \text{ instruction execution time}}{999 \times 1 \text{ instruction execution time}} = \frac{1000}{999} \approx 1.001001$$

This optimization is probably not worth the effort. If, however, the programmer is able to eliminate a single instruction from within a loop that executes 400 times, then the speedup for this example program is more significant:

$$\text{speedup} = \frac{1000 \times 1 \text{ instruction execution time}}{(1000 - 400) \times 1 \text{ instruction execution time}} = \frac{1000}{600} \approx 1.666666$$

SUMMARY

The basic operation of a computer system has the processor continuously fetch and execute instructions as given in the fetch and execute cycle. Programs are stored in memory. The PC contains the address of the next instruction to be fetched. It is modified during the execution of each instruction. For control instructions, the execution of the instruction may explicitly modify the PC. For other instructions, the hardware must modify the PC to point to the instruction following the one completing its execution.

Performance figures for computer systems can vary a great deal based on what software tools are used, the implementation of the architecture, and the program used to benchmark the system. A single performance figure does not predict the system's performance for all programs. The true test of the speed of a computer system is to execute the programs that will be used in a normal workload.

PROBLEMS

1. Diagram a computer system, showing the CPU, memory, PC, and ALU. Use arrows to show how data and instructions travel to the various components.

2. How many wires connect a processor to memory?

3. Detail the memory operations needed to fetch and execute the assembly language instruction

```
sub X, Y, Z
```

4. List the six steps of the instruction fetch and execute cycle. Identify those steps that require a memory access for an arithmetic instruction.

5. List the six steps of the instruction fetch and execute cycle. Identify those steps that require a memory access for a control instruction.

6. Write a detailed instruction fetch and execute cycle for a processor that keeps the PC in memory instead of the processor.

7. Write an expression for the result calculated in variable `sum` in Figure 2.5.

8. Write an expression for the total number of instructions fetched and executed for the program fragment given in Figure 2.5, assuming the value of variable `limit` may be changed.

9. Show how the MIPS performance statistic is calculated for Figure 2.6.

10. A program is worked on to gain some performance enhancement. Before the enhancement, the program takes 2 seconds to execute. After the enhancement, the program takes 1.5 seconds to execute. What speedup has been attained?

11. A program is worked on to gain some performance enhancement. The portion of the program that is worked on accounts for 40% of the program's execution time. This portion of the program shows a speedup of 3. What speedup is attained for the program? What speedup is attained if the worked on portion of the program can be entirely eliminated?

12. A computer processor is manufactured in a newer technology that results in each instruction executing in 1/3 the time, as compared with the same processor manufactured in an older technology. What speedup has the processor attained?

13. Briefly explain why the MIPS performance number is not a good measure of performance.

CHAPTER 3

SASM—SIMPLE ABSTRACT LANGUAGE

A programming language provides a method for the programmer to describe precisely the data structures and the algorithms to be performed on those data structures. This chapter introduces a powerful assembly language, SASM, that allows the creation of useful programs. Its power comes from allowing a high level of abstraction. It is similar to high-level languages such as Pascal or C in the amount of work that is accomplished with individual instructions. Its syntax is similar to a traditional assembly language.

Any programming language must provide ways of specifying four types of operations. First, the language must provide a way to specify the **type** of a variable. This implies the range of values the variable can be assigned and the ways it can be used. Some languages, such as FORTRAN, allow implicit declaration depending on the name chosen for the variable. Second, the language must have a way of specifying arithmetic operations such as addition and multiplication. Third, the language must provide control structures that allow looping and conditional execution. Fourth, a programming language must provide a way to communicate with the user of the program created in the programming language.

This chapter discusses aspects of assembly language programming, such as when and why assembly language code is written. It then focuses on the details of the SASM programming language. Most programming examples are given in both C and SASM. Each of the four necessary operation types is discussed in turn. At the end of the chapter is a complete program example.

3.1 ASSEMBLY AND COMPILATION

A goal of programming language design is to provide an environment to maximize the efficiency of the programmer. The structure of the programming language should make it easy to write programs correctly and quickly. The programming language should also foster programs that make it easy for a programmer unfamiliar with a program to read and understand how it works for the purpose of modifying it. In addition to assisting in the programming process, however, a programming language should be designed so that it can be executed efficiently on a computer. Programs should make the best use of the hardware so that they execute as rapidly as possible, using as few resources as possible.

Unfortunately, these two goals—programmer efficiency and hardware efficiency—are frequently incompatible. Often, an unsophisticated algorithm is easily written and easily understood, but slow to execute. A more obscure algorithm might use resources more efficiently or take advantage of certain features of the computer that make the algorithm run efficiently.

Why Write Assembly Language Programs?

Years ago, hardware efficiency was extracted at the expense of the programmer's time. If a fast program was needed, then it was written in assembly language. Compilers were capable of translating programs from high-level languages, but they generated assembly language programs that were relatively inefficient as compared with the same programs written by a programmer in assembly language. Programmers often found it necessary to optimize the assembly language code created by the compiler for two reasons. The first is that memory space was often quite limited. A programmer could write code that fit in the available space when a compiler could not. The second reason that assembly code was written was to achieve acceptable performance. A programmer could write code that executed faster than the code generated by a compiler.

This is no longer the case. Compilers have improved to the point that they can generate code comparable to, or better than, the code most programmers can generate. There are two main reasons why the use of compiler-generated code has become common. Advances in compiler technology have greatly improved the quality of the assembly language code generated. Writing in assembly language may result in little or no improvement over the best code a compiler can generate. In many cases it is hard to find ways to improve the code generated by a high-quality compiler. The second reason is that there is little benefit derived by improving the execution speed of the assembly language. Many computers today execute so rapidly that it is not necessary to optimize code at the assembly language level.

It has become increasingly rare for programmers to find it necessary to write assembly language code. However, there are several special reasons why it might be necessary. First, there are features of the computer that can be accessed with assembly language that are not well captured in a high-level language. Programs that must use those features may need to be written, at least partially, in assembly language. Critical parts of an operating system are an example of code that is often written in assembly language for this reason. A second reason for needing assembly language programming may be the critical constraints for a program. An example is a program that must fit in a very small amount of memory. Another example is a program that must execute in a highly predictable amount of time. Sometimes the reason for writing in assembly language is simply the unavailability of a good compiler. This last reason should become increasingly rare as compiler technology becomes more widely established.

Compiler writers must understand how to write programs in assembly language before they can write compilers. For a compiler to produce efficient code, a compiler writer must be able to assess the costs and benefits of various code implementations. There are often several ways to implement the same code, and the best way often depends on details that are specific to the implementation of the targeted computer. These details vary from machine to machine.

Where SASM Fits In

SASM is similar to the intermediate language that a compiler might generate. It is not difficult to translate high-level language code into SASM, and it is straightforward to translate SASM code into Pentium code. SASM therefore provides a good starting point for the introduction of computer architecture for a programmer who knows a high-level language.

In general, this book presents the simplest, most obvious sequence of instructions. As is typical of modern high-level languages, ease of understanding is emphasized over efficiency of the program. This is consistent with the way compilers generate efficient assembly language code. Using a more-or-less direct translation, a compiler initially creates a program in an intermediate language that is often an abstraction of the assembly language of the targeted computer. Then the compiler invokes a program, known as an **optimizer,** to improve the speed of the program without changing its behavior. Either during the optimizations or afterward, the assembly language of the abstract computer is translated into the assembly language of the target computer, then translated into machine code.

3.2 VARIABLE DECLARATION

Like all high-level languages, C provides a means for declaring the type of a variable. Declaration is for the benefit of the compiler or assembler, which must know how much space to allocate for specific variables. Different variable types can take on different values and require different amounts of space. It is important that sufficient space, but not more, be set aside.

SASM understands three simple types: integers, characters, and floating point. The declaration of a variable is accomplished by giving a variable a name and a type. Integers are declared using the following syntax. An integer declaration in C is

```
int variablename {= value};
```

The SASM declaration of an integer or floating point variable looks like

```
{ variablename } dd value
```

For the definitions, optional words are in braces ({}). When an identifier is used to give a name to a variable, such as `variablename`, it is a **label**. In both C and SASM, identifiers follow the rule that they start with a letter, and can be followed by letters or digits. A space character marks the end of the variable name. Variable names and labels may not be reserved words, which are listed in Appendix A. There are many of them. The `dd` gives information about the amount of memory space needed for the variable. The label indicates how the variable is to be referenced. The `value` is a constant that will be assigned to the variable as an initial value. If there is no value in the variable declaration, the assembler gives an error.

The declaration

```
ten dd 10
```

sets aside space for a variable named `ten`, and initializes its value to 10. The declaration

```
counter dd ?
```

sets aside space for a variable named `counter`, but does not give it an initial value. The question mark character tells the assembler to set aside space, but not bother with an initial value. Variable `ten` is of type integer. Variable `counter` could be either an integer or a floating point type variable.

A floating point variable is also declared using `dd`. This is because the amount of memory required for an integer and a floating point variable is the same. The `value` of a floating point variable is given by the following syntax. A floating point value contains an optional sign (+ or -) and a set of digits that may contain a decimal point, and may be followed by an exponent specification. The exponent specification is the letter `E` or `e` followed by an optional sign and an integer. The following examples are all legal floating point values, and they all specify the same value.

```
136.42
1.3642E2
+13.642e1
0.13642e+3
13642.e-2
```

The SASM character type declaration is similar to the SASM integer type declaration. The SASM declaration of a character type variable looks like

```
{ variablename } db value
```

The word `db` gives information about the size of a character type variable. The label `variablename` specifies the variable name. Like integer declarations, the value portion gives an initial value. One syntax for `value` is that of a single character enclosed in single quote marks.

The declaration

```
sentinel db 'z'
```

identifies the variable named `sentinel` to be a character, and initializes its value to be the character 'z.' A declaration without a value portion will generate an error from the assembler.

Other characters such as the newline character are specified using the ASCII character code, as described in Chapter 5. The newline character in SASM can be declared:

```
newline db 0ah
```

Declarations are information given to the assembler about how to *create* the program, not how to execute it. They are therefore set apart within a program in a section that specifies how memory is to be allocated. The memory is divided into two distinct areas for assembly purposes, one for instructions, known as the **code** or **text** space, and one for variables, known as the **data** space. In SASM, declarations can occur anywhere, but they must be separated from code by the use of a **directive**. A directive gives information to the assembler about the program. The data declarations section is indicated by preceding one or more declarations by the directive `.data`, as in

```
.data
var1   dd 0
var2   db 0
```

Code is distinguished in SASM by preceding it with the directive `.code`. There may be multiple `.data` and `.code` sections in a program.

3.3 ARITHMETIC OPERATIONS

An assignment statement in C can involve the evaluation of expressions composed of operators, variables, and constants. In C, as in most languages, all operators are either unary or binary. High-level languages such as C and Pascal go to great lengths to define how to evaluate an expression by defining the order in which the operators are applied. Thus the C statement

```
answer = a - b + c;
```

is defined precisely to be

```
answer = ( a - b ) + c;
```

and not

```
answer = a - ( b + c );
```

SASM Instructions	Equivalent C Statement	Notes
`move x, y`	`x = y;`	
`moveb x, y`	`x = y;`	both x and y are characters
`movezx x, y`	`x = y;`	move character to integer
`movesx x, y`	`x = y;`	move character-sized integer to integer
`ineg x`	`x = -x;`	sets condition codes
`iadd x, y`	`x = x + y;`	sets condition codes
`isub x, y`	`x = x - y;`	sets condition codes
`imult x, y`	`x = x * y;`	
`idivi x, y`	`x = x / y;`	
`irem x, y`	`x = x % y;`	
`fpadd y, x`	`y = y + x;`	y and x are floating point values; x may not be a constant
`fpsub y, x`	`y = y - x;`	y and x are floating point values; x may not be a constant
`fpmul y, x`	`y = y * x;`	y and x are floating point values; x may not be a constant
`fpdiv y, x`	`y = y / x;`	y and x are floating point values; x may not be a constant

Figure 3.1 Arithmetic operations is SASM.

In fact, the evaluation of a C statement involves a series of binary or unary operations, performed on constants and variables in a well-defined order. SASM makes this order explicit by requiring that each operation be specified explicitly, and that the result be assigned to a variable.

Figure 3.1 gives SASM's arithmetic instructions and their C equivalents. An instruction consists of an operation specification, known as the **mnemonic** or **opcode**, and one or two operand specifications. An operand is either (1) the name of a variable or (2) a constant. For example, consider the C program fragment

```
int area_triangle, width, height;
...
area_triangle = ( width * height ) / 2;
```

This statement could be translated into the following SASM code fragment:

```
.data
area_triangle      dd 0
width              dd ?
height             dd ?
tmp                dd ?

.code
move        area_triangle, width
imult       area_triangle, height
idivi       area_triangle, 2
```

For all arithmetic instructions, the first operand specifies the destination of the result, and the second operand is a source. The `move` instruction is equivalent to a simple C assignment statement. The value assigned to the first (destination) operand variable given in the `move` instruction is the value of the second (source) variable. The value of the source variable is unchanged by the `move` instruction. The C assignment statement

```
A = B;
```

could be translated to the SASM instruction

```
move    A, B
```

In general, an instruction set architecture is defined with respect to the number of operands in arithmetic instructions. SASM arithmetic instructions are two-operand instructions because the instruction set is based on the Pentium architecture. The Pentium architecture is defined with two-address instructions. In a **two-address architecture**, one of the operands is both a source and a destination. Two operands are required as sources for the instruction's operation. The result is placed back into one of the operands, overwriting it.

It is also common to see **three-address architectures**. The arithmetic instructions will contain three operands. Two will be source operands, and one will be a destination operand. A three-address assembly language instruction to perform an add might look like

```
add A, B, C
```

where the contents of variable `B` are added to the contents of variable `C`. The result is then placed back into variable `A`. From an assembly language programming standpoint, a three-address instruction set is preferable, since it can take fewer instructions to accomplish the same task. However, both two- and three-address architectures have the same functionality.

The `iadd`, `isub`, and `imult` instructions perform the integer operations that are specified in C by the operators `+`, `-`, and `*`, respectively. Instructions equivalent to these operators are defined in SASM where the operands are integers. Operand types should not be mixed in one instruction. Integer division is specified by the `idivi` instruction, and the modulus (or remainder) function is specified by the `irem` instruction. The `idivi` instruction corresponds to integer division in C, and `irem` corresponds to the C `%` function.

SASM contains a set of instructions to perform floating point operations. These instructions are separate from the instructions that do integer operations. Floating point and integer operands may not be mixed in an instruction. Comparisons between floating point values require an understanding of the representation used for floating point values. The representations for floating point values are discussed in Chapter 5. Any comparisons must be accomplished using the logical and integer arithmetic instructions. Note that the underlying Pentium architecture provides many more floating point instructions than the four given SASM arithmetic instructions. However, this set is sufficient to implement any necessary function. SASM provides no method for allowing the programmer to determine the method used for rounding.

```
/* a simple C program to average 3 integers */
main()
{
        int avg;
        int i1 = 20;
        int i2 = 13;
        int i3 = 82;

        avg = (i1 + i2 + i3) / 3;
}
```

```
;a simple SASM program to average 3 integers
title average program
.486
.model flat, stdcall
.stack 1000h
include sasmacros.inc

.data
avg     dd ?            ; integer average
i1      dd 20           ; first number in the average
i2      dd 13           ; second number in the average
i3      dd 82           ; third number in the average

.code
main:
        move            avg, i1
        iadd            avg, i2
        iadd            avg, i3
        idivi           avg, 3          ; get integer average
        done
end
```

Figure 3.2 C and SASM versions of a program that averages three integers.

A Simple SASM Program

Figure 3.2 contains the code for an exceptionally simple program that finds the average of the three integers contained in the variables `i1`, `i2`, and `i3`. This example illustrates several important parts of a program not yet specified. The program is shown in both C and SASM.

SASM programs can be documented by adding comments. The first line of the SASM program is a comment. A comment in C is marked by surrounding it with the character strings `/*` and `*/`. SASM comments are formed on a line-by-line basis. Within any line of a program, anything that follows a `;` (semicolon) character is considered to be a comment. Therefore, a comment may appear on the same line as an instruction or declaration by placing a semicolon between the end of the instruction or declaration and the comment itself. A comment may also appear by itself on a line that begins with the `;` character. Comments may not span lines.

Following the comment at the beginning of the program is a line that gives the program a `title`. A title is optional, and it does not need to be at the beginning of the source code.

The title in the SASM program is followed by several lines containing directives. These directives give the assembler information about how to assemble the program. The `.486` directive tells the assembler that the architecture assumed for the assembly language program is the Intel 486. The Pentium architecture is remarkably similar to the 486. Since the 486 architecture predates the Pentium, programming tools that work for the 486 architecture (but not yet for the Pentium architecture) may be used.

The `.model` directive specifies the programmers choice of memory addressing. The Pentium architecture gives a programmer several choices in how to access memory. The model that this book uses exclusively is called the flat model.

The `.stack` directive is unnecessary for programs that do not use the stack. Stacks and their usage are discussed in Chapters 8 and 10. This directive specifies the amount of memory to be set aside for a stack.

The line in the program

```
include sasmacros.inc
```

is what allows the programmer to specify SASM instructions while producing code that will execute Pentium code. The file `sasmacros.inc` defines **macros** to provide the illusion of SASM instructions. Without the inclusion of this file, the SASM instructions will not be available, since their translations to Pentium code will be missing. Macros give the programmer a method of substituting text of one form with text of another form.

Every SASM program needs to have the first instruction to be executed within the program marked. One method for marking this entry point is by the use of a special label. For programs that use the macros to provide SASM instructions, this label is `main`.

What appears to be the instruction `done` in the code is another macro that prompts the user to press any character on the keyboard, and then waits for a key to be pressed. When a key is pressed, the macro does a small amount of housekeeping and then exits.

The end of a program is indicated by the single word `end`. The end of a program is marked for the benefit of the assembler.

Within the program in Figure 3.2, the variable `avg` is declared to be an integer. Because of this, the instruction `idivi` only gives the integer portion of the average. The remainder is lost. For the given variable values, the variable `avg` will contain the value 38, not $38\frac{1}{3}$.

3.4 CONTROL STRUCTURES

The assembly language instructions presented so far are not sufficient to form a usable programming language. C provides two categories of **structured statements** or **control structures**: conditionals and iteratives. An example of the first category is an **if statement**. It provides the capability for conditional execution of a statement. If the condition in the if statement evaluates to true, then the statement is executed. Otherwise it is skipped. Here is a C if statement.

```
if (a < b)
        c = a + b;
```

When the if statement is executed, the first thing that occurs is a comparison. The value of a is compared against the value of b. If a is indeed less than b, then the conditional evaluates to `true`, and the statement associated with the if statement is executed. In this case, the sum of a and b is calculated and assigned to variable c. If the conditional evaluated to `false`, then the statement is not executed. It is skipped. This is conditional execution; depending on the value of the condition, a statement may or may not be skipped.

An example of the second category is a **repetitive statement**, which is used to implement a **loop.** C examples of repetitive statements are `for`, `while`, and `do-while` loops. Both categories of statements are made possible by the assembly language construct called a **branch** or **jump**. These are **control instructions**, and the simplest is the equivalent of the C `goto` statement.

More complex control instructions combine conditional execution with a `goto` statement. This powerful set of instructions is the only mechanism provided in SASM to enable looping constructs. While this limitation may seem restrictive initially, there are very good reasons for it, since this restriction closely reflects the underlying hardware restrictions. The use of `goto` is generally discouraged in high-level languages because it makes programs difficult to analyze and debug. If the compiler is implemented correctly, however, and the high-level language program is well structured, the use of control instructions at the assembly language level introduces no new concerns. Compilers produce assembly language code using control instructions.

Figure 3.3 summarizes SASM's control instructions. SASM (and the underlying Pentium architecture) depend on condition codes for control decisions. Many of the arithmetic instructions set the condition codes. Figure 3.4 contains a partial list of the condition codes. The zero flag (ZF) gets set to 1 when a result is 0. It is cleared otherwise. The sign flag indicates when a value is negative. The sign flag is set to 1 when a result is negative. It is cleared when a result is 0 or positive. The `compare` instruction exists in the instruction set to set the condition codes explicitly.

SASM Instructions	Operation	Notes
`br label`	unconditional branch	goto label
`bgz label`	branch if greater than 0	if ZF=SF=0, goto label
`bgez label`	branch if greater than or equal to 0	if ZF=1 or SF=0, goto label
`blz label`	branch if less than 0	if SF=1, goto label
`blez label`	branch if less than or equal to 0	if SF=1 or ZF=1, goto label
`bez label`	branch if equal to 0	if ZF=1, goto label
`bnz label`	branch if not equal to 0	if ZF=0, goto label
`compare x, y`		does the operation x - y to set condition codes x and y are integers
`compareb x, y`		does the operation x - y to set condition codes x and y are characters

Figure 3.3 Instructions enabling conditional execution in SASM.

Flag	Name	Value
ZF	zero flag	ZF = 1 if value is zero
SF	sign flag	SF = 1 if value is negative

Figure 3.4 SASM condition codes

Note that an unconditional control instruction can be constructed from a conditional one. As an example, the SASM instruction

```
br      next
```

could also be implemented with the code fragment

```
move    temp, 0
compare temp, temp
bez     next
```

Also note that not all the given SASM control instructions are necessary to the instruction set. For example, the SASM instruction `bgez` can be synthesized using the following code fragment.

```
          ;branch to L1 if x >= y
          compare      x, y
          bgz          L1
          bez          L1
          .
          .
          .
L1:       ; code to execute if x >= y
```

Figure 3.5 shows a C `if-then-else` statement and two possible SASM assembly language equivalents. The statement tests if `AA` is positive. If `AA` is positive, it assigns to `BB` the value of `CC/AA`. Otherwise, it assigns `BB` the value `AA + 10`. All three code fragments implement the same function. Note that the first SASM equivalent reverses the sense of the comparison, and the second reverses the order of the `if` and `else` statements.

So far, labels have been used only to identify variable names. Labels are also used to identify an instruction or variable declaration. When the program is assembled, the assembler allocates storage space for both program instructions and data. Each label must be unique. When a label is attached to an instruction or to data, the assembler associates a memory location with the label.

Two versions of SASM code are given in Figure 3.5 to illustrate a point. There are numerous ways to program any given high-level language control structure. Based on the specific program, code written one way might execute more efficiently than code written another. This fact can be used to advantage by a sophisticated compiler or assembly language programmer.

A compound conditional can be built out of multiple control instructions. Figure 3.6 shows an example of a C compound conditional statement. One of the two conditions must evaluate to `true` if the statements within the `if` statement are to be executed. The SASM

C statement

```
if (AA > 0) then
    BB = CC / AA;
else
    BB = AA + 10;
```

Possible SASM equivalent

```
              compare     0, AA
              blez        else_part
              move        BB, CC
              idivi       BB, AA
              br          end_if
else_part:    move        BB, AA
              iadd        BB, 10
end_if:
```

Another possible SASM equivalent

```
              compare     AA, 0
              bgz         if_part
              move        BB, AA
              iadd        BB, 10
              br          end_if
if_part:      move        BB, CC
              idivi       BB, AA
end_if:
```

Figure 3.5 SASM code fragments implementing the C `if-then-else` statement.

code uses two control instructions to implement the structure of the compound conditional. If `AA` is not equal to `BB`, then the `bez` branch is not taken, and the second comparison is made. If `AA` and `BB` are equal, then the branch is taken to the code within the `if` statement. If both conditionals turn out to be false, then the unconditional control instruction, `br`, modifies the PC such that it contains the address `end_if`.

A second example of a compound conditional is given in Figure 3.7. It shows an example containing a logical `and` together with a logical `or`. In C, the evaluation of the `and` is completed before the `or`. The equivalent SASM code to implement the `if` statement reverses some of the conditions. This reversal has the effect of reducing the number of instructions necessary to implement the complete test.

C statement

```
if ( (AA == BB) || (XX < YY) ) {
        AA = AA + 1;
        BB = BB - 1;
        YY = AA + XX;
}
```

SASM equivalent

```
                compare         AA, BB
                bez             do_if
                compare         XX, YY
                bgez            end_if
do_if:          iadd            AA, 1
                iadd            BB, -1
                move            YY, AA
                iadd            YY, XX
end_if:
```

Figure 3.6 SASM code implementing a C compound conditional.

C statement

```
if ( (AA == BB) && (XX == YY) || (ZZ < 0) ) {
        AA = AA + 1;
        XX = ZZ;
}
```

SASM equivalent

```
                compare         AA, BB
                bnz             check_ZZ
                compare         XX, YY
                bez             do_if
check_ZZ:       compare         ZZ, 0
                bgez            end_if
do_if:          iadd            AA, 1
                move            XX, ZZ
end_if:
```

Figure 3.7 SASM code implementing a C compound conditional.

C statement

```
result = 1;
counter = exponent;
while (counter > 0) {
        result = result * base;
        counter = counter - 1;
}
```

SASM equivalent

```
              move          result, 1
              move          counter, exponent
              compare       counter, 0
while_1:      blez          end_while
              imult         result, base
              isub          counter, 1
              br            while_1
end_while1:
```

Figure 3.8 SASM code to calculate base^{exponent} using a `while` loop.

An equivalent to a C `while` loop is straightforward to build out of SASM instructions. Figure 3.8 contains both a C version and a SASM version of a `while` loop that implements a power function. It calculates base^{exponent}, where `exponent` is assumed to be a positive integer. The result is assigned to the variable `result`. Note that the variables `base` and `exponent` are not changed by the execution of the loop, like the C implementation. The `compare` instruction is necessary to set the condition codes before they are tested at the top of the loop. A `compare` instruction is not required within the loop, because the `isub` instruction correctly sets the condition codes based on the value placed in the variable `counter`. The control instructions test the condition codes; they do not set the condition codes.

A C `for` loop can also be formed from SASM instructions. Figure 3.9 contains a C `for` loop and an SASM translation of the loop. Before the loop is entered, the loop induction variable `counter` is initialized to 1. At the top of the loop is a test to see if the loop induction variable is greater than the given ending value (`exponent`). If it is greater, the branch is taken, and the loop is exited. This is done by a `compare` instruction followed by the conditional control instruction `bgz`. The last statement in the `for` loop is an unconditional branch back to the top of the loop. Before branching back to the top, the loop induction variable is incremented by 1. Notice that although the high-level language looping construct can define that a `for` loop implicitly increments the loop induction variable, SASM does not. A SASM equivalent must explicitly contain an instruction to add one to the loop induction variable. Incrementing an induction variable is such a common operation that some assembly languages provide a mechanism for implicitly incrementing a variable, just as high-level languages do.

C statement

```
result = 1;
for (counter = 1; counter <= exponent; counter++) {
        result = result * base;
}
```

SASM equivalent

```
        move       result, 1
        move       counter, 1    ; initialize loop induction variable

        ; exit loop when counter > exponent
for_loop:
        compare    counter, exponent
        bgz        end_for
        imult      result, base
        iadd       counter, 1    ; increment loop induction variable
        br         for_loop
end_for:
```

Figure 3.9 SASM code to calculate $base^{exponent}$ using a `for` loop.

3.5 COMMUNICATION WITH THE USER

The final necessary item for an assembly language is some form of communication with the user. The communication is between the computer and the user of the program. For simplicity, assume that all input is communication from the user, and it comes from a keyboard. All output communication from the computer to the user goes to a display (or screen).

Figure 3.10 contains SASM communication instructions. There is one **input** instruction. It reads one character of data from a keyboard, and places the data in the variable specified as an operand. There are four **output** instructions. Each displays the data specified by the operand variable.

SASM Instructions	Equivalent C Statement	Notes
`get_ch ch`	`ch = getc(stdin);`	
`put_ch ch`	`printf("%c", ch);`	
`put_i x`	`printf("%d", x);`	
`put_fp fl`	`printf("%f", fl);`	
`put_str stringname`	`printf("%s", stringname);`	

Figure 3.10 SASM communication instructions.

The SASM `put_ch` instruction sends a single character as output. The SASM instruction

```
put_ch variable
```

is equivalent to the C statement

```
printf("%c", variable);
```

In order to inject a new line into the output, the newline character, given in C by '`\n`', is explicitly printed. The newline character can be declared by the directive

```
newline       db     0ah
```

Printing out this character forces the cursor to move to the beginning of the next line.

The output operation `put_str` takes a special form of string, and outputs it to the screen. The string is essentially an array of characters, and the final character of the string is the null character. The null termination tells the operating system when the end of the string has been reached and it should stop printing characters.

One way to declare a string that is null terminated is to use the directive

```
string1 db 'howdy!', 0
```

This directive declares a string of 7 characters, and labels it `string1`. The first 6 characters are assigned to be the characters in the string, and the final character is the null character. When declared as a null-terminated string, the string is printed out to a display by using the single instruction

```
put_str string1
```

The `put_str` instruction is a powerful instruction for displaying messages, but it is in fact a simple procedure that calls `put_ch` repeatedly. Here is the SASM code to write the message `howdy!`, using only `put_ch` instructions.

```
put_ch 'h'
put_ch 'o'
put_ch 'w'
put_ch 'd'
put_ch 'y'
put_ch '!'
```

The structure of the input and output instructions is similar to that of C. The SASM input instruction

```
get_ch  user_char
```

is equivalent to the C `getc` statement

```
user_char = getc(stdin);
```

C code

```
while ( (ch = getc(stdin)) != 'Z' );
printf("Z encountered\n");
```

SASM equivalent

```
.data
z_char          db     'Z'
message         db     'Z encountered', 0ah, 0
ch              db     ?

.code
put_loop:       get_ch          ch
                compareb        ch, z_char
                bnz             put_loop
                put_str         message
```

Figure 3.11 C and SASM code to read characters until the character 'Z' is encountered.

Figure 3.11 gives both C and SASM code fragments that read characters typed on the keyboard until the character 'Z' is encountered. It then prints out the message

```
Z encountered
```

3.6 A SASM PROGRAM

Figures 3.12 and 3.13 contain a simple, complete program that prints out for the user the sum of the first 25 positive integers. Figure 3.13 contains a SASM version of the C program given in Figure 3.12.

```
#include <stdio.h>
main()
{
        int n;          /* number of integers to sum */
        int sum;        /* running sum of the first n integers */
        int i;          /* integer to be added into sum, from 1 to 25 */

        n = 25;         /* calculate the sum */
        sum = 0;
        for (i=1; i<=n; i++)
                sum = sum + i;
        printf("The sum of the first %d integers is %d\n", n, sum);
}
```

Figure 3.12 C program that sums the first 25 positive integers.

```
; SASM program to sum the integers 1 through 25

.486
.model flat, stdcall
.stack 1000h

include sasmacros.inc
title sumints program

.data
n           dd      ?       ; number of integers to sum
sum         dd      ?       ; running sum of integers
i           dd      ?       ; the integers, loop induction variable
str1        db      'The sum of the first ', 0
str2        db      ' integers is ', 0
newline     db      0ah

.code
main:
        move        n, 25           ; set number of integers to sum
        move        sum, 0          ; at 25
        move        i, 1
for_loop:
        compare     i, n            ; loop until i reaches n
        bgz         done_for
        iadd        sum, i
        iadd        i, 1
        br          for_loop
done_for:
        put_str     str1            ; print out results
        put_i       n
        put_str     str2
        put_i       sum
        put_ch      newline
        done
end
```

Figure 3.13 SASM program that sums the first 25 positive integers.

SUMMARY

SASM has ways of implementing all the features of a high-level language: declarations, arithmetic operations, control structures, and communication with the user. SASM code looks like assembly language code. Each instruction or declaration is on its own line, and instructions are written with a mnemonic followed by one or more operands. The SASM language acts like an assembly language. Each instruction has a fixed number of operands and performs a single, well-defined operation. All operations in an assembly language are explicit, unlike some operations in high-level languages.

PROBLEMS

1. Draw a diagram of a skeleton SASM program. Identify the different parts of the program, what pieces are optional, and where instructions and data belong.

2. Explain how to implement a boolean-type variable in SASM. What is the variable's type, and how is it used?

3. Write a SASM declaration for

   a. a user-entered character called `char`

   b. the newline character

   c. an integer called `sum`.

4. Write a SASM declaration for

   a. a logical variable called `flag`

   b. the null-terminated string "`Please enter a character:`"

   c. the constant `pi`.

5. Write a SASM code fragment for the following C code:

```
if (i < 20) {
        i++;
}
```

6. Write a SASM code fragment for the following C code:

```
if (int1 > int2) && (int3 == int4) {
        int1 = int2 * int5;
}
```

7. Write a SASM code fragment for the following C code:

```
if (count > 200) {
        int1 = int2 - 10;
}
else {
        int1 = int2 + 10;
        count++;
}
```

8. Write a SASM code fragment for the following C code. Assume all variables are integers.

```
if (a == b) {
        if (c < d) {
                a = c * d;
                c = c - 2;
        }
}
```

9. Write a SASM code fragment for the following C code. Assume all variables are integers.

```
while (count < limit) {
        int1 = (int2 + int3 + int4 + int5) / 4;
        count ++;
}
```

10. Write a SASM code fragment for the following C `for` loop. Assume all variables are integers.

```
for (i=2; i<=z ; i++) {
        a = i % 2;
        if (a == 0)
                sum = sum + i;
}
```

11. Write a SASM code fragment for the following C code. Assume all variables are integers.

```
{
int     a, b, c, d, i;

        b = 13;
        for (i = 2; i <= a; i++) {
                c = b * i;
                if ( c != 0 )
                {
                        d = b - a;
                        d = d % c;
                }
        }
}
```

12. Are constants included in SASM? How is a constant specified and used in SASM?

13. Write a SASM code fragment that decides if the integer variable `value` is evenly divisible by 3. If `value` is evenly divisible, it should set the variable `flag` to 1, and if `value` is not evenly divisible, then it should set `flag` to 0.

14. Write a SASM program that prints out a sequence of *n* Xs, where *n* is a positive integer initialized in the declarations section of the program.

15. Write a SASM program that prints out the alphabet.

16. Write a SASM program that calculates the area of a triangle using integer variables.

17. Write a SASM program that calculates the area of a triangle using floating point variables.

18. Write a SASM program that calculates the perimeter and area of a rectangle using integer variables.

19. Write a SASM program that calculates the perimeter and area of a rectangle using floating point variables.

20. Write a SASM program that calculates the greatest common divisor of two integers.

21. Write a SASM program that counts the number of punctuation marks in a paragraph entered by the user.

22. Write a SASM program that reads a line of user input, and prints the line back out for the user with all lower-case letters converted to upper-case letters.

CHAPTER

4

NUMBER SYSTEMS

One of the most important functions of a computer is to maintain values for variables. The notation, or **representation**, used to represent mathematical values is critical in determining the cost of operations to be performed with respect to those values. No matter how quickly a computer can do calculations, the time required to execute common operations limits its performance. Thus it is critical to choose representations that make possible the fastest possible execution of the most important and most common operations.

The representation of numerical values is made difficult because of the discrete nature of computer representation. Only a finite number of unique values can be represented in a digital computer, regardless of how large the computer is. Yet there are an infinite number of integers. Even worse, there are an infinite number of rational numbers between any two integers, and an infinite number of irrational numbers between any two rational numbers, and even an infinite number of rational numbers between any two irrational numbers. How can all these numbers be represented? The answer, quite simply, is that they cannot all be represented *exactly*. Only a finite subset of numbers can be represented. This immediately introduces problems for arithmetic operations. What if a result has no representation?

Of the numbers that can be represented, the chosen method of representation affects the difficulty in performing arithmetic operations. This chapter demonstrates this concept—that the same arithmetic operation may be trivial or complex depending on the representation chosen for the numbers. This concept is true for traditional representations of numbers as well as for computer representation. This chapter concentrates on traditional representations, and Chapter 5 discusses the methods used to represent mathematical values in computers.

4.1 NUMBERS AND THEIR REPRESENTATION

In the earliest representations of numbers, people used a **unary** number system. The number 1 was represented by a single mark, 2 by two such marks, 3 by three marks, and so on. For small numbers, this system is adequate, and in fact makes simple addition and subtraction quite easy. It has several serious limitations. First, the number of symbols necessary to represent a number grows directly with the size of the number; so it is tedious to represent large numbers. Second, only positive integers can be represented in this way.

Representation of large numbers can be made easier to read by grouping the marks together, such as

If this technique is used very often, the group may come to be thought of as a new symbol, representing a larger number. This procedure can be applied repeatedly. For example, 5 can be represented by **V**, 10 by **X**, 50 by **L**. The symbol **V** was likely derived from

Using such notation, any positive integer can be represented as a sum of these symbols. Numbers can still be added together easily, and with the concept of making change (five **I**s for one **V**), it is not hard to subtract. Neither negative numbers nor nonintegers can be represented, however. Furthermore, most numbers can be represented in a variety of ways. Fifteen, for example, can be represented by **IIIII IIIII IIIII**, **IIIIIVV**, **VVV**, **VX**, as well as other combinations. This may seem unimportant, but it makes much more difficult the apparently simple question of whether two representations are representing the same value. Notice that the order of the symbols does not affect the value. Fifteen can be represented either as **VX** or as **XV**. A defined order reduces redundant representations, although it does not eliminate them. Simply sorting the symbols within a representation greatly reduces the number of ways that a given number can be represented. In fact, it guarantees there will always be a single, unique way to represent positive integers with the minimum number of symbols. Yet no matter how many symbols are introduced, there will always be numbers much larger than the value of the largest symbol, and such numbers can only be represented by repeating the largest symbol many times.

Roman Numeral	Decimal Value
I	1
V	5
X	10
L	50
C	100
D	500
M	1000

Figure 4.1 Roman numeral definitions.

Roman Numerals

A slight enhancement to the above scheme is to introduce an ordering of the symbols. Roman numerals are sorted by decreasing values. Assigning a conventional order to the symbols makes it possible to convey information by the *position* of the symbol. Violations of the ordering rule have defined meanings. Thus a symbol representing a smaller value preceding a symbol representing a larger value means that the smaller value represents a negative value. **IX** represents the value nine while **XI** represents the value eleven. This rule further reduces the size of the longest representations, but it still does not provide representations for negative values or nonintegers, or even zero. Figure 4.1 contains a set of symbols that are traditionally used to express numbers as Roman numerals.

Uniqueness is particularly important when comparing two representations to determine which is larger. In order to assure uniqueness, it is necessary further to restrict the order of the symbols: Only a single smaller symbol of any type may precede a larger one, and only symbols representing powers of ten (**I**, **X**, **C**, and so on) may be placed out of order. This rule guarantees that there is a unique and shortest representation for every number. This unique representation can easily be determined, and other representations can be converted into the unique form.

While the ordering introduces a unique representation for each number, it makes mathematical operations like addition much more difficult. Here is one possible algorithm for addition:

1. Convert all position-sensitive symbols into a position-insensitive form and sort by the values of the symbols. This conversion eliminates negative values, creating numbers that are not legal Roman numerals but are nevertheless unambiguous. Examples: **IV → IIII, IX → VIIII, CM → DCCCC.**
2. Merge the two position-insensitive representations into a single position-insensitive representation by sorting the symbols by value.
3. Starting with lowest-valued symbols, combine lower-value types into higher-value types. Examples: **IIIII → V, VV → X, XXXXX → L.**
4. Create legal Roman numerals by converting back to the unique format.

As an example, add the numbers **XIX** (19) and **MXMV** (1995).

1. **XIX → XVIIII**
   MXMV → MDCCCCLXXXXV
2. **XVIIII + MDCCCCLXXXXV → MDCCCCLXXXXXVVIIII**

3. **MDCCCCLXXXXXVVIIII → MDCCCCLXXXXXXIIII**
MDCCCCLXXXXXXIIII → MDCCCCLLXIIII
MDCCCCLLXIIII →MDCCCCCCXIIII
MDCCCCCCXIIII → MDDXIIII
MDDXIIII → MMXIIII
4. **MMXIIII → MMXIV**

4.2 WEIGHTED POSITIONAL NOTATION

Roman numerals have many limitations. They need many different symbols to represent arbitrarily large numbers. They cannot represent nonintegers, or even negative integers. Elementary arithmetic operations are tedious. Roman numerals are best used for obfuscation. The notion of ordering is an important concept that can be extended and employed in representations to overcome these limitations. The decimal number system includes a set of ten symbols representing the first ten integers (including zero), and uses the position of the symbols to indicate value. By assigning each position the appropriate power of ten, any possible sequence of the ten digits represents a unique integer. That integer is a weighted sum of the digits. Given a sequence of n digits, $d_0, d_1, d_2, \ldots, d_{n-1}$, the summation

$$d_0 \times 10^0 + d_1 \times 10^1 + d_2 \times 10^2 + \cdots + d_{n-1} \times 10^{n-1} = \sum_{i=0}^{n-1} d_i \times 10^i$$

has a unique value for every possible combination of the n digits. Conversely, every positive integer can be represented by some unique sequence. This key result has the additional property that the shortest sequences represent the smallest numbers. This is useful, since small numbers like five, eight, or fifteen need to be written down much more often than a number like three million, eight-hundred sixty-two thousand, four hundred fifty-one. Note, however, that the technique is not unique to a decimal system. Any positive integer value can be used as the **radix** or **base** for a weighted positional representation. For radix r, the first r integers, including zero, are given unique symbols, collectively called radix-r digits. Then for a sequence of n such digits, $s_0, s_1, s_2, \ldots, s_{n-1}$, if $s_{n-1} \neq 0$, the summation

$$N = s_0 b^0 + s_1 b^1 + (s_2 b^2) + \cdots + s_{n-1} b^{n-1} = \sum_{i=0}^{n-1} s_i b^i$$

yields the unique positive integer N. While either order could be used, the near-universal convention used for representing numbers is to write the symbols left to right by descending weight, $s_{n-1} s_{n-2} \ldots s_3 s_2 s_1 s_0$. This is a **weighted positional notation**.

The symbol carrying the most weight, s_{n-1}, is designated the **most significant digit**, while the symbol carrying the least weight, s_0, is designated the **least significant digit**.

For bases less than or equal to ten, a subset of the ten decimal digits can be used to represent the symbols. For example, only 0 and 1 are necessary for **binary** (radix two), and 0–7 for **octal** (radix eight). For bases larger than ten, such as **hexadecimal** (radix sixteen), new symbols must be introduced. It is common to use the first letters of the alphabet to represent the next symbols in order: *a* is used to represent ten, *b* to represent eleven, *c* for twelve, and so on. That convention is used here. For example, the hexadecimal sequence *18d* represents the decimal value

$$\begin{aligned} & 1 \times 16^2 + 8 \times 16^1 + d \times 16^0 \\ &= 1 \times 256 + 8 \times 16 + 13 \times 1 \\ &= 256 + 128 + 13 \\ &= 397_{\text{ten}} \end{aligned}$$

Hexadecimal representations containing the symbols *a-f* are easily recognized as such, but the sequence *315* could be the hexadecimal representation for 789_{ten}, the octal representation for 205_{ten}, or the decimal representation for 315_{ten}. In text a subscript is often used to indicate which is intended, as in the previous sentence (also written as 789_{10}). Using subscripts in programming languages is cumbersome; so different methods are employed. A common hexadecimal representation is given by the sequence `0x`, followed by the digits. For example, the hexadecimal sequence given above could be represented by `0x18d`. An alternative representation in code, and the method used by SASM, is to follow the digits by the letter 'h.' The same example represented in SASM code would be `18dh`. A hexadecimal representation in code is required to start with a digit. Therefore, if the hexadecimal value starts with a letter, a leading 0 is added. This is done to distinguish a hexadecimal value (that begins with a letter) from a symbol. An octal representation is indicated in SASM by using the single suffix letter 'q.' The number 27_{ten} is represented in hexadecimal as `1bh` and in octal as `33q`. Interestingly enough, most programming languages provide no convention for representing numbers in binary. SASM does recognize binary values as those that have the suffix letter 'b.'

Since the radix *r* can be any positive integer, the question naturally arises: What is the best value for *r*? The best choice for a computer is different than for humans, since the problems being solved are different, and therefore the costs of solving the problems are different. It is fairly easy to argue that radix ten is not optimal for either computers or humans, although it is less clear what radix would be optimal for all human uses. The choice of radix ten resulted from anatomical reasons. A larger radix would make counting by using fingers more difficult. So why not a smaller radix, say five? A smaller radix requires more digits to represent a large number. The largest integer that can be represented with three radix-five digits is $444_{\text{five}} = 124_{\text{ten}}$, while three radix-ten digits can represent an integer up to 999_{ten}, a number more than 8 times as large. Increasing the radix has a cost, because more unique symbols are required. The cost may be measured by space taken up by the symbol, time to draw the symbol, or difficulty of distinguishing the symbols. However that cost is measured, the cost of increasing the number of symbols is substantial.

Representing numbers in radix four means discriminating among four symbols, whereas radix two (binary) numbers only require discriminating between two symbols. Notice that a sequence of two binary symbols can represent the integers 0, 1, 2, and 3; so two binary digits can be used to substitute for a single radix-four digit. Since three binary digits can represent the integers 0, 1, 2, 3, 4, 5, 6, and 7, three binary digits can be used to represent a single octal (radix-eight) digit. Likewise, four binary digits can be used to represent a single hexadecimal (radix-sixteen) digit.

Digital circuitry provides an inexpensive way to design computers, and it easily discriminates between two values. With most technologies used in computers, discriminating

Decimal	Binary	Octal	Hexadecimal
0	0	0	0
1	1	1	1
2	10	2	2
3	11	3	3
4	100	4	4
5	101	5	5
6	110	6	6
7	111	7	7
8	1000	10	8
9	1001	11	9
10	1010	12	a
11	1011	13	b
12	1100	14	c
13	1101	15	d
14	1110	16	e
15	1111	17	f
16	1 0000	20	10
17	1 0001	21	11
18	1 0010	22	12
19	1 0011	23	13
20	1 0100	24	14

Figure 4.2 Values given in various radices.

only between two values is far cheaper than even three, and succeeding values become increasingly difficult. Thus numbers are represented by binary values. Because triplets of binary digits can easily be represented with a single octal digit, and quadruplets of binary digits can be represented with a single hexadecimal digit, errors are much less likely if humans work in either octal or hexadecimal. It is easy to convert integers between binary and either of these radices, and with a little practice, many people can do it by inspection. Converting to other radices, particularly decimal, is more difficult. On the other hand, representing numbers in octal or hexadecimal representation makes some operations easier for humans than the binary representation. For the decimal number 500, for example, it is much easier to remember the hexadecimal representation $1f4_{\text{sixteen}}$, or the octal representation 764_{eight}, than it is to remember the binary $1\ 1111\ 0100_{\text{two}}$. For the most part, representation of numbers in either hexadecimal or octal is simply a shorthand way of indicating binary representation. Figure 4.2 shows representations of the decimal values 0–20 in various radices.

Negative Numbers

The weighted positional notation introduced can be easily extended to represent zero and negative integers. Zero can be represented by violating the rule that the most significant symbol is not zero. Since a symbol is defined in any radix to represent zero, it is unambiguous to represent the number zero simply with the single symbol 0. Note that any single symbol unambiguously represents a number, regardless of radix, though the use of a letter as a symbol potentially introduces ambiguity with a single-letter variable name. Assigning symbols to the smallest negative integers leads to some interesting methods for representing negative numbers, since positive and negative numbers of different weights can now be mixed to form a positive or negative number. In addition to increasing the number of symbols required, such schemes do not readily yield a unique representation.

Alternatively, negative numbers can be specified by introducing a single additional symbol and specifying that it goes only at the beginning of the sequence. The symbol – is conventionally used to identify a negative number. Either the absence of the – symbol or the optional symbol + is used to indicate a positive value. Indicating negative numbers in this way requires the introduction of an additional symbol, two additional symbols if + is used. This may seem unimportant, but in a computer where numbers are represented in binary, the addition of a + or – symbol is problematic. The computer must be able to distinguish among three symbols: –, 0, and 1. Introducing a new symbol in this way would increase the number of symbols to three. For this and other reasons, other methods are used to represent negative numbers in a computer. These methods are discussed in Chapter 5, but the key idea is that if the computer is to distinguish between only two symbols, it must be able to recognize by the format of the representation whether the symbol is a binary digit or something else.

4.3 TRANSFORMATIONS BETWEEN RADICES

A number can be represented in a variety of ways. An integer can be represented using weighted positional notation with any radix. Since the representation used in a computer is not a decimal format, it is often necessary to determine the equivalent representation of a number with respect to a different radix. This section describes methods for performing such conversions.

There are three radices involved in the conversion of a representation. Two of these radices are the radix of the original representation and the radix of the final representation. Arithmetic algorithms may be applicable in any radix, but they are *performed* with respect to a particular radix. Therefore, the third radix involved in the conversion is the radix in which the arithmetic is performed. Addition yields the same result regardless of the representation. For addition of two numbers represented in decimal, a radix ten algorithm is naturally used, though one could convert both representations to radix two, perform the addition in binary, then convert the result back to decimal.

A computer must do all arithmetic in binary if it has only a radix-two arithmetic unit. The examples and methods given in this section are not radix specific in that they can be applied with respect to arithmetic in any radix. Since nondecimal arithmetic has not been introduced, all arithmetic in this chapter is decimal. The choice of conversion method is dictated by the radix of the arithmetic.

For decimal arithmetic, the algorithms convert decimal representations to another radix or they convert representations from another radix into decimal. Note that if binary arithmetic were employed, the natural radix would be two, and the conversions would be defined as converting to or from binary representations. It is important to stress, however, that none of the algorithms is specific to a radix.

Conversion into Decimal

Consider first the case of converting into decimal. The method relies on the definition of a number in weighted positional notation. The weighted positional notation is a sum of products. The method computes each of the terms and takes their sum. A number N represented in radix r by the n radix-r digits is written as a sequence of digits concatenated together with the most significant digit on the left.

$$d_{n-1}d_{n-2}\cdots d_2d_1d_0$$

This representation can be converted to radix ten simply by performing the following decimal summation.

$$N = \sum_{i=0}^{n-1} d_i r^i$$

An example is shown in Figure 4.3, where the binary number $10\ 0110_{\text{two}}$ is converted to radix ten.

A second example is shown in Figure 4.4, where the hexadecimal number $3b2_{\text{sixteen}}$ is converted to radix ten.

The formula can be rewritten to eliminate the exponentiation by recognizing the following equality:

$$N = \sum_{i=0}^{n-1} d_i r^i = d_0 + r(d_1 + r\{d_2 + r[d_3 + \cdots + r(d_{n-2} + rd_{n-1})]\cdots\})$$

binary representation	$= 10\ 0110_{\text{two}}$
decimal representation	$= 1\times 2^5 + 0\times 2^4 + 0\times 2^3 + 1\times 2^2 + 1\times 2^1 + 0\times 2^0$
	$= 38_{\text{ten}}$

Figure 4.3 Translation of a binary number to its decimal representation.

hexadecimal representation	$= 3b2_{\text{sixteen}}$
decimal representation	$= 3\times 16^2 + b\times 16^1 + 2\times 16^0$
	$= 3\times 16^2 + 11\times 16^1 + 2\times 16^0$
	$= 946_{\text{ten}}$

Figure 4.4 Translation of a hexadecimal number to its decimal representation.

For example, the hexadecimal representation $3b2_{\text{sixteen}}$ is converted as follows:

$$
\begin{aligned}
\text{hexadecimal representation} &= 3b2_{\text{sixteen}} \\
\text{decimal representation} &= 2 + 16_{\text{ten}}(b + 16_{\text{ten}} \times 3) \\
&= 2 + 16_{\text{ten}}(11_{\text{ten}} + 16_{\text{ten}} \times 3) \\
&= 2 + 16_{\text{ten}} \times 59 \\
&= 2 + 944 \\
&= 946
\end{aligned}
$$

Likewise, the binary representation of a number can be converted:

$$
\begin{aligned}
\text{binary representation} &= 11101_{\text{two}} \\
\text{decimal representation} &= 1 + 2\{0 + 2[1 + 2(1 + 2 \times 1)]\} \\
&= 1 + 2[0 + 2(1 + 2 \times 3)] \\
&= 1 + 2(0 + 2 \times 7) \\
&= 29
\end{aligned}
$$

Converting from Decimal

Presented here are two methods for converting from a representation in radix ten into another radix. The first calculates the least significant digit first. The method employs repetitive division. This method could be used to convert between numbers with a radix other than ten, but the radix of the arithmetic would need to be the radix of the original number.

To convert a number from radix ten to radix r, divide the number N by the radix r. Integer division provides an integer quotient and an integer remainder. The single-digit remainder is the least significant digit of the radix r representation. Now divide the quotient by r, again acquiring a quotient and remainder. The new remainder is the second-least-significant digit. Divide the new quotient by r to yield the third-least significant digit, and so on until the quotient is zero, in which case the final remainder is the most significant digit. Figure 4.5 gives an example of conversion of the decimal number 80_{ten} into binary.

Division	Quotient	Remainder
$80_{\text{ten}}/2$	40_{ten}	0
$40_{\text{ten}}/2$	20_{ten}	0
$20_{\text{ten}}/2$	10_{ten}	0
$10_{\text{ten}}/2$	5	0
5/2	2	1
2/2	1	0
1/2	0	1

binary representation: 1010000_{two}

decimal representation: 80_{ten}

Figure 4.5 Division method for translating a decimal number to its binary representation.

Figure 4.6 gives an example of conversion of the decimal number 946_{ten} into hexadecimal.

Division	**Quotient**	**Remainder**
$946_{ten}/16_{ten}$	59_{ten}	2
$59_{ten}/16_{ten}$	3_{ten}	$11_{ten} = b$
$3/16_{ten}$	0	3

hexadecimal representation: $3b2_{sixteen}$
decimal representation: 946_{ten}

Figure 4.6 Division method for translating a decimal value to its hexadecimal representation.

A second algorithm for converting from the radix ten employs a subtraction-of-powers method. This method calculates the most significant digit first by guessing the appropriate value, in the same way that long division involves guessing each digit of the quotient, then verifying that it is correct. To convert the radix-*B* representation, $b_{n-1}b_{n-2}\cdots b_2b_1b_0$, of the number

$$N = \sum_{i=0}^{n-1} b_i B^i$$

to the radix-*C* representation, $c_{m-1}c_{m-2}\cdots c_2c_1c_0$

$$N = \sum_{i=0}^{m-1} c_i C^i$$

the idea is to guess the most significant digit, c_{m-1}. The first guess is the position of the most significant digit, that is, the value of *m*. This value can be determined by the following criterion: *m* is the smallest integer for which $C^m > N$.

Having determined *m*, the value of the most significant digit, c_{m-1}, can be determined by the following criterion: c_{m-1} is the largest digit such that

$$c_{m-1}C^{m-1} \le N$$

Once c_{m-1} is determined, c_{m-2} is found by recognizing that it must be the largest digit such that

$$c_{m-2}C^{m-2} \le N - c_{m-1}C^{m-1}$$

This process is continued, determining digits c_{m-3}, c_{m-4}, and so on until c_0 is determined.

Figure 4.7 shows an example of this method applied to determine the binary representation of the number 43_{ten}. Note that guessing is particularly easy in binary, since the only two possibilities are zero and one, and both are easy to test by inspection.

Figure 4.8 shows an example to determine the hexadecimal representation of the number 946_{ten}.

$$2^5 < 43_{ten} < 2^6 \qquad m = 6$$
$$43_{ten} - 2^5 = 11_{ten}$$
$$11_{ten} - 2^3 = 3$$
$$3 - 2^1 = 1$$
$$1 - 2^0 = 0$$
$$43_{ten} = 2^5 + 2^3 + 2^1 + 2^0$$

binary representation: 101011_{two}
decimal representation: 43_{ten}

Figure 4.7 Subtraction-of-powers method for translating a decimal number to its binary representation.

$$16^2 < 946_{ten} < 16^3 \qquad m = 3$$
$$946_{ten} - 3 \times 16^2 = 178_{ten} \qquad c_2 = 3$$
$$178_{ten} - 11 \times 16^1 = 2 \qquad c_1 = 11_{ten} = b$$
$$2 - 2 \times 16^0 = 0 \qquad c_0 = 2$$

hexadecimal representation: $3b2_{sixteen}$
decimal representation: 946_{ten}

Figure 4.8 Subtraction-of-powers method for translating a decimal representation to its hexadecimal representation.

Powers of Two

Of particular interest is converting between bases that are both powers of two. Because any representation based on a power of two can easily be converted to binary representation, these conversions are particularly easy. The algorithm from binary to radix 2^a is simple: Group the binary digits together in groups of a, starting from the least significant digit. Add leading zeros if necessary to obtain a whole number of groups. Substitute for each group the equivalent symbol in radix 2^a. For example, the binary number

$$1110110010_{two}$$

is grouped for octal ($a = 3$) as

$$001 \quad 110 \quad 110 \quad 010_{two}$$

It is translated into octal as

$$1662_{eight}$$

Likewise, the same number can be converted into hexadecimal ($a = 4$)

$$1110110010_{two}$$

$$0011 \quad 1011 \quad 0010_{two}$$

$$3b2_{sixteen}$$

Conversion to binary is even simpler. Convert each symbol in radix 2^a into the equivalent binary string of a digits, concatenate the result, and drop any leading zeros:

$$a45_{\text{sixteen}}$$

$$1010 \quad 0100 \quad 0101_{\text{two}}$$

$$101001000101_{\text{two}}$$

In this text, binary numbers are usually grouped by fours to facilitate conversion to hexadecimal representation by inspection.

Two methods have actually been given, one for converting to a larger power of two, one for converting to a smaller. Note that no arithmetic operations are being performed in these methods.

4.4 REPRESENTATION OF NONINTEGER NUMBERS

Precise representation of numbers is important in a computer, even for extremely large or small numbers. Physics calculations often use the speed of light, approximately 3.0×10^8 meters per second. Chemistry calculations invariably involve Avogadro's number, approximately 6.022×10^{23} atoms per mole. The mass of the earth is approximately 5.98×10^{24} kilograms. These are examples of very large numbers that must be representable. Some extremely small numbers come from the same fields of study. The charge on an electron is approximately -1.60×10^{-19} coulombs. Planck's constant is approximately 6.63×10^{-27} erg seconds. Computer representations must allow for this huge **range** of values. The representation must also allow for **precise** values. For example, using a value for π of 3.14 might introduce small errors into final results. The value 3.1415927 has a higher precision, but it is still only an approximation. Both a large range and high precision must be captured in the representation chosen for numbers.

There are several reasons why integer-only representation and arithmetic are preferred in computers. Many problems can be solved with integers alone, and many program variables need be assigned only integer values. (Loops are normally executed an integral number of times.) Another important property of integer arithmetic is that addition, subtraction, and multiplication are **closed** under the integers. Any mathematical computation starting with integers and employing only these operations will have only integer results. Division can also be defined so that it is also closed over integers by using a proper fraction for a remainder. While only a finite number of integers can be represented, it is possible to represent all integer values within a very wide **range**. If all the integers within a range are representable, then addition, subtraction, and multiplication have the property that a result is either representable or out of the range. Real numbers, on the other hand, do not have this property, because between any two real numbers, regardless of how close they are together, additional real numbers exist. The computer with representations of real numbers must deal with approximate results, since simple arithmetic operations such as taking the average of two almost equal numbers generate results that cannot be represented exactly. Approximate representation gives rise to errors that, while very small, nevertheless accumulate with repetition, creating some surprising problems with convergence and even the correctness of the result. A direct result of the need to round is that noninteger multiplication is not commutative, $xy \neq yx$, on many computers. The ability to represent results exactly in integer arithmetic gives a strong incentive to restrict representations to integers.

Extending Weighted Positional Notation to Include Nonintegers

Nonrepeating decimal numbers can be represented simply as a ratio of two integers, one of which is a power of 10. For example, the number 2.98 is a rational number that can be represented as

$$\frac{298}{10^2}$$

This fact forms the basis for extending weighted positional notation to include nonrepeating rational numbers. If a number N has X decimal digits, it can be represented exactly by the integer ratio

$$\frac{10^X \times N}{10^X}$$

A period (the decimal point) is placed appropriately to indicate the magnitude of the denominator. The decimal point is simply a shorthand way of identifying the number as a rational number where the denominator is a power of 10. This concept extends to any radix, and adding a period in the middle (called a **radix point** since it is not decimal) is a concise way of representing the set of rational numbers that can be represented in that radix as a ratio with a denominator equal to a power of the radix. As an example, the number

$$13.875_{\text{ten}} = \frac{111_{\text{ten}}}{8}$$

can be represented in octal as 15.7_{eight}, since

$$\frac{111_{\text{ten}}}{8} = \frac{157_{\text{eight}}}{8} = \frac{15.7_{\text{eight}} \times 8^1}{8^1} = 15.7_{\text{eight}}$$

Repeating decimal numbers are also rational numbers, but they cannot be represented as a ratio with the denominator equal to a power of ten. Repeating pattern numbers occur in any radix. For example, the number $\frac{1}{3}$ cannot be represented in either decimal or binary except as a repeating pattern.

$$\frac{1}{3} = 0.33333\ldots_{\text{ten}} = 0.\bar{3}_{\text{ten}} = 0.01010101\ldots_{\text{two}} = 0.\overline{01}_{\text{two}}$$

The bar notation is used to indicate the sequence of digits that repeats. By extending the weighted positional notation to include a radix point as demonstrated above, a large and well-spaced subset of the rational numbers can be represented. This set includes all the rational numbers that can be represented as a ratio where the denominator is a power of the radix. By representing the repeating-pattern numbers to a large number of places, even the repeating-pattern numbers can be closely approximated. Computers are capable of representing exactly any rational number as a ratio of two integers. The subset of nonrepeating patterns in the radix used for representation is a reasonable subset of the rational numbers, and this subset is well supported on most computers.

Conversion of Fractions

The algorithms of Section 4.3 (Transformations between Radices) can be extended to convert nonintegers. For example, converting a decimal fraction into binary can be accomplished with the following algorithm. An improper fraction (a noninteger greater than one) is represented as

$$f_{n-1}f_{n-2}\cdots f_2 f_1 f_0 . f_{-1} f_{-2} f_{-3}\cdots$$

It is treated as the sum of an integer and a proper fraction. The integer is converted using the techniques discussed earlier. The binary representation of a proper fraction F has the form

$$F = .f_{-1}f_{-2}f_{-3}\cdots$$

The fraction is converted one digit at a time, beginning with its most significant digit. For the binary case, the most significant digit f_{-1} of the fraction F is either zero or one. It is one if and only if

$$F \geq \frac{1}{2^1}$$

Multiplying the fraction F by two results in an improper fraction. The integer portion of the result gives the most significant bit, f_{-1}. The proper fraction is used to find the next most significant bit, f_{-2}. f_{-2} is one if and only if the fraction is at least $\frac{1}{2}$. Multiply the proper fraction by 2. The integer portion of the resulting improper fraction gives the next bit, f_{-2}. This process is repeated as long as required. The binary representation of the original fraction is determined exactly if the proper fraction becomes 0. The pattern of bits will eventually repeat in all cases.

Two examples of this technique are given in Figures 4.9 and 4.10. The example given in Figure 4.9 expresses values in proper fractions. The example in Figure 4.10 uses decimals. This technique can be extended to convert a decimal fraction to any other radix. A similar algorithm exists for converting a noninteger represented in any radix into decimal representation.

Approximate Values

There are generally two categories of numbers that must be represented in a computer. One category includes the numbers that can be expressed exactly using mathematics. These include the integers, all rational numbers (the ratio of two integers), and some (irrational) constants such as π, e, and $\sqrt{2}$. The second category consists of experimentally

$$1\frac{5}{8} = 1 + \frac{5}{8} \qquad f_0 = 1$$

proper fraction: $\frac{5}{8}$

$$2 \times \frac{5}{8} = 1 + \frac{1}{4} \qquad f_{-1} = 1$$

$$2 \times \frac{1}{4} = 0 + \frac{1}{2} \qquad f_{-2} = 0$$

$$2 \times \frac{1}{2} = 1 + 0 \qquad f_{-3} = 1$$

binary representation: 1.101_{two}

decimal representation: $1\frac{5}{8}$

Figure 4.9 Conversion of the number $1\frac{5}{8}$ to binary.

$3.6 = 3 + 0.6$		$f_1 f_0 = 11$
	proper fraction: .6	
2×0.6	$= 1 + .2$	$f_{-1} = 1$
2×0.2	$= 0 + .4$	$f_{-2} = 0$
2×0.4	$= 0 + .8$	$f_{-3} = 0$
2×0.8	$= 1 + .6$	$f_{-4} = 1$

binary representation: 11.1001_{two}
decimal representation: 3.6_{ten}

Figure 4.10 Conversion of the decimal representation of the number 3.6_{ten} to binary.

derived numbers. This category includes numbers that have been determined by experimental measurement and calculation. Values of numbers in this category are known only approximately, though some are known with remarkable precision. In other words, there is an inherent error associated with the second category of numbers. Such experimental values can actually be thought of as a pair of exactly known constants, representing the endpoints of the range of values within which the measured value is thought to be. If the endpoint is not known exactly, or cannot be represented exactly, an exact number can always be selected by increasing the range slightly. This introduces additional possible error, and therefore should be minimized as much as possible. For example, a number measured with a tool that is accurate to 0.01% can be represented by a range of values, from 0.01% less than the measured value to 0.01% greater than the measured value. If a measurement taken with this instrument gives a reading of 78.962 meters, the interval of possible values can be expressed as 78.962±0.01% meters. Computing the endpoints of the range, and rounding down for the smaller number, up for the larger, gives a range with endpoints of 78.9541 and 78.9699 meters.

When computations are performed using experimentally derived constants, the size of the interval, expressed as a percent of the value, generally does not shrink, but there are reasons why it might grow. Subtracting one experimentally derived constant from another

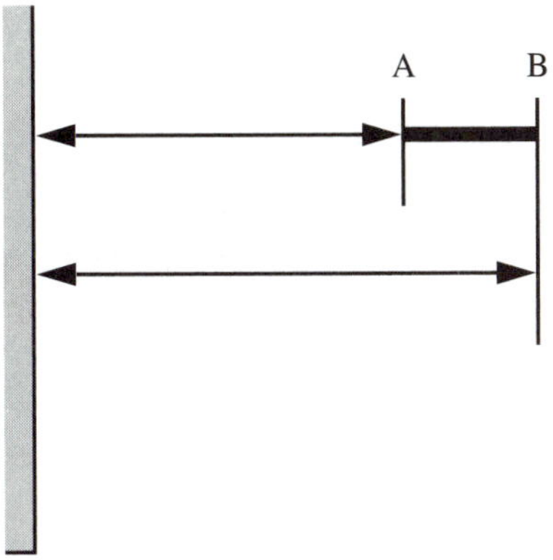

Figure 4.11 Measuring the distance from A to B.

results in a new interval that can be determined by computing the four exact results from the endpoints of the ranges of the two constants. The two extreme values represent a new interval, which may be much larger, as a percent of the result, than either of the two original constants. If the endpoints of such intervals can be represented precisely, the exact range of the result can be determined. Again, the interval can be widened to account for an inability to represent the endpoint precisely. Continuing with the above example, suppose that the line segment AB shown in Figure 4.11 is being determined by measuring the distance from the wall to A, and the distance from the wall to B, and taking the difference. If A is measured to be 78.962 meters, and B is measured to be 81.527 meters, the accuracy of the instrument indicates that B is in the range of 81.527±0.01% meters, with minimum and maximum values of 81.5188 and 81.5352, respectively. Subtracting A from B gives an approximate value of 81.527 – 78.962 = 2.565 meters. This result is not accurate within 0.01%, however, since it could be as small as 81.5188 – 78.9699 = 2.5489 meters or as large as 81.5352 – 78.9541 = 2.5811 meters. Notice that the difference of either of these endpoints is much more than 0.01%. The result is only accurate to about 1.3%.

Computer designers strive to provide efficient ways for representing numbers that permit rapid computation without greatly increasing the range of error in the process. Integers over a wide range of values can be represented exactly, and there are ways to extend the representation of integers to arbitrarily large values. Rational numbers can be represented exactly as a ratio of two integers. Irrational numbers can be represented with an arbitrarily high degree of precision, so that the error introduced by their imprecise representation can be guaranteed to be acceptably small. Approximate values can be represented by providing a sufficiently large set of rational numbers so that the endpoints of an interval can be closely approximated. These techniques, known as **interval arithmetic**, can be employed to determine the precision of answers.

Scientific Notation

A large set of rational numbers can be represented using two integers. The denominator contains a power of the radix, and the exponent alone can be used to specify the denominator, since it will always be an integer. A slightly different way of representing the same subset of rational numbers using integers is **scientific notation**. This form is capable of representing many rational numbers with three integers, an **exponent** x, a **significand** or **mantissa** s, and a radix or base r. The standard form is

$$\text{number} = s \times r^{x}$$

The extended weighted positional notation is used to represent the significand and the exponent, and the radix for that notation usually is the same as the radix r. In the standard form, the significand is not an integer. It can always be made into an integer by multiplying it by a fixed power of the radix and subtracting the appropriate integer constant from the exponent. For example, the number 15.625 is normally represented in scientific notation as 1.5625×10^{1}. It can be represented exclusively with integers as 15625×10^{-3}.

Normalization

It would be perfectly reasonable to require that the significand always be an integer, but scientific convention places a different restriction on the significand. It must be assigned within a range of values to guarantee uniqueness. In radix ten, the significand normally must lie within the range of one and ten. Adjusting the significand to satisfy this criterion, with compensation of the exponent to maintain the same value, is known as **normalization**. Standard scientific notation defines normalization to meet the following rule:

$$1 \leq s < r$$

where s is the significand, and r is the radix. This rule implies that, in the extended weighted positional notation with no leading zeros in the significand, the radix point always occurs just to the right of the first significant symbol. The examples of physical constants given at the beginning of this section are normalized.

Precision and Accuracy

Note that standard scientific notation can be converted into a notation exclusively using integers by multiplying the significand appropriately to move the radix point all the way to the right, and subtracting the appropriate amount from the exponent. Thus an equivalent form, which would also guarantee uniqueness, would be to require the significand to be an integer. No digits may be dropped from the significand, even if the least significant digit in the integer is zero. Scientific notation carries with it additional information: an indication of the **accuracy** of the representation. In fact, scientific notation provides *only* representation of approximate values. The value 1.5625×10^{1} is really 15.625 ± 0.0005. It represents a range of values between 15.6245 and 15.6255. The value 1.56250×10^{1} represents a range of values between 15.62495 and 15.62505, because it represents the interval 15.6250 ± 0.00005. Note that scientific notation is inherently intended for experimentally derived, or approximate, representation. There is no way to represent the integer 2 exactly using scientific notation. The representation $2.0000000000 \times 10^{0}$ only approximately represents the integer 2, and zero cannot be represented at all.

Representation of approximate values is appropriate in scientific computations, where measured or calculated numbers are only known approximately. In the sciences, the assessment of the accuracy of a measurement is a critical aspect of an experiment, and the concept of **significant digits** is used to maintain an estimate of the maximum accumulated error. This technique provides rule-of-thumb approximations to the techniques of interval arithmetic. Because error analysis need only be estimated approximately, using the concept of significant digits can save a great deal of computation while maintaining a rough estimate of the accuracy of the results.

Computations that create new values must obey rules about significant digits. For example, if the diameter of a circle is measured to be 13.7 ± 0.05 centimeters, the measured value is accurate to three decimal digits. It has three significant digits. Regardless of the accuracy to which π is known, the circumference of the circle can be computed only to three significant digits. Using a calculator with a π key, the calculation of the circumference, $\pi \times 13.7$, produces the result 43.039819360. If it is set to give the result in scientific notation, it produces the result 4.3039818×10^1. The answer is incorrect because it does not take significant digits into account. While the printed result is within the range of values, it is misleading because it implies far more accuracy than is warranted from the measured data. If the diameter happens to be measured accurately to six significant digits, and is in fact 13.7000 ± 0.00005 centimeters, the result can be expressed more accurately as 43.0398. The calculator does not know how to round, because it is not given information about the accuracy of the measurement.

The calculator has a fixed **precision**. This is determined by the maximum number of significant digits it is capable of computing and representing correctly. However, the **accuracy** of the computation is limited by the lesser of the two: the precision of the representations and computations, and the accuracy of the values used in the computation. The accuracy can never be more, and is usually less, than the precision of the calculator.

SUMMARY

Whether for longhand calculations or the internal use of a computer, the representation chosen can dramatically affect the difficulty in performing a mathematical operation. Just as addition and multiplication are difficult using Roman numerals, addition and subtraction can be made easier or more difficult by the choice of representation for a computer. Careful studies have determined the best representations for integers. The representations that permit fast implementations of addition and additive inverse are chosen because of the frequency and generality of these operations.

Weighted positional representation makes possible efficient representation and computation. The use of radix two introduces the requirement for converting from one base to another. Several algorithms were given for performing such conversions, both for integers and for nonintegers.

Only a finite number of unique values can be represented in a computer. The notion of integers can be extended to include fractions. A much wider range of numbers can be represented by the use of an exponent such as that used in scientific notation. The representation of very large or very small numbers does not require greater precision, however, and computer representations can exploit this fact.

PROBLEMS

1. Give an algorithm for determining the unique, shortest symbol string for Roman numerals.
2. For an arbitrary string of Roman numeral symbols, give an algorithm for determining the correct Roman numeral representation.

3. Using a calculator, determine the minimum number of keystrokes necessary to get it to overflow.

4. Give the decimal representation of the octal number 467q. Give the octal representation of the decimal number 467.

5. Give binary for the octal number 467q. What decimal value does this represent?

6. Give the decimal representation of the hexadecimal number 123h. Give the hexadecimal representation of the decimal number 123.

7. What is decimal value of the radix-five number 3411?

8. What is the radix-five value of the decimal number 98?

9. Fill in the missing entries of the following table.

Binary	Octal	Decimal	Hexadecimal
101100b			
11101100b			
	1267q		
	63q		
		90	
		63	
			63h
			0abfh

10. Fill in the missing entries of the following table.

Binary	Ternary (radix three)	Decimal
1100b		
11011001b		
	1012	
	221	
		82
		16

11. Suppose that you are given the cost of storing values: It costs $X - 1$ units of cost for a component that can remember any of X unique symbols ($X \geq 2$). In other words, it costs one unit to store a binary digit, two units to store a ternary digit, three units to

store a quad digit, and so on. You are to select a radix for storing numbers in weighted positional notation. What radix would you choose to store large numbers for the lowest price?

12. Suppose that each symbol costs the same amount, that is, a digit that can take on one of X integer values costs X units. Suppose that you can spend up to 120 units. What integer value for X allows you to represent the largest positive integer in weighted positional notation?

13. Give binary representations for the following fractional decimal values:

a. 64.5

b. 0.025

c. 18.0625

14. Give radix-4 representations for the following fractional binary values:

a. 1011.010110

b. 1.011

c. 1111.0001

15. Give an algorithm for converting a fraction represented in decimal to a fraction represented in octal.

16. Give an algorithm for converting a noninteger represented in binary into its decimal representation.

CHAPTER
5
DATA REPRESENTATION

A number is a mathematical concept. There is only one fifteen, yet the number fifteen can be represented many different ways. When a mathematical operation is performed, the representation of the numbers in no way affects the result. Adding seven to eight gives a result of fifteen regardless of the representations used for seven, eight, and fifteen. However, the representation can profoundly impact the effort needed to compute the representation of the result. In fact, it is often necessary to change the representation of a number in order to apply a particular algorithm to determine the resulting representation. For example, in Chapter 4 it was shown that addition was possible, although difficult, using Roman numerals. Longhand addition is difficult, and multiplication is nearly impossible. In fact, any person today asked to perform a multiplication given two numbers represented as Roman numerals would surely convert the numbers to decimal representation, perform the multiplication, then convert the

15	15.0	3×5	$\sqrt{225}$
$7 + 8$	$11 \times 1.\overline{36}$	$\sum_{i=0}^{3} 2^i$	$\sum_{n=1}^{5} n$
$1 \times 10^1 + 5 \times 10^0$	15×16^0	$1 \times 8^1 + 7 \times 8^0$	$2^3 + 2^2 + 2^1 + 2^0$
15_{ten}	f_{sixteen}	17_{eight}	1111_{two}
XV	fifteen	`0xf`	$2^4 - 2^0$
	IIIII IIIII IIIII	$\sum_{i=1}^{\infty} \frac{(4 \ln 2)^i}{i!}$	

Figure 5.1 Various representations for the number fifteen.

result back to Roman numerals. That is much simpler than performing the multiplication directly in the Roman numeral representation, though such an algorithm exists. The algorithm for doing addition is completely different for Roman numerals than for conventional decimal representation.

5.1 NUMBERS VERSUS THEIR REPRESENTATION

A number can be represented many different ways. Figure 5.1 gives a sample of ways the number fifteen can be represented.

The representation of a number greatly impacts the efficiency of mathematical operations. Different representations make certain arithmetic operations easier relative to other mathematical operations. For example, representing all numbers by their logarithms would be highly effective in a context where multiplication and division are common operations and addition and subtraction are rare. Addition and subtraction are inherently less complex than multiplication and division, and representing numbers with their logarithms makes multiplication and division easy; add or subtract their logarithms, respectively. On the other hand, addition or subtraction of numbers represented by their logarithms is difficult because the antilogarithms of each of the numbers must be determined before the addition or subtraction can be performed. After this, the logarithm of the result can be determined.

Scientific notation is a useful representation when dealing with numbers that are extremely large or extremely small. Operations involving numbers with large differences in magnitude can be handled more gracefully in scientific notation than in conventional decimal representation. Both addition and multiplication are more complicated than for conventional decimal representation.

Choosing an appropriate representation for numbers is critical in building an efficient computer. The representation must be such that a set of primitive operations can be performed efficiently, and the primitives must be such that all important operations can be performed in a reasonable manner. Rarely used operations can be expensive (that is, slow), but they must be possible. Two of the most important primitives are addition and negation. Negation is the operation that calculates an **additive inverse.** The additive inverse of X is a number Y for which the equation $X + Y = 0$ is true. If addition and negation can be performed efficiently, then subtraction readily follows, as does comparison. Multiplication and division can be achieved by a sequence of additions, negations, and comparisons. For general-purpose computers, the most important representation is one that permits simple, fast algorithms to be applied (1) to do the addition of two integers and (2) to determine the additive inverse of an integer.

Mapping Infinite Sets to Finite Sets

In mathematics, a variable can assume an infinite set of values. Even if values are restricted to integers, the set of possible values is still infinite. For a computer to distinguish distinct values, the values must have unique representations. Memory cells can only distinguish a finite number of unique states. If a symbol takes on one of M possible values, the number of unique representations that can be constructed from a sequence of N symbols is M^N. Consider a 3-digit decimal number. Decimal digits may be one of ten possible values; so $M = 10$. Since $N = 3$, 10^3 numbers can be represented. They are the integers in the range 0 to 999.

Because it is easy to build a simple electronic circuit that can distinguish between two states, computers are conventionally built to operate on binary digits, or **bits**. Associating a symbol (either 0 or 1) with each of the two possible states of the bit, a sequence of N bits can represent 2^N unique values. In order for the computer to perform arithmetic, each of these 2^N unique representations must be associated with a set of mathematical values, for example, with the integers in the interval 0 to $2^N - 1$. Then operations such as addition must be defined and hardware designed so that whatever representations are supplied, the representation of the correct resulting value is generated.

The size of a memory cell for a representation determines the number of unique values that can be represented. The decision about how to represent numbers, and the hardware to perform the primitive operations on them, is made when the hardware is designed. Often more than one representation is facilitated for different classes of numbers. For example, most computers have a different way of representing integers and reals. Once these decisions have been made and the computer is built, only a finite number of unique representations can be stored in a memory cell. If a unique representation is assigned to each of the consecutive non-negative integers, the size of the memory cell determines the largest integer that can be represented. There are techniques, known as **multiple-precision** arithmetic, for representing larger numbers with multiple memory cells, but most computers are not designed to support operations on these numbers very well, and execution of primitive operations on variables represented in multiple precision is much slower.

While the computer design is being specified, the value of the largest representable integer can be made arbitrarily large by increasing the size of the memory cell. Once the memory cell size is specified, the maximum representable integer has been determined. By specifying sufficiently large memory cells, arbitrarily large integers can be represented, but the cost of memory is increased. The amount of work the processor must do when it performs operations on these large integers is also increased. More important, while the largest representable value may be very large, it is nevertheless easy to create simple programs that will require a value that is still larger. As an example, any calculator can be made to overflow in only a handful of operations. The computer designer must be careful to select a memory cell that is large enough to permit the efficient representation of nearly all integers that will be used in most programs. Selecting a memory cell larger than that only adds cost and may actually slow down the computer. Even so, the programmer will always be faced with the fact that certain operations will result in a value that cannot be represented.

This chapter discusses ways of representing various kinds of data in fixed-size cells. It presents binary representations for integers, nonintegers, and characters. The emphasis is on choosing representations that permit easy manipulation by a computer. In the case of integers, the emphasis is on efficient implementation of addition and negation. For characters, the emphasis is on efficient comparison.

Binary Representation

The natural way to represent non-negative integers in a computer is through the use of binary, weighted positional notation. The binary sequence $s_{n-1}s_{n-2}\ldots s_2s_1s_0$ is the representation assigned to the integer

$$\sum_{i=0}^{n-1} s_i 2^i$$

where n is the number of bits. Since the binary digit s_i is either zero or one, the sum can also be represented by the sum of the powers of two where the corresponding bit is one. For example, the binary number represented by 100101 is

$$2^0 + 2^2 + 2^5 = 37_{\text{ten}}$$

SASM and the Pentium processor on which it is based number the bits right to left, beginning with zero, as shown in Chapter 4, but this numbering is not universal. In fact, many computers number the bits in the reverse order, with the **most significant bit** (msb), numbered 0 and the **least significant bit** (lsb), numbered $n - 1$. For historical reasons, numbering the bits from the most significant end to least significant end is known as **big endian**, while numbering in the reverse order is known as **little endian**.

Because computers have fixed-size memory cells, a number is represented with a fixed number of bits. Unlike longhand notation, where it is customary to leave out leading zeros, the computer representation includes leading zeros for all but the very largest numbers it can represent. Most computers today store numbers in memory cells that are either 32 or 64 bits; so they can represent either 2^{32} = 4,294,967,296 or 2^{64} = 18,446,744,073,709,551,616 unique values. Examples in this book are for 32 bits, or in some cases for eight bits. Figure 5.2 displays some 8- and 32-bit sample representations of positive integers.

Decimal Representation	BINARY REPRESENTATION	
	8-bit Binary	32-bit Binary
0	0000 0000	0000 0000 0000 0000 0000 0000 0000 0000 0000
1	0000 0001	0000 0000 0000 0000 0000 0000 0000 0000 0001
2	0000 0010	0000 0000 0000 0000 0000 0000 0000 0000 0010
3	0000 0011	0000 0000 0000 0000 0000 0000 0000 0000 0011
4	0000 0100	0000 0000 0000 0000 0000 0000 0000 0000 0100
5	0000 0101	0000 0000 0000 0000 0000 0000 0000 0000 0101
6	0000 0110	0000 0000 0000 0000 0000 0000 0000 0000 0110
7	0000 0111	0000 0000 0000 0000 0000 0000 0000 0000 0111
8	0000 1000	0000 0000 0000 0000 0000 0000 0000 0000 1000
.	.	.
.	.	.
.	.	.
36		0000 0000 0000 0000 0000 0000 0000 0010 0100
37		0000 0000 0000 0000 0000 0000 0000 0010 0101
38		0000 0000 0000 0000 0000 0000 0000 0010 0110
.	.	.
.	.	.
.	.	.

Figure 5.2 Some sample binary representations of positive integers.

5.2 REPRESENTATION OF INTEGERS

The representation of a non-negative integer using binary, weighted positional notation is called **unsigned** integer representation. An $(n + 1)$-bit unsigned integer representation can represent the range of values from 0 to $2^{n+1} - 1$. In order to simplify the expressions for ranges represented and value represented, $n + 1$ bits are used instead of n bits.

Formally, an $(n + 1)$-bit sequence

$$b_n b_{n-1} b_{n-2} \ldots b_2 b_1 b_0$$

represents the integer

$$\sum_{i=0}^{n} (b_i \times 2^i)$$

Sign Magnitude

In many applications, it is useful to be able to assign negative integer values to a variable. Yet a fixed-size memory cell limits the number of unique values representable. Assigning some of the values to negative numbers means that fewer positive values can be assigned. In a binary number system, adding a single extra bit doubles the number of unique values

SIGN MAGNITUDE	
Representation	**Value Represented**
0000 0011	3
1000 0111	–7
0000 0111	7
1111 1111	–127
0000 0000	0
1000 0000	0

Figure 5.3 Sign magnitude examples.

that can be represented. An extra bit might be used to distinguish between positive and negative values. Such a bit would be interpreted as a **sign bit**. The unsigned integer within this representation is the **magnitude**. This representation is called sign magnitude.

By convention, a zero in the sign bit is understood to mean that the integer represented is positive or zero, and a one means that the integer represented is negative or zero. The sign bit is placed to the left of the magnitude. Figure 5.3 contains examples of 8-bit sign magnitude integers.

Given an $(n + 1)$-bit sign magnitude number, the range of values that can be represented includes the integers from $-(2^n - 1)$ to $(2^n - 1)$. As an example, consider 8-bit sign magnitude representation. The largest-magnitude negative integer representable in the 8 bits is –127, and the largest-magnitude positive integer is +127.

The integer represented in $(n + 1)$-bit sign magnitude is

$$(-1)^{b_n}\left(\sum_{i=1}^{n-1} b_i \times 2^i\right)$$

Sign magnitude representation associates a sign bit with a magnitude that represents zero. There are therefore two representations for the value zero. This observation is important. Besides representing one fewer unique value, the circuitry that compares sign magnitude integers and does arithmetic operations is more complicated than that needed for comparing numbers in other representations. This is a result of having two distinct representations for the integer value zero.

One's Complement

A historically significant integer representation is **one's complement**. This representation came about in the search for a representation that simplifies the hardware that performs addition and subtraction, while keeping the additive inverse easy to compute. The representation makes using a single adder circuit for both unsigned integers and one's complement integers possible.

The representations for the positive integer values in one's complement are the same as those in sign magnitude representation. The representations for the negative values differ. A negative value is calculated by forming the **bit-wise complement** of the positive representation. In any binary representation, the bit-wise complement function is particularly easy to compute: For each bit in the representation, if the bit is one, it becomes zero, and if the bit is zero, it becomes one. A trivial hardware circuit can be made to **invert** all the bits in a representation. Forming the bit-wise complement of a one's complement representation is the operation that calculates an additive inverse. This operation is called **taking the one's complement**.

Figure 5.4 contains examples of one's complement representations. Like sign magnitude, one's complement has two representations for zero. The values of one's complement integers range from $-(2^n - 1)$ to $2^n - 1$, for $n + 1$ bits. With 4 bits, the values range from –7 (bit pattern `1000`) to 7 (bit pattern `0111`).

ONE'S COMPLEMENT	
Representation	**Value Represented**
0000 0011	3
1111 1000	–7
0000 0111	7
1111 1111	0
0000 0000	0
1000 0000	127

Figure 5.4 One's complement examples.

Two's Complement

The major drawback of one's complement representation is that it has two distinct representations for the integer value zero (see Figure 5.4). **Two's complement** representation fixes this problem, while maintaining the ease of computing an additive inverse and doing addition.

A circular number line helps to visualize the representations and the values represented in complement representations. Figure 5.5 contains a number wheel, showing value represented for all possible combinations of four-bit one's and two's complement representations.

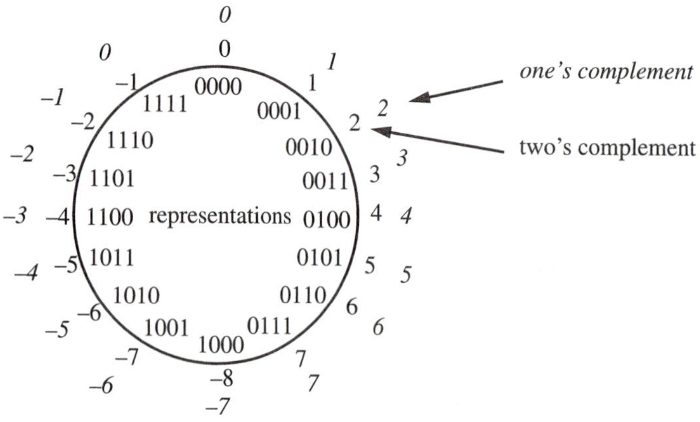

Figure 5.5 Complement representations and values.

The additive inverse of a two's complement integer can be obtained by taking the one's complement and adding the constant 1. This operation of calculating the bit-wise complement followed by adding 1 is referred to as **taking the two's complement**. The two's complement representation for a negative integer is found by determining the additive inverse of its positive representation. Figure 5.6 shows the 8-bit, two's complement representations for several integers.

TWO'S COMPLEMENT	
Representation	**Value Represented**
0000 0011	3
1000 0111	–121
0000 0111	7
1111 1111	–1
0000 0000	0
1000 0000	–128

Figure 5.6 Two's complement examples.

Since all bit patterns represent unique integers in two's complement, $n + 1$ bits can represent 2^{n+1} values. These values range from $-(2^n)$ to $2^n - 1$. For 5 bits, values of –16 (bit pattern `10000`) to 15 (`01111`) can be represented.

It is important to distinguish between the additive inverse operation, also known as negation, and the complement operations. Computing the additive inverse is a mathematical operation, independent of the representation being used.

Taking the one's complement of a number is an operation on a representation, namely inverting all the bits. In one's complement representation, computing the additive inverse is accomplished by taking the one's complement. Taking the two's complement of a number is also an operation on a representation. If the representation is two's complement, then taking the two's complement is equivalent to computing the additive inverse. Note that it is a well-defined operation to take the one's complement of a two's complement representation, a sign magnitude representation, or even an unsigned representation, even if the result is not what is expected. The same is true for taking the two's complement; the additive inverse is computed on the symbol sequence *as if it were* a two's complement representation.

Two's complement representation, having only a single representation for zero, has the asymmetrical property that one more negative value than positive value is represented. This phenomenon introduces a special consideration. The most negative number representable (1000···000) has no additive inverse within a fixed precision. The usual algorithm to take the two's complement for this representation returns the same representation. By applying the algorithm, it seems that the number is its own additive inverse. This is of course incorrect, and it is an example of **overflow**. Overflow is the situation that results whenever the result of a computation is outside the range of values that can be represented. Overflow is further discussed in Chapter 6.

Biased Representation

Yet another way to represent both positive and negative integer values is **biased** representation. Biased representation uses unsigned representation to represent a range of values other than 0 to

$2^{n+1} - 1$. Each value has a **bias** added in order to place it within the range of unsigned representation. The choice of the bias depends on the range of values to be represented. If the unsigned integer representation includes integers from zero to M, then subtracting approximately $M/2$ from the unsigned interpretation would give a set of values ranging from approximately $-M/2$ to $+M/2$. This gives a bias of either 2^n or $2^n - 1$ for an $(n + 1)$-bit representation. For an 8-bit representation, that means a bias of either 127 or 128.

As an example, a three-bit biased integer representation with a bias of 4 (called biased-4) has the values as given in Figure 5.7.

Representation	Unsigned Value Represented	Biased-4 Value Represented
000	0	–4
001	1	–3
010	2	–2
011	3	–1
100	4	0
101	5	1
110	6	2
111	7	3

Figure 5.7 Three-bit biased-4 representation.

Formally, a biased-B representation of an $(n + 1)$-bit sequence represents the integer

$$\left(\sum_{i=0}^{n} b_i \times 2^i\right) - B$$

The biased value represented can easily be computed from the unsigned representation. If the unsigned representation has a value N, the biased value represented is $N - B$ for a biased-B representation.

Notes on Integer Representations

Figure 5.8 shows bit patterns for various interpretations of 8-bit binary encodings. It gives the decimal integer represented for each of the representations: unsigned, sign magnitude, two's complement, one's complement, biased-127, and biased-128. Some general observations are appropriate here. First, the representation of positive integers is identical for all representations except the biased ones. Second, in the complement and sign magnitude representations, the most significant bit identifies the sign of the number. It is one for negative numbers and zero for positive numbers. Third, exactly the same values are represented by two's complement and biased-128 notations. In fact, the representations of a given integer are the same in both except that the most significant bit is always inverted.

Figure 5.9 summarizes the ranges and values represented for the various integer representations using an $(n + 1)$-bit sequence $b_n b_{n-1} \cdots b_2 b_1 b_0$. Virtually all modern computers use a two's complement representation for integers. SASM assumes a 32-bit two's complement representation for integers.

Representation	VALUE REPRESENTED					
	Unsigned	**Sign Magnitude**	**Two's Comp.**	**One's Comp.**	**Biased-127**	**Biased-128**
0000 0000	0	0	0	0	−127	−128
0000 0001	1	1	1	1	−126	−127
0000 0010	2	2	2	2	−125	−126
0000 0011	3	3	3	3	−124	−125
0000 0100	4	4	4	4	−123	−124
0000 0101	5	5	5	5	−122	−123
0000 0110	6	6	6	6	−121	−122
0000 0111	7	7	7	7	−120	−121
0000 1000	8	8	8	8	−119	−120
0000 1001	9	9	9	9	−118	−119
0000 1010	10	10	10	10	−117	−118
0000 1011	11	11	11	11	−116	−117
0000 1100	12	12	12	12	−115	−116
0000 1101	13	13	13	13	−114	−115
0000 1110	14	14	14	14	−113	−114
0000 1111	15	15	15	15	−112	−113
0001 0000	16	16	16	16	−111	−112
0001 0001	17	17	17	17	−110	−111
0001 0010	18	18	18	18	−109	−110
0001 0011	19	19	19	19	−108	−109
0001 0100	20	20	20	20	−107	−108
0001 0101	21	21	21	21	−106	−107
0001 0110	22	22	22	22	−105	−106
0001 0111	23	23	23	23	−104	−105
.	.	.	.	.	.	.
.	.	.	.	.	.	.
.	.	.	.	.	.	.
0111 1000	120	120	120	120	−7	−8
0111 1001	121	121	121	121	−6	−7
0111 1010	122	122	122	122	−5	−6
0111 1011	123	123	123	123	−4	−5
0111 1100	124	124	124	124	−3	−4
0111 1101	125	125	125	125	−2	−3
0111 1110	126	126	126	126	−1	−2
0111 1111	127	127	127	127	0	−1
1000 0000	128	0	−128	−127	1	0
1000 0001	129	−1	−127	−126	2	1
1000 0010	130	−2	−126	−125	3	2
1000 0011	131	−3	−125	−124	4	3
1000 0100	132	−4	−124	−123	5	4
1000 0101	133	−5	−123	−122	6	5
1000 0110	134	−6	−122	−121	7	6

Figure 5.8 Decimal values for the various integer representations.

Representation	VALUE REPRESENTED					
	Unsigned	Sign Magnitude	Two's Comp.	One's Comp.	Biased-127	Biased-128
1000 0111	135	−7	−121	−120	8	7
.	.	.	.	.	.	.
.	.	.	.	.	.	.
.	.	.	.	.	.	.
1111 1000	248	−120	−8	−7	121	120
1111 1001	249	−121	−7	−6	122	121
1111 1010	250	−122	−6	−5	123	122
1111 1011	251	−123	−5	−4	124	123
1111 1100	252	−124	−4	−3	125	124
1111 1101	253	−125	−3	−2	126	125
1111 1110	254	−126	−2	−1	127	126
1111 1111	255	−127	−1	0	128	127

Figure 5.8 *Continued*

Format	Range	Value Represented
Unsigned	$0 \le I < 2^{n+1}$	$= \sum_{i=0}^{n} b_i \times 2^i$
Sign magnitude	$-(2^n) < I < 2^n$	$I = (-1)^{b_n} \sum_{i=0}^{n-1} b_i \times 2^i$
One's complement	$-(2^n) < I < 2^n$	$I = \left(\sum_{i=0}^{n-1} b_i \times 2^i\right) - b_n(2^n - 1)$
Two's complement	$-(2^n) \le I < 2^n$	$I = \left(\sum_{i=0}^{n-1} b_i \times 2^i\right) - b_n(2^n)$
Biased-B	$-B \le I < 2^{n+1} - B$	$I = \left(\sum_{i=0}^{n} b_i \times 2^i\right) - B$
For the $(n + 1)$-bit representation $b_n b_{n-1} \cdots b_2 b_1 b_0$		

Figure 5.9 Ranges and values represented for the integer representations.

Sign Extension

The specification of the representation of an integer in a computer generally specifies a fixed precision (number of bits). Eight, 16, 32, and 64 bits are commonly used for integer representation. It is occasionally necessary (see multiplication in Chapter 6) to convert the representation of an integer from one size to another. The most common situation is where an integer is expanded from an 8- or 16-bit representation to a 32-bit representation. The SASM code fragment

```
.data
variable1     dd     ?
variable2     db     ?
.code
.
.
.
iadd   variable1, variable2
.
.
.
```

contains an example of this common case. The variable `variable1` must maintain the same value while changing its size from 8 to 32 bits.

The algorithm used to increase the number of bits of an unsigned integer without changing the value represented is straightforward. Place the original integer into the least significant portion of the larger-precision representation. Assign zeros to all the bits that have not been filled by the original integer. This example shows an 8-bit unsigned integer transformed into a 16-bit unsigned integer.

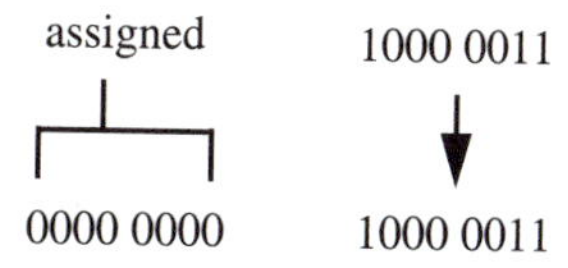

The SASM instruction `movezx` provides this zero-extension operation.

Sign magnitude representations are also easy to expand. The sign bit of the smaller-precision representation is placed into the sign bit (most significant bit) of the larger-precision representation. The magnitude is placed into the least significant portion of the larger-precision representation. The remaining bits are assigned to be zeros, as shown in this example:

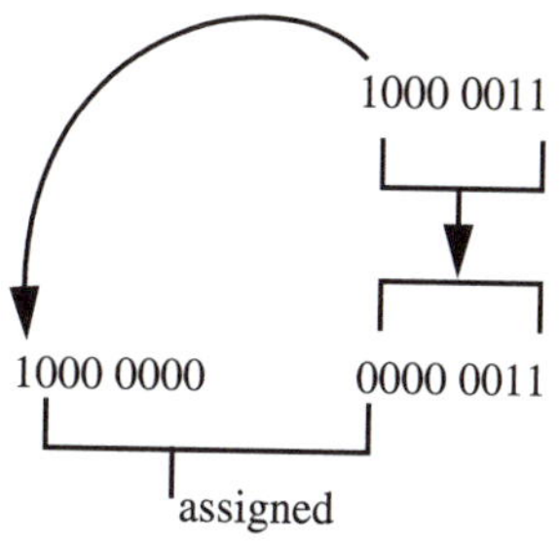

Complement integers are **sign extended**. The original representation is placed into the least significant bits of the larger-precision representation. Then the most significant bit of the original representation is propagated throughout the most significant bits of the larger-precision representation. For a positive number, a zero is propagated.

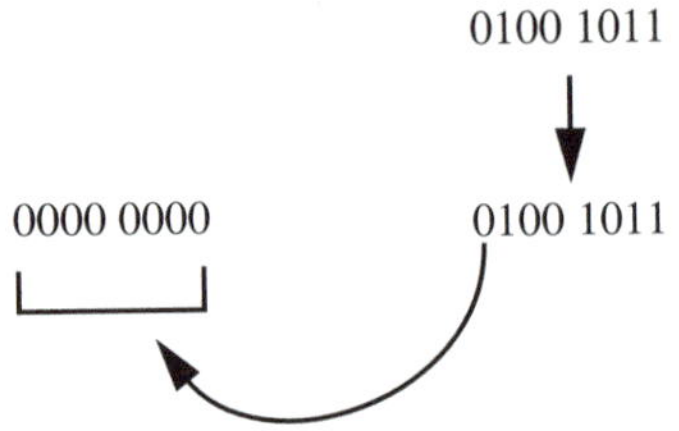

For a negative number, a one is propagated.

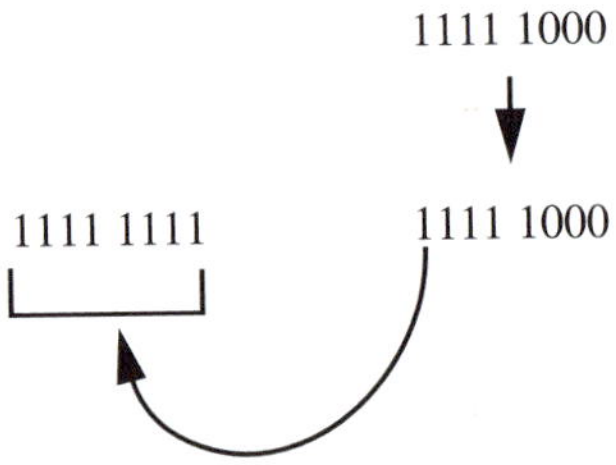

5.3 CHARACTERS

In a programming language, a variable is assigned a value. For many variables, this value is a numerical value, but the notion of type in the language introduces the concept that a variable can take on a set of values that need not be numerical. Within each type, it is necessary to provide a unique representation for each allowable value. The most common, non-numerical type is a **character**. Computers often communicate with the outside world by reading or writing a sequence of characters, called a **string**. A keyboard must assign a binary value to a variable when a character is typed, such as the 'A' key. This value must then be transmitted to the computer. The assignment of characters to values is largely arbitrary, but must be agreed upon by all the various devices that communicate in this way. Certain sets of character assignments have been standardized and are widely used.

The most prominent is the American National Standards Institute (ANSI) standard known as the **American Standard for Computer Information Interchange**. **ASCII,** as it is commonly known, assigns unique representations to 128 characters. These include some nonprinting characters such as the character `esc`. It is transmitted when the 'escape' key is typed. Both the 'shift' key and the 'control' key have the effect of modifying the mapping of keys to characters; so pressing either key (or both) changes the character transmitted to the computer. In this way it is possible to transmit more unique characters than there are

Dec	Hex	Char	Dec	Hex	Char	Dec	Hex	Char	Dec	Hex	Char
0	0	nul	32	20	sp	64	40	@	96	60	`
1	1	soh	33	21	!	65	41	A	97	61	a
2	2	stx	34	22	"	66	42	B	98	62	b
3	3	etx	35	23	#	67	43	C	99	63	c
4	4	eot	36	24	$	68	44	D	100	64	d
5	5	enq	37	25	%	69	45	E	101	65	e
6	6	ack	38	26	&	70	46	F	102	66	f
7	7	bel	39	27	'	71	47	G	103	67	g
8	8	bs	40	28	(	72	48	H	104	68	h
9	9	ht	41	29	)	73	49	I	105	69	i
10	a	nl	42	2a	*	74	4a	J	106	6a	j
11	b	vt	43	2b	+	75	4b	K	107	6b	k
12	c	np	44	2c	,	76	4c	L	108	6c	l
13	d	cr	45	2d	-	77	4d	M	109	6d	m
14	e	so	46	2e	.	78	4e	N	110	6e	n
15	f	si	47	2f	/	79	4f	O	111	6f	o
16	10	dle	48	30	0	80	50	P	112	70	p
17	11	dc1	49	31	1	81	51	Q	113	71	q
18	12	dc2	50	32	2	82	52	R	114	72	r
19	13	dc3	51	33	3	83	53	S	115	73	s
20	14	dc4	52	34	4	84	54	T	116	74	t
21	15	nak	53	35	5	85	55	U	117	75	u
22	16	syn	54	36	6	86	56	V	118	76	v
23	17	etb	55	37	7	87	57	W	119	77	w
24	18	can	56	38	8	88	58	X	120	78	x
25	19	em	57	39	9	89	59	Y	121	79	y
26	1a	sub	58	3a	:	90	5a	Z	122	7a	z
27	1b	esc	59	3b	;	91	5b	[	123	7b	{
28	1c	fs	60	3c	<	92	5c	\	124	7c	|
29	1d	gs	61	3d	=	93	5d	]	125	7d	}
30	1e	rs	62	3e	>	94	5e	^	126	7e	~
31	1f	us	63	3f	?	95	5f	_	127	7f	del

Figure 5.10 Decimal and hexadecimal values for the ASCII character code.

keys. The ASCII code for characters is given in Figure 5.10. Each of the 128 characters is assigned a unique combination of the seven bits that define the ASCII character. The seven bits are most often numbered from 0 to 6, with bit 0 being the least significant bit. While the characters are not numbers (in the sense that numerical operations can be performed on them), each character has a representation that is also the representation for a 7-bit unsigned binary integer. In this way, the letter 'a' is associated with the decimal integer 97, the letter 'b' is associated with the decimal integer 98, and so on. Note also that the character '7' is associated with the decimal integer 55, not the decimal integer 7.

While the ordering of bits within the character is arbitrary, it must be agreed upon. The characters in the ASCII code were assigned in a specific order to expedite the execution of

```
.data
the_int         dd      ?       ; the user-entered integer
digit           dd      ?       ; the digit that a character represents
char            db      ?       ; a character of user-entered input

.code

        move            the_int, 0
each_char:
        get_ch          char
        compareb        char, '9'     ; check that character read is a
                                      ; digit
        bgz             not_a_digit
        movezx          digit, char   ; char -> integer conversion
        isub            digit, 48
        blz             not_a_digit
        imult           the_int, 10   ; the_int = (the_int * 10) + digit
        iadd            the_int, digit
        br              each_char     ; continue processing characters
                                      ; until the character read is
                                      ; not a digit
```

Figure 5.11 SASM code fragment to translate a character string into an integer representation.

common operations. One operation that is often performed on strings of characters is **sorting**. In order to sort, it is necessary to determine which of two characters comes first in the alphabet. By assigning the character encoding in lexicographical order, this task is made easy; the representations of the two characters are treated as two integers. An integer comparison identifies the character ordering. However, all lower-case letters are determined to occur after all the upper-case letters. Although this is not true lexicographical order, additional range tests can be used to determine case. Once the case of a letter is determined, comparisons are straightforward.

The procedure for comparing characters can be extended to include nonalphabetical characters as well. One particularly useful comparison is on the digits. Because of the ordered assignment of the digits (0–9), it is possible to determine if the value is a digit by checking that it is within the decimal range 48–57. If the character representation is treated as an unsigned integer and 48 is subtracted from that integer, the result is an unsigned representation of the digit.

Converting the ASCII character string representation of an integer to its integer representation is essential due to the way many input and output devices operate. The data that devices transmit are characters. Yet often an integer representation is required. Therefore, the character string that represents an integer must be translated into its corresponding integer representation before it can be used by a program. Figure 5.11 contains a SASM code fragment that translates a character string into its integer representation. The code is written for positive integers.

5.4 FLOATING POINT REPRESENTATION

Many computers support noninteger representations using a form reminiscent of scientific notation. This form is known as **floating point** representation. Variables that are declared type `real` in Pascal or `float` in C and other programming languages are usually represented internally as floating point numbers.

While there is a variety of floating point formats and alternatives, a single standard has recently emerged and has come to be almost universally used. The standard is known as the IEEE Floating Point Standard (FPS). Debate continues as to the merit of some of the details of this standard versus other, older formats, but it is widely agreed that there is benefit in a universal standard. It appears that for the foreseeable future, FPS will be supported on all new computers. Unless otherwise stated, discussions in this book relate specifically to representations defined in the FPS.

Like scientific notation, the representation for floating point numbers is broken into two parts, one specifying the mantissa and the other the exponent. The exponent is represented as an 8-bit, biased-127 integer. The mantissa is represented as a variant of a scaled, sign magnitude integer, where the value is normalized. **Scaled** means that the integer is implicitly divided by a constant, in this case 2^{23}.

A magnitude of a number N represented in floating point is determined by the mantissa m and exponent e:

$$N = m \times 2^e$$

Since N can be positive or negative, the sign of the mantissa is represented explicitly with a sign s, which is zero for a positive mantissa and one for a negative mantissa:

$$N = (-1)^s \times m \times 2^e$$

Normalization places the value of the mantissa greater than or equal to one, and less than the radix. The radix is 2; so normalization of the mantissa requires that

$$1 \le \mathrm{m} < 2$$

Because of this range limitation, m can always be represented in binary in the form

$$1.b_{-1}b_{-2}b_{-3}\ldots$$

In the FPS single-precision format, the precision is given as 24 bits; so m can be represented by the binary sequence

$$1.b_{-1}b_{-2}b_{-3}\cdots b_{-21}b_{-22}b_{-23}$$

where

$$m = 1 + \sum_{j=-1}^{-23} b_j \times 2^j = 1 + \sum_{j=-23}^{-1} b_j \times 2^j$$

Factoring out of the summation the quantity 2^{-23} gives

$$m = 1 + 2^{-23} \times \sum_{j=-23}^{-1} b_j \times 2^j \times 2^{23} = 1 + 2^{-23} \times \sum_{j=-23}^{-1} b_j \times 2^{j+23}$$

Changing induction variables to $i = j + 23$ has the effect of numbering the bits starting with zero in the least significant digit:

$$m = 1 + 2^{-23} \times \sum_{i=0}^{22} b_{i-23} \times 2^i$$

Renumbering the binary bits accordingly by substituting $b_x = f_{23+x}$ gives

$$1.b_{-1}b_{-2}\cdots b_{-22}b_{-23} = 1.f_{22}f_{21}\cdots f_1 f_0$$

The value m takes the form

$$m = 1 + \frac{\left(\sum_{i=0}^{22} f_i \times 2^i\right)}{2^{23}}$$

The summation in this equation is in the form of the unsigned integer

$$F = \sum_{i=0}^{22} f_i \times 2^i$$

The mantissa in the FPS single-precision format, $f_{22}f_{21}\ldots f_1 f_0$ represents the integer value

$$F = \sum_{i=0}^{22} f_i \times 2^i$$

and

$$m = 1 + \frac{F}{2^{23}}$$

The exponent e is a biased-127 representation; so

$$e = \left(\sum_{i=0}^{7} e_i \times 2^i\right) - 127$$

Again recognizing the summation as an integer

$$E = \sum_{i=0}^{7} e_i \times 2^i$$

$$N = (-1)^s \times m \times 2^e$$

$$m = 1.f_{22}f_{21}\cdots f_1f_0 = 1 + \frac{f_{22}f_{21}\cdots f_1f_0}{2^{23}}$$

Conversion to *S, F,* and *E*	Conversion to *s, m,* and *e*
$F = (m-1)\times 2^{23}$	$m = 1 + \frac{F}{2^{23}}$
$E = e + 127$	$e = E - 127$
$S = s$	$s = S$

Figure 5.12 Representation of IEEE FPS single-precision floating point numbers.

and

$$e = \mathrm{E} - 127$$

Thus the floating point number N can be represented explicitly by the unsigned integers E and F and the sign bit S.

Figure 5.12 summarizes the relationship between *s, e,* and *f,* the terms of the floating point value, and *S, E,* and *F,* the unsigned integers used to represent them. The mantissa for the single-precision format is represented with 23 bits of fraction *F.*

The IEEE FPS stores its fields in an order different from what might be expected. The format is

S	*E*	*F*

There are three fields in the format. *S* is the sign of the mantissa, and it is referred to simply as the sign. *E* is referred to as the exponent, although this is not quite correct; it is the biased integer representation for the exponent. *F* the fractional part of the mantissa. The sign field *S* is a single bit. The exponent *E* is eight bits, and the fraction *F* is 23 bits. This format is known as **single precision**. In a 64-bit format, known as **double precision**, the exponent field is 11 bits and is a biased-1023 integer representation. The significand is 53 bits, and it is normalized the same as a single-precision number.

The number of bits allocated for the exponent and fraction fields within the fixed-precision format has an effect on the range of values that can be represented. Discussion and compromise went into defining the standard, where the exponent field is fixed at eight bits and the fraction field is fixed at 23 bits. If the precision of the representation is held constant, and the size of the exponent field is increased, the magnitude of the exponent that can be represented increases. This gives a larger range for representable values. This also has the effect of reducing the number of bits used for the mantissa. The same number of unique and exact values will be able to be represented, independent of the number of bits allocated for each field. Yet with fewer bits for the mantissa and more for the exponent, the representable values will be spaced farther apart from each other.

In the single-precision format, the exponent E can take on integer values in the range

$$0 \le \mathrm{E} < 256$$

However, the maximum and minimum values (represented with all ones and with all zeros) both have special interpretations, providing representations for zero and other special values. Therefore, the value of the exponent e is restricted to the range of integer values

$$-126 \le e < 128$$

Zero is represented by $F = E = 0$, regardless of the sign bit. Another special representation is NaN, which stands for Not-a-Number. Infinity is the value assigned to the results of arithmetic operations that are too large positive or too large negative to have a representation. Division by zero results in a representation for ∞. NaN is the value assigned when operations have no well-defined mathematical result, such as division of $+\infty$ by $-\infty$. These representations are shown in Figure 5.13.

Symbol	Definition
$+\infty$	$S = 0, E = 255, F = 0$
$-\infty$	$S = 1, E = 255, F = 0$
NaN	$S = 0, E = 255, F \neq 0$

Figure 5.13 Special representations in the FPS.

For the IEEE single-precision floating point number represented by the string $z_{31}z_{30}\ldots z_1z_0$, a mathematical expression for the value represented is

$$(-1)^{z_{31}} \times \left(1 + 2^{-23}\sum_{i=0}^{22} z_i \times 2^i\right) \times 2^{\left(\sum_{i=0}^{7} z_{i+23} \times 2^i\right) - 2^7 - 1}$$

Zero and the Hidden Bit

The integer F used in specifying a floating point number can take any integer value from zero to $2^{23}–1$. The mantissa takes on a magnitude between one and $2 - 2^{-23}$. For the mantissa m, there is an implicit 1 at the beginning.

$$m = 1.f_{22}f_{21}\cdots f_1f_0$$

As with scientific notation, there is no way to represent the number zero, since the mantissa must be at least one. One way to include zero would be to represent explicitly the digit to the left of the binary point,

$$f_{23}.f_{22}f_{21}\cdots f_1f_0$$

Doing this has several advantages. First, it seems more natural, since this digit appears in scientific notation. Second, it readily permits the representation of zero. Third, it permits the representation of unnormalized representations, which is sometimes important during intermediate steps in a computation. Many computers previously have used a floating point representation that explicitly includes the digit to the left of the binary point, and though it is not included in the IEEE FPS representation, it is still sometimes useful to be able to refer to it. It is commonly called the **hidden bit**.

Since the FPS does not explicitly represent the hidden bit, a special representation for zero is required. The chosen way is to use the minimum value for the exponent $e = -127$. Thus E must be a positive unsigned integer. The FPS defines zero as the case where $E = F = 0$. Note that the sign bit S is not specified; so there are two representations for zero.

The mantissa in a floating point representation has a fixed precision. There is no provision for varying the number of symbols; so, unlike scientific notation, nothing can be inferred from the floating point number about the accuracy of the number being represented. There is a maximum accuracy, restricted by the precision of the representation and the numerical algorithms employed.

Example: IEEE FPS Representation of 17.15

It takes several steps to get the floating point value 17.15 in the FPS single-precision format. The first step is to get the binary values for 17 and 0.15. 17 is 10001. The fraction can be calculated using the algorithm given in Chapter 4.

		Digits of Fraction
2×0.15	$= 0.30$	$msb = 0$
2×0.30	$= 0.60$	0
2×0.60	$= 1.20$	1
2×0.20	$= 0.40$	0
2×0.40	$= 0.80$	0
2×0.80	$= 1.60$	1
2×0.60		

The repeating binary fraction is $0.00\overline{1001}$.

The next step is to normalize the mantissa:

$$17.15_{ten} = 10001.00\overline{1001}_{two}$$
$$= 1.00010010\overline{1001}_{two} \times 2^{4}_{ten}$$

Bias the exponent:

$$4 + 127 = 131_{ten} = 10000011_{two}$$

Note that 17.15 is a positive number. Its sign will be 0.

Put the values into the correct fields, remembering that the leading one in the fraction is not represented. It is the hidden bit. The repeating digits in the mantissa that extend beyond the given precision are truncated in this example.

sign	exponent	significand
0	10000011	00010010011001100110011

Floating point representations are often given in hexadecimal. The hexadecimal for this example is `0x41893333`.

Example: Decimal Value of the Representation 0xc2508000

Finding the decimal value represented when given an IEEE FPS single-precision representation expressed in hexadecimal is primarily a process of reversing the steps given in the previous example. To find the decimal value represented by 0xc2508000, first break up the value into the FPS fields:

sign	exponent	significand
1	10000100	10100001000000000000000

Take the bias out of the exponent field to get the value represented:

$$10000100_{two} = 132_{ten}$$

$$132 - 127 = 5$$

Express the mantissa and exponent together in their normalized form, remembering to add back in the hidden bit.

$$1.10100001000000000000000_{two} \times 2^{5}_{ten}$$

Express this mixed-radix result in an unnormalized binary form:

$$110100.001\ 0000\ 0000\ 0000\ 000$$

This is the value

$$52.125$$

in floating point representation. The inclusion of the sign bit completes the example. The IEEE single-precision FPS value 0xc2508000 represents the decimal value –52.125.

5.5 A LITTLE EXTRA ON COMPLEMENT REPRESENTATION

As an alternative to the intuitive approach, consider the mathematical derivation of complement representation. Complement representation represents negative numbers by adding a large **bias** to all negative numbers, creating positive numbers in unsigned representation. The idea is that a negative number is represented as a very large positive number by subtracting its magnitude from a positive integer. The bias is chosen so that any negative number representable appears as if it were larger than the largest positive number representable. That is, the largest representable positive numbers are reserved for representation of negative numbers.

If the bias B is chosen carefully, the subtraction operation can be performed by a simple operation on each symbol in the representation. In decimal representation, if the bias is chosen to be $B = 9{,}999$, then the additive inverse of any number N up to, but not including, 5,000 can be uniquely represented by the number $B - N$. The choice of $B = 9{,}999$ means that $B - N$ can be determined by inspection; each digit d_i is replaced by $9 - d_i$. For example, the complement representation of the number $-1{,}257$ is $9{,}999 - 1{,}257 = 8{,}742$. This representation is known as **nine's complement**.

One's complement representation of integers derives from the need to exploit the easy computability of taking the one's complement. The idea is that if negative integers can be accommodated by the adder, and the additive inverse of a positive number can be easily determined, then addition and subtraction are straightforward. The representation of positive numbers is the same as for unsigned integers, where the most significant bit is always zero. The representations for large unsigned integers—those where the most significant bit is one—are reserved for the negative values to be represented. Now the bias is introduced by subtracting it from the positive representation only if the most significant bit is one. That is, the one's complement representation has the following form:

$$\left(\sum_{i=0}^{n-1} b_i \times 2^i\right) - b_n \times B$$

where B is the bias, and the representation has $n + 1$ bits. If b_n is a positive number, the number represented is the same as for the unsigned representation. If b_n is negative, however, the number represented is a negative number. The value for B that satisfies these constraints can be derived. Let I be represented by the binary sequence

$$b_n b_{n-1} b_{n-2} \cdots b_2 b_1 b_0$$

Let $\bar{I}$ represent the result of taking the one's complement of I. Letting $\bar{b}_j = 1 - b_j$ for all j, $\bar{I}$ is represented by the sequence

$$\bar{b}_n \bar{b}_{n-1} \bar{b}_{n-2} \cdots \bar{b}_2 \bar{b}_1 \bar{b}_0$$

and has the value

$$\left(\sum_{i=0}^{n-1} \bar{b}_i \times 2^i\right) - (\bar{b}_n \times B) = \left(\sum_{i=0}^{n-1} (1 - b_i) \times 2^i\right) - [(1 - b_n) \times B]$$

The one's complement representation chooses the additive inverse of I to be $\bar{I}$, the result of taking the one's complement of I; so

$$I + \bar{I} = 0$$

This results in the equation

$$\left(\sum_{i=0}^{n-1} b_i \times 2^i\right) - (b_n \times B) + \left(\sum_{i=0}^{n-1} (1 - b_i) \times 2^i\right) - [(1 - b_n) \times B] = 0$$

Solve the equation for B:

$$\sum_{i=0}^{n-1} b_i \times 2^i + \sum_{i=0}^{n-1} (1 - b_i) \times 2^i = b_n \times B + (1 - b_n) \times B$$

$$\sum_{i=0}^{n-1} b_i \times 2^i + \sum_{i=0}^{n-1} (1 - b_i) \times 2^i = B$$

$$\sum_{i=0}^{n-1} [b_i \times 2^i + (1 - b_i) \times 2^i] = B$$

$$\sum_{i=0}^{n-1} 2^i = B$$

Observing that

$$\sum_{i=0}^{n-1} 2^i = 2^n - 1$$

yields the result

$$B = 2^n - 1$$

This result shows that a bias of $B = 2^n - 1$ can be used with the representation above, and therefore the value for the integer I is

$$\left(\sum_{i=0}^{n-1} b_i \times 2^i \right) - b_n \times (2^n - 1)$$

Thus it has been shown that the additive inverse of a one's complement representation is found by inverting each bit of its representation.

Assigning B the value 2^n results in two's complement representation. The integer represented is

$$\left(\sum_{i=0}^{n-1} b_i \times 2^i \right) - b_n \times 2^n$$

The mathematical basis for **sign extension** of complement representation results from the fact that the most significant bit is subtracted instead of added. Thus, for an $(n + 1)$-bit two's complement representation

$$I = \left(\sum_{i=0}^{n-1} b_i \times 2^i\right) - b_n \times 2^n$$

$$I = \left(\sum_{i=0}^{n} b_i \times 2^i\right) - 2 \times b_n \times 2^n$$

$$I = \left(\sum_{i=0}^{n} b_i \times 2^i\right) - b_n \times 2^{n+1}$$

Now to represent the integer I as an $(m + 1)$-bit two's complement representation requires that

$$I = \left(\sum_{i=0}^{m} b'_i \times 2^i\right) - (b'_m \times 2^{m+1})$$

for some set of binary variables b'_i. Assigning $b'_j = b_j$ for $0 < j \le n$ yields

$$\left(\sum_{i=0}^{n} b_i \times 2^i\right) - b_n \times 2^{n+1} = \left(\sum_{i=0}^{m} b'_i \times 2^i\right) - b'_m \times 2^{m+1}$$

$$= \left(\sum_{i=0}^{n-1} b'_i \times 2^i\right) + \left(\sum_{i=n}^{m-1} b'_i \times 2^i\right) - b'_m \times 2^{m+1}$$

$$= \left(\sum_{i=0}^{n-1} b_i \times 2^i\right) + \left(\sum_{i=n}^{m-1} b'_i \times 2^i\right) - b'_m \times 2^{m+1}$$

Subtracting

$$\sum_{i=0}^{n-1} b_i \times 2^i$$

from each side and rearranging terms yields

$$b'_m \times 2^m - (b_n \times 2^n) = \sum_{i=n}^{m-1} b'_i \times 2^i$$

The only assignment of boolean values to the variables b'_j that can satisfy this equality is if $b'_j = b_n$, for $n + 1 \leq j \leq m$. Thus the bit that identifies the sign, b_n must be propagated to the left.

SUMMARY

This chapter demonstrated how different types of data can be represented. Integers can be represented in several different ways. Floating point numbers can be represented by integers. The ASCII code for character representation forms a standard with useful properties.

By far the most widely used representation for integers today is two's complement. However, other representations are used. For example, the mantissa in the FPS uses sign magnitude representation (with an implicit leading one), while the exponent uses the biased-127 representation. All these representations are carefully defined mathematically so that the mathematical operations performed on them can be correctly implemented.

PROBLEMS

1. Longhand multiplication is performed by breaking the multiplier into terms, one for each digit, determining the partial sum for each term, then adding them together. Roman numerals can also be broken into terms, one for each symbol. Devise an algorithm to perform multiplication directly for numbers represented as Roman numerals.

2. Give an unsigned binary representation of the following decimal integers:

a. 320

b. 70

c. 128

d. 31

e. 25

f. 84

3. Give the decimal representation of the following unsigned binary integers:

a. 101110

b. 0101

c. 1111

d. 101111101

e. 111111

f. 10101010

4. How many binary digits (bits) does it take to represent the decimal value 4005?

5. What is the range of a 6-bit unsigned integer representation? A 6-bit two's complement integer?

6. What number does 100 0001 represent? Is it possible to tell? If not, what extra information is needed?

7. Fill in the missing entries of the following table. All binary numbers are 8 bits.

Decimal Value	2's Complement	Sign Magnitude	1's Complement
–68			
		0110 1100	
	1000 1000		
			1010 1010
	0101 0101		
		0110 0101	
38			
			0111 1111
125			
0			

8. Fill in the missing entries of the following table. All binary numbers are 8 bits.

Decimal Value	Unsigned	Biased-4
–2		
	0011 0000	
		0100 0001
18		

9. Give 16-bit representations for the following 8-bit integers:

a. 1010 1010 (one's comp.)

b. 0101 0000 (two's comp.)

c. 1111 1111 (unsigned)

d. 0111 1101 (sign magnitude)

e. 1111 1111 (sign magnitude)

f. 1010 1010 (two's comp.)

10. Give an algorithm for turning a 16-bit sign magnitude integer into an 8-bit sign magnitude integer. Are there cases where no algorithm can be found that works? If so, identify the cases, and explain why no algorithm will work.

11. What range of integer values does SASM allow? Give the bit pattern for the largest and smallest (most negative) integers.

12. What are the ASCII character codes for the characters '?,' 'M,' 'm,' and the null character?

13. Give the IEEE FPS single-precision floating point representation for the decimal value 1.0.

14. Give the IEEE FPS single-precision floating point representation for the decimal value 100.0.

15. Give the IEEE FPS single-precision floating point representation for the number -83.7_{ten}.

16. Give the IEEE FPS single-precision floating point representation for the number 64.5_{ten}.

17. Give the IEEE FPS single-precision floating point representation for the number -1.025_{ten}.

18. What decimal value is represented by the IEEE FPS single-precision representation, given in hexadecimal as 0x45ac0000?

19. What decimal value is represented by the IEEE FPS single-precision representation, given in hexadecimal as 0xc480 0000?

20. What decimal value is represented by the IEEE FPS single-precision representation, given in hexadecimal as 0x3fe0 0000?

21. What would happen to the range and spacing of representable floating point values if the allocations of bits in the IEEE FPS single-precision format were changed to have 7 bits of exponent and 24 bits of fraction?

22. What is the result of taking the additive inverse of a number twice? Will the result be positive or negative?

23. A positive number has the same representation in one's complement and in two's complement. Suppose its representation is interpreted as two's complement, and its additive inverse is determined. Now this representation is interpreted as one's complement, and its additive inverse is determined. Whether interpreted as one's complement or two's complement, the result will be the same, since it is a positive number. What is the relationship between this result and the original number?

24. Show mathematically that two integers that have a sum of zero have one's complement representations that are bit-complementary.

25. Write a SASM program that reads in an integer and then prints it back out again. Note that the difficult part of this program is that the characters read in must be translated to integers.

26. Write a SASM program that reads in 3 integers (where the integers are separated by a single space on one line), adds them up, and then prints out the result. Note that the difficult part of this program is that the characters read in must be translated to integers.

27. Write a SASM program that prints out an integer without using the SASM `put_i` instruction.

CHAPTER 6

ARITHMETIC AND LOGICAL OPERATIONS

At the heart of a computer is an Arithmetic/Logical Unit (**ALU**) that is capable of performing a well-defined, and limited, set of arithmetic and logical functions on one or two variables. Among the most basic, and most important, of the operations are addition and negation. A computer that can perform addition and negation can do subtraction easily, and it can be programmed to do multiplication and division as a series of additions and subtractions. The ALU must implement algorithms to perform these operations, and these algorithms are surprisingly similar to those employed to perform equivalent longhand operations. Unfortunately, the longhand operations are long and tedious.

The precise algorithms to be performed depend on the representation of the integers: A given bit string represents a different value in sign magnitude than in two's complement representation. In fact, the compelling arguments for choosing one representation over another revolve around the relative efficiency in implementing the simple arithmetic operations for each representation.

Because a finite number of values can be represented within a data type, computer hardware must do arithmetic on a fixed number of bits. Today's computers often use 32 or 64 bits for integer arithmetic. Even with this large number of bits, arithmetic operations may sometimes produce results that are not representable. When a result value does not have a representation, then **overflow** has occurred. Rules can be derived for any arithmetic operation and any integer representation to determine when overflow has occurred. **Detection** of overflow is recognizing when it has occurred. Detection is important, because a lack of detection means that wrong results are used as if they were correct.

Arithmetic on integers includes the operations addition, subtraction, multiplication, integer division, and the modulus function. Logical operations include operations to aid in masking and merging of data. These are usually expressed in terms of inversion (taking the one's complement) and the logical `and` and `or` functions. They are most often performed on an entire word in a bit-wise fashion.

This chapter describes the manipulation of bits that computer hardware must perform in order to carry out logical and arithmetic instructions. Algorithms for the arithmetic operations focus primarily on algorithms based on two's complement integer representation, because this representation is nearly universally employed for integers.

6.1 LOGICAL OPERATIONS

Most programming languages allow logical manipulations on data. C provides `and`, `or`, and `not` operators. SASM provides these, plus others. Typically, the variables used in logical operations are not representations of integers, but rather other, non-numerical quantities, such as characters. Logical operations are defined for boolean variables. A boolean variable can only have one of two values and therefore can be represented in a single bit. An instruction normally specifies a set of operands, where each operand has a fixed precision. Each bit can be a separate boolean variable. A boolean operation is applied simultaneously for each bit in the cell. A unary boolean operation has a single input. Of the four possible unary operators shown in Figure 6.1, the only interesting one is the inverse function, often referred to as the `not` operator. Note that this operation is the same as taking a one's complement.

Figure 6.1 is an example of a **truth table**. Such a table defines a function explicitly by enumerating every possible combination of inputs and specifying the output for each case. A **true** value is represented by a 1, and a **false** value is represented by a 0.

	Output			
Input	ZERO	ONE	INVERSE	SAME
0	0	1	1	0
1	0	1	0	1

Figure 6.1 Unary logical operations.

Input		Output					
a	**b**	**and**	**or**	**nand**	**nor**	**xor (exclusive or)**	**xnor (equality)**
0	0	0	0	1	1	0	1
0	1	0	1	1	0	1	0
1	0	0	1	1	0	1	0
1	1	1	1	0	0	0	1

Figure 6.2 Truth table for logical operations.

SASM Instruction	C Equivalent	Notes
`lnot x`	`x = ~x;`	
`land x, y`	`x = x & y;`	sets condition codes
`lor x, y`	`x = x | y;`	sets condition codes
`lxor x, y`	`x = x ^ y;`	sets condition codes

Figure 6.3 SASM logical operations.

There are sixteen distinct boolean functions that can be performed on two variables. Again, they can be described by a truth table. Figure 6.2 gives the truth table for some common binary boolean operations. Each possible combination of the input variables **a** and **b** is represented as a distinct row in the table. For example, the `and` function is true only if both **a** and **b** are true—the last line in the table. For the `or` function, the result is true if either **a** or **b** (or both) is true.

SASM provides instructions that perform logical operations. The instructions may be used only with variables declared with `dd,` although the interpretation of the content does not assume anything about the implied representation of integers. The logical operations are performed bit-wise on the operands. This means that each bit of result is formed by operating on the corresponding bit of the operands. Bit 0 of the result is formed by doing the operation on bit 0 of each of the operands. Bit 1 of the result is formed by doing the operation on bit 1 of each of the operands, and bit 21 of the result is formed by doing the operation on bit 21 of each of the operands. Figure 6.3 contains a table of SASM logical instructions.

Logical operations are often used when multiple variables are stored together. Since a computer has a fixed-size memory cell, it is more efficient to store multiple variables within a single cell. For example, if a cell consists of 32 bits, it can hold a 32-bit integer in a cell, or it can hold up to four characters in a cell. The process of extracting a portion from a cell is accomplished by **masking**, an operation that selects part of a cell for future operations. For example, if a cell contains 32 bits, numbered 0 to 31 from left to right, separate (8-bit) characters might be stored using bits 0–7, 8–15, 16–23, and 24–31. In order to access the individual characters, for example, to print them, it is necessary to extract them, one at a time. Suppose, for example, that a memory cell contains the four characters `Char` from left to right. This could be declared in SASM by

```
cell   dd    43686172h
```

A **mask** can be used to extract the appropriate bits. The following four masks can be used to extract the characters in the four positions, regardless of the character represented.

```
mask1  dd     ff000000h
mask2  dd     00ff0000h
mask3  dd     0000ff00h
mask4  dd     000000ffh
```

The SASM instruction

```
land   cell, mask1
```

would overwrite the variable `cell` with the value 0x43000000. The leftmost character is extracted from the variable `cell` by using a mask and a logical operation.

If it were desired to replace the capital 'C' in the variable `cell` with a lower-case 'c', this can be accomplished by a logical operation combined with the use of a mask. A SASM code fragment to clear (mask out) the capital 'C' and merge in a lower-case 'c' is given in Figure 6.4. After the code fragment has been executed, the variable `cell` would contain the value 0x63686172.

As another example of the use of logical operations, consider the case where many boolean variables are kept together in a single, integer-sized variable. A common operation will be to clear one of the boolean variables. This involves forcing a zero into the bit position corresponding to the variable. For an example, assume the bits are numbered 0–31 from right to left, and bit 12 is the boolean variable to be cleared. The SASM code fragment in Figure 6.5 will clear the bit.

```
.data
cell                    dd     43686172h
mask1                   dd     0ff000000h
not_mask1               dd     ?
little_c                dd     63000000h

.code
            move               not_mask1, mask1
            lnot               not_mask1
            land               cell, not_mask1
            lor                cell,little_c
```

Figure 6.4 SASM example of masking and merging.

```
.data
bool_vars               dd     ?

.code
            land bool_vars, 0ffffefffh
```

Figure 6.5 SASM code fragment to clear bit 12 of a variable.

6.2 SHIFT OPERATIONS

While logical operations are employed to merge and extract individual variables or fields, it may also be necessary to **align** the variables to be merged. Alignment places a specific portion of a cell at a specific bit position. For example, printing a character in SASM requires that the character be in positions 7–0 (with bits numbered 0–31, right to left). For each character to be printed when characters are packed into an integer-sized variable, an alignment is required. In general, it is necessary to be able to **shift** the position of bits within a cell in order to align them appropriately. This requirement results in a second set of operations known as **shifting.** A shift operation moves the bits within the cell by shifting them right or left. There are three types of shift operations: logical, rotate, and arithmetic.

Logical Shift

A **logical right shift** moves the bits within a cell right one position. The rightmost bit (the least significant bit if the cell is interpreted as an integer) of the original cell is discarded. The leftmost bit (msb) is assigned the value 0. Figure 6.6 diagrams the bit movements for a logical right shift of one bit. A logical right shift of the 8-bit quantity 1000 1011 gives 0100 0101.

A **logical left shift** moves the bits within a cell left one position. The leftmost bit (the most significant bit if the cell is interpreted as an integer) of the original cell is discarded. The rightmost bit (lsb) is assigned the value 0. Figure 6.7 diagrams the bit movements for a logical left shift of one bit. A logical left shift of the 8-bit quantity 1000 1011 gives 0001 0110.

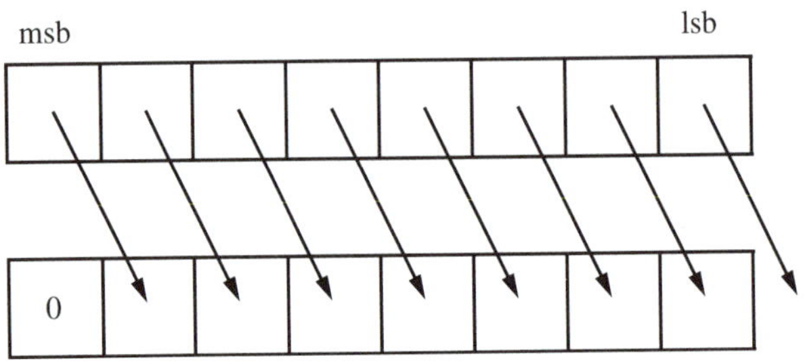

Figure 6.6 Logical right shift one bit.

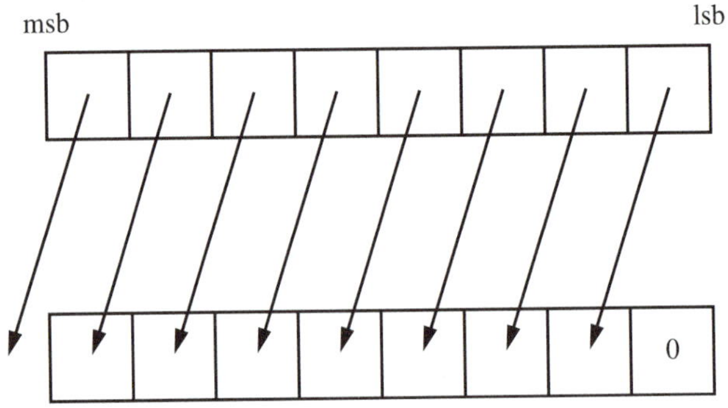

Figure 6.7 Logical left shift one bit.

The description here implies that the bits are shifted by one position. In fact a shift instruction will often have an integer parameter that sets how many times the one position shift operation is applied.

Rotate

A **rotate** operation shifts the bits within a cell without discarding. A **rotate right** shifts bits to the right. Instead of throwing away the rightmost bit (lsb), it is placed in the most significant position of the rotated cell. Figure 6.8 diagrams the bit movements for a rotate right of one bit. A rotate right by one bit of the 8-bit quantity 10001011 gives 11000101. A rotate right by four bits of the same 8-bit quantity 10001011 gives 10111000.

A **rotate left** shifts bits to the left. Instead of throwing away the leftmost bit (msb), it is placed in the least significant position of the rotated cell. Figure 6.9 diagrams the bit movements for a rotate left. A rotate left by one bit of the 8-bit quantity 10001011 gives 00010111. A rotate left by three bits of the same 8-bit quantity 10001011 gives 01011100.

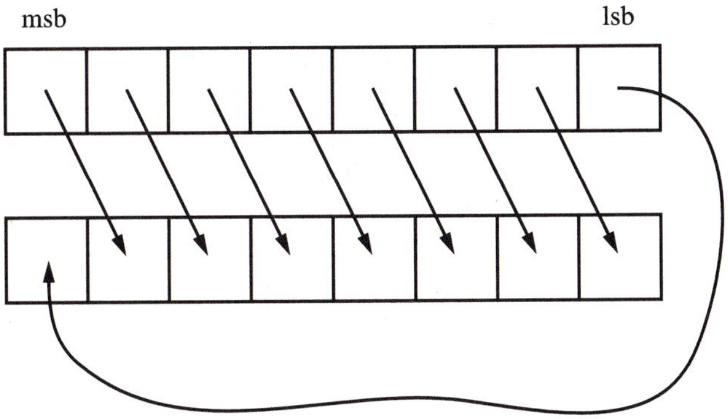

Figure 6.8 Rotate right one bit.

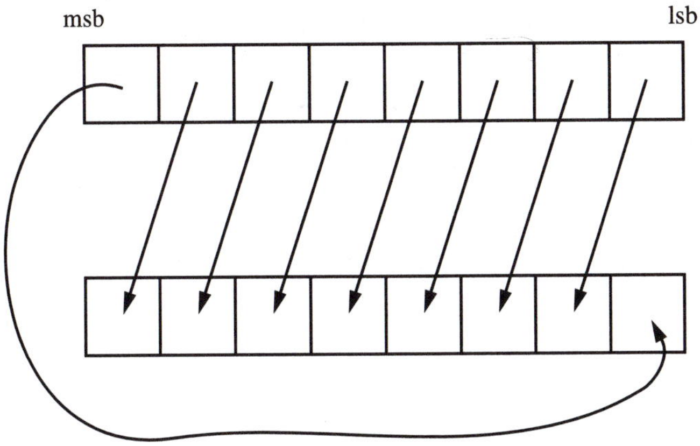

Figure 6.9 Rotate left one bit.

Note that rotate is different from a logical shift in that no information is lost: Any rotate instruction has an inverse operation. Note also that every rotate left operation has an equivalent rotate right operation. Thus it is redundant to have both rotate right and rotate left instructions.

Arithmetic Shift

A shift operation performed on a positive integer has a simple mathematical interpretation; a right shift is equivalent to (integer) division by two; a left shift is equivalent to multiplication by two. This observation is important enough that it has been extended to include negative integers. For a two's complement representation, positive or negative, a logical left shift results in multiplication of the value by two (assuming no overflow). An arithmetic left shift produces the identical result to a logical left shift. An arithmetic left shift of the 8-bit quantity 0000 1011 gives 0001 0110.

For a two's complement representation, positive or negative, division by two is accomplished with a logical right shift if the sign bit is extended, rather than zero-filling from the left. An arithmetic right shift replicates the sign bit rather than zero filling. Figure 6.10 diagrams the bit movements for an arithmetic right shift of one bit. An arithmetic right shift of the 8-bit quantity 1000 0000 gives 1100 0000. An arithmetic right shift is a different operation than a logical right shift.

Figure 6.11 contains a table of SASM shifting instructions. Some of the shifting instructions have no C equivalents given, because their definition in C is implementation dependent. Each of the instructions has one operand. The operand is shifted by one place according to the instruction type. The result is then placed back into the first operand, overwriting its original value. Note that there is no arithmetic left shift instruction. It would be redundant because it is the same operation as a logical left shift.

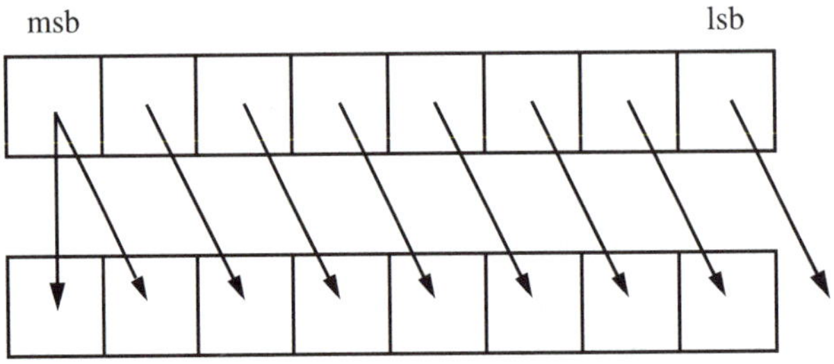

Figure 6.10 Arithmetic right shift one bit.

SASM Instruction	C Equivalent	Notes
`llsh x`	`x << 1;`	logical left shift by 1 bit; sets condition codes
`rlsh x`		logical right shift by 1 bit; sets condition codes
`rash x`		arithmetic right shift by 1 bit; sets condition codes
`rrot x`		rotate right by 1 bit; sets only CF condition code

Figure 6.11 SASM shifting instructions.

6.3 ADDITION AND SUBTRACTION

For the logical and shifting operations, each bit of the result can be computed relatively easily. One bit from each of the input variables is all that is needed to determine a given bit of the output. Arithmetic operations are inherently more complex than this, because there is no simple relationship between the bits in the input variables and the corresponding bits in the output variables. In fact, some bits in the output variable depend on the value of every single bit of both input variables. Thus addition and subtraction are inherently more complex to implement than logical and shifting operations. This is the reason that so much care must be taken to choose the appropriate representation.

Unsigned Addition and Subtraction

The algorithm for addition of unsigned integers is the same regardless of base—the same algorithm taught in school for longhand addition. The algorithm starts at the least significant end of the integers, adding corresponding columns. At each column, both a sum digit and a carry for the next column are generated. Figure 6.12 gives an example of this using decimal integers.

```
  4672
+ 3608
------
  8280
```

Figure 6.12 Unsigned decimal addition.

More formally, given three values *X*, *Y*, and *Z*, their unsigned $(n + 1)$-bit representations give

$$X = \sum_{i=0}^{n} x_i \times 2^i$$

$$Y = \sum_{i=0}^{n} y_i \times 2^i$$

$$Z = \sum_{i=0}^{n} z_i \times 2^i$$

respectively. If *Z* is the sum of *X* and *Y*, then it might be expected that for $0 \le j \le n$,

$$z_j = x_j + y_j$$

Unfortunately, it is not this simple, because *x*, *y*, and *z* are boolean variables, and can have only the value zero or one. Thus if $x_j = 1$ and $y_j = 1$,

$$x_j + y_j = 2 \ne z_j$$

since z_j also can only have the value zero or one. Beginning with the least significant bit position, if $x_0 = 1$ and $y_0 = 1$, we know that both *X* and *Y* are odd numbers. So *Z* must be even, and therefore $z_0 = 0$. However, z_1 is affected by this result, referred to as a **carry**. The rule involves modulo arithmetic:

$$z_0 = (x_0 + y_0) \bmod 2$$

If a carry is generated in bit position j, it indicates a sum of 2×2^j. That is, it has twice the weight of the position generating it, and it must be added to the next bit position, $j + 1$. It is called c_{j+1}. Thus for bit positions $1 \le j \le n$, there are three terms that must be added together, x_j, y_j, and c_j. Since each of these variables is also a boolean variable, their maximum sum is three; so in general

$$z_j = (c_j + x_j + y_j) \bmod 2$$

$$c_j = (c_{j-1} + x_{j-1} + y_{j-1}) \text{ div } 2$$

where c_0 is assumed to be zero. Figure 6.13 illustrates all possible cases by giving the truth table for binary addition. Note that as j increases, the computation of the z and c variables become increasingly complex

$$c_0 = 0$$

$$z_0 = (x_0 + y_0) \bmod 2$$

$$c_1 = (c_0 + x_0 + y_0) \text{ div } 2 = (x_0 + y_0) \text{ div } 2$$

$$z_1 = (c_1 + x_1 + y_1) \bmod 2 = \{[(x_0 + y_0) \text{ div } 2] + x_1 + y_1\} \bmod 2$$

$$c_2 = (c_1 + x_1 + y_1) \text{ div } 2 = [(x_0 + y_0) \text{ div } 2 + x_1 + y_1] \text{ div } 2$$

$$z_2 = (c_2 + x_2 + y_2) \bmod 2 = \{[(c_1 + x_1 + y_1) \text{ div } 2] + x_2 + y_2\} \bmod 2$$

$$\begin{aligned} c_3 &= (c_2 + x_2 + y_2) \text{ div } 2 \\ &= \{[(x_0 + y_0) \text{ div}_2 + x_1 + y_1] \text{ div } 2 + x_2 + y_2\} \text{ div } 2 \end{aligned}$$

$$\begin{aligned} z_3 &= (c_3 + x_3 + y_3) \bmod 2 \\ &= (\{[(x_0 + y_0) \text{ div } 2 + x_1 + y_1] \text{ div } 2 + x_2 + y_2\} \text{ div } 2 + x_3 + y_3) \bmod 2 \end{aligned}$$

In other words, each variable z_j is a function not only of x_j and y_j, but also every variable that is less significant than x_j and y_j.

c_j	x_j	y_j	z_j	c_{j+1}
0	0	0	0	0
0	0	1	1	0
0	1	0	1	0
0	1	1	0	1
1	0	0	1	0
1	0	1	0	1
1	1	0	0	1
1	1	1	1	1

Figure 6.13 Truth table for binary addition.

```
carries: 11111100        carries: 01100110
         01110010                 10110001
       + 00101110               + 00010011
         --------                 --------
         10100000                 11000100
```

Figure 6.14 Unsigned binary addition examples.

The hardware necessary to compute such a complex set of functions is substantial, and an enormous amount of research and design effort have gone into solving this problem since the beginning of the computer age.

Two examples of unsigned addition are given in Figure 6.14 . Both are 8-bit examples, with carries given above the columns.

One further point needs to be made here. The largest number that can be represented as an unsigned integer in $n + 1$ bits is

$$\sum_{i=0}^{n} 2^i = 2^{n+1} - 1$$

If the sum of two representable integers is larger than $2^{n+1} - 1$, there is a carry out of position n, and an incorrect answer is computed. Throwing away the carry out, c_{n+1}, results in modulo 2^{n+1} addition. Since the correct result is not representable, overflow occurs. Overflow can be detected in an unsigned addition calculation when the carry out from the most significant bit, c_{n+1}, is 1. Within the computer's fixed precision, the unsigned addition algorithm is more formally stated as

$$Z = (X + Y) \bmod 2^{n+1}$$

Overflow occurs if

$$(X + Y) \bmod 2^{n+1} \neq X + Y$$

Subtraction on unsigned integers is defined for positive results only. Therefore, an integer can only be subtracted from one of equal or larger magnitude. A truth table can be defined to help with subtraction, as given in Figure 6.15. The unusual aspect of the truth table is that there is no result for the subtraction of 1 from 0. In that case, borrowing from the next column is done (as in decimal subtraction). When working in a binary system, the amount borrowed from a more significant column is 2_{ten} (10_{two}). To illustrate subtraction that must use borrowing, consider the simple case of subtracting 6 from 8 as shown in Figure 6.16.

a	b	a – b
0	0	0
0	1	borrow
1	0	1
1	1	0
10	1	1

Figure 6.15 Truth table for binary subtraction.

```
      1
    0 10 10
  0 1 0 0 0
- 0 0 1 1 0
-----------
  0 0 0 1 0
```

Figure 6.16 Unsigned subtraction with borrowing.

Sign Magnitude Addition and Subtraction

The addition of two sign magnitude integers follows an algorithm similar to the one for unsigned integers. If two integers represented in sign magnitude are of the same sign, the unsigned addition algorithm is applied to the magnitudes. The sign of the result is set separately, and is the same as the integers being added. Figure 6.17 shows two examples of addition on sign magnitude integers that have the same sign. The examples are given for 8-bit represntations. Any carry out from the most significant bit of the magnitude is thrown away.

If the two integers to be added are of opposite signs, however, the addition algorithm cannot be applied. It is defined only for integers of like sign. Alternatively, the problem can be redefined. The addition can be turned into a subtraction of the additive inverse of one of the integers, since

$$X + Y = X - (-Y)$$

The subtraction of sign magnitude integers does unsigned subtraction on the magnitudes, with the sign bit set separately. The smaller-magnitude integer is subtracted from the larger-magnitude integer, and the sign will be the same as the integer with the larger magnitude. So the determination of the sign of the result requires a comparison. Figure 6.18 shows a single 8-bit example of sign magnitude addition that must be redefined as a subtraction operation.

```
carries: 1110000        carries: 0001000
       0 0101001               1 1110100
     + 0 0011010             + 1 0000100
     -----------             -----------
       0 1000011               1 1111000
```

Figure 6.17 Sign magnitude addition examples.

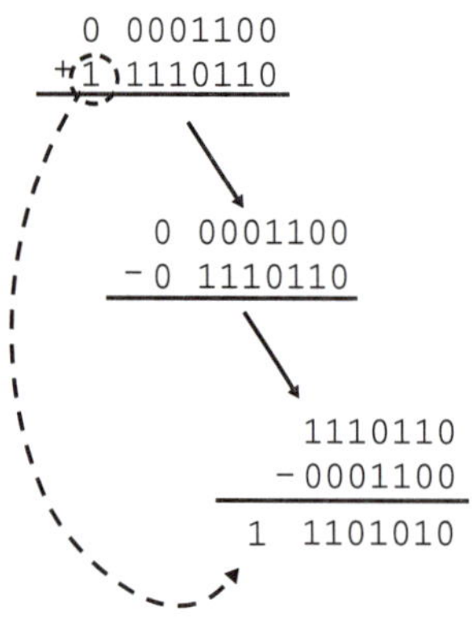

Figure 6.18 Sign magnitude addition example.

Subtraction of sign magnitude integers follows much the same algorithm as addition. Subtraction is only performed on integers of like sign. Unsigned subtraction is used on the magnitudes, with the smaller magnitude integer subtracted from the larger. The sign of the result is determined by the order of the subtraction. If the order of the subtraction is unchanged, then the sign will be the same as the integers. If the order of the subtraction is changed, then the sign bit will also be inverted. Figure 6.19 gives two simple 4-bit examples of sign magnitude subtraction on integers of the same sign.

Sign magnitude subtraction on integers that do not have the same sign redefines the problem to perform addition on an additive inverse. For integers of opposite sign, the problem $X - Y$ is redefined to be $X + (-Y)$. The sign of the result is set the same as the signs of the integers within the addition. Figure 6.20 contains two 6-bit examples of sign magnitude subtraction on integers that do not have the same sign.

The comparison operation, the determination of what operation to perform (addition or subtraction), and the requirement of hardware to do both addition and subtraction make hardware complicated. Not only is this method complicated; its implementation is also slow. The reason is that a comparison operation must be performed to decide which operand is larger before the subtraction is performed. The way a computer normally does a comparison of two integers is by subtracting one from the other. Thus the situation arises that the computer must subtract one number from another before it knows which of two possible subtractions to perform. The best way to perform this operation is simply to do both subtractions. The results of the incorrect subtraction (subtracting the larger magnitude from the smaller) include the indication of an invalid result. Thus the correct result can be determined, but only after the two subtractions have been performed.

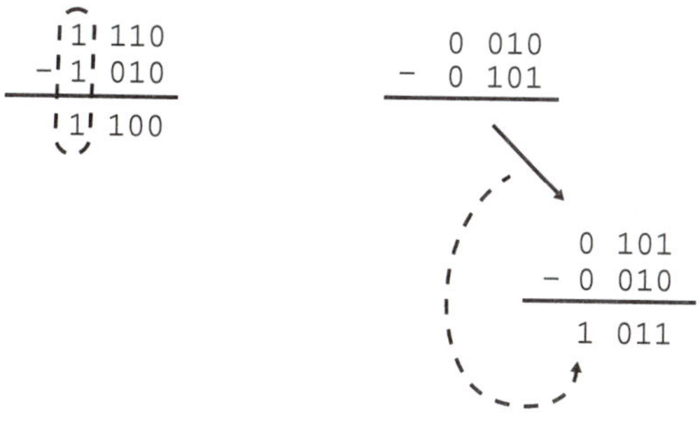

Figure 6.19 Sign magnitude subtraction examples.

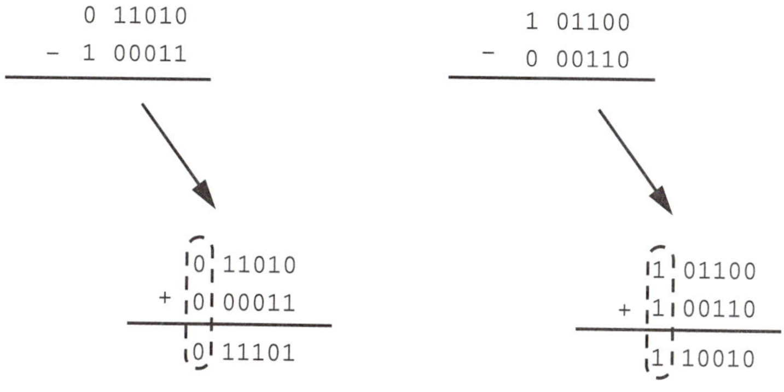

Figure 6.20 Sign magnitude subtraction on integers of different signs.

The detection of overflow in addition of sign magnitude integers is straightforward. If both addends are of the same sign, and there is a carry out from the most significant bit (msb) of the magnitudes, then overflow has occurred. Note that overflow will never occur when adding two numbers of different signs.

Two's Complement Addition and Subtraction

Two's complement representation makes addition simpler. There is only one addition algorithm regardless of the operands' sign. A further benefit is that subtraction can be performed simply by computing the additive inverse and applying the addition algorithm. The operation $X - Y$ becomes $X + (-Y)$.

The elegance of two's complement representation is that the addition algorithm for unsigned integers *is the same algorithm* used to perform addition on both positive and negative integers. This means that the same hardware can be used for both unsigned and two's complement addition. This surprising fact results from the relationship between the interpretation of an integer as an unsigned number and its interpretation as a two's complement number.

Since the addition hardware defined does arithmetic modulo 2^{n+1}, the representation of the unsigned result is also the correct result for two's complement. The result of the adder will always produce the correct result, if the correct result is representable. Figure 6.21 presents two examples of 8-bit two's complement addition that have representable results.

A result that is not representable is the case of overflow. The conditions that signal overflow are different for unsigned and two's complement representations. Overflow in two's complement representation does not necessarily occur when there is a carry out of the most significant bit during an addition. It is only when both addends are of the same sign, and the result is of the opposite sign, that overflow has occurred. Figure 6.22 shows two examples of overflow in the addition of two's complement integers. One results in a carry out from the most significant bit, and the other does not.

Subtraction of two's complement integers is redefined as the addition of an additive inverse. An example of this is presented in Figure 6.23. The detection of overflow is the same as for addition. After the subtraction has been redefined as the addition of an additive inverse, the resulting addition calculation is checked for overflow.

```
  11100100        11110000
+ 11001110      + 00110000
----------      ----------
  10110010        00100000
```

Figure 6.21 Two's complement addition examples.

```
  00000101              11010101
+ 01111100            + 10101001
----------            ----------
  10000001              01111110
 OVERFLOW               OVERFLOW
(WITH CARRY OUT)
```

Figure 6.22 Examples of overflow in two's complement addition.

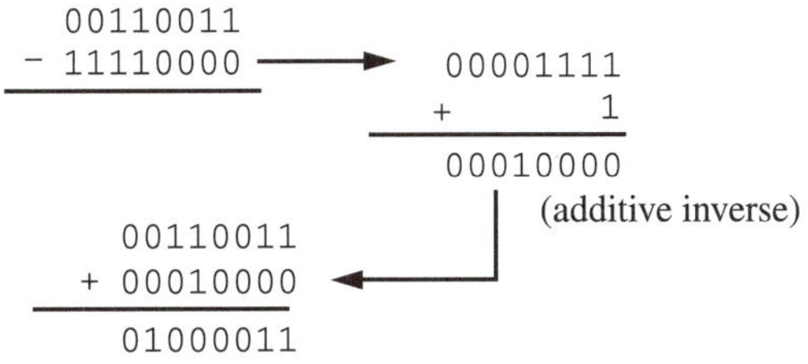

Figure 6.23 Two's complement subtraction.

One's Complement Addition and Subtraction

One's complement addition and subtraction depend on building hardware that does arithmetic modulo $2^{n-1} - 1$. As it turns out, this is not hard. The carry out from the most significant bit in addition indicates a number greater than 2^{n+1}. This requires that 1 must be added to the result to generate the correct answer. The adder previously discussed can be adapted to do this. The restriction that c_0 is always 0 is modified. The carry out of the most significant bit, c_n, becomes the carry in of the least significant bit, c_0. Note that one's complement addition will be slower than two's complement addition, since two addition operations may need to be performed. Subtraction of one's complement integers can be accomplished in the same manner as two's complement subtraction. The subtraction $X - Y$ becomes the addition $X + (-Y)$.

6.4 MULTIPLICATION

The multiplication of integers also proceeds in a manner analogous to the longhand multiplication of decimal numbers. To understand the method, it is important to understand why longhand multiplication works. Consider the product, Z, of two integers, X and Y. Assume that their representation is unsigned. The algorithm readily extends to complement representation, since addition and multiplication by powers of two are the only operations being applied.

For unsigned integers, X and Y,

$$X = \sum_{i=0}^{n} x_i \times 2^i$$

$$Y = \sum_{i=0}^{n} y_i \times 2^i$$

and the product Z is

$$\begin{aligned} X \times Y &= \left(\sum_{i=0}^{n} x_i \times 2^i\right) \times \left(\sum_{i=0}^{n} y_i \times 2^i\right) \\ &= \sum_{i=0}^{n} \left[x_i \times 2^i \times \left(\sum_{j=0}^{n} y_j \times 2^i\right)\right] \\ &= \sum_{i=0}^{n} x_i \times 2^i \times Y \end{aligned}$$

```
     1000 (8)
   × 0110 (6)
     0000
    1000
   1000
 + 0000
  0110000 (48)
```

Figure 6.24 Unsigned multiplication example.

Thus the product of X and Y can be broken into a summation. Each nonzero term of the summation will be a product of Y and a power of two. This algorithm can be implemented by repetitive multiplications of Y, conditionally adding the terms into the product, as appropriate.

Figure 6.24 gives an example of the longhand version of the multiplication algorithm on unsigned binary integers. The longhand algorithm works because this implicit product of a power of two is accomplished by shifting the multiplicand left by the appropriate amount in forming the terms to be added. In base two the multiplication part is even simpler, since in base two the multiplicand can be only zero or one.

A problem does arise in the range of the answers. Notice that if $0 \le X$, and $Y \le 2^n - 1$, then

$$0 \le X \times Y < 2^{2n} - 2^{n+1} + 1 < 2^{2n}$$

Thus it may take as many as $2n$ bits to represent the product of two numbers that can each be represented in n bits. In general, this causes problems. One solution is to allow larger integers for the result. It is common for a computer to compute a product and require two integer variables for result storage. If the product does not result in overflow in a single integer, this is easily determined, and only the least significant half of the result need be further considered. If the product will not fit in a single integer, the integer with the most significant half of the product contains the additional information. A conventional n-bit adder can be used to perform arithmetic on variables that require two integers (and therefore must be treated as two variables) to store, but the algorithms are tricky, even for simple operations like addition and subtraction.

The algorithm for multiplication of unsigned integers can be extended to work for two's complement integers. By sign extending both the multiplier and the multiplicand to the size needed for the result, the algorithm will work unchanged. The result will be in the least significant $2n$ bits, where n is the number of bits in the operands before sign extension. Notice that by sign extending the operands, the result produced would be $4n$ bits long. The most significant $2n$ bits are not part of the result, and must be discarded. Figure 6.25 shows four examples of this algorithm applied to 4-bit two's complement integers. The sign extension is not necessary in the case where both operands are positive.

An alternative algorithm for multiplication of two's complement integers takes into account the sign of the multiplier. When the multiplier is negative, the wrong result is generated if the unsigned multiplication algorithm is applied. Instead of sign extending the multiplier and multiplicand, the partial products can be sign extended to the precision required for the product. This method works for a positive multiplier. When the multiplier is negative, the problem is redefined by multiplying the additive inverse of both multiplier and multiplicand. The problem $X \times Y$ becomes $-X \times -Y$.

```
sign extension
           11111101 (-3)                00000101 (5)   <—— multiplicand
         × 00000110 (6)               × 11111101 (-3)  <—— multiplier
           00000000                     00000101
          11111101                     00000000
         11111101                     00000101
        00000000                     00000101
       00000000                     00000101
      00000000                     00000101
     00000000                     00000101
  + 00000000                   + 00000101
           11101110 (-18)               11110001 (-15)


           11111000 (-8)                11111000 (-8)
         × 00000111 (7)               × 11111000 (-8)
           11111000                     00000000
          11111000                     00000000
      + 11111000                      00000000
           11001000 (-56)            11111000
                                    11111000
                                   11111000
                                  11111000
                               + 11111000
                                        01000000
```

Figure 6.25 Two's complement integer multiplication.

```
                    000110 (6)                        000010 (2)
                  × 111011 (-5)                     × 110001 (-15)
                       ↓                                 ↓
sign extension      111010 (-6)                       111110 (-2)
                  × 000101 (5)                      × 001111 (15)
              111111111010                      111111111110
              000000000000                      111111111100
            + 111111101000                      111111111000
              111111100010 (-30)              + 111111110000
                                                111111100010 (-30)
```

Figure 6.26 Two's complement multiplication by sign extension of partial products.

Two examples of this multiplication algorithm appear in Figure 6.26. The 6-bit operands require 12 bits of precision for the result. Therefore, the partial products are sign extended to 12 bits. And, since the multiplier is negative, the problem is redefined as the multiplication of the additive inverses of both multiplier and multiplicand.

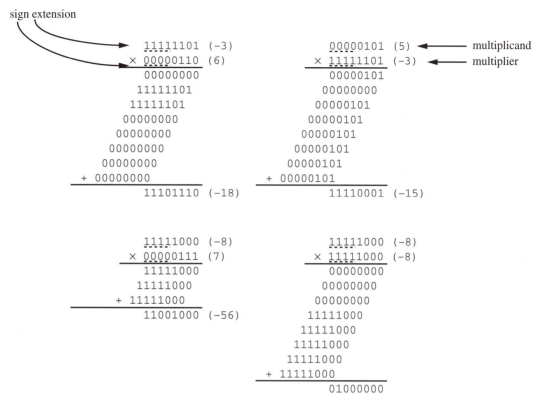

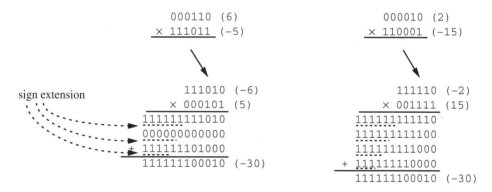

```
.data
X               dd      ?              ; multiplier
Y               dd      ?              ; multiplicand
ls_sum          dd      0              ; least significant portion of result
ms_sum          dd      0              ; most significant portion of result
bit_sum         dd      ?
bit_mask        dd      00000001h
bit_test        dd      ?

.code
          compare     0, X           ; if negative multiplier, get
          blz         do_mult        ; additive inverses of X and Y
          lnot        X
          iadd        X, 1
          lnot        Y
          iadd        Y, 1
do_mult:
          move        bit_test, bit_mask
          land        bit_test, X ; get appropriate multiplier bit
          bez         shift          ; skip addition if bit is 0
          iadd        ms_sum, Y      ; add partial sum
shift:
          move        bit_sum, 1     ; get lsb of ms_sum into ls_sum
          land        bit_sum, ms_sum
          lor         ls_sum, bit_sum
          rrot        ls_sum         ; move the lsb of ls_sum to msb
          rash        ms_sum         ; maintain sign of ms_sum
          llsh        bit_mask       ; set up to work on next bit
          compare     bit_mask, 0
          bgz         do_mult        ; done when the 1 in bit_mask is
                                     ; shifted to msb position
          move        bit_sum, 1     ; final iteration
          land        bit_sum, ms_sum
          lor         ls_sum, bit_sum
          rrot        ls_sum
          rash        ms_sum
```

Figure 6.27 SASM implementation of 32-bit two's complement multiplication.

Surprisingly, the adder necessary to perform an n-bit multiplication does not need to be more than n bits. This is because each row in the table of partial sums consists of no more than n bits; so at most n result bits can be affected. An example of this is shown in the SASM implementation of 32-bit two's complement multiplication as given as the code fragment in Figure 6.27. It provides a 64-bit result. The least significant 32 bits of result are placed into the variable `ls_sum`, and the most significant 32 bits of result are placed into the variable `ms_sum`. The program works correctly for any pair of two's complement numbers, X and Y. The program also provides examples of merging and masking, since the appropriate multiplier bit must be extracted, and the result is spread across two variables.

The product of two n-bit quantities can always be represented in $2n$ bits. Thus overflow never occurs. If the result is restricted to n bits, overflow may occur. While overflow is not simple to detect, the SASM algorithm has an easy test for overflow. If the variable `ls_sum` is positive, then `ms_sum` must be zero. If the variable `ls_sum` is negative, then `ms_sum` must be -1.

6.5 DIVISION

There is no simple division algorithm for two's complement integers. The unsigned division algorithm is analogous to that used for longhand division of decimal integers. Figure 6.28 shows an example of longhand division on an unsigned binary and decimal value. The guess that must be made in decimal arithmetic is difficult, but in binary it is trivial; either it goes one time or it doesn't. So the algorithm repeatedly subtracts the divisor, properly aligned.

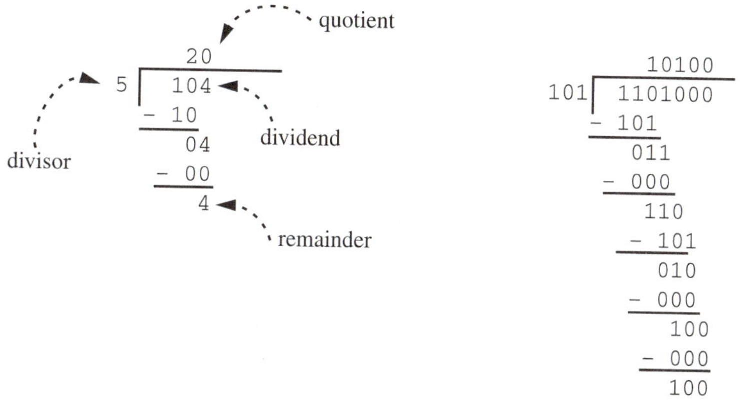

Figure 6.28 Integer division on decimal and unsigned binary numbers.

No convenient algorithm exists for division of sign magnitude and complement integers. Accommodating them requires calculating the absolute value of both divisor and dividend, and doing unsigned division with the absolute values. The sign needed for the result can be determined in advance. If a negative result is needed, then the additive inverse of the positive quotient is taken.

Overflow does not occur in integer division. Both the quotient and remainder are always guaranteed to be less than or equal to the dividend.

An exception case that must be handled is division by zero. The result of division by zero is not defined. To handle this case, a check is usually made for a zero divisor. When a zero divisor is detected, a reasonable implementation is to stop the program from executing, and forward the information that a division by zero occurred to the operating system.

SUMMARY

The computer hardware that does arithmetic and logical operations (the ALU) on integers is a critical portion of a computer processor, because it contributes in such a large way to the processor's speed. This ALU is heavily utilized by all programs, and therefore must be designed to operate as efficiently as possible. The choice of integer representation affects the speed of the algorithm that can be implemented. Two's complement integer representation is chosen because it makes addition both simple and quick. Subtraction becomes the addition of an additive inverse; so a separate piece of hardware to do subtraction is not necessary. Multiplication and division can also be implemented by repeated additions or subtractions.

PROBLEMS

1. Fill in the missing entries of the following table. Do the logical operations bit-wise on the 8-bit binary values.

x	**y**	not **x**	**x** and **y**	**x** or **y**
00000000	11111111			
	00000000	11111111		
11110000	01010101			

2. Fill in the missing entries of the following table. Do the logical operations bit-wise on the 8-bit binary values.

x	**y**	**x** xor **y**	**x** nand **y**	**x** nor **y**
00000011	00111111			
	00000000	11111111		
11110000	01010101			

3. Write a SASM code fragment that sets bit 30 of variable `xx` if bit 18 of variable `yy` is set. Make sure that the other bits of variable `xx` are unchanged from their initial value. Bits are numbered from the right, starting with 0.

4. Do unsigned addition on the following 8-bit integers. Identify which (if any) of the operations results in overflow. Show a check of your work by converting to decimal.

```
  11011001        00110100        00000001
+ 00101110      + 01101101      + 01111111
----------      ----------      ----------
```

5. Do sign magnitude addition on the following 8-bit integers. Identify which (if any) of the operations results in overflow. Show a check of your work by converting to decimal.

```
  11011001       00110100       00000001
+ 00101110     + 01101101     + 01111111
```

6. Do two's complement addition on the following 8-bit integers. Identify which (if any) of the operations results in overflow. Show a check of your work by converting to decimal.

```
  11001010       00110001       00000001
+ 00101100     + 01111110     + 11111111
```

7. Do two's complement addition on the following 20-bit integers (given in hexadecimal). Identify which (if any) of the operations results in overflow.

```
  3b008       94c21       0ccde
+ 0cf05     + 60332     + f037a
```

8. Do two's complement subtraction on the following 8-bit integers. Identify which (if any) of the operations result in overflow. Show a check of your work by converting to decimal.

```
  11011001       00110100       00000001
- 10101110     - 01101101     - 01111111
```

9. Give an algorithm for doing subtraction on 4-bit one's complement integers.

10. Do the following multiplications in two's complement representation. Convert the decimal numbers to 8-bit two's complement representation first, and then show the multiplication.

a. 33×4
b. -1×4
c. 22×-5
d. -18×-16

11. Do the following two's complement multiplication. Identify which calculations (if any) results in overflow for 12-bit words. Show your work. Show a check of your work by converting to decimal.

```
  000111      011110      011011      111111
× 000110    × 110111    × 010100    × 101111
```

12. Do the following long division, and identify the remainder of the division. Do the work both in decimal and unsigned binary.

a.23 / 4

b.240 / 8

13. The numbers 10 and -15 are stored in sign magnitude representation in a computer that performs only 16-bit two's complement arithmetic. After the computer adds the two numbers, what is the sign magnitude interpretation of the result?

14. Suppose that the SASM instruction `llsh` were not available. Can the same functionality be accomplished using `rrot` and logical operations? If so, give an example showing how.

15. Suppose that the SASM instruction `rash` were not available. Can the same functionality be accomplished using `rrot` and logical operations? If so, give an example showing how.

16. Define the tests for detection of overflow in one's complement addition and subtraction.

17. Which is faster: one's complement subtraction or two's complement subtraction? Why?

18. Specify an algorithm that detects overflow in the case of a 32-bit multiplication that requires more than 32 bits of precision for its result.

CHAPTER 7

FLOATING POINT ARITHMETIC

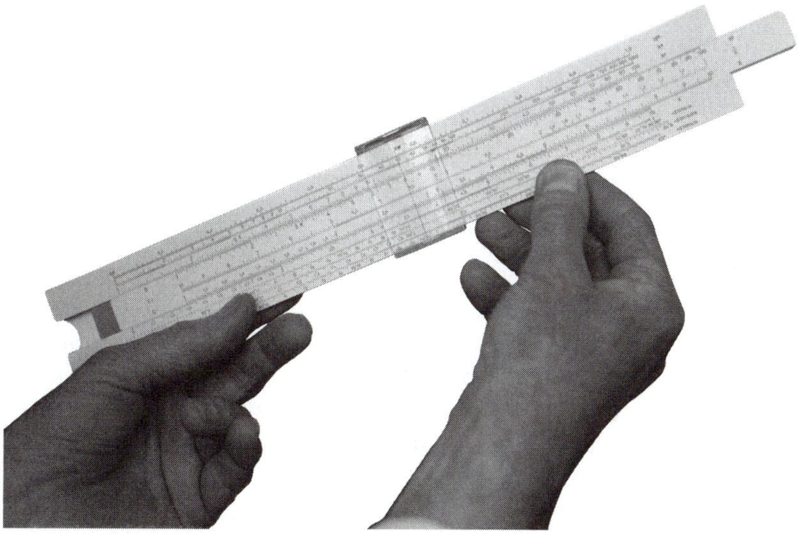

The representation and manipulation of floating point numbers are among the most critical aspects of a computer design. Particularly for the fastest of computers and other computers that must perform precise mathematical operations, the speed of execution of arithmetic operations on floating point numbers is important. In fact, one of the key measures used to indicate a rough measure of performance for a scientific computer is the number of floating point operations that can be performed per second (FLOPS). FLOPS stands for FLoating point Operations Per Second.

Floating point operations are inherently more complex than their equivalent integer operations, in the same way that operations on numbers represented in scientific notation are more complex than those represented as simple strings of digits with a radix point. Addition and subtraction are harder because the exponents must be compared to facilitate the alignment of the radix points. Multiplication is hard because the exponents must be added together, and the resulting representation may have to be normalized.

This chapter discusses algorithms for performing the basic floating point operations. At the end of the chapter, advanced topics relating to floating point operations are covered. As with integer arithmetic, there are a small number of primitive operations that are performed repeatedly. All floating point arithmetic can be accomplished by treating the individual parts of the floating point representation as integers and performing shifting operations and integer arithmetic on them.

As with integers, the representation of floating point numbers critically affects the ease with which these primitive operations can be performed. At one time nearly every computer manufacturer had its own representation for floating point numbers. Today the IEEE Floating Point Standard is widely accepted, and the examples here are given in this representation.

7.1 HARDWARE VERSUS SOFTWARE CALCULATIONS

All general-purpose computers must be able to do arithmetic on real numbers. There is a choice for how the calculations are done, either in hardware or in software. The choice is made during the design of the computer. A hardware implementation provides circuitry that does the floating point arithmetic. It will be much faster than a software implementation. A software implementation requires significantly less computer hardware. It uses program code (much like a procedure or function), and it utilizes integer arithmetic to do floating point arithmetic.

A variety of design alternatives is possible. In general, more expensive solutions use more hardware but run faster, while less expensive solutions depend on software and run slower. The variation in both cost and performance may be dramatic; hardware-supported floating point operations may execute several orders of magnitude faster than a software implementation. Thus the computer designer is faced with design choices to increase performance by increasing the cost. There are many examples of this, resulting in dramatic variations in both the cost and performance of computers.

The computer designer also may have multiple choices for a hardware design. Some designs result in much faster, but more expensive, implementations than others. An example can be seen in the case of shifting operations. It is much simpler to build hardware that only shifts the bits in an operand by a single position. This restriction can be reflected in the instruction set by defining only instructions that shift by a single bit. No loss of generality results, because the programmer can always achieve an arbitrary shift by writing a simple loop that executes the shift instruction as many times as required. Such code is tedious for the programmer, however. It also requires more memory, both for code and extra variables.

Given that the decision has been made to provide shift instructions with variable shifts, the hardware designer can still implement the shift instruction in a variety of ways. A fast way uses a circuit known as a **barrel shifter**, which allows the arbitrary shift to occur all at once, but is very expensive. A slower implementation might implement the equivalent of a program loop in hardware, using only a simple shifter capable of shifting a single bit. The hardware then could use a **sequencer** to serialize the shifts and keep track of the count.

7.2 ADDITION AND SUBTRACTION

The addition of two numbers represented in scientific notation can be broken down into a series of arithmetic operations on integers. Consider the addition of the numbers 2.25×10^0 and 1.340625×10^2. The addition proceeds as follows. First the numbers are represented in signed positional notation, including their decimal point:

$$2.25 + 134.0625$$

Their decimal points are lined up:

$$\begin{array}{r} 2.25 \\ +\ 134.0625 \\ \hline \end{array}$$

The addition operation is the same as for integer addition (ignoring the decimal point), as can be seen by zero-filling to the right until the two operands are aligned:

$$\begin{array}{r} 2.2500 \\ +\ 134.0625 \\ \hline \end{array}$$

Now the addition is performed:

$$\begin{array}{r} 2.2500 \\ +\ 134.0625 \\ \hline 136.3125 \end{array}$$

Finally, the number is converted back into scientific notation, 1.363125×10^2. Note that the first number has only three significant digits (±0.005); so the accuracy of the result is only good to two decimal digits, and the correct answer is 1.3631×10^2. Using this knowledge, an alternative technique could be used, namely, rounding the digit with the greater precision to that of the lesser:

$$\begin{array}{r} 2.25 \\ +\ 134.06 \\ \hline 136.31 \end{array}$$

The computer has no concept of accuracy, only precision. It therefore always computes results as if the accuracy were limited only by the precision. Thus the computer obtains the answer of 1.363125×10^2.

Recall the representation of FPS numbers from Chapter 5:

$$N = (-1)^s \times m \times 2^e$$

Conversion to *S, F, E*	**Conversion to *s, m, e***
$F = (m - 1) \times 2^n$ $E = e + 127$ $S = s$	$m = 1 + F/2^n$ $e = E - 127$ $s = S$

E and F are the unsigned interpretation of the bit patterns of the exponent and fraction fields, respectively. For floating point representation, the integer portion of the mantissa is always one, and it is assumed that the accuracy is 24 bits. Shifting to align the radix points results in more than 24 bits. In order not to lose the most significant bit, the number with the smaller exponent is shifted right.

The addition of two numbers represented in the FPS is performed analogously to the decimal example above. The following example adds the floating point numbers 2.25 and 134.0625. The single-precision format for the number 2.25, including the hidden bit in parentheses, is

S	**E**	**F**
0	1000 0000	(1) 001 0000 0000 0000 0000 0000

The single-precision format for the number 134.0625 is

S	**E**	**F**
0	1000 0110	(1) 000 0110 0001 0000 0000 0000

Aligning the radix points is a matter of shifting the fraction corresponding to the smaller exponent and incrementing its exponent until the exponents of the two representations match. For the example, the floating point number representing 2.25 is shifted. Its fraction must be right shifted by six places such that its exponent **E** will be 134_{ten}. In this way

S	**E**	**F**
0	1000 0000	(1) 001 0000 0000 0000 0000 0000

becomes

0	1000 0110	(0) 000 0010 0100 0000 0000 0000

after radix-point alignment. Note that the hidden bit is now 0 for the representation shifted.

Now that the radix points have been aligned, the addition can proceed. Note that only the mantissas are added. The exponent of the result is the same as the exponent of the numbers being added.

0	1000 0110	(0) 000 0010 0100 0000 0000 0000
+0	1000 0110	(1) 000 0110 0001 0000 0000 0000
0	1000 0110	(1) 000 1000 0101 0000 0000 0000

This result is already normalized. Since the larger mantissa is greater than one and less than two, in no case can the sum of the two mantissas be as large as four. In general, when adding two positive mantissas, the range of the resulting mantissa is

$$1 \leq m < 4$$

If $m < 2$, it is already normalized. If $m \geq 2$, it must be normalized. Only a single shift is required, since m cannot be as large as four. Normalizing is therefore a matter of shifting the mantissa right by one position and adding one to the exponent. An example that requires normalization is the addition of 134.0625 and 255.0625. The representation of 255.0625 is

S	**E**	**F**
0	1000 0110	(1) 111 1111 0001 0000 0000 0000

The addition is written as

```
 0     1000 0110     (1) 111 1111 0001 0000 0000 0000
+0     1000 0110     (1) 000 0110 0001 0000 0000 0000
-----------------------------------------------------
 0     1000 0110    (11) 000 0101 0010 0000 0000 0000
```

Notice that the sum has overflowed the position of the hidden bit. Shifting the mantissa right by one position and incrementing the exponent, the result becomes

```
0     1000 0111    (1) 100 0010 1001 0000 0000 0000
```

So far the examples have assumed only positive mantissa and exponents. The exponents can be positive or negative, with no change in the algorithm, with the interpretation that the selection of "the smaller" exponent means "more negative." The biased-127 representation makes this interpretation simple: The smaller number represented will always have a smaller value for E, the unsigned interpretation.

Negative mantissas must also be handled correctly. Since the sign bit S determines the sign of the mantissa, the mantissa is a variant of sign magnitude representation. Negative numbers can be handled correctly by assuring that the additions are performed correctly. Since addition on sign magnitude representations are difficult, it is easiest on most computers to convert the mantissa to a two's complement representation for addition, converting the result back to sign magnitude. Here is the addition of the first example performed again, but this time with a sign changed:

$$2.25 + (-134.0625) = -131.8125$$

The numbers are represented in exactly the same way except that the sign bit S of the addend is inverted. The representation for –134.0625 is

```
S      E                      F
1    1000 0110    (1) 000 0110 0001 0000 0000 0000
```

The smaller number is again determined by the exponent, and the addition proceeds. The mantissas are converted to two's complement representation for the addition:

```
(0) 000 0010 0100 0000 0000 0000
```

becomes

```
0000 0000 0000 0010 0100 0000 0000 0000
```

and the additive inverse of

```
(1) 000 0110 0001 0000 0000 0000
```

is represented as

```
1111 1111 0111 1001 1111 0000 0000 0000
```

After the addition is performed in two's complement,

```
  0000 0000 0000 0010 0100 0000 0000 0000
+ 1111 1111 0111 1001 1111 0000 0000 0000
------------------------------------------
  1111 1111 0111 1100 0011 0000 0000 0000
```

the result is converted back to sign magnitude, with

```
1111 1111 0111 1100 0011 0000 0000 0000
```

yielding

```
(1) 000 011 1101 0000 0000 0000
```

The single precision FPS representation of the result is

```
S       E                      F
1   1000 0110   (1) 000 0010 1101 0000 0000 0000
```

Alternatively, a hand calculation doing sign magnitude subtraction of the mantissas gives the same result.

```
  0   1000 0110   (1) 000 0110 0001 0000 0000 0000    (134.0625)
- 0   1000 0110   (0) 000 0010 0100 0000 0000 0000        (2.25)
------------------------------------------------------------------
  1   1000 0110   (1) 000 0011 1101 0000 0000 0000   (-131.8125)
```

The sign of the result is negative because the order of the operands is changed in order to subtract the smaller-magnitude mantissa from the larger-magnitude mantissa.

Normalization becomes more complex with the introduction of negative mantissas. For numbers of the same sign, the magnitude of their sum can be no less than the larger number and no greater than twice the larger number. With numbers of opposite sign, the magnitude of their sum can be arbitrarily small–zero, if the numbers are equal in magnitude. In the case of addition of numbers of opposite sign, the result may have to be normalized as many positions as there are precision. Notice that there is a large loss of accuracy in such a case. If two experimentally derived numbers are approximately the same size, the accuracy of their difference is small. For example, if two distance measurements have been taken, with the results of 135.901 and 135.861 meters, respectively, their difference is

```
  135.901
- 135.861
---------
  000.040
```

meters. However, this number, 0.04, has only two digits of significance, and even the second is suspect. The computer, of course, is not able to take this loss of accuracy into account, and will produce a result dependent only on its precision. It is the responsibility of the programmer to recognize the loss of significance in such a calculation.

Subtraction can be achieved with a trivial extension, since taking the additive inverse of a number in floating point representation involves inverting the sign bit *S*. The subtraction of 135.861 from 135.901 would be treated as follows. The value 135.901 in single-precision FPS format is:

```
S       E                      F
0   1000 0110   (1) 000 0111 1110 0110 1010 0000
```

The value 135.861 in single-precision FPS format is:

```
S      E                  F
0   1000 0110   (1) 000 0111 1101 1100 0110 1010
```

The mantissas are converted to two's complement and added.

```
  0000 0000 1000 0111 1110 0110 1010 1000
+ 1111 1111 0111 1000 0010 0011 1001 0110
-----------------------------------------
  0000 0000 0000 0000 0000 1010 0011 1110
```

The unnormalized result is therefore

```
S      E                  F
0   1000 0110   (0) 000 0000 0000 1010 0011 1110
```

It is normalized by shifting the mantissa left until the leading one moves into the hidden bit position. It will need to be shifted left 12 positions. The exponent is adjusted by subtracting 12.

```
S      E                  F
0   1000 0110   (0) 000 0000 0000 1010 0011 1110
```

becomes

```
S      E                  F
0   0111 1010   (1) 010 0011 1110 0000 0000 0000
```

This is the representation for 0.040.

If the two numbers being compared are identical, the resulting subtraction will result in a mantissa of zero. No amount of shifting will move a one into the hidden bit position. This case must be recognized explicitly, and the representation for zero, $E = F = 0$, obtained. Remember that this result does not indicate the numbers are necessarily identical, simply that their difference is smaller than can be determined from the accuracy of the measurements and the precision of the computer.

Another important case is the subtraction of two numbers that vary enormously in magnitude. If the exponents of the numbers vary by more than the precision of the mantissa (24), the result of shifting will be to obtain zero for the mantissa of the smaller number. The result, therefore, is just the larger number.

7.3 MULTIPLICATION

The multiplication of two floating point numbers is actually simpler than floating point addition. Like multiplication of numbers in scientific notation, the following steps are taken:

1. Do unsigned multiplication on the mantissas.
2. Add the exponents.
3. Normalize the result.
4. Set the sign bit of the result.

The multiplication of the mantissas is the same as multiplication of two unsigned numbers. Remember that the number of bits required for a result will be twice the number of bits in the mantissa. Some of the least significant bits will be discarded to maintain the same precision within the single-precision representation.

Here is an example of multiplication of two floating point numbers in a shortened format. The format is modified by eliminating the 16 least significant bits of the mantissa, giving the mantissa only seven bits instead of the 23 bits in the single-precision FPS format. The example performs the multiplication of 18.0 and 9.5. The value 18.0 is represented in the modified single-precision format as

S	E	F
0	1000 0011	(1) 001 0000

The value 9.5 is represented in the modified single-precision format as

S	E	F
0	1000 0010	(1) 001 1000

The mantissas are first multiplied. Note that the hidden bit is also part of the multiplication.

```
            1.0010000
          × 1.0011000
  -------------------
             00000000
            00000000
           00000000
          10010000
         10010000
        00000000
       00000000
   +  10010000
  -------------------
      101010110000000
```

Placing the radix point gives a mantissa of

```
1.01010110000000
```

The exponents are added. This is accomplished by adding the true exponents. Unsigned addition could be performed directly on the biased-127 representations, though a correction must be made to account for the introduction of a double bias. Addition of biased-127 representations could also be achieved by unbiasing one of the integers—that is, subtracting 127 from it—then applying two's complement addition. The result would be the biased-127 representation of the sum.

```
    e     E
    4  1000 0011
  + 3  1000 0010
  ---
    7  1000 0110
```

The sign of the result is based on the signs of the two numbers being multiplied. Figure 7.1 gives the sign of the result. Note that the sign bit of the result is the same as the logical exclusive or operation.

Multiplier Sign	Multiplicand Sign	Result Sign
0	0	0
0	1	1
1	0	1
1	1	0

Figure 7.1 Sign bit for multiplication.

The mantissa of the result for the example is already normalized; so no shifting need be done. Remember that the leading one (hidden bit) of the mantissa is not stored. The result of the multiplication is represented in the modified single-precision format as

S	E	F
0	1000 0110	(1) 010 1011

7.4 DIVISION

The division of floating point numbers follows a pattern of operations similar to that of multiplication. The steps to accomplish floating point division are as follows:

1. Do unsigned division on the mantissas.
2. Subtract the exponent of the divisor from the exponent of the dividend.
3. Normalize the result.
4. Set the sign bit of the result.

This series of steps results in **true division**.

The sign bit of the result is set according to the truth table in Figure 7.2. Note that the table is the same as for multiplication.

Divisor Sign	Dividend Sign	Quotient Sign
0	0	0
0	1	1
1	0	1
1	1	0

Figure 7.2 Sign bit for division.

An alternative algorithm for division is called **division by reciprocal** or **reciprocal division**. This method performs division by determining the multiplicative inverse (reciprocal) of the divisor, and multiplying:

$$\frac{Q}{D} = Q \times \frac{1}{D}$$

The reciprocal of the mantissa can be determined by a technique of successive approximation, using multiplication and addition. One technique starts with an approximate value and achieves successively more accurate approximations via **Newton–Raphson iteration**. To compute R, the reciprocal of the divisor D, the following equation is applied iteratively:

$$R_{n+1} = R_n \times (2 - R_n D)$$

The initial value for R, R_0, can be anything, but gives a better result if close. The value required for D must be scaled to be in the range $1 \le D < 2$. This scaling is easily done in hardware by use of an arithmetic shift. The iteration converges quadratically—with each iteration, the result has twice as many bit positions that are significant as the previous iteration. It is therefore particularly effective for computations involving very high precision. For computers having very high-speed multipliers, reciprocal division can be accomplished faster than true division, and it does not require division hardware, only a multiplier and a small amount of additional logic.

Some computers simply provide multiplicative inverse as an instruction, leaving the programmer to use it and multiplication to achieve division. Others use this technique of successive approximation to acquire the multiplicative inverse of the divisor, then perform multiplication.

True division is required to comply with the floating point standard. This is because the calculation of a multiplicative inverse is inexact. When the multiplicative inverse is multiplied by the quotient, the incorrect result may be obtained. Consider the example of the division

$$\frac{3.0}{3.0}$$

True division will calculate 1.0 as its result. The multiplicative inverse of 3.0 is $0.\overline{33}$, and division by reciprocal will compute the product

$$3.0 \times 0.\overline{33}$$

to the precision limits of the hardware. The result may be $0.\overline{99}$, or it may be rounded to be the correct result, depending on the method of rounding used.

7.5 ADVANCED TOPICS

In this section some important issues relating to floating point manipulation are discussed: rounding, standards for the design of floating point hardware, overflow, and underflow.

Rounding

The set of integers representable in a given type exhibits an important property not present for floating point numbers. For the five standard arithmetic operations defined over integers (addition, subtraction, multiplication, integer division, and the modulus function), the operations are well defined and the resulting value is unambiguous; either the value is representable or it is not. All these operations generate integer results. Thus the test for overflow is conceptually simple; if the mathematical result is outside the range of integers representable, overflow has occurred. Otherwise, the result is exact.

The situation is more complex for floating point numbers. For some operations the mathematical result is a number that is not representable. Consider, for example, two floating point representations that are adjacent; that is, there are no representable values between them. Taking their average—for example, by adding them together and dividing by two—is a well-defined mathematical operation that generates a result that is not representable. This cannot be regarded as overflow, because the result is not out of the range of representable numbers, and the desired result is that the "closest" representable number be assigned. The selection of this approximation is referred to as **rounding**, and is a critical concern. No matter what policy is chosen, a small amount of error is introduced into the computation whenever rounding occurs. Undesirable effects of rounding include the following.

1. Errors tend to accumulate over time. For algorithms that iterate many times, it is important that errors tend to cancel each other out. For example, if a sum is being accumulated by repeatedly adding the value 100/3, rounding to the nearest integer after each addition will produce the series of sums that begins with 33, 66, 99, 132, and 165. This rounding method therefore introduces a systematic error of close to 1%.
2. Operations performed in a different order might give a different result. In fact, on many computers floating point addition is not commutative! A computation adding a to b may yield a different result than adding b to a.
3. Exact comparison of two floating point variables is infeasible. Subtracting one from the other may yield a result that is very close to zero, but not exactly, since there are many representable values very close to zero. Thus algorithms that converge by generating successively more accurate approximations must be tested for convergence by specifying when successive answers differ by less than ε, a small constant determined by the precision of the representation.

Consider the decimal number 0.458962. In decimal, the representable number allowable may be close to this value with only four digits. The choice would be either 0.4589 or 0.4590. Two algorithms are often taught: **rounding** and **truncation**. Truncation is simple: Discard the excess digits. Rounding is slightly more complicated: Determine the halfway point between the adjacent values and select the nearest. The rule is particularly tricky because an arbitrary choice is made—rounding up—in the case of a tie. The tie case is common. Notice that for a random set of values, this rule rounds up more often than down, introducing a systematic bias.

Four rules for rounding are defined in the IEEE Floating Point Standard. Others are possible, but they are not presented. Note that these rules are specific to radix-2 rounding. The standard specifies that the programmer should be allowed to choose the method of rounding. An implementation of these methods requires that bits to the right of the 23 bits of mantissa be maintained throughout any computation. They are called the guard bit, round bit, and sticky bit, with the sticky bit being placed at the least significant position past the end of the mantissa. For computations, the guard and round bits act as extra bits of precision. The sticky bit is set whenever any bit less significant than the round bit would be set.

- **Round toward zero**. This method truncates the magnitude of the number to the correct number of bits. The absolute value of the result is never larger than the absolute value of the initial value. The mantissa of a result for a single-precision calculation such as

mantissa	extra bits for rounding
`1.10100000000000000000011`	`111`

  leads to the mantissa

```
1.10100000000000000000011
```

  after rounding toward zero. The extra bits carried through a calculation (for their purpose in rounding) are truncated.

- **Round toward positive infinity**. The number chosen is the least positive value having a representation and not arithmetically less than the unrounded value. The mantissa of a result for a single-precision calculation such as

mantissa	extra bits for rounding
`1.10100000000000000000011`	`111`

  leads to the mantissa

```
1.10100000000000000000100
```

  after rounding toward positive infinity. A negative value after calculation

mantissa	extra bits for rounding
`1.10100000000000000000011`	`111`

  leads to the mantissa

```
1.10100000000000000000011
```

  after rounding toward positive infinity.

- **Round toward negative infinity**. The number chosen is least negative value having a representation and not arithmetically greater than the unrounded value. The mantissa of a result for a single-precision calculation such as

mantissa	extra bits for rounding
`1.10100000000000000000011`	`111`

  leads to the mantissa

```
1.10100000000000000000011
```

after rounding toward negative infinity. A negative value after calculation

mantissa	extra bits for rounding
1.10100000000000000000011	111

leads to the mantissa

1.10100000000000000000100

after rounding toward negative infinity.

- **Round to nearest**. This is rounding as taught in school, but with a different rule for breaking ties. When the two nearest representable values are equally near, the rounding is chosen so that the least significant bit of the result is always zero. The mantissa of a result for a single-precision calculation such as

mantissa	extra bits for rounding
1.10100000000000000000011	111

leads to the mantissa

1.10100000000000000000100

after rounding toward the nearest representation. An example of the case where the two representable values are equally near is

mantissa	extra bits for rounding
1.10100000000000000000011	100

The choices for representable values are

1.10100000000000000000100

and

1.10100000000000000000010

For this case, the representation ending in a 0 is chosen. The choice will be

1.10100000000000000000100

Rounding to nearest is most commonly used, and is generally suggested. It is easy to implement, and creates fewer problems with systematic error than always rounding up in the case of a tie.

Standards

A large issue in floating point arithmetic deals with compatibility. For a variety of reasons, two computers may compute a slightly different answer for the same program. Although the error may be small, it is easy to write a program that will amplify an arbitrarily small difference into an arbitrarily large difference. Some programs do this inadvertently. For example, the test for convergence must be related to the maximum rounding error that can occur. If a program that terminates normally on one computer is run on a computer with less precision (and therefore greater maximum rounding error), the test for convergence may never succeed and the program never terminate.

A standard for floating point arithmetic is a set of guidelines to follow in the design of floating point hardware. All machines that follow the guidelines exactly will generate the same results. Those that do not follow the standard may generate slightly different results. Virtually all architectures now follow the same standard: the IEEE Floating Point Standard.

The standard defines virtually every aspect relating to the processing of floating point numbers. One important (and much argued) detail is the allocation of bits within a single-precision or double-precision representation. The discussion settles around how many bits should be given to the exponent versus those given to the mantissa. Increasing the number of bits in the exponent will increase the range of possible values. Numbers of greater magnitude can be represented. Since the size of a single-precision floating point number is fixed, however, increasing the bits available for the exponent decreases the bits available for the mantissa. The total number of values that can be represented exactly is fixed. In essence, the representable numbers are spread farther apart. Therefore, precision and sometimes accuracy are lost.

The standard also defines special representations for infinity and for results that cannot be numbers (**NaN**—Not a Number). An attempt to divide by zero results in a representation for infinity.

There are computers that do not follow the floating point standard. Some machines follow only part of the standard, but not all of it. Reasons for this are varied. Some of these machines were built before the standard was designed. Computers can be designed and built less expensively if they do not follow the entire standard.

Overflow and Underflow

Like integer arithmetic, overflow can occur as a result of floating point operations. Overflow occurs when the exponent of the normalized result is outside the range of values representable. As an example, if the biased exponent E of a single precision normalized result should be $1\ 0000\ 1110_{two}$, then overflow has occurred. The biased exponent of a single precision number must be eight bits.

The IEEE Floating Point Standard assigns special meaning for the extreme values of the exponent. This slightly decreases the range of representable range of values. The smallest number that can be represented in the normal way has an exponent of $e = -126$ (E = 00000001). The largest number that can be represented in the normal way has an exponent of $e = 127$ (E = 11111110). If the biased-127 representation is 11111111_{two}, the exponent e would ordinarily be 128_{ten}. This value for the exponent, however, is reserved, and the interpretation of the other fields is modified. Specifically, if the fraction F is zero, then the value is defined to be either positive or negative infinity, depending on the sign bit S. That is, the value is $-1^S \times \infty$. For any nonzero value of F, the value is NaN.

Zero is represented by $E = F = 0$:

```
S       E                          F
0   0000 0000   (0) 000 0000 0000 0000 0000 0000
```

or

```
S       E                          F
1   0000 0000   (0) 000 0000 0000 0000 0000 0000
```

As with all sign magnitude representations, there are two representations for zero.

Underflow occurs when a result is too close to zero to be represented. Although the error is exceedingly small, the fact that underflow occurs is as important as when overflow occurs. For example, repetitively dividing a number by a positive constant results in successively smaller values, but mathematically, the result is never zero. Using floating point operations, the value will eventually underflow, returning the value zero after some iteration. Until underflow occurs, the computation is reversible; multiplying by the constant the same number of times will return the original number. Once underflow occurs, any number of multiplications will still produce the result of zero.

A technique for increasing the range of representable numbers near zero can be employed by giving up precision gradually. Effectively, the very small numbers are spread farther apart than they otherwise would be, extending much closer to zero. This is accomplished by **denormalizing** a number. The idea may best be conveyed by an example. Consider the number one, which is represented in single-precision FPS with

```
S       E                          F
0   0111 1111   (1) 000 0000 0000 0000 0000 0000
```

If this value is repetitively divided by two, the fraction F will not change, but the exponent E will be reduced by one with each division by two. After 126 divisions, the representation becomes

```
S       E                          F
0   0000 0001   (1) 000 0000 0000 0000 0000 0000
```

Now, if division by two is performed again, the result will be 0:

```
S       E                          F
0   0000 0000   (?) 000 0000 0000 0000 0000 0000
```

Remember that a special definition of zero is necessary because of the hidden bit, and the fact that the mantissa can never be smaller than 1.0. If the definition of the mantissa is modified, however, for the special case when $E = 0$, it is possible to represent still smaller values. For this case, the hidden bit is defined to be zero, not one. With this redefinition, representation of much smaller numbers is possible. The 127th division yields the representation:

```
S       E                          F
0   0000 0000   (0) 100 0000 0000 0000 0000 0000
```

This number is denormalized, since $m < 1.0$. It also has only 23 significant digits, not the 24 (including the hidden bit) that floating point numbers normally have. Another division by two gives:

S	E	F
0	0000 0000	(0) 010 0000 0000 0000 0000 0000

Division by two can be repeated until F finally loses its last significant bit, going from one to zero. Thus the smallest (denormalized) representable number is 2^{-149}:

S	E	F
0	0000 0000	(0) 000 0000 0000 0000 0000 0001

This increase in range does not come without a cost. All numbers in the denormalized form have lowered precision. Note that the smallest representable value, 2^{-149}, has only a single bit of precision. In general, it is not possible to reverse an operation that resulted in a denormalized number, due to the loss in precision. In the example chosen, the process is reversible because the loss of significant digits does not result in rounding error.

The extension of the range by decreasing precision is known as **graceful underflow**. Notice that the introduction of denormalized representation does not introduce multiple representations in general. Since the exponent, e, is -126 in all cases, each value of the mantissa defines a unique value except for the special case of zero.

SUMMARY

The requirements of floating point computation are critical for scientific computing and other applications that require high-precision computation. The support for floating point representation is a key issue in the design of a computer. While the details sometimes seem tedious, an understanding of their implementation and the decisions made along the way are critical for understanding one of the most basic capabilities of the computer.

Hardware support for floating point operations is expensive, and may be unjustified in applications where little floating point computation is required. Software emulation of floating point operations may take orders of magnitude longer than hardware implementation to complete programs that make extensive use of floating point.

PROBLEMS

1. Give a method for detection of overflow when doing single-precision floating point addition.
2. Give a method for detection of overflow when doing single-precision floating point multiplication.
3. Using a 7-bit mantissa, do the following floating point additions:
   a. 3.6 + 10.1
   b. 205.0 + 1.0
   c. 18.25 + 5200.0
   d. – 65.0 + 106.0

4. Using a 7-bit mantissa, do the following floating point subtractions:
   a. 80.0 – 26.5
   b. 128.0 – 129.0
   c. – 8.4 – 18.0

5. Using a 7-bit mantissa, do the following floating point multiplications:
   a. 20.0×3.0
   b. 1.6×-2.25
   c. 0.005×100.0

6. Round the following mantissas by rounding toward zero:

	mantissa	extra bits for rounding
a.	`1.10100000000000000000101`	`010`
b.	`1.10100000000000000000101`	`100`
c.	`1.10100000000000000000000`	`111`

7. Round the following mantissas by rounding toward positive infinity:

	mantissa	extra bits for rounding
a.	`1.10100000000000000000101`	`010`
b.	`1.10100000000000000000101`	`100`
c.	`1.10100000000000000000000`	`111`

8. Round the following mantissas by rounding toward negative infinity:

	mantissa	extra bits for rounding
a.	`1.10100000000000000000101`	`010`
b.	`1.10100000000000000000101`	`100`
c.	`1.10100000000000000000000`	`111`

9. Round the following mantissas by rounding to nearest.

	mantissa	extra bits for rounding
a.	`1.10100000000000000000101`	`010`
b.	`1.10100000000000000000101`	`100`
c.	`1.10100000000000000000000`	`111`

10. Convert 0.3 to the nearest IEEE single-precision floating point representation. What is the difference between the value of the representation and 0.3?

11. For arithmetic done in IEEE single-precision floating point format, give a positive, nonzero number x that when added to 1.0 produces the result x. A restatement of the problem is: Give a value for x such that $x > 0$ and $x + 1.0 = x$.

12. The value 1,000,000.0 can be exactly represented in IEEE single-precision floating point format. What is the next larger floating point value that can be exactly represented in IEEE single-precision floating point format? Give both its decimal value and its bit pattern.

13. Give bit patterns for two IEEE single-precision floating point numbers whose addition would result in a denormalized number.

14. On some computers floating point multiply is actually faster than floating point addition. Since multiplication is more complex than addition, this is surprising. Why might it be faster?

15. The Control Data 6600 had no hardware for fixed-point multiply. It did have hardware for floating point multiply. Do you think fixed-point multiply would be faster by performing successive fixed-point additions or by converting from fixed to floating point, performing floating point addition, then converting back to fixed point? Why?

16. Give a SASM code fragment that checks if the value of a variable is a single-precision floating point representation for the value 0.

17. Give a SASM code fragment that checks if the value of a variable is a negative single-precision floating point representation.

18. Give a SASM code fragment that checks if the value of a variable is a single-precision floating point representation of Not A Number (NaN).

19. Write a SASM program that calculates the diameter and area of a circle given the radius in single-precision floating point representation.

CHAPTER

8

DATA STRUCTURES

Assembly programmers and architects often think in terms of simple data such as characters, integers, and floating point numbers. Real programs are rarely designed in terms of such limited abstractions. Instead, abstractions such as lists, trees, stacks, files, and databases are used. Each of these abstractions can be constructed from simpler components, and these components may themselves be constructed of simpler ones. At the bottom levels are the familiar addresses, characters, integers, and floating point numbers.

Suppose that a program is being designed to operate on a data structure such as a sorted list. Procedures such as `InsertElement`, `DeleteElement`, and `PrintList` must be written. There are several different implementations of the abstract data structure called a list. Suppose it is to be implemented as a **linked list**. Each node of this list will contain a field that has the actual data, and additional fields that point to the next and previous elements in the list. The next and previous pointer fields will be addresses, while the list data might be composed of a complex data structure (which is made up of simpler fields).

The data associated with this program must be ordered within memory. While high-level languages provide ways of accessing data, assembly languages do not. It is therefore necessary for assembly language code to explicitly calculate the locations of data within the structure. This chapter explores the manipulation and accessing of data within data structures. Three important data structures—the array, the stack, and the queue—are presented.

8.1 MEMORY AS AN ARRAY

Up until now, memory has been described as something that could be accessed symbolically, that is, by providing a label as an address. Although memory is in fact just a collection of cells with no inherent ordering, it is convenient to assign numerical values as addresses for the cells, making it possible to order the cells and specify relationships among them. It is customary to assign unsigned integers for memory addresses.

The computer memory itself is organized as a gigantic, one-dimensional array, and all uses of memory are simply allocations of part of this array. Suppose that the entire computer memory is a single large array. In C, the array might have the following declaration.

```
char m[size_of_memory];
```

Even though each character requires only seven bits, by convention memory is typically allocated in 8-bit cells, where each cell is known as a **byte**. Each array element is a separate byte, with each element having a unique address.

Addressability

A **memory cell** is the unit of memory that has a unique address associated with it. For a memory having individual memory cells that hold eight bits, assigning one byte per cell is straightforward. Each memory location contains one byte, and each memory location has its own unique address. An addressing scheme where each byte of memory has a unique address is called **byte addressing**. A 32-bit integer requires 4 bytes on a byte-addressable architecture. Alternatively, it is possible to make all memory cells 32 bits instead of 8. Each 32-bit cell is given its own unique address. This addressing scheme is called **word addressing**. Word addressability introduces the new problem of how more than one character is fit into one memory cell. It would be wasteful to have 32-bit memory cells and store only one character per cell. Making memory cells 32 bits does not solve the underlying problem of matching addressability to data size. There are other data types that require more than 32 bits.

Each architecture uses its own terms to describe the sizes of data. It is common among modern computers to use the term **word** to designate the amount of memory allocated for storing an integer. Many of the most popular computers today work primarily with 32-bit integers, and designate a word as 32 bits. As technology improves, more and more computers will designate a word as 64 bits. To maintain consistency within an architecture developed when the size of an integer was 16 bits, some architectures refer to 16-bit cells as words and

32-bit cells as **longwords** or **doublewords,** even though their current computers deal with 32- or 64-bit integer quantities. The Pentium architecture does this. A 16-bit quantity is a word, and a 32-bit quantity is a doubleword. In this book the term **doubleword** indicates the size of a memory cell required to hold an integer.

The storage of a doubleword requires four bytes in SASM. Since SASM is implemented to be byte addressable, there are four addresses associated with each doubleword. By convention, the smallest of the four addresses is used to indicate the address of the doubleword. The ordering of the bytes within the doubleword must then be specified. The numbering may be big endian, where bytes are numbered from the most significant end of the doubleword to the least significant. Figure 8.1 shows an example of big endian numbering of bytes within a doubleword. The figure identifies the byte address within the byte. Remember that the contents of a real memory do not contain their addresses. The alternative numbering of bytes within a doubleword is little endian, where the bytes are numbered from least significant to most significant end. Figure 8.2 shows little endian numbering of bytes within doublewords. Again, the figure shows the address of each byte within the byte.

Some architectures place an additional restriction on the storage of integers: They require that doublewords be **aligned.** This means that the doubleword address, that is, the smallest of the byte addresses pointing to the doubleword, is a multiple of four. This restriction arises from the capabilities designed into the hardware of the memory system. The Pentium architecture does not have this restriction. Doublewords may be placed at any address. Note that consecutive doublewords in a byte-addressable machine have addresses that differ by four whether they are aligned or not.

doubleword address				
0	0	1	2	3
4	4	5	6	7
8	8	9	10	11
12				

Figure 8.1 Big endian numbering of bytes within words.

doubleword address				
0	3	2	1	0
4	7	6	5	4
8	11	10	9	8
12				

Figure 8.2 Little endian numbering of bytes within words.

8.2 ARRAYS

Assembly languages do not generally have instructions that include the notion of an array. A block of memory can be allocated with a single directive, where the first element is given a label. The block is just a portion of memory, and the assembly language has no notion of how the block is subdivided. The implementation of arrays requires a method for declaration and a method for accessing elements.

The **array** is the most important and most general data structure, particularly for a low-level view of the computer. It is important because *all other data structures can be implemented from an array.* In fact, the feasibility of a given data structure is largely a question of the difficulty of implementing it from an array.

In any language, an array declaration requires only that a correct amount of memory space be allocated for the array, and that a label (address) be tied to the first element of the array. The assembly language declaration of an array is a straightforward extension to the declarations already given. A C program would declare an array of seven characters with

```
char ar[7];
```

An SASM program might declare this same array for the seven characters with the directive

```
ar db 7 dup(0)
```

This declaration is of a seven-element array of byte-sized elements. Each element is initialized to be the null character, which has the ASCII character code of all zeros. The declaration used for allocating space for an array is an extension to the syntax for declaring a simple variable. Added to the end of the declaration is the number of elements in the array followed by the word `dup` and the initial contents of the elements within parentheses. From Chapter 3, the SASM declaration of a simple character variable looks like

```
{variablename} db value
```

The declaration that includes the option of specifying the number of character array elements is of the form

```
{variablename} db initial value, initial value, . . .
```

or

```
{variablename} db numelements dup(initial value)
```

The space for an array of integers or real numbers can be allocated by replacing the type specification `db` with `dd`. The declaration from above,

```
ar db 7 dup(0)
```

allocates seven (not eight) consecutive bytes of memory, associates the label `ar` with the first element, and initializes all the elements. Figure 8.3 shows how this array might be placed in memory. For this example, the starting address of the array is 100.

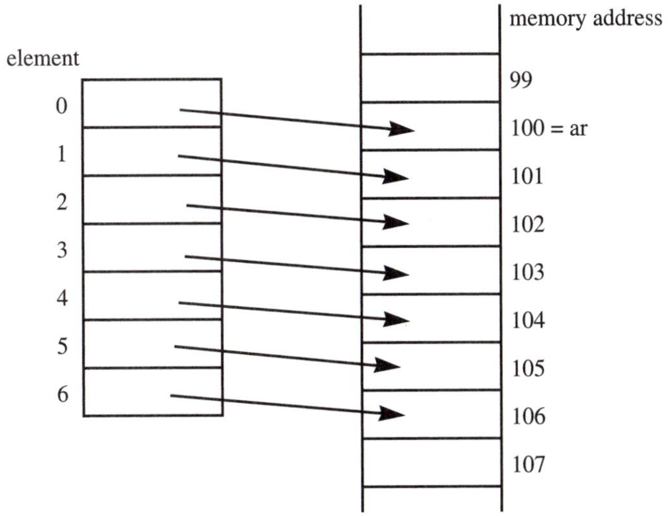

Figure 8.3 A one-dimensional array mapped into memory.

A byte or doubleword in memory can be accessed by specifying its address with the SASM syntax

```
M(address)
```

or

```
m(address)
```

The variable `address` must contain the address to be accessed. Note that the programmer has no control over the location of an array within memory. The **starting address** (also called the **base address**) can be determined using the SASM `la` instruction. The `la` mnemonic stands for load address. The instruction takes the address assigned to the source operand, and places the address into the destination operand. The destination operand must be a doubleword, because all addresses are 32 bits.

Array elements can be accessed by using an offset from the starting address. The SASM code to place the character 'g' in the fourth element of the array shown in Figure 8.3 could be

```
la     address, ar
iadd   address, 3
moveb  m(address), 'g'
```

For this example, the `la` instruction would place the value 100, the array's starting address, into the variable `address`. Since element numbering starts at 0, the fourth byte of the array is at address 103, an offset of 3 from the starting address. The `iadd` instruction calculates the address of the fourth element. The `moveb` instruction then places the character into memory at the calculated location.

Array elements need not be characters, or even bytes. They might be integers, or floating point numbers, or small arrays. Therefore, the size of an array element is not always one byte, although all elements must be the same size. Because of the requirement that elements be the same size, a formula for finding the address of an array element can be specified, taking into account the number of distinct addresses associated with a single array element. The formula presumes a byte-addressable memory.

$$\text{byte address of element } x = \text{starting address} + \text{size\_of\_element} \times x$$

This formula also presumes that the first element of the array is numbered 0. The size_of_element is the number of bytes in a single array element. Note that if size_of_element is one, the formula refers to an array of bytes.

Figure 8.4 shows an array integers. A five-element integer array is mapped into memory starting at location 72. Following the SASM definition, there are four bytes allocated for one integer; so the size of each element is four. The last (fifth) element in the array, element number 4, is stored at location 72 + 4(4) = 88.

The amount of space required to store an array of integers is four times larger than the space required to store an array of bytes. The total space required to store an array is the product of the number of elements in the array and the size of an array element. Thus an array of ten integers requires 40 bytes of memory. This space could be allocated with

```
ar db 40 dup(0)
```

or

```
ar dd 10 dup(0)
```

or

```
ar db 40 dup(?)
```

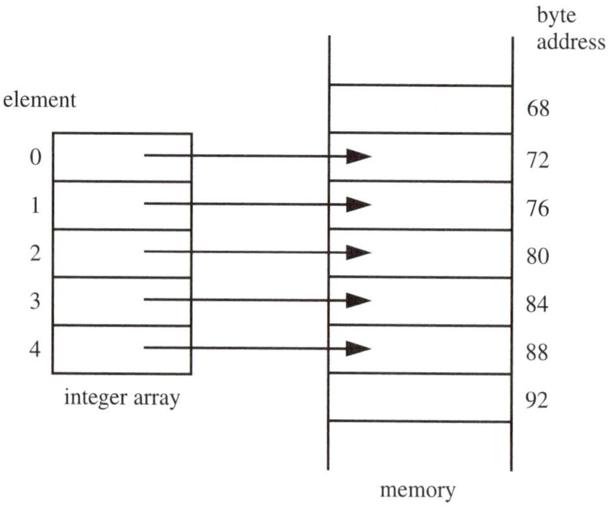

Figure 8.4 A one-dimensional array of integers mapped into memory.

Variables have an implied type. This type is sometimes inferred from the variable declaration. Thus a declaration of `dd` indicates an integer or float, while `db` indicates a character. Unfortunately, the implementation of array declarations does not convey the type of the array elements. For the instruction

```
la i, ar
```

`i` must be a doubleword, but there is no way to infer the type of an array reference, such as

```
move M(i), M(j)
```

Two-Dimensional Arrays

The following conventions are used to describe a two-dimensional array in the discussion that follows. An array is given as an $r \times c$ array, where r refers to the number of rows, and c refers to the number of columns in the array. An element of the array will be specified in the format `[y, x]`, where `y` is the row number and `x` is the column number. Figure 8.5 illustrates an array that follows these conventions.

A SASM declaration must allocate enough memory to store the entire array. The number of elements in the array is the number of rows times the number of columns. For the C array

```
char ar_2D[row_elements, col_elements];
```

the number of elements in the array can be calculated with

$$\text{number\_of\_elements} = \text{row\_elements} \times \text{col\_elements}$$

The value of number_of_elements can then be used to determine the amount of memory space needed for the array. The number of bytes needed for the array is found by multiplying the number of elements times the size (in bytes) of each element:

$$\text{array\_size} = \text{number\_of\_elements} \times \text{size\_of\_element}$$

A SASM declaration for the array requires the constant array_size. For the sample two-dimensional array in Figure 8.5, the declaration could be

```
ar_2D db 15 dup(0)
```

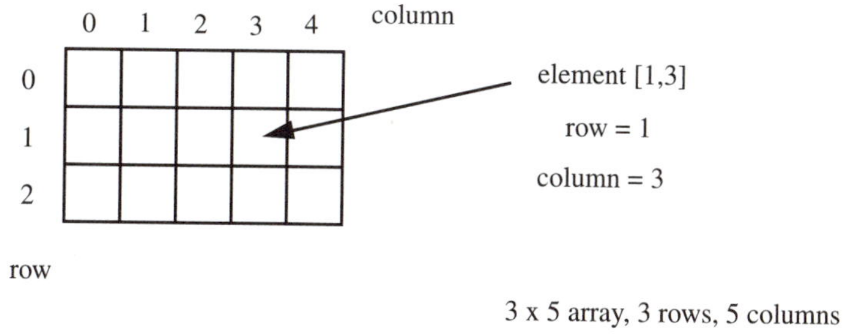

Figure 8.5 A sample two-dimensional array.

if each element is a byte. Note that this declaration could also be used for a one-dimensional array of 15 bytes. The declaration provides no distinction for the dimensions of the array.

Storage Order

Memory is organized as a one-dimensional array. Allocating memory space for a two-dimensional array requires mapping the array into this one-dimensional space. To do this, the two-dimensional array can be thought of as an array of arrays. Each row can be thought of as a separate array, and these arrays are placed into memory contiguously. This storage order is known as **row-major order**. Accessing an element in the third row consists of finding its address by skipping over the first two row arrays and addressing the appropriate element in the third array.

Figure 8.6 shows a 3×4 array stored in memory in row-major order. The element number is shown inside the memory location that would contain the element.

If the array is stored as a sequence of arrays consisting of the columns instead of rows, the order is known as **column-major order**. The same array used in Figure 8.6 is shown in column-major order in Figure 8.7. Notice that the memory address of the individual elements depends on the storage order. Many programming languages allocate arrays in row-major order, although FORTRAN uses column-major order, and some languages leave the decision up to those who implement a compiler.

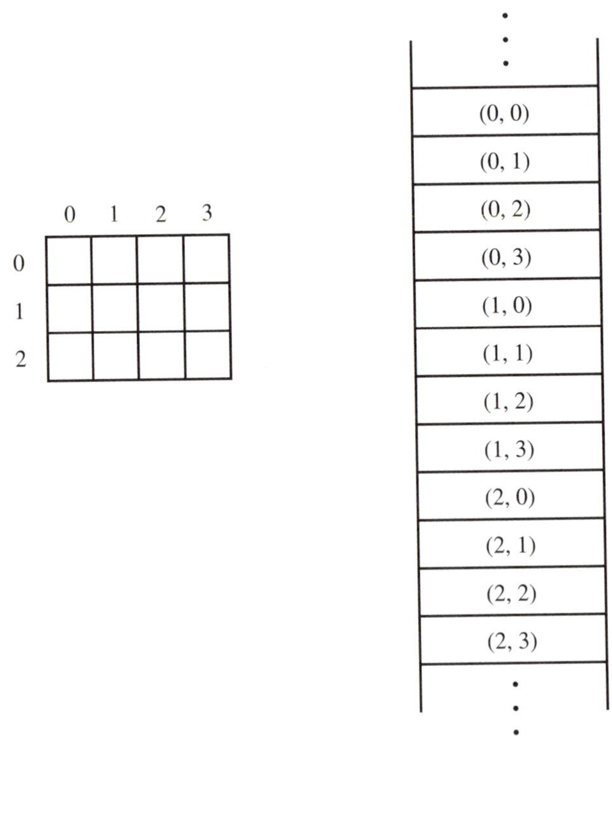

Figure 8.6 A two-dimensional array stored in row-major order.

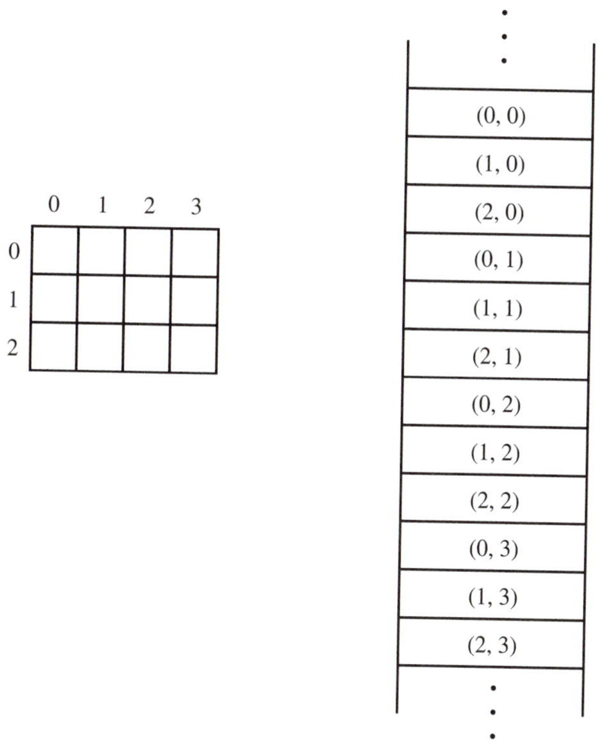

Figure 8.7 A two-dimensional array stored in column-major order.

Address Calculation

The address calculation of a two-dimensional array element includes a computation to skip over entire rows (or columns). The amount of storage allocated for individual rows (columns) is determined by the number of elements in a row (column), not the index limits. The general formula for calculating the address of an array element must take into account the size of the array elements. If the variable size_of_element is the number of bytes in one element, then the byte address of the element [y,x] can be specified as

$$\text{starting address} + \text{size\_of\_element} \times y \times \text{number of columns} + \text{size\_of\_element} \times x$$

for row-major order. For column-major order, it is

$$\text{starting address} + \text{size\_of\_element} \times x \times \text{number of rows} + \text{size\_of\_element} \times y$$

As an example, consider the C array declared

```
char ar_2D[3, 4];
```

The number of elements can be calculated by

$$\text{number\_of\_elements} = 3 \times 4 = 12$$

A SASM declaration for the array is

```
ar_2D db 12 dup(0)
```

The address of array element `[1,3]` is calculated as follows. The formula for row-major ordering is used, since arrays in C are always stored in row-major order. The byte address of element `ar_2D[1,3]` is

$$\text{ar\_2D starting address} + 1 \times 1 \times 4 + 1 \times 3 = \text{ar\_2D starting address} + 7$$

As an example of SASM code that manipulates an array, consider a seven-by-five (7 × 5) array of integers. A code fragment is needed to reinitialize each element in the third column of the array to zero. Figure 8.8 shows this array before and after the initialization code has been executed. Assume that the array is stored in row major order. Figure 8.9 contains a SASM code fragment that clears the third column of the array.

This code fragment can be written in various ways. The code fragment in Figure 8.9 calculates the address of each element of the third column, then assigns the value zero as the contents of that address. The loop changes the value of the row being worked on each time through the loop. When all the rows have been worked on, the loop is exited.

Figure 8.8 A 7 × 5 array of integers before and after code execution.

	0	1	2	3	4
0	13	8	78	54	67
1	52	22	–2	–9	6
2	0	44	63	53	22
3	23	0	21	43	46
4	8	83	77	99	–4
5	–3	10	98	8	87
6	96	13	43	7	43

The array in its initial state

	0	1	2	3	4
0	13	8	0	54	67
1	52	22	0	–9	6
2	0	44	0	53	22
3	23	0	0	43	46
4	8	83	0	99	–4
5	–3	10	0	8	87
6	96	13	0	7	43

The array after the code fragment has been executed

```
.data
array               db 140 dup(0) ; bytes for a 7 x 5 array of integers
row                 dd ?
col                 dd ?
base                dd ?
address             dd ?
elements_in_row     dd 5
elements_in_col     dd 7
elem_size           dd 4

.code
              move        row, 0
              move        col, 2
              la          base, array
loop_1:       compare     row, elements_in_col
              bez         next
              move        address, row
              imult       address, elements_in_row
              iadd        address, col
              imult       address, elem_size   ; 4 bytes in each element.
              iadd        address, base        ; Gives the address
                                               ; of the desired element
              move        M(address), 0        ; clear the element
              iadd        row, 1               ; set up for the next row
              br          loop_1
next:         ; more code can go here
```

Figure 8.9 SASM code fragment to clear the third column of an array.

A more efficient, but possibly less clear, code fragment to reinitialize the elements of the third column is contained in Figure 8.10. It calculates the number of bytes in a row, and then adds that amount to the address each time through the loop. The code is more efficient because there is less code within the loop.

8.3 STACKS

Most cafeterias have a stack of trays. Diners take trays from the top of the stack, use them, and then return them for cleaning. The clean trays are then put back onto the top of the stack. Once a clean tray is put into the stack, it is the first tray taken off the top. This stack of cafeteria trays is an analogy to a data structure called a **stack**. Stacks are often used in programming when data will need to be used in the reverse order that it is generated. A stack is essential in implementing recursive procedure calls (see Chapter 11). Another term commonly used to describe a stack is **LIFO**, an acronym for Last In First Out.

An example where data is generated in the reverse order from which it is needed might be in doing an integer-to-ASCII character conversion. A common algorithm for calculating the characters from the integer determines digits from the least significant digit to

```
.data
array               db 140 dup(0)        ; bytes for a 7 x 5 array of integers
bytes_in_row        dd ?
total_bytes         dd ?
end_of_array        dd ?
base                dd ?
elements_in_row     dd 5
elements_in_col     dd 7
elem_size           dd 4
address             dd ?

.code
            la          base, array
            move        address, base
            iadd        address, 8          ; address contains the first
                                            ; element to initialize
            move        bytes_in_row, elem_size
            imult       bytes_in_row, elements_in_row
            move        total_bytes, bytes_in_row
            imult       total_bytes, elements_in_col
            move        end_of_array, total_bytes
            iadd        end_of_array, base
loop_1:     compare     address, end_of_array
            bgz         next
            move        M(address), 0       ; clear the element
            ; set up for next row
            iadd        address, bytes_in_row
            br          loop_1
next:       ; more code can go here
```

Figure 8.10 More efficient code fragment to clear the third column of an array.

the most significant digit. Yet this order is the reverse from which they need to be printed out. A stack is easily utilized to hold the digits until they are ready to be printed out.

The abstraction that operates as a stack has two well-defined operations, **push** and **pop**. Push is the operation that places a new item at the top of the stack. Pop retrieves the top item from the stack. An additional operation for a stack is a test if the stack is empty. Obviously, if the stack has no elements, it cannot supply one. Another operation that results from implementation limitations is the test for a full stack. In the abstract, a stack can grow without limitation. Implementations, however, are constrained in various ways by memory limitations. Therefore, real stacks may have the limitation that there is no more room to push another item on the stack. In this case, the stack is said to be full.

Stack Implementation and Example

A stack can be implemented in many ways: by an array, by a linked list, or even by a tree data structure. The following examples show the implementation of a fixed-size element stack by the use of an array and a variable, known as the **stack pointer**. The stack pointer identifies the next available array element that is currently unused within the stack. It is an address. The variables that implement a stack of 100 doublewords could be declared in SASM as

```
a_stack         dd 100 dup(0)
a_sp            dd ?
```

The declaration for the stack pointer, `a_sp`, cannot provide an initial value. The address desired is the address of the first element of the array `a_stack.` It would be useful if the declaration could allow for a **static** initialization of the stack pointer. The value is known before the program is run. However, there is no mechanism for doing this in SASM. Code is written to initialize the value of `a_sp` using the `la` instruction. The code fragment that initializes `a_sp` in this way is

```
                .data
a_stack         dd 100 dup(0)
a_sp            dd ?
                .code
                la              a_sp, a_stack
                isub            a_sp, 4
```

In this case, the variable is initialized **dynamically**, that is, while the program is running. Note that if the stack data structure contains integers, each element pushed onto the stack occupies precisely one doubleword. In this implementation, the stack pointer identifies the item already at the top of the stack. This implementation also presumes that the stack is growing from the beginning of the array (smaller addresses) toward the end of the array (larger addresses). A stack could also be implemented such that the stack pointer identified the next available location for data. It is also common to see implementations that place items into the end of the array first. In that case, the stack would grow from the end of the array toward the beginning of the array (from larger addresses towards smaller addresses).

Putting an item onto the top of the stack is a **push** operation. The push operation on the stack declared above is accomplished by the following SASM code. The value of the variable `x` is pushed onto the stack.

```
iadd            a_sp, 4
isub            M(a_sp), x
```

Taking an item off the top of the stack is a **pop** operation. The pop operation on the stack declared above is accomplished by the following SASM code. The top of stack item is popped into the variable `x`.

```
move            x, M(a_sp)
isub            a_sp, 4
```

Figure 8.11 shows the state of a stack from its initial state through three push operations and one pop operation. The stack's initial state shows the stack pointer pointing to a location outside the boundary of the stack, since the stack is empty. After each push operation, the stack pointer points to a full location. Note that as a result of the pop operation,

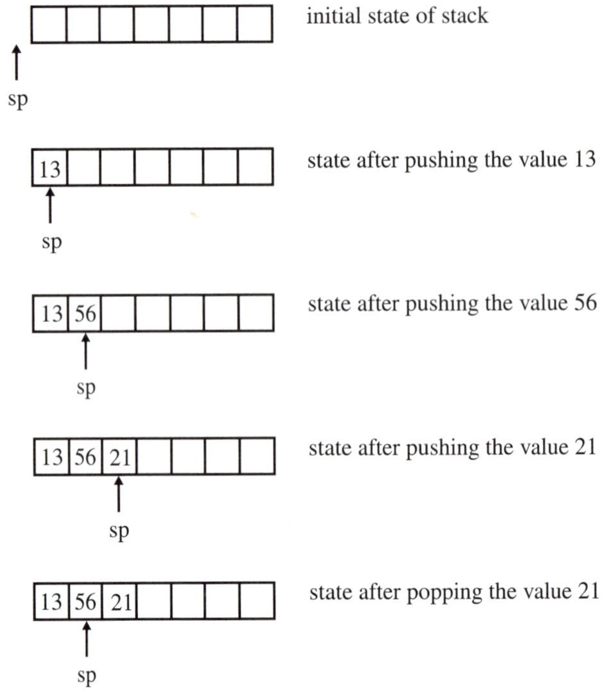

Figure 8.11 The results of push and pop operations.

the top of stack item is copied to another location, yet the value is still present in the first empty location. The implementation of a pop operation does not remove an item from the stack; it merely changes the stack pointer so the next push operation will overwrite that location.

Figure 8.12 contains an example SASM code fragment that prints out a positive integer. The integer is iteratively converted to the ASCII characters that must be printed, so that only the SASM `put_ch` instruction is used for output. A stack is used to hold the characters, because the characters are generated in the reverse order that they must be printed. The stack is declared as an array of bytes. In this implementation, the stack pointer identifies the empty location at the top of the stack. The stack grows from smaller addresses toward larger addresses.

The stack of characters is implemented as an array of bytes. An alternative implementation could use an array of doublewords as a stack. The code would be modified by using `move` instructions instead of the `moveb` instruction. This variation would work fine with respect to the output instruction `put_ch`, since the instruction defaults to printing out the byte at the address given. The address of a doubleword variable is also the address of its least significant byte. The array of doublewords wastes memory space as compared to the array of characters.

Full and Empty Stacks

A push operation to a full stack causes problems. For the implementation of a stack using an array and a stack pointer, a push to a full stack would overwrite memory locations that are not part of the array's allocation. It might destroy one or more variables by overwriting

```
.data
ch_stack        db 50 dup(0)
a_sp            dd ?          ; top of stack pointer
bottom          dd ?          ; bottom of stack
bias            dd 48         ; decimal value of ASCII character '0'
number          dd ?          ; integer to be printed
digit           dd ?          ; digit to be printed

.code
                la            a_sp, ch_stack
                la            bottom, ch_stack
loop_top:       move          digit, number
                irem          digit, 10
                iadd          digit, bias
                moveb         M(a_sp), digit     ; push character
                iadd          a_sp, 1            ; onto stack
                idivi         number, 10
                compare       number, 0
                bgz           loop_top

print_it:       isub          a_sp, 1            ; pop character
                put_ch        M(a_sp)
                compare       a_sp, bottom
                bgz           print_it
```

Figure 8.12 SASM code fragment to print out a positive integer using a stack.

them. This type of error in the program may be difficult to find, since variables not explicitly accessed are changed.

A pop operation on an empty stack also causes problems. This programming error may be more difficult to find than the push to a full stack. It is likely that the pop operation would return the value of a memory location outside the bounds of the stack, and then the program would continue without changing any variables. The value popped from the stack might be used in calculations without causing a program error.

There is no boundary checking implied in assembly language code. Checking for a full stack is a matter of identifying when a push operation would result in writing to a memory location that is not part of the stack's memory allocation. The check for an empty stack is similar. Before a pop operation, a check is made to see if the operation would result in accessing a memory location that is not part of the stack's memory allocation. A robust program will always check for a full stack before any push operation, and it will check for an empty stack before any pop operation.

The SASM code fragment in Figure 8.13 is the same as that in Figure 8.12, but with boundary checking. As part of a push operation, there is a check to make sure that the stack is not full. There is a check to make sure that the stack is not empty before a pop operation. If an error is encountered, then the code prints out an appropriate error message and exits. These error conditions should never be encountered when a finished program is running. The checks may lead the programmer to discover and eliminate program bugs.

```
.data
ch_stack             db 50 dup(0)
a_sp                 dd ?          ; top of stack pointer
bottom               dd ?          ; bottom of stack
top                  dd ?          ; stack boundary
bias                 dd 48         ; decimal value of ASCII character '0'
number               dd ?          ; integer to be printed
digit                dd ?          ; digit to be printed
push_error           db 'Attempt to push item into full stack', 0ah, 0
pop_error            db 'Attempt to pop item from an empty stack', 0ah, 0

.code
                     la            a_sp, ch_stack
                     la            bottom, ch_stack
                     move          top, bottom
                     iadd          top, 50
loop_top:            move          digit, number
                     irem          digit, 10
                     iadd          digit, bias
                     compare       a_sp, top            ; check for full stack
                     bgez          bad_push
                     moveb         M(a_sp), digit       ; push character
                     iadd          a_sp, 1              ; onto stack
                     idivi         number, 10
                     compare       number, 0
                     bgz           loop_top

print_it:            compare       a_sp, bottom         ; check for empty stack
                     blez          bad_pop
                     isub          a_sp, 4              ; pop character
                     put_ch        M(a_sp)
                     compare       a_sp, bottom
                     bgz           print_it

                     ; other code for after the printing goes here


bad_push:            put_str       push_error
                     done
bad_pop:             put_str       pop_error
                     done
```

Figure 8.13 A SASM code fragment with bounds checking.

8.4 QUEUES

People making airline reservations by telephone expect to be served "fairly." The order in which calls are handled is expected to be first come first served (FCFS), also called first in first out (**FIFO**). This concept is so important in the United States that often the initial recorded message for telephone calls explicitly states that calls will be answered in the order received. A computer is often used to maintain a FIFO order of waiting calls.

A **queue** is a data structure that maintains FIFO ordering, and is sometimes called a **FIFO**. This abstract data structure has two operations, **enqueue** and **dequeue**. Enqueue and dequeue are conceptually similar to the stack operations push and pop. Enqueue puts an element into the queue, while dequeue removes an element. The difference between the queue and the stack is that the queue elements are dequeued in the same order that they are enqueued; so the element that has been enqueued the longest is dequeued first.

Queue Implementation

Like a stack, there are many implementations of queues. A linked list implementation of a queue is commonly employed. Another implementation uses an array and pointers, similar to that described for a stack, though the queue is slightly more difficult. The queue has two ends, the **head** and the **tail**. Elements are inserted at the tail of the queue, and they are retrieved from the head of the queue. One implementation of a queue uses an array. Figure 8.14 shows queue operations on part of a queue implied to be implemented out of an array.

Maintaining pointers to the head and tail of the queue within the array encounters a problem; the data tend to "walk" through the array as elements are enqueued and

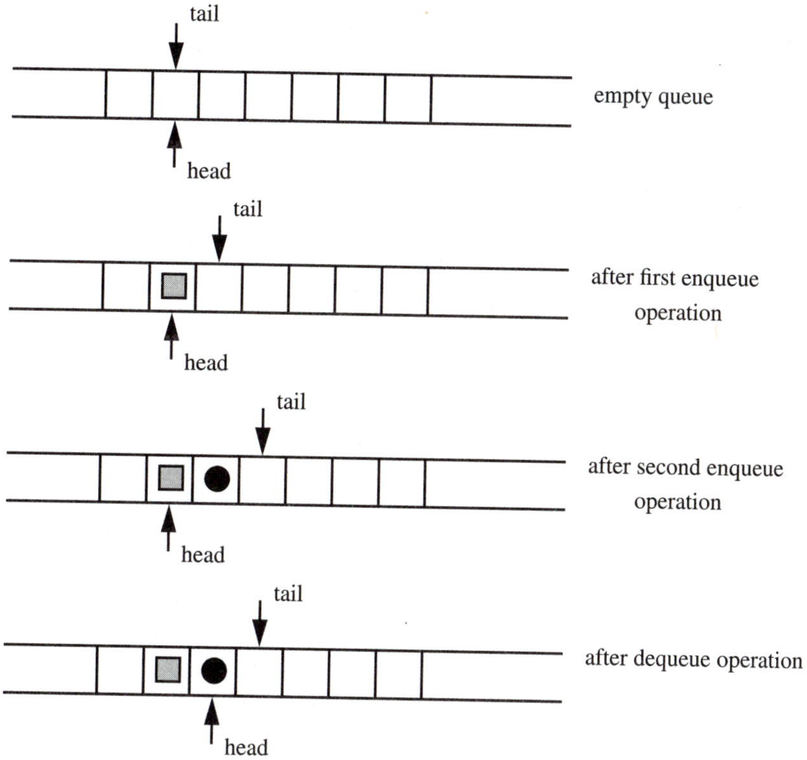

Figure 8.14 Enqueue and dequeue operations on a queue.

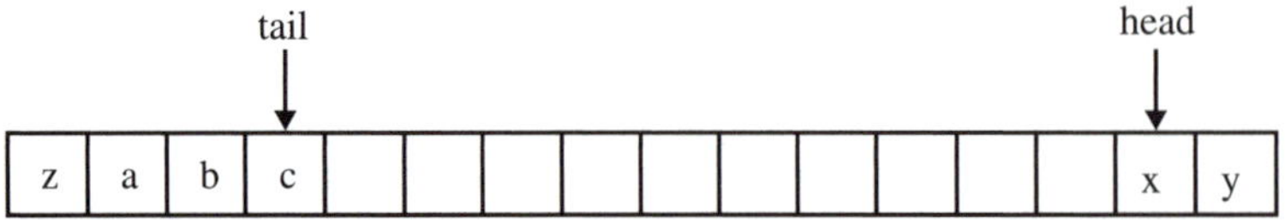

Figure 8.15 An array implementation of a queue with data that has wrapped around to the beginning of the array.

dequeued. Eventually, the tail pointer reaches the end of the array. A naive solution might be to copy the data structure periodically to keep the enqueued data within the array. This is inefficient when the queue is large and mostly full a large portion of the time. A better implementation allows the empty array elements to be reused and allows the data to walk through the array. As the end of the array is reached, the tail pointer wraps around to use the empty elements at the beginning of the array. A diagram of an array implementation of a queue that has wrapped around is shown in Figure 8.15. This idea can be implemented by employing modulo arithmetic to compute the array element to be referenced. The head and tail indices can simply be maintained as a count of the total number of elements dequeued and enqueued, respectively. If the modulo operation is applied before each array access, the effect is that the queue becomes a **circular buffer**. Successive accesses go to consecutive locations until the end of the array is reached, at which point the next access is to the beginning of the array. The head and tail indices can both walk around the array, with the head "chasing" the tail around the queue.

Like a stack, a queue may be either empty or full. If empty, the dequeue operation must not return an invalid element. If full, the enqueue operation must not destroy an element already in the queue by overwriting it. If the operations are written carefully, only tests for equality of the head and tail pointers are needed to implement checks for full or empty queues.

An example of a SASM program that utilizes a queue is given in Figure 8.16. The queue is a circular buffer, and it is implemented out of an array. The program simulates a queue of waiting telephone calls. It requires the program user to enter data in order to enqueue and dequeue waiting calls. The program determines which waiting telephone call is to be handled next. When a telephone line is answered, the caller is placed on hold, and a single-character name followed by a newline character is entered identifying the waiting line. The call is then enqueued, awaiting its turn. When a person becomes available to take a call and presses the return key (entering no character name), the program dequeues and prints the single character name of the next call to be taken. The program is implemented as an infinite loop, waiting for more calls to be enqueued.

Note that if there are fewer than 64 telephone lines, the queue will never be full; so the branch to `full_queue` should never be taken. When there are no callers waiting and a sales representative attempts to fetch the next call, the dequeue operation branches to the label `empty_queue`, and prints the appropriate message.

The queue is implemented so that there is always one empty, unused element. Therefore, the maximum number of calls that can be enqueued is one fewer than the number of array elements allocated. For this program, 64 elements are allocated; so a full queue will have 63 calls enqueued. This implementation simplifies the tests for a full or empty queue.

```
 title queue program
; This program simulates a queue of calls to be answered.
.486
.model flat, stdcall
.stack 1000h
include sasmacros.inc

.data
queue         db 64 dup(0)          ; array to hold queue
head          dd 0                  ; head offset
tail          dd 0                  ; tail offset
linenum       db ?                  ; phone line to be enqueued
nextline      db ?                  ; phone line to be dequeued
tmp_addr      dd ?
char          dd ?
str1          db 'Which line is ringing? ', 0
str2          db 'The next line to be answered is ', 0
str3          db 'Enqueuing line ', 0
empty         db 'No calls waiting. ', 0
full          db 'ERROR: queue is full. Exiting program.',0

.code
main:
main_loop:              ; infinite loop
       put_str      str1
       get_ch       linenum
       compareb     linenum, 0ah          ; see if character is newline
       bez          dequeue
       get_ch       char                  ; throw away newline if have a valid
                                          ; character entered
enqueue:
       put_str      str3
       put_ch       linenum
       put_ch       0ah
       iadd         tail, 1               ; update tail index
       irem         tail, 64              ; modulo queue size
       compare      tail, head            ; full queue if tail == head
       bez          full_queue
       la           tmp_addr, queue
       iadd         temp_addr, tail
       moveb        M(tmp_addr), linenum; put linenumber in queue
       br           main_loop

dequeue:
       compare      head, tail            ; empty queue if tail == head
       bez          empty_queue
       iadd         head, 1               ; update head pointer
       irem         head, 64              ; modulo queue size
```

Figure 8.16 SASM program to simulate call waiting with a queue.

```
        la          tmp_addr, queue
        iadd        tmp_addr, head
        moveb       nextline, M(addr)    ; get linenumber from queue
        put_str     str2
        put_ch      nextline
        put_ch      0ah
        br          main_loop

empty_queue:
        put_str     empty
        br          main_loop
full_queue:
        put_strfull
        done                             ; exit program if error

end
```

Figure 8.16 *Continued*

SUMMARY

The implementation of data structures in assembly language requires mechanisms for manipulating addresses. Thinking of memory as one large array, data structures can be implemented by allocating and accessing select portions of the array. The array data structure is straightforward to implement in SASM. It can also provide the basis for the implementation of other data structures.

A stack is a basic data structure that can be implemented in a variety of ways. One simple way to implement a stack is to use an array and a pointer, known as the stack pointer. A queue can also be implemented in many ways. A simple method uses an array as a circular buffer, with two pointers, known as the tail pointer and the head pointer, to keep track of the head and the tail of the queue.

An array is made up of fixed-sized elements, making it possible to compute the address of individual elements from the indices. Stacks and queues are not restricted to fixed-sized elements, since the addresses of elements are not computed from indices. The information must be kept regarding the size of each element in the queue so that the pointers can be adjusted by the appropriate amount. That information can be stored along with the data in the queue itself, however. Thus both queues and stacks can contain variable-sized elements.

A stack is a critical data structure for implementing procedure call and return mechanisms. Using a stack for storage of return addresses allows nested procedure calls and recursive program implementation. A stack used in this manner is explored in Chapter 11.

PROBLEMS

1. What is the difference between a word-addressable memory and a byte-addressable memory?

2. Is whether a memory system is byte addressable or word addressable reflected in an architecture's instruction set?

3. What is the address of the sixth element of a 15-element array that starts at memory location 40 if
   a. elements are characters?
   b. elements are integers?
   c. elements are single-precision floating point numbers?
   d. elements are 7 bytes in length?

4. What is the base address of a SASM array that has byte elements, where element 26 is located at address 54?

5. What is the address of the tenth element of an array of integers, where the base address of the array is 2000?

6. Write a SASM code fragment to calculate the address of the twelfth array element of an array declared by
   a. `chars db 60 dup(0)`
   b. `ints dd 25 dup(0)`

7. Write a SASM declaration for an 8×10 array of
   a. bytes
   b. doublewords

8. What is the byte address of element [8, 10] of a 12×11 two-dimensional array? The array is stored in row-major order, and the first element of each row and column is numbered 0. The base address of the array is 1000, and each element of the array is a doubleword.

9. Redo Problem 8 assuming that the array is stored in column-major order.

10. Write a SASM code fragment that calculates the address of element `[j,i]` for a two-dimensional array with the following specifications: there are `row` rows, `col` columns, and the number of bytes per element is in the variable `size`. The array is stored in row-major order. How does the code change if the array is stored in column-major order?

11. Redo Problem 10 given that `j=3`, `i=8`, `row=60`, `col=24`, and `size=8`. Can the code be written in such a way that only the declarations change?

12. Write a SASM code fragment that copies a two-dimensional array stored in column-major order to an analogous array stored in row-major order. Use a 6×8 array of integers.

13. Write a SASM declaration for a stack that contains room for 100 elements where the stack has
a. integer-sized elements
b. character-sized elements

14. For the example code presented in Figures 8.9 and 8.10, determine which set of code is more efficient. Use the number of SASM instructions executed as a measure of efficiency. What happens to the efficiency of each set of code if the array size is smaller?

15. Modify the code given in Figure 8.9 so that the row index is checked each time through the loop to make sure it is within the bounds of the array. If the row index is not within the bounds of the array, have the code branch to label `bounds_error`. At label `bounds_error`, have the code print an error message and exit the program.

16. Does it matter whether the elements within a stack are pushed at the start of the array or at the end of an array?

17. Rewrite SASM code for the stack's push and pop operations assuming that the stack grows from the end of the array toward the start, and the stack pointer points to a full location at the top of the stack.

18. Write a SASM code fragment that prints out an integer, one character at a time. Use a stack to hold the characters that form the integer.

19. Write a SASM program that reads a single line of input, and then prints it out in reverse order. For example, if the user types

```
Here is a line to reverse.
```

then the output of the program will be

```
.esrever ot enil a si ereH
```

20. Write a SASM program that determines if a string entered by the user is a **palindrome**. A palindrome is a string that is the same forward and backward. For example, the word `radar` is a palindrome, and the word `Radar` is not a palindrome.

21. Write a SASM program that does matrix multiplication on two 8×8 integer matrices.

22. Modify the SASM program in Figure 8.16 such that if the queue is full when a new call comes in, the program prints out the list of waiting calls, clears the queue, and enqueues the new call.

CHAPTER 9

USING REGISTERS FOR EFFICIENCY

The SASM language captures many of the features of a genuine assembly language. However, it is not a practical language, because it supports abstractions not provided by a real assembly language. Those abstractions allow the SASM programmer to ignore practical details of the architecture that a true assembly language must deal with.

One of the details ignored so far is that instructions must also be stored in memory, and memory has fixed-size cells. The format used to store the information in an instruction is critical in determining the efficiency and performance of an architecture. Most computers have more than one kind of memory. The memories vary in their size, their speed, and their use. Assembly languages normally expose some of these memories to the programmer, who is then responsible for making the most effective use of the resources. This may mean, for example, that additional instructions must be inserted just to copy values from one memory to another.

A real assembly language has no notion of a data type. Data in memory are not self-identifying. The bits at a memory location have no inherent meaning—the meaning is determined by how an instruction uses them. A doubleword in memory might be interpreted as an unsigned integer, a floating point number, a character, several characters, or part of an instruction.

The assembly language for a real computer exposes these details to the programmer. It is the responsibility of the programmer (or the compiler generating the assembly language program) to assure that integer variables are added together using an integer add instruction, and that memory cells containing instructions are not interpreted as floating point operands.

This chapter exposes some of the real features that an assembly language exposes to the programmer.

9.1 INSTRUCTIONS AND EFFICIENCY

After an instruction is fetched, but before it can be executed, all the relevant information about the instruction must be known to the processor. The information includes the operation to be performed, the source operands to be used in the operation, and the destination for the result. To continue the instruction fetch and execute cycle, the address of the next instruction must also be determined.

Because a significant portion of all memory accesses are to fetch instructions, the organization and efficient handling of memory accesses to fetch instructions is critical to the performance of a computer. A fixed size for all instructions simplifies things. The fetching of the instruction and the calculation of the address of the next instruction are primary examples. It is trivial to determine where one instruction ends and the next begins if all instructions require the same amount of memory. Delineating instructions becomes difficult if instructions can vary in size. In addition, more time will be required to fetch an instruction that does not fit into a single word on a computer that fetches exactly one word at a time. Many architectures have some instructions that could easily be packed into less space, perhaps even packing two instructions into the space of one. These architectures are designed not to pack these instructions into a smaller space because of the benefits of fixed-size instructions.

While having a fixed size for all instructions is desirable, not all architectures have a fixed size for instructions. The Pentium is an example of an architecture with variable-length instructions. An instruction set with variable-length instructions can have the benefit that many instructions (those most commonly used) will be able to be encoded in a very small size. There will be no unused bits within an instruction simply to match the fixed size of other longer instructions. This means that the total amount of memory needed for a program's code could be quite small. At the point in time when the architecture the Pentium evolved from was specified, the savings in code size allowed by variable-length instructions was more important to the designers than the consequences of variable-length instructions.

Other things being equal, small instructions are better than large ones. While this may seem obvious, its importance cannot be overstated. Large instructions not only take up more memory, but they may require more time to fetch from memory. Consider how much memory is necessary to specify completely a single assembly language add instruction.

```
add a, b, c
```

opcode	address	address	address
add	a	b	c

Figure 9.1 The format of an add instruction.

This addition instruction has three operands. Two will be source operands, and one will be a destination operand. If the first operand (a) is the destination, then the implied operation of this instruction is to add the value of variable b to the value of variable c and place the result into variable a. An architecture that allows three operands in an instruction is referred to as a **three-address architecture**, or a **three-address instruction set**.

The instruction is broken into parts; individual fields consist of a contiguous set of bits within the instruction. The addition instruction consists of four fields, as shown in Figure 9.1. One field is an **opcode**. It corresponds to the mnemonic of an assembly language instruction, and it indicates that the instruction is to perform an add operation. It also implicitly gives information about how the other fields are interpreted. The different kinds of instructions have different kinds of specifiers. For an add instruction, each of the three additional fields contains information about the operands being accessed. The opcode must be represented in a field large enough to specify uniquely each possible opcode. Most computers have fewer than 256 instructions; so an 8-bit opcode field is a reasonable size. Notice that drastically reducing the number of instructions would result in only a small reduction in the space required for the opcode. Only 64 instructions can be represented with a 6-bit opcode.

Variables a, b, and c each require an address to specify their memory location. Addresses in many architectures are 32-bit unsigned integers. A 6-bit opcode and the three addresses will therefore require at least 102 bits. Fetching 102 bits from memory in order to execute a single instruction puts a heavy load on the memory. Memory accesses take more time than arithmetic and logical operations in modern processors. If each memory access transfers 32 bits of data, then the fetch and execution of this addition instruction would require 7 memory accesses. The first 4 accesses would fetch the instruction itself. Each of the source operands would be loaded, and then the result would be stored in the location specified by the destination operand. Note that the number of bits required for the instruction is more than the total number of bits in the three operands that are loaded/stored. One of the limiting factors in a computer's performance is its ability to read instructions and data as fast as it can process them. Reducing the size of an instruction reduces the size of the program in memory. More important, it reduces the time and the amount of hardware needed to fetch an instruction. There are ways to reduce the size of instructions. Some techniques are so simple and effective that virtually all modern computers use them.

One motivation for a technique to reduce instruction size comes from the observation that computer programs exhibit a property known as **locality of reference**. Locality is the property that, even for large programs, a small and predictable set of variables tends to be referenced much more often than other variables. In other words, locality is an indication that memory is *not* referenced randomly. The fact that certain variables are much more likely than others to be referenced can be exploited by creating special, concise ways of specifying an operand in the common cases.

Reduce Instruction Size

Pronouns are used in the English language to reduce the length of a sentence. When an object is mentioned repeatedly, it is named the first time to clearly indicate what it is. After that, the object can be referenced using the pronoun "it." Ambiguity occurs only if there is more than one possible object to be referred to as "it." In an instruction set, an instruction must specify the full, unambiguous address of a variable upon first reference. After that, the variable may be either implicitly referenced by context, or an abbreviated name may be used. The specification must be stated explicitly. In natural language, ambiguity is often interesting, puzzling, or amusing. Ambiguity in a computer program is never desirable.

The address of a variable can often be inferred from its context. This would eliminate the requirement of explicitly placing the address in an instruction. A shorter instruction is the result. SASM's **two-address instruction set** does this. One operand specification is used as both one of the source operands and as the destination of the result. Rather than the general three-address instruction

```
add a, b, c
```

SASM offers

```
iadd a, b
```

This two-address format requires two instructions to accomplish the same task as one instruction in the three-address format. The SASM code sequence to accomplish the equivalent of the three-address addition instruction is

```
move a, c
iadd a, b
```

It is often the case that the full generality of a three-address instruction is not needed. Incrementing a variable or computing a running sum are two cases where a three-address instruction is not needed. A two-address instruction set reduces the size of instructions, thereby making the instruction fetch faster. It does not always require more instructions to accomplish its task than it would in three-address format. An example is the assembly language implementation of the C assignment statement

```
a = a + b + c;
```

It would be translated into at least two instructions on a three-address architecture.

```
add a, a, b
add a, a, c
```

The two-address (SASM) implementation also takes two instructions,

```
iadd a, b
iadd a, c
```

and yet the two-address format has shorter instructions.

A further shortening of the instruction results in a **one-address instruction set**. The required second source operand can be implied as part of an instruction definition. Many early computers used the concept of an **accumulator**, a special memory cell that can be a source and is the destination of most instructions' results. The accumulator may be thought of as a temporary variable from the viewpoint of the programmer. Each arithmetic operation implies the use of the accumulator as a source operand and/or result destination. The addition instruction in the one-address format can be characterized by the following C statement:

```
Accumulator = Accumulator + x;
```

Since the variable `Accumulator` is implied, a one-address instruction has the format

```
add x
```

The three-address addition instruction

```
add a, b, c
```

written in C as

```
a = b + c;
```

can be synthesized out of a sequence of three C statements.

```
Accumulator = b;
Accumulator = Accumulator + c;
a = Accumulator;
```

Note that a `move` instruction must be treated specially in the one-address architecture. It requires two distinct operations: moving *to* the accumulator, and moving *from* the accumulator. A one-address architecture defines an instruction such as

```
sta variable
```

to assign the value of the accumulator to `variable`. The mnemonic `sta` stands for store accumulator. A one-address architecture defines an instruction such as

```
lda variable
```

to assign the value of `variable` to the accumulator. The mnemonic `lda` stands for load accumulator. The following code sequence accomplishes the equivalent of the three-address addition instruction, but in the one-address format:

```
lda c
add b
sta a
```

The use of a single-address instruction set need not increase the number of instructions required as much as might be expected. For example, the C assignment statement

```
Avg= ( a + b + c + d ) / 4;
```

requires four instructions in the three-address format:

```
add Avg, a, b
add Avg, Avg, c
add Avg, Avg, d
div Avg, Avg, 4
```

In SASM (a two-address format), the implementation of this C assignment statement becomes the five-instruction sequence

```
move Avg, a
iadd Avg, b
iadd Avg, c
iadd Avg, d
idivi Avg, 4
```

A one-address implementation requires six instructions:

```
lda a
add b
add c
add d
div 4
sta Avg
```

The code size can be further reduced if it happens either that one of the variables `a`, `b`, `c`, or `d` is already in the accumulator from a previous instruction, or that `Avg` can be left in the accumulator for the succeeding instruction. This does not happen as often as one might hope. Computers that restrict instructions exclusively to the one-address format have fallen out of favor in recent years, but variations on this technique have appeared on many computers in the past, and likely will reappear in the future.

9.2 REGISTERS

A second way to take advantage of the locality of references to memory is to use abbreviated names. People with long names are often given nicknames by their friends or family. In general, shortened forms are convenient to use because they are used often and can be said quickly. Care must be exercised to avoid ambiguity. In a similar manner, it is possible to designate that certain addresses are to be referenced frequently, and therefore should be given short, convenient names. In this case, a short and convenient name requires that an address must be specified in fewer bits. The easiest way to do this is to create a second, small memory. Having only a small number of locations, an address can be specified in fewer bits. A memory containing 256 locations, for example, would require only $\log_2 256 = 8$ bits of address.

A syntax must be introduced into the assembly language to reference this second smaller memory. The second memory might be distinguished from main memory by using a prefix such as the letter "r" together with an address to refer to the location. If there are 256 locations in this second memory, the largest address within the second memory would be 255. Thus it would be possible to represent an address as an 8-bit unsigned integer. Including three such addresses within a three-address instruction only requires 24 bits; so a 32-bit instruction could contain an 8-bit opcode and still specify three such operands. For example, the instruction

```
add r12, r15, r200
```

could be written to have the same effect as the instruction

```
add a, b, c
```

Variable `a` would be placed and kept in the second smaller memory at location 12, `b` would be at location 15, and `c` would be at location 200.

The second memory is commonly designed into architectures, and it is called a **register set** or **register file**. An individual location within the register file is referred to as a **register**.

The instruction format using registers for operands is fully general for variables that are already present in the register file. It is restrictive in the sense that only variables within the register file can be accessed. Any variable could be assigned to a register, and this is where the locality is exploited. The variables that are used most often are assigned more or less permanently to individual registers. Other variables that are not assigned to locations in the register file can be temporarily assigned to a location within it. The values of such variables must be copied into the appropriate register location when the register is bound to the variable, and copied back to the original memory location when the register is unbound. Thus many different variables can share a single register location during the course of a program.

The concept of using registers has been tested and shown to be so effective that virtually all modern computers use registers in some capacity. The registers are designed to be part of the processor, not part of memory. This further reduces the number of memory accesses for instructions that take their operands from the register file.

Special Registers

Because the register number is a constant (not a variable) within the register designation for an operand, a syntax is required in the assembly language to denote a register. Examples of the syntax used to indicate register number 3 as an operand could be

r3 R3 $3 3

Other architectures (like the Pentium) give each register its own name.

Some registers are designed for general-purpose use, and others are used for special purposes. The most prominent example of a special-purpose register is the program counter (PC). Sometimes a register is specified for holding the address of a frequently accessed region of memory. A stack pointer is an important example of this type. Frequently used constants are sometimes permanently stored in a register. There are several architectures that designate one register that always contains the constant zero. It is traditionally implemented as a register instead of being contained within the memory.

9.3 LOAD/STORE ARCHITECTURES

Some architectures fully specify the addresses of each operand within an instruction. Such machines are known as **memory-to-memory architectures**. While they are appealing because of the simplicity of their assembly language, memory-to-memory architectures do not provide a good tradeoff between cost and speed. Their value is primarily pedagogical. The assembly language SASM defines a memory-to-memory architecture.

For architectures designed today, the instruction set is designed such that most instructions get their operands exclusively from registers, and calculated results get written back to registers. The only instructions that access data from main memory are those that move individual operands between registers and memory. A **load** instruction copies the value from memory into a register, and a **store** instruction copies the value within a register into memory. Architectures that restrict the accessing of operands in memory to load and store instructions are known as **load/store** architectures. A load instruction would have the form

```
load rX, var_name
```

which would load the value of the variable `var_name` into register `X`. A store instruction would have the form

```
store var_name, rX
```

which would store the content of the register `X` into the memory location bound to the variable `var_name`.

9.4 ADDRESSING MODES

Registers supply source operands and receive results faster than memory. Arithmetic and logical instructions that keep operands in registers can be short because they need only specify registers to identify their sources and destinations. Memory addresses cannot be eliminated from code completely. Even if arithmetic instructions do not restrict operands to being in registers, some instructions (loads and stores) must be capable of moving operands between the registers and main memory. Consider the information needed to specify a load instruction. In addition to the opcode, the instruction must specify the address of the data to be read. It must also specify the register into which the data are to be loaded. While the destination register can be specified with few bits, the address may be large. An opcode, a register specification, and a 32-bit address cannot all be placed into a fixed-size, 32-bit instruction. Another class of instructions that must specify main memory addresses are branch instructions. Together with an opcode, a 32-bit target address of a taken branch cannot fit into a fixed-size, 32-bit instruction. There are a variety of ways to handle this limitation.

By combining the use of registers together with allowing flexibility in instruction format, an address can be specified within an instruction in many different ways. An **addressing mode** within an instruction defines how to get the **effective address** for an operand. The effective address is used to get the operand. For a load instruction, the effective address is the location in memory where the operand is. For a control instruction, the effective address is the target address that will be placed in the PC.

The following is a partial list of addressing modes. They show what is required to obtain an effective address for a single operand. Not all machines have the capability to offer all addressing modes. Since it takes space within an instruction to allow the programmer a choice of addressing modes, many architectures make their instructions shorter (and easier to decode) by fixing the addressing mode for all operands.

1. If an instruction may be of variable size, the effective address may be placed directly in the instruction. The address is a constant that happens to be stored within an instruction. Note that the hardware must know about this format so that it can adjust the PC appropriately when executing the instruction. This instruction format is shown containing a single operand.

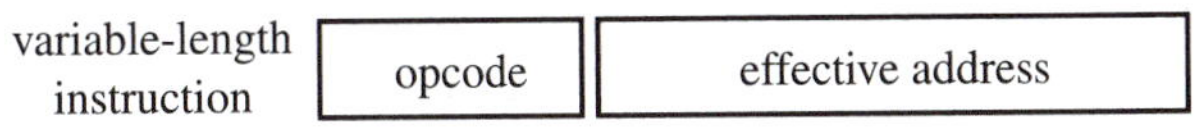

   This addressing mode is called **direct**.
2. The instruction might specify a register that contains the effective address, instead of specifying the address itself.

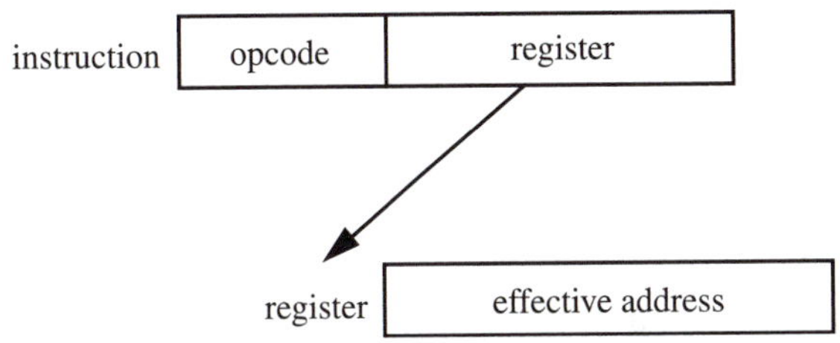

   This addressing mode is called **register direct**. This mode's capability is important when the address itself is a variable. The Pentium processor offers this addressing mode and calls it register indirect.
3. An addressing mode may be specified with a small constant and a register. The effective address is computed by adding together the contents of the register and the constant.

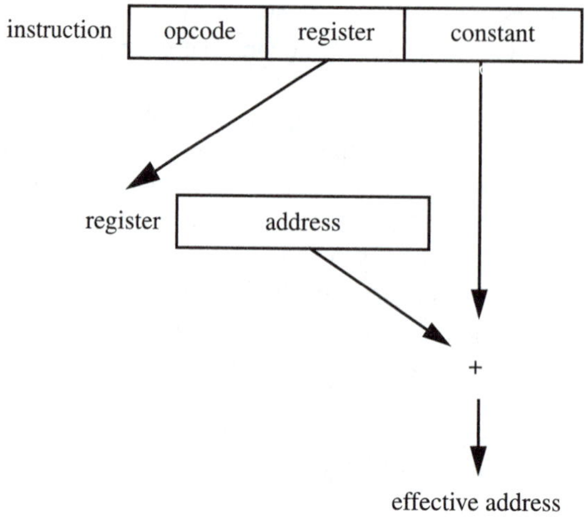

This addressing mode is known as **base displacement**. Note that if the constant is zero, then this is the same as a register direct addressing mode.

4. An effective address might be specified by adding together the contents of the two registers.

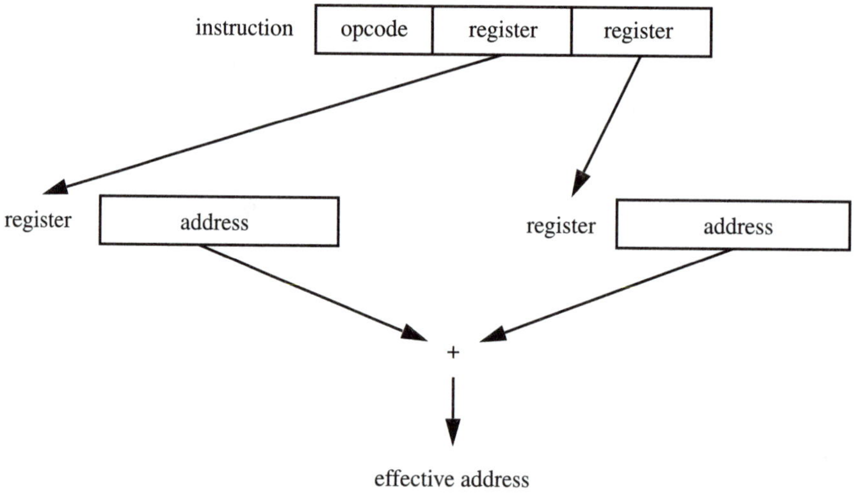

One use of this addressing mode might be to generate the address of an array element. If one of the registers contains the base address of the array, and the other contains the offset from the base to the desired element, then this form of addressing calculates the element's address without any extra instructions. The Pentium processor has an addressing mode like this and calls it base-indexed mode.

5. If the value of a constant is known when a program is written, it would be convenient to place the value directly into the instruction. No added memory accesses are required, since the instruction fetch has the effect of bringing in the operand as well.

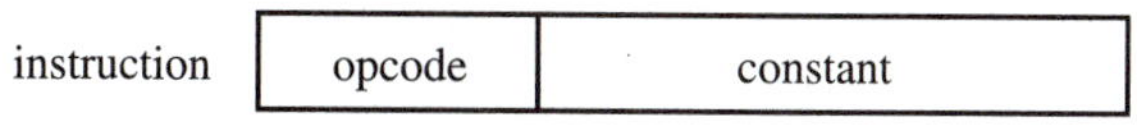

This addressing mode is known as **immediate**. The effective address of the operand is the address of the instruction itself. If an implementation of an architecture that offers immediate addressing mode needs the effective address, then the address can be taken from the PC. The diagram shows a fixed-size instruction containing the constant. The constant must be small enough to fit in the fixed-size instruction. Variable-length instructions can allow for many sizes of immediate operands.

6. **Register addressing mode** is where the operand is contained in a register.

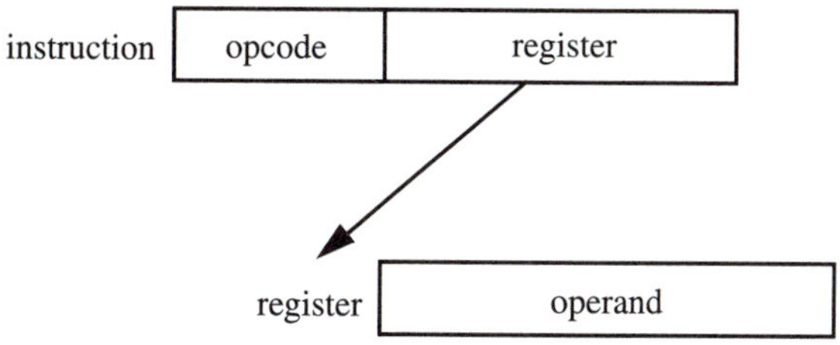

Since the operand is in a register, there is no memory access involved in getting the operand. Referring to an effective address for register addressing mode does not make sense.

7. An addressing mode that facilitates dereferencing pointers places the address of the address within the instruction.

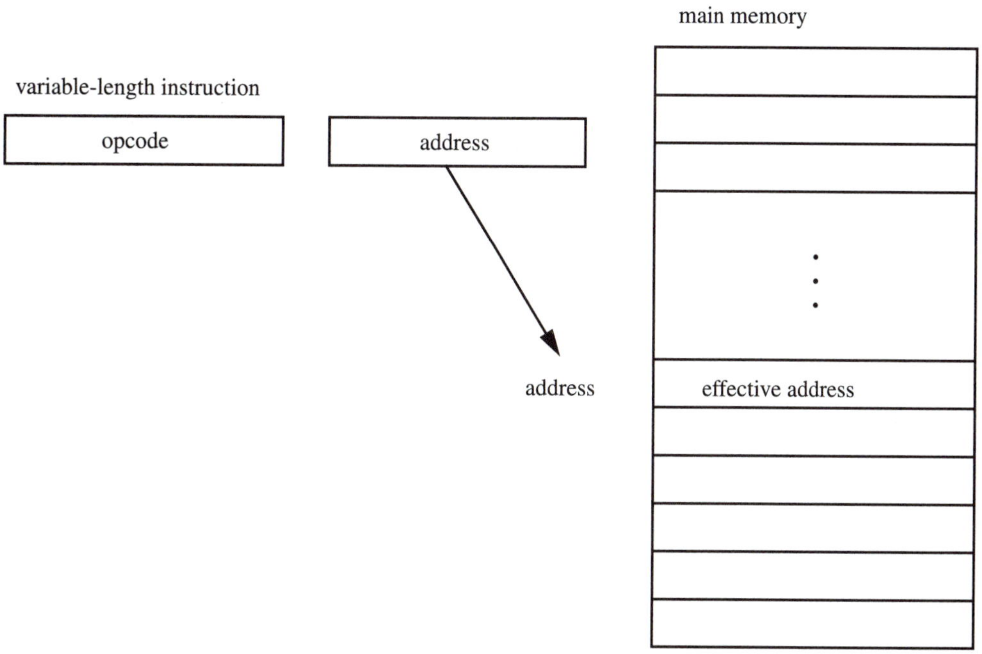

Note that this addressing mode requires a memory access in order to get the effective address. For the instruction that loads data, this **indirect addressing mode** would require two memory accesses. The first memory access loads the effective address, and the second memory access loads the data.

8. A **register indirect addressing mode** is similar to indirect addressing mode. The address of the effective address is in a register, instead of being contained within the instruction.

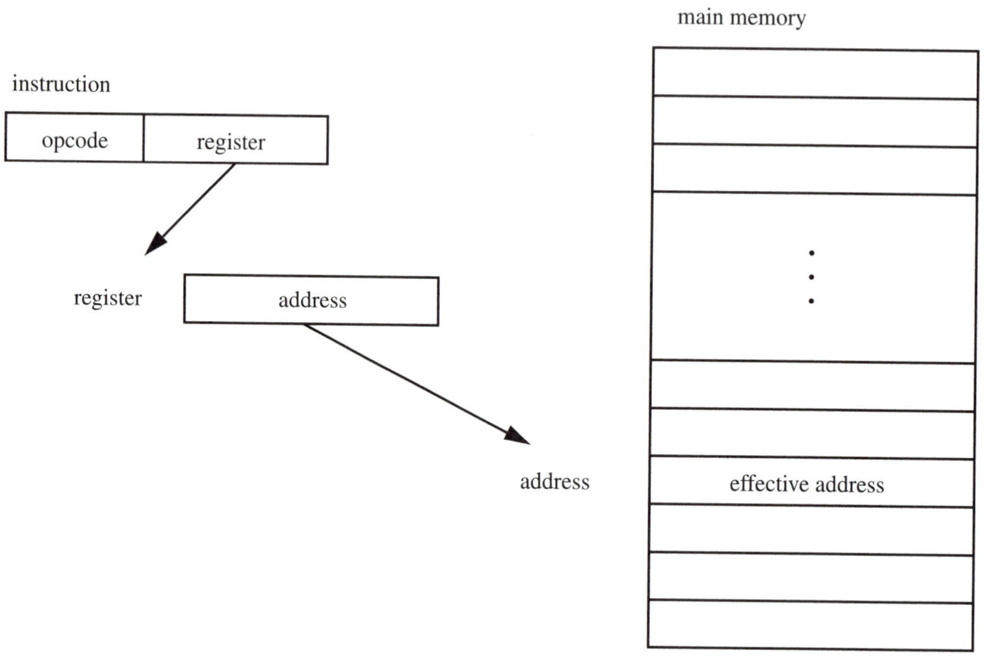

This addressing mode can reduce instruction size compared to indirect addressing mode. It is possible to fit a register specification in fewer bits than an address requires. It requires the same number of memory accesses as an indirect addressing mode.

9. A **PC relative addressing mode** is one that uses the program counter to come up with an effective address. One common use of a PC relative addressing mode is within a control instruction. For a taken branch, an effective address is calculated and placed into the program counter.

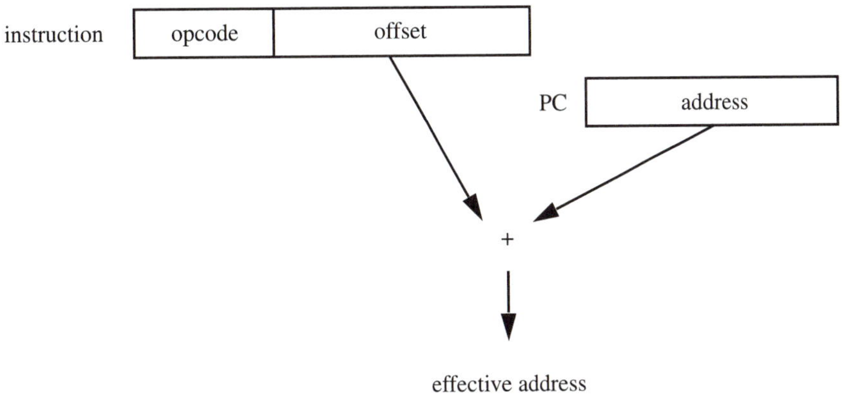

One implementation uses available bits within the instruction for an offset field. The program counter contains the address of the branch instruction. By adding together the offset field and the program counter, the effective address calculated is relative to the branch instruction. Immediate addressing mode may be considered PC relative. The effective address points to the instruction. The program counter contains the address of the instruction; so the effective address is contained in the program counter.

Computers offer a variety of methods for specifying addressing modes. A typical method of specifying addressing modes on a load/store architecture is to let the instruction specify the addressing mode. The mode for each operand is implied by the instruction, and therefore requires no bits to specify a programmer's choice of addressing mode. All operands for arithmetic and logical instructions will use register mode. In a load/store architecture, only two classes of instructions specify addresses: load/store instructions and control instructions. The addressing mode for operands in these instructions will also be fixed and implied by the instruction.

Other architectures, particularly those developed before the 1980s, give a choice of addressing mode to the programmer. Extra bits associated with each operand specify an addressing mode for the operand. The variety of addressing modes can be large. This may have the effect of requiring instructions to be of variable length.

The performance of architectures with variable-length instructions can be affected. It may require more than one memory access to fetch the entire instruction. The performance of the decode hardware can also be affected. When the instruction does not have fixed-size fields containing operand specification, the decode hardware must decode one operand at a time, to identify the boundaries between operand specifications. This is done serially, thereby reducing performance.

SUMMARY

The cause of poor performance in the implementation of an assembly language like SASM is the large number of memory accesses associated with every instruction fetch and execution. To reduce the number of memory accesses, virtually all modern computer architectures include registers. The use of general purpose registers reduces the size of instructions. It can also reduce the number of memory accesses required for operand access.

Load/store architectures further reduce the number of memory accesses to fetch and execute an instruction by requiring that all operands for arithmetic and logical instructions be in registers. The only instructions to specify operands that are in memory are loads and stores. Loads and stores move data to/from registers.

Addressing modes give the programmer flexibility in the specification of operand location. Architectures that allow a wide variety of addressing modes may result in a reduced number of instructions within a program, as compared to the same program written for a load/store architecture. However, fewer instructions do not necessarily imply faster execution. Performance may be lost due to the implementation of variable-length instruction execution and an increased number of memory accesses.

PROBLEMS

1. How many bits would an instruction require if a three-address format were used in SASM?

2. Identify two different code sequences where a three-address architecture will require fewer instructions than a two-address architecture.

3. Describe a benefit of a two-address architecture over a three-address architecture. Describe a benefit of a three-address architecture over a two-address architecture.

4. Write a code fragment that subtracts the contents of variable `y` from variable `x` and places the result into variable `z` if

   a. a three-address instruction set is used

   b. a two-address instruction set is used

   c. a one-address instruction set is used

5. If the opcode field of an instruction is defined to contain 7 bits, how many instructions does the architecture have?

6. An architecture is defined to have a register file with 64 registers. How many bits will be used within an instruction to specify a register?

7. If an instruction may use one of 16 different addressing modes for each of its two operands, how many bits are required in the instruction to specify addressing mode?

8. An addressing mode is defined for an instruction. It includes specifications for two registers. An effective address is calculated by adding together the contents of the two

registers. How might this addressing mode be used to access an element of a two-dimensional array?

9. Suggest an equivalent implementation for the SASM instruction

```
iadd xx, yy
```

on a load/store architecture. Assume that the load/store architecture has plenty of registers, and that it has a three-address format for its add instruction.

10. Identify a case where a register direct addressing mode would be useful.

11. Identify a case where a base displacement addressing mode would be useful.

12. Identify a case where an indirect addressing mode would be useful.

13. Identify a case where a PC relative addressing mode would be useful.

14. An **autoincrement** addressing mode is like a register direct addressing mode, but with the added feature that the register containing the address is incremented after the address is used. Draw a diagram to show the use of an autoincrement addressing mode. What quantity should be added to the address?

15. Identify a case where an autoincrement addressing mode would be useful.

CHAPTER

10

THE PENTIUM ARCHITECTURE

The Pentium architecture is derived from earlier Intel architectures, the 486, the 386, the 286, and originally from the 8086. In 1979, when the 8086 architecture was released, the market was eagerly awaiting the first single chip processors. These first processors overcame many technical difficulties. The packaging available did not provide enough I/O pins to send signals on and off the chips, and the process technology limited the number of transistors on a chip. Some of the original design decisions appear odd when compared with more modern architectures.

By maintaining backward compatibility with earlier releases in its architectural family, the Pentium maintains a market gathered over time. There is a huge body of software written for the Pentium and its previous processors.

Oddities and what computer architects see as inconsistencies in the architecture occur due to the long development and things that appeared in the 8086. These types of things make the description of the architecture long, with lots of details and exceptions (compared with other more modern architectures). This chapter aims to detail a portion of the Pentium instruction set. Omitted from the description are many of the more esoteric instructions.

10.1 GENERALITIES

The Pentium instruction set is very large as compared with other more modern architectures. The original 8086 instruction set is comparable in size to other architectures designed in the same time period. With each new processor in the family of architectures, new instructions have been added, while keeping all previous instructions, to maintain backward compatibility.

The Pentium architecture has a two-address instruction set. The first operand in the list of operands for any instruction is the destination of the result. For instructions with two operands, the first operand is both a source and a destination. It gets overwritten with the result.

There are both general-purpose registers and special-purpose registers. The 16-bit registers implemented in the earlier members of the family were extended to 32 bits in the later architectures in the x86 family.

It is not a load/store architecture. Operands may come from memory or registers as specified by the programmer.

Addressing modes are programmer specified; they are not implied by the instruction. Many instructions have restrictions on the addressing modes allowed for operands.

Control instructions are based on condition codes. The condition codes are kept in a special-purpose register called EFLAGS.

The directives used in Pentium assembly language programs are the same as already presented for SASM. They do not change for Pentium assembly language. Note that directives are not part of an architecture's specification.

10.2 REGISTERS

There are eight general-purpose 32-bit registers available in the Pentium. They are given the names EAX, EBX, ECX, EDX, EBP, ESI, EDI, and ESP. Earlier versions of the architecture had 16-bit or 8-bit registers. The letter 'E' in the name of the register distinguishes the 32-bit registers from the 16-bit versions. Entire registers or portions of the 32-bit registers can be used. This is different from most other architectures where an entire register is always used, not a portion of a register. Of these eight registers, EBP and ESP have specific uses that are not general purpose. EBP is a frame pointer, as described in Chapter 11. ESP is a stack pointer, also as described in Chapter 11. A diagram of the registers is in Figure 10.1.

Further deviation from general-purpose register usage is that certain classes of instructions imply the use of a register. The implied use of a register means that it does not require bits within the machine code for addressing mode and operand specification. Therefore, the instruction can be more tightly encoded, possibly making the instruction shorter.

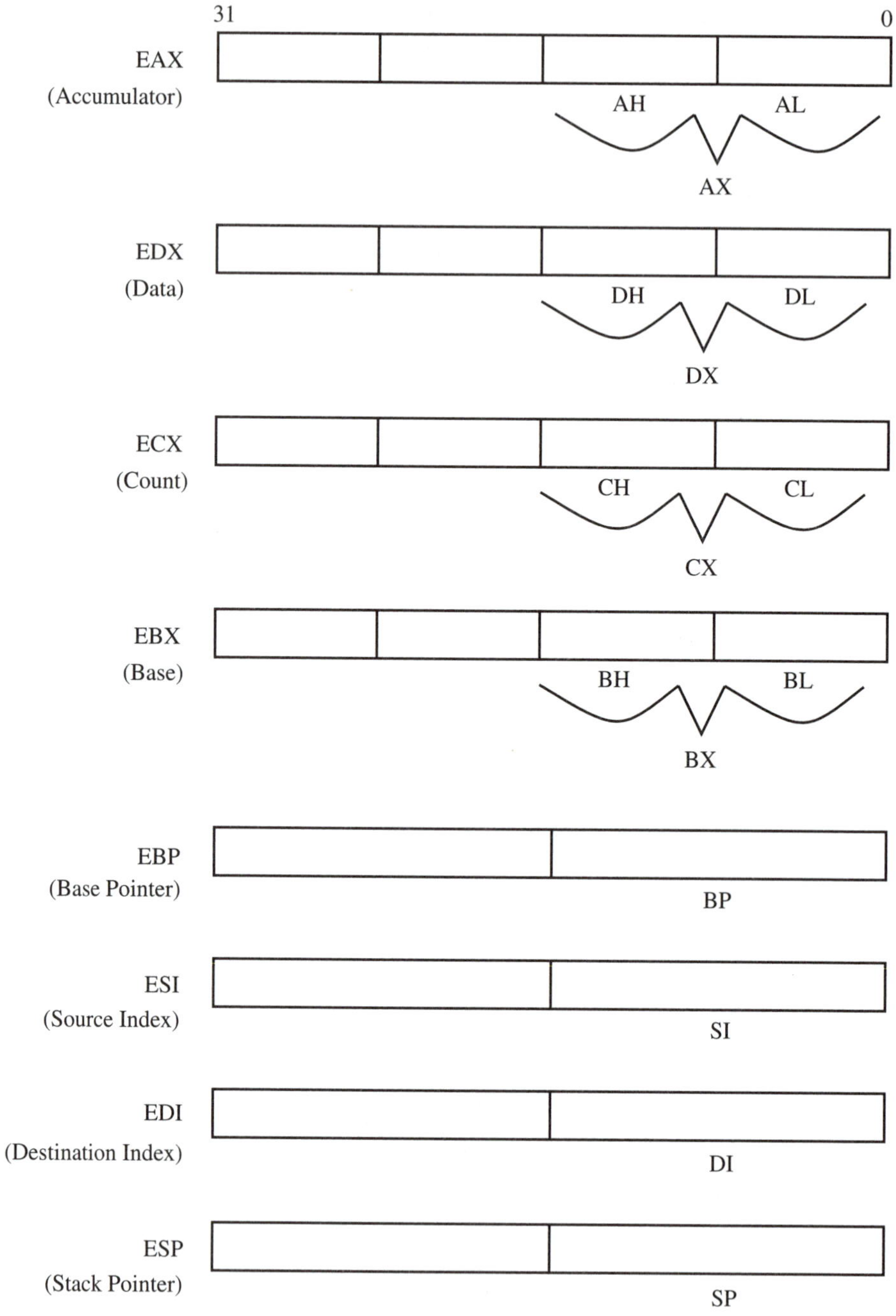

Figure 10.1 General register designations.

Flag	Name	Bit Number	Purpose
OF	Overflow flag	11	Set when result exceeds integer range
SF	Sign flag	7	Set when result is negative
ZF	Zero flag	6	Set when result is zero
PF	Parity flag	2	Set when least significant byte of result has an even number of bits set
CF	Carry flag	0	Set when there is a carry out from the most significant bit of result

Figure 10.2 EFLAGS specification.

The syntax for using registers as operands places the register name in the code as an operand. The register names are therefore reserved words. The register names may be written using all capital letters, as in EAX, or in lower-case letters, as in eax.

Writing code that makes effective use of registers places variables in registers, as opposed to keeping the variables in memory. For example, the loop induction variable of a for loop belongs in a register. The variable is never stored in memory. Its initial value is placed directly in a register, and the instructions requiring the variable always access the register where it is stored. The Pentium processor makes it easy to keep variables in memory with its large variety of addressing modes. The performance of any processor (with registers) will increase if its registers are effectively used.

The condition codes are kept in a register called EFLAGS. It is a 32-bit register, where fewer than 32 bits correspond to condition codes. The condition codes relevant to control instructions presented in this chapter are given in Figure 10.2.

There are also several more registers on a Pentium processor that deal with addressing. They are called segment registers and are used when the programmer uses a segmented memory model. These registers are not used in this book. They are 16-bit registers named CS, DS, SS, ES, FS, and GS.

10.3 MEMORY MODEL

A modern approach to using memory implements Intel's flat memory model. It is this model that is presented in this book. The memory model presumes that memory provides one large contiguous set of memory locations that a program may access. This **address space** can be accessed by using an address that is given as a single unsigned 32-bit integer. The range of addresses available to the program is not broken into pieces; it is flat. This flat memory model is supported by the 386 and more recent processors in the x86 family architecture.

The memory model supported and used in previous processors within the family of architectures is called a segmented model. The Pentium also supports this model, but it allows the programmer to choose which memory model is used. This unique segmented model can be attributed to the technological limitations of the earliest processors in the x86 family. Addresses were limited to 16 bits. This amount of memory is not large enough for both the code and the data of many programs. The segmented model increases this size,

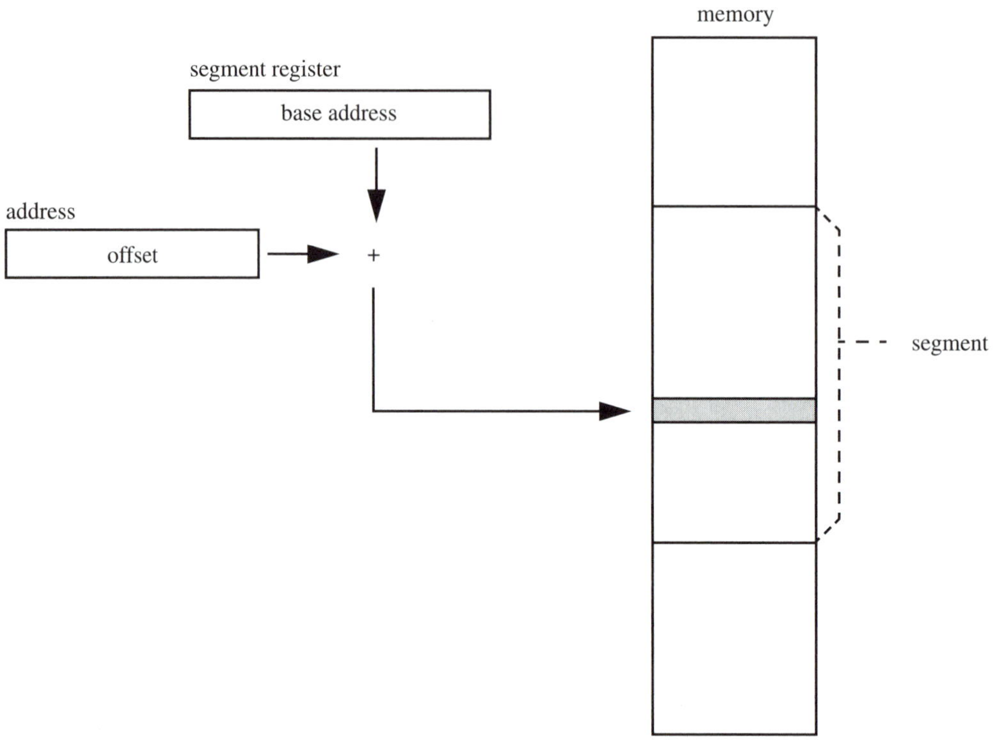

Figure 10.3 Memory access in a segmented memory model.

giving 2^{20} = 1 Mbyte of accessible memory. In the segmented model, the various pieces of a program are divided up into **segments**. The code goes into one segment, the data into another, and the stack is placed into a third segment. Each segment is given its own address space of up to 64 Kbytes in length. A set of registers, called **segment registers**, are used to provide information about each segment. One piece of information within a segment register identifies a segment's base address in memory. The 16-bit address is an offset from a specific segment base address. Figure 10.3 diagrams the use of the segmented memory model in addressing memory.

As technological limitations were overcome, the later processors in the x86 family expanded address size to 32 bits. The segmented memory model works the same, but each segment can utilize its own 32-bit address space. Segments can be up to 4 Gbytes in length.

10.4 ADDRESSING MODES

The Pentium allows a wide variety of addressing modes to be used for operands in instructions. The programmer is given the choice of addressing modes for operands. In addition, the syntax used to specify addressing modes within assembly language code is less restrictive than other assembly languages. For the following examples containing addressing modes, the Pentium `mov` instruction is used. It copies data from the source operand to the destination operand. Like many Pentium instructions, the `mov` instruction has the restriction that one of its operands use register mode. This has the effect of reducing the size of the instruction's machine code.

Not all available addressing modes are presented. To maintain backward compatibility with earlier versions of the x86 architecture, each instruction works with a wide variety of operand sizes. Both 8-bit and 16-bit operands must work. A few 8-bit operands are presented here, and the 16-bit size is ignored.

An operand that uses **register mode** implies that the contents of the register will be used as the operand. The syntax for register mode gives the name of the register. As an example, the Pentium instruction

```
mov EAX, ECX
```

uses register mode for both its operands. The contents of register ECX is copied into register EAX.

An **immediate mode** operand places the value of the immediate directly in the code. The Pentium instruction

```
mov EAX, 0aabb0100h
```

places the bit pattern 1010 1010 1011 1011 0000 0001 0000 0000 into register EAX. Note that it makes no sense (and is not allowed) to use an immediate addressing mode for the destination register.

Pentium addressing modes for memory operands come in a general form. The flat address space presented allows for any addressing mode that may be expressed as

$$\text{base register} + (\text{index register} \times \text{scaling factor}) + \text{displacement}$$

There are some special cases that limit which registers can be used in combination, but this scheme is extremely flexible in comparison to other architectures. The scaling factor is a constant, limited to the values 1, 2, 4, or 8. The addressing mode descriptions that follow utilize subsets of this general addressing mode specification.

This flexible Pentium addressing mode allows for several modes unnamed as yet. For example, the instruction

```
mov EDX, [EDI][EBP+8]
```

calculates an effective address by adding together the contents of register EDI, the contents of register EBP, and the constant 8. Intel calls this addressing mode base-indexed with displacement. This addressing mode could be used to access an element of a two-dimensional array. One register contains the base address of the array. The other register contains an offset from the base address to the element, and the constant identifies the field desired within the array element.

A **register direct** (called register indirect by Intel) addressing mode uses the contents of a register as an effective address. The syntax for a register direct addressing mode in Pentium assembly language uses square brackets around the name of the register. The example Pentium instruction

```
mov [EAX], EDX
```

uses a register direct addressing mode for the destination operand. The instruction copies the contents of register EDX into the location pointed to by the contents of register EAX. Register EAX is a base register, if the general addressing mode given above is considered.

Base displacement (called based or indexed by Intel) addressing mode allows an 8- or 32-bit displacement to be added to the contents of a register and used as an effective address. For example, the source operand in the Pentium instruction

```
mov EBX, 16[EAX]
```

uses a base displacement addressing mode. The instruction adds the decimal value 16 to the contents of register EAX as the calculation of an effective address. The contents at that effective address are then copied into register EBX. Alternative syntax for a base displacement addressing mode is

```
mov EBX, [EAX+16]
```

or

```
mov EBX, [EAX]16
```

Register EAX is the base register, and the constant 16 is the displacement.

A **direct** addressing mode is also available. The effective address is contained within the instruction. Pentium syntax for a direct addressing mode places the symbol for the address in the assembly language code. An example that uses a direct addressing mode for the second operand is

```
mov EBX, table
```

The contents at the location pointed to by the label `table` are copied into register EBX.

The availability of many addressing modes leads to a difficulty in assembly language specification. The size of the data pointed to by an effective address is not defined. Often, an instruction operates on a specific size of data. In the Pentium architecture, the size of data is not always well defined, because a single assembly language mnemonic represents an instruction that works on differing operand sizes. Therefore, it is sometimes necessary to specify further the size of data desired. This is done with the directives

```
byte ptr
```

and

```
dword ptr
```

When needed, a directive is placed within the instruction, just before the operand that it describes. For example, the Pentium move instruction does not specify the amount of data to be moved. Consider the move instruction

```
mov    EAX, [EBX]
```

Register EBX contains an address. That address could be assumed to point to a byte or a doubleword. Register EAX has space for 32 bits; so a default amount of data to move would be the 32-bit doubleword pointed to by the address. To make this explicit, the directive is used

```
mov    EAX, dword ptr [EBX]
```

The use of the directive can change the amount of data transferred. The Pentium instruction

```
mov    EAX, byte ptr [EBX]
```

loads the byte at the address contained in register EBX into register AL, the least significant byte of register EAX. Alternatively, a byte transfer can be specified without the directive by

```
mov    AL, [EBX]
```

10.5 INSTRUCTION SET

This section details many of the instructions in the Pentium instruction set. Only a subset of the Pentium's large instruction set is given. Those instructions not described provide either redundant functionality or are omitted due to antiquated purposes. Those instructions are rarely included on more recently developed architectures, because the data types they support are no longer commonly used. An example of this is the set of decimal string instructions on the Pentium. The decimal arithmetic instructions are those that operate on binary coded decimal strings. BCD data types are only rarely used today. More recently developed architectures do not support the BCD data type at all. The set of instructions that operate on strings have functionality that can be implemented using other code. They are not discussed.

For a complete description of all instructions, see *Pentium Processor Family Developer's Manual, Volume 3: Architecture and Programming Manual.*

The use of some other instructions not described may lead to more efficient code. The code is more efficient due to fewer bytes required for the machine code.

The size of the operands is important. They must match, so that the architecture executing the instruction explicitly knows how much data it is operating on. Many of the instructions will perform the same function on different sizes of data.

Data Movement Instructions

Each of the instructions from SASM that copy data from one location to another has a direct Pentium equivalent. The difference between the SASM and the Pentium code is in the restriction of where the operands are located. SASM omits all notion of registers, and the Pentium generally requires that one of its operands use register mode as its addressing mode.

Several examples of the `mov` instruction are given in the section above on Addressing Modes. Figure 10.4 lists instructions that fall into the category of data movement. The

Instruction	Operands	Notes
mov	reg, r/m r/m, reg reg, immed r/m, immed	data copy first operand is used as source and overwritten as destination
movsx	reg, r/m8	data copy with sign extension
movzx	reg, r/m8	data copy with zero extension
lea	reg, m	load effective address

Figure 10.4 Pentium data movement instructions.

Operand Type	Definition
reg	register mode operand
reg8	8-bit register mode operand
r/m	32-bit operand can be register mode, or any addressing mode of the general form
r/m8	8-bit operand can be register mode, or any addressing mode of the general form
immed	operand is a 32-bit immediate
immed8	operand is an 8-bit immediate
m	operand is a symbol, giving an address in memory

Figure 10.5 Operand types.

instruction column gives the mnemonic for the opcode of the instruction. The **operands** column defines the number and addressing modes allowed for the operands. Figure 10.5 contains a more detailed description of the abbreviations used to describe the allowable operands and addressing modes.

The SASM `la` instruction does the same operation as the Pentium `lea` instruction. The difference between the two is that the Pentium instruction requires that the address be placed into a register instead of another location within memory. An example of this instruction is

```
lea EBX, table
```

This instruction places the address assigned to the label `table` into register EBX. Note that this is a different function from the instruction

```
mov EBX, table
```

The `mov` instruction will take the 32-bit doubleword at address `table` and copy it to register EBX.

SASM provides data copy instructions with zero extension or sign extension. The same functionality is provided by the Pentium instruction set with the `movsx` and `movzx` instructions. The difference between the two is that the Pentium instruction requires that the result must be placed in a register.

Integer Arithmetic Instructions

All architectures have instructions for doing integer arithmetic. The variations between architectures include the data types supported, number of operands, flexibility of addressing modes available for operands, and variety of integer arithmetic functions provided as instructions. The integer arithmetic instructions available on the Pentium are detailed in Figure 10.6. The variety of Pentium arithmetic instructions is larger than those offered in SASM. SASM offers fewer instructions to reduce programmer choice and simplify code. Some of these Pentium instructions provide redundant functionality. For example, the instruction

```
inc ECX
```

does the same arithmetic operation as

```
add ECX, 1
```

The `inc` instruction is part of the instruction set (although redundant) because it provides a frequently needed operation. The machine code for the `inc` instruction is one byte shorter than that of the `add` instruction. Some efficiency in the instruction fetch may occur due to the shorter instruction.

Integer multiplication has the complication that the result produced may need up to twice as many bits as the operands. Architectures deal with this in a variety of ways. Some architectures set aside specific registers for receiving the result. The Pentium allows this by restricting one of the source operands to be in register EAX. The most significant half of the product is placed in register EDX, and the least significant half of the product is placed in register EAX. Another method for dealing with the large precision of the product is to throw away the most significant bits of the product. The Pentium allows this by placing the least significant half of the product into one of the 32-bit registers.

Integer division is also complicated by the number of bits required for operands and results. The Pentium architecture requires twice as many bits for the dividend as for the divisor. It therefore uses two registers concatenated together to perform 32-bit division. The most significant half of the dividend must be in EDX, and the least significant half of the dividend must be in register EAX. Division creates two results, a quotient and a remainder. Register EDX is overwritten with the resulting remainder, and register EAX is overwritten with the resulting quotient.

Instruction	Operands	Notes
add	reg, r/m r/m, reg reg, immed r/m, immed	two's complement addition EFLAGS set based on result first operand is used as source and overwritten as destination
inc	reg r/m	increment operand EFLAGS (except CF) set based on result
sub	reg, r/m r/m, reg reg, immed r/m, immed	two's complement subtraction EFLAGS set based on result
dec	reg r/m	decrement operand EFLAGS set based on result
neg	r/m	additive inverse EFLAGS set based on result (CF is cleared if result=0, set otherwise)
mul	EAX, r/m	unsigned multiplication EDX:EAX ← EAX * r/m CF and OF flags are cleared if EDX=0, and they are set otherwise SF and ZF are undefined
imul	r/m reg, r/m reg, r/m, immed	two's complement multiplication complex setting of EFLAGS EDX:EAX ← EAX * r/m reg ← reg * r/m reg ← r/m * immed
div	r/m	unsigned division does EDX:EAX / r/m, EAX = quotient, EDX = remainder EFLAGS are undefined
idiv	r/m	two's complement division does EDX:EAX / r/m, EAX = quotient, EDX = remainder EFLAGS are undefined
cmp	reg, r/m r/m, immed r/m8, immed8 r/m, immed8	subtracts source from destination to set EFLAGS sign extended source is subtracted from destination

Figure 10.6 Pentium integer arithmetic instructions.

Logical Instructions

Every architecture provides a way to perform logical operations. At a minimum, an architecture could provide a nand operation, since all other logical functions can be built from nand operations. Some architectures provide more logical instructions than the Pentium's `not`, `and`, `or`, and `xor` (exclusive or) instructions. Except for the `not` instruction, these

Instruction	Operands	Notes
not	r/m r/m8	logical not (one's complement operation)
and	reg, r/m reg8, r/m8 r/m, reg r/m8, reg8 r/m, immed r/m8, immed8	logical and EFLAGS set based on result first operand is used as source and overwritten as destination
or	reg, r/m reg8, r/m8 r/m, reg r/m8, reg8 r/m, immed r/m8, immed8	logical or EFLAGS set based on result first operand is used as source and overwritten as destination
xor	reg, r/m reg8, r/m8 r/m, reg r/m8, reg8 r/m, immed r/m8, immed8	logical xor EFLAGS set based on result first operand is used as source and overwritten as destination
test	r/m, reg r/m8, reg8 r/m, immed r/m8, immed8	logical and to set EFLAGS EFLAGS set based on result operands are not changed

Figure 10.7 Pentium logical instructions.

instructions require two operands. The first operand is both a source and a destination for the result of the logical operation.

Figure 10.7 details the logical instructions.

Figure 10.8 details the shift category of instructions. The condition code CF is set by the arithmetic and logical shift instructions. The bit shifted out of the operand (which does not appear in the result) is placed into CF.

Floating Point Arithmetic Instructions

The Pentium implements floating point arithmetic instructions in hardware. The processor has a physically separate set of hardware that does floating point operations. It is called the FPU, standing for Floating Point Unit. Given that this hardware was specified much more recently than other portions of the architecture, the design is different. It does meet the specifications of the IEEE floating point arithmetic standard.

The FPU contains eight general-purpose floating point registers, plus several other registers that maintain state and status information about the FPU. The general-purpose floating point registers are 80 bits wide. Single-precision or double-precision values are placed within those 80 bits in an extended format specified by Intel. Figure 10.9 contains a diagram of the registers.

Instruction	Operands	Notes
sal	r/m, 1 r/m, CL r/m, immed8	shift left arithmetic destination is shifted by amount specified in source operand ZF and SF set based on result
shl	r/m, 1 r/m, CL r/m, immed8	shift left logical destination is shifted by amount specified in source operand ZF and SF set based on result
sar	r/m, 1 r/m, CL r/m, immed8	shift right arithmetic destination is shifted by amount specified in source operand ZF and SF set based on result
shr	r/m, 1 r/m, CL r/m, immed8	shift right logical destination is shifted by amount specified in source operand ZF and SF set based on result
rol	r/m, 1 r/m, CL r/m, immed8	rotate left destination is rotated by amount specified in source operand OF and CF affected
ror	r/m, 1 r/m, CL r/m, immed8	rotate right destination is rotated by amount specified in source operand OF and CF affected

Figure 10.8 Pentium shifting instructions.

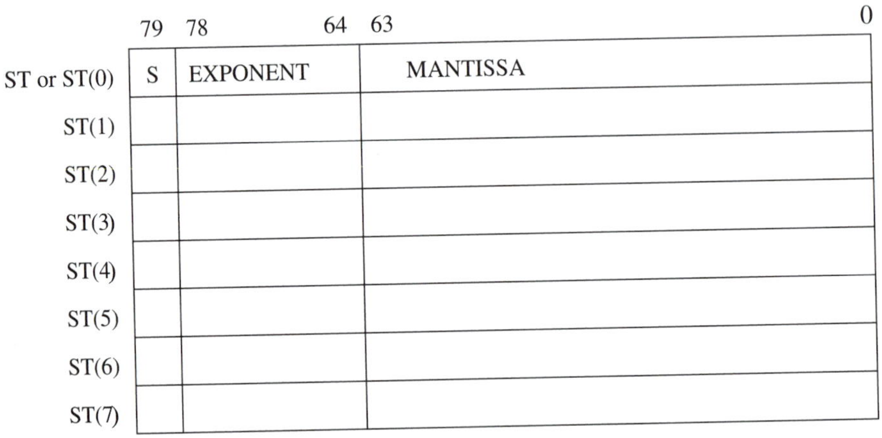

Figure 10.9 Pentium FPU register file.

This register file is organized as a stack maintained by the hardware. The register within the file that is the current top of the stack is referred to as ST or ST(0). All floating point instructions specify operands relative to ST.

A subset of the Pentium floating point instructions are given in Figure 10.10. Like the non-FPU instructions, the programmer is given great freedom in the specification of the operands. Allowable operands are explained by Figure 10.11.

Instruction	Operands	Notes
finit	*no operands*	initialize the FPU sets ST
fld	 m32 m64 ST(i)	load floating point value push m32 operand onto FPU stack push m64 operand onto FPU stack push ST(i) onto FPU stack, i is calculated before top of stack pointer is changed
fldz	*no operands*	load floating point value 0.0
fst	 m32 m64 ST(i)	store floating point value copy ST to m32 copy ST to m64 copy ST to ST(i)
fstp	 m32 m64 ST(i)	store floating point value and pop ST pop ST to m32 pop ST to m64 pop ST to ST(i), i is calculated before top of stack pointer is changed
fadd	 m32 m64 ST, ST(i) ST(i), ST	floating point add ST gets ST + m32 ST gets ST + m64 ST gets ST + ST(i) ST(i) gets ST + ST(i)
faddp	 ST(i), ST	floating point add and pop ST ST(i) gets ST(i) + ST, then pop ST
fsub	 m32 m64 ST, ST(i) ST(i), ST	floating point subtract ST gets ST - m32 ST gets ST - m64 ST gets ST - ST(i) ST(i) gets ST(i) - ST
fsubp	 ST(i), ST	floating point subtract and pop ST ST(i) gets ST(i) - ST, then pop ST
fsubr	 m32 m64 ST, ST(i) ST(i), ST	floating point subtract, operands reversed ST gets m32 - ST ST gets m64 - ST ST gets ST(i) - ST ST(i) gets ST(i) - ST
fmul	 m32 m64 ST, ST(i) ST(i), ST	floating point multiply ST gets m32 * ST ST gets m64 * ST ST gets ST * ST(i) ST(i) gets ST * ST(i)

Figure 10.10 Pentium floating point instructions. *Continued on next page*

Instruction	Operands	Notes
fmulp	 ST(i), ST	floating point multiply and pop ST ST(i) gets ST(i) * ST, then pop ST
fdiv	 m32 m64 ST, ST(i) ST(i), ST	floating point divide ST gets ST / m32 ST gets ST / m64 ST gets ST / ST(i) ST(i) gets ST(i) / ST
fdivp	 ST(i), ST	floating point divide and pop ST ST(i) gets ST(i) / ST, then pop ST
fdivr	 m32 m64 ST, ST(i) ST(i), ST	floating point divide, operands reversed ST gets m32 / ST ST gets m64 / ST ST gets ST(i) / ST ST(i) gets ST / ST(i)
fdivrp	 ST(i), ST	floating point divide, operands reversed and pop ST ST(i) gets ST / ST(i), then pop ST
frndint	*no operands*	round floating point to integer, using current rounding mode ST gets ST, rounded to an integer
fchs	*no operands*	change sign ST gets -ST
fcom	 m32 m64 ST(i)	compare floating point values, setting FPU flags C0-C3 compare ST with m32 compare ST with m64 compare ST with ST(i)
ftst	*no operands*	test floating point value, setting FPU flags C0-C3 compare ST with 0.0
fxam	*no operands*	test floating point value, setting FPU flags C0-C3 set C0-C3 according to type of ST
fstsw	AX	copy FPU status word to AX

Figure 10.10 *Continued*

A Pentium code fragment that uses floating point instructions is given in Figure 10.12. The example calculates the area of a circle, using an approximation for π. The instruction

```
fld    ST(0)
```

duplicates the item at the top of the stack. The first multiply instruction computes the square of the radius.

Operand Type	Definition
m32	32-bit (single precision) operand, addressing mode of the general form
m64	64-bit (double precision) operand, addressing mode of the general form
ST ST(0)	current top of stack
ST(i)	register at i away from ST, $0 \leq i \leq 7$

Figure 10.11 FPU instruction operand specification.

```
.data
pi          dd     3.14159        ; an approximation
radius      dd     6.823E+1
area        dd     ?

.code
; compute the area of a circle
      fld     pi
      fld     radius
      fld     ST(0)          ; duplicate radius on stack
      fmulp   ST(1), ST      ; radius * radius
      fmulp   ST(1), ST      ; pi * (radius squared)
      fstp    area
```

Figure 10.12 Pentium code fragment to calculate the area of a circle.

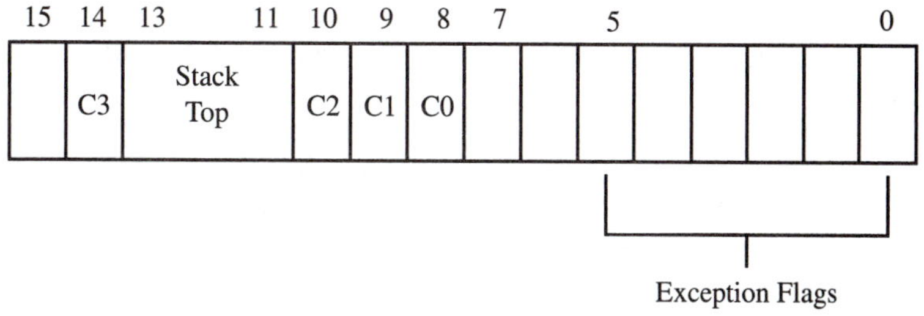

Figure 10.13 The FPU Status Word.

The floating point instructions `fcom`, `ftst`, and `fxam` set condition code bits. The four bits, called C3, C2, C1, and C0, are separate and different from the condition code bits in the EFLAGS register. These bits are contained in a register called the FPU Status Word, as diagrammed in Figure 10.13. The setting of the condition codes C3, C2, and C0 for the `fcom` instruction is given by the table in Figure 10.14. If a control decision will be based on the settings of the condition codes, the Pentium instruction `fstsw` is used to copy the FPU Status Word to register AX. Further masking and testing of register AX is used to set the EFLAGS register. Then control instructions are based on the settings of the

Comparison	C3	C2	C0
ST > operand	0	0	0
ST < operand	0	0	1
ST = operand	1	0	0
Either operand is NaN	1	1	1

Figure 10.14 FPU Status Word condition code settings for `fcom` or `ftst` instruction.

Type in ST	C3	C2	C1	C0
unsupported	0	0	sign of ST	0
NaN	0	0	sign of ST	1
normal	0	1	sign of ST	0
infinity	0	1	sign of ST	1
zero	1	0	sign of ST	0
empty	1	0	sign of ST	1
denormal	1	1	sign of ST	0

Figure 10.15 FPU Status Word condition code settings for `fxam` instruction.

EFLAGS register. The `ftst` instruction compares the contents of ST against 0.0. The table in Figure 10.14 is also used to give the condition code settings for the `ftst` instruction, with the assumption that the operand is 0.0. The `fxam` instruction is used to set condition code bits according to the type of floating point value. It provides a clean way to check if a representation is for one of the special values, like NaN. Figure 10.15 gives a table showing the setting of the condition code bits after the `fxam` instruction for the various types of values in ST.

Control Instructions

The control instructions available on the Pentium allow for both unconditional and conditional changes in control flow. Intel calls all these instructions jumps on the Pentium. The jump instructions base decisions on the condition codes in the EFLAGS register. Figure 10.16 lists the Pentium control instructions. The Pentium has two names for many of the control instructions. Either can be used, since both names refer to the same instruction (and opcode).

Input/Output Instructions

The task of making input and output work belongs in the operating system of a computer. Very few modern computers provide instructions that directly access I/O devices

Instruction	Operands	Notes
jmp	m	unconditional jump
jg jnle	m	jump if greater than 0 (SF xor OF) or ZF = 0
jge jnl	m	jump if greater than or equal to 0 SF xor OF = 0
jl jnge	m	jump if less than 0 SF xor OF = 1
jle jng	m	jump if less than or equal to 0 (SF xor OF) or ZF = 1
jns	m	jump if not negative SF = 0
jo	m	jump if overflow OF = 1
js	m	jump if negative SF = 1
je jz	m	jump if zero ZF = 1
jne jnz	m	jump if not zero ZF = 0

Figure 10.16 Pentium control instructions.

Macro	Operands	Notes
put_ch	r/m	character is in least significant byte of 32-bit operand
get_ch		character will be in AL, the least significant byte of register EAX
put_str	m	operand is name of null terminated string

Figure 10.17 Pentium I/O macros.

and perform I/O functions. Even on architectures that do provide I/O instructions, the programmer writing applications is not given access to these instructions. The architecture is designed such that only the operating system is allowed to execute the I/O instructions. Instead, the programmer is given a mechanism to request I/O functionality.

The illusion of I/O instructions is provided by the macros given in Figure 10.17. A standard library of I/O functions is utilized to do the input and output. These macros are a subset of the macros provided by SASM, but their usage is changed slightly. Both `put_ch` and `get_ch` implicitly use register EAX.

10.6 CODE EXAMPLES

Given the Pentium's large instruction set and wide variety of addressing modes, the programmer has many decisions to make when writing any program. In addition, programs with the same functionality can be written in many different ways. All the SASM instructions are implemented using Pentium instructions. For example, the functionality of the SASM instruction

```
imult  int2, int1
```

can be implemented using the Pentium code fragment

```
mov     EBX, dword ptr int1
mov     EDX, dword ptr int2
imul    EDX, EBX
mov     dword ptr int2, EDX
```

Note that this code fragment does not implement the SASM syntax of `M(x)`. The variables to be multiplied are assumed to be in variables `int1` and `int2`. The Pentium `imul` instruction differs from its SASM equivalent, `imult`, in the allowable addressing modes for operands and in the implied location of the result. For the Pentium instruction, the result is always restricted to a register. The SASM instruction has no notion of registers; so its implementation must include copying the result from a register to the destination operand in memory.

Figure 10.18 contains a code fragment that counts the number of 1s within variable `xx` located in memory. It is presumed that variable `xx` will be assigned a value before this

```
.data
xx        dd      ?

.code
                  .
                  .
                  .
                  mov           EAX, 00000001h     ; mask
                  mov           ECX, 32       ; test all 32 bits of xx
                  mov           EDX, 0        ; counter of # of bits set

test_bit:         test          EAX, xx
                  jz            next_bit
                  inc           EDX
next_bit:         ror           xx, 1
                  dec           ECX
                  jnz           test_bit
```

Figure 10.18 Pentium code fragment.

code fragment is executed. The code fragment uses a loop that checks each bit within `xx`. The check is accomplished using the `test` instruction. Each bit is checked after a rotate instruction places the bit into the least significant position within the 32-bit doubleword. This code fragment shows registers being used to hold variables. The variable that keeps a count of the number of ones seen resides in register EDX. Register ECX is a counter used to determine the number of loop iterations. A mask used in the `test` instruction resides in register EAX. Alternatively, some or all of the variables could reside in variables within memory. By keeping the variables in registers, there may be some improvement in performance due to fewer memory accesses.

Figure 10.19 contains a simple Pentium assembly language program that prints out the alphabet in lower case. The program works with characters using 32-bit registers. Therefore, care must be taken to match the types of operands. An explicit comparison is done to determine when the loop that prints the characters should exit. The loop could alternatively be written as a for loop that iterates 26 times to print out the characters of the alphabet. Note that the only variable in the data section of memory is for the newline character. All other variables are placed exclusively in the registers. The newline character could have been passed to the `put_ch` macro as an immediate. That would eliminate the need for any variables in memory. The performance of the program should be improved by placing as many variables as possible into registers, as opposed to placing these same variables in memory. It reduces the number of memory accesses generated by the program.

```
title alphabet printing program

; This program prints out the lower case alphabet.
.486
.model flat, stdcall
.stack 1000h
INCLUDE Pmacros.inc

.data
newline        dd      0ah      ; newline character

.code
main:
               mov          EAX, 97        ; 'a' is 97
               mov          EDX, 122       ; 'z' is 122
print:         cmp          EAX, EDX
               jg           all_done
               put_ch       EAX
               inc          EAX
               jmp          print

all_done:      put_ch       newline
               done
end
```

Figure 10.19 Pentium program to print out the lower-case alphabet.

SUMMARY

The Pentium architecture is derived from earlier architectures. Its instruction set is large, and only a subset of its instructions have been detailed in this chapter. The many instructions can use a wide variety of addressing modes for operands. This is different from many of the more recently designed architectures classified as load/store architectures. Load/store architectures generally fix the addressing mode for each operand of an instruction. Allowing such a variety of addressing modes gives the Pentium assembly language programmer (or a compiler) a great deal of programming freedom.

The number of registers in the Pentium is few as compared with other more recently designed architectures. Therefore, assembly language code uses more variables located in memory, rather than in registers.

PROBLEMS

1. Give two Pentium code fragments that implement the SASM instruction

```
isub counter, 1
```

2. Give a Pentium code fragment that implements the SASM instruction

```
move dest, src
```

3. Give a Pentium code fragment that implements the SASM instruction

```
irem int2, int1
```

4. Give a Pentium code fragment that implements the skeleton of a high-level language for loop.

5. Write a Pentium code fragment that reads in a single line of characters entered by the user and counts the number of characters.

6. Write a Pentium code fragment that sets (places a 1) in bit 14 of register ECX without changing the values of the other bits.

7. What is the maximum number of memory accesses that the code fragment in Figure 10.18 could generate? Assume (for simplicity) that the fetch of each instruction generates one memory access.

8. How many memory accesses does the program in Figure 10.19 generate? Assume (for simplicity) that the fetch of each instruction generates one memory access.

9. Write a Pentium code fragment that reads in an integer.

10. Write a Pentium code fragment that prints out a null-terminated string without using the `put_str` macro.

11. Write a Pentium code fragment that prints out an integer.

12. Write a Pentium code fragment that calculates the area of a triangle given single-precision floating point variables containing the height and width of the triangle.

13. Write a Pentium code fragment that prints out a single-precision floating point value in the format ±1.??????????????????????? × 2^e. The mantissa is printed in binary, where each of the 23 '?' characters in the format is a single bit of the representation's mantissa. The true exponent, e, is a base-ten integer.

14. Write a Pentium code fragment that sums each of the 10 integer elements of the array declared as

```
int_array dd 10 dup(0)
```

15. Give the skeleton of a Pentium program.

16. Write a Pentium program that reads in a single line of characters entered by the user and prints the line back out in the opposite order. For example, if the user enters

```
Here is a string to reverse.
```

then the program prints out

```
.esrever ot gnirts a si ereH
```

17. Write a Pentium program that reads in an integer entered by the user and then prints the integer out.

18. Write a Pentium program that decides if a string entered by the user is a palindrome. A palindrome is a string that is the same written forward as it is written backward. For example, the string

```
RadaR
```

is a palindrome.

CHAPTER 11

PROCEDURES

A high-level language programmer uses procedures for several reasons. Code becomes modular, facilitating later modification. The writing of code within a modular program can be done by more than one programmer. All that is necessary is that the functionality and parameters of the different procedures be well defined.

A compiler needs to generate assembly language code for implementing procedure calls, returns, and parameter passing. There are many correct ways for doing these tasks. The high-level language specifies rules for syntax and functionality, and a compiler will implement a set of conventions. The conventions vary from computer to computer, and they vary from language to language. This chapter discusses how procedures are implemented at the assembly language level.

```
.code
       .
       .
       .
       lea EAX, rtn1
       jmp proc
rtn1:
       .
       .
       .
       done

proc:          ; procedure code here
       .
       .
       .
       jmp [EAX]
```

Figure 11.1 Procedure call and return mechanism.

11.1 PROCEDURE CALL AND RETURN MECHANISMS

There are four steps that need to be accomplished in order to call and return from a procedure.

1. Save return address
2. Procedure call
3. Execute procedure
4. Return to the saved return address

Each of these steps is straightforward. The first step (save return address) might be accomplished using the Pentium `lea` instruction.

```
lea    EAX, ret_addr
```

The return location must be identified with a label (`ret_addr` in this example). This return address is saved in register EAX. The procedure call step needs to transfer control to the first instruction within the procedure. This can be accomplished with an unconditional branch (`jmp`) instruction. Execution of the procedure follows. The return requires a branch or jump to the address saved in the first step. A code fragment using this basic mechanism is shown in Figure 11.1.

11.2 DYNAMIC STORAGE ALLOCATION

Placing a return address in a register works fine as long as there are no nested procedure calls. A nested call is a procedure call within the body of a procedure. If a nested procedure is invoked, the value held in the register containing the return address will be overwritten. To avoid the loss of return addresses, a safe place for storing return addresses is

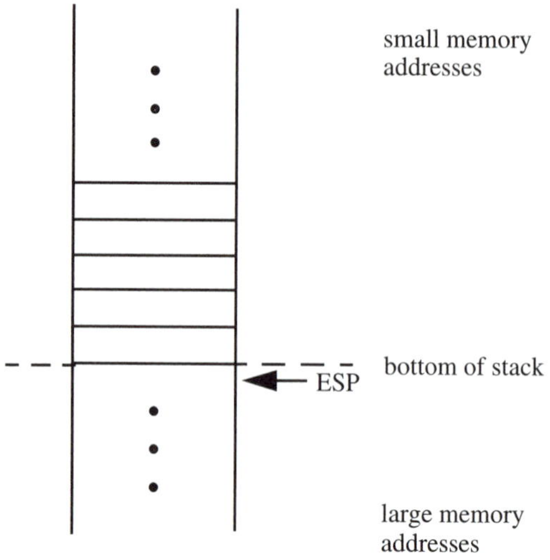

Figure 11.2 Initial (empty) state of the system stack.

needed. For each procedure that has been invoked but not completed, a return address must be saved. Note that once a procedure has returned, the space for the return address is no longer needed, and can be reused (for example, to store a return address for a newly invoked procedure). A method that can dynamically allocate space for procedures when they are invoked and deallocate the space when they return is needed. **Dynamic allocation** sets aside space while the program is running.

The amount of memory required to save all the return addresses is therefore limited only by the number of nested levels of procedure calls permitted. In many modern programming languages this limit is very large. To provide space for storing many return addresses, a stack is employed.

Many computer systems implement a stack as part of the environment provided when a program is running. This stack is referred to as the **system stack**. It is such an important and frequently used structure that some computers provide assembly language support for accessing the stack efficiently. The Pentium architecture system stack has its bottom of the stack (also known as the base) at a very large memory address. The size of the stack is given by the programmer in a `.stack` directive. As items are pushed on the stack, it grows toward smaller memory addresses. Register ESP is a stack pointer for the system stack. It contains the address of the data currently at the top of the stack. It is initialized prior to the beginning of a program's execution. Figure 11.2 shows a diagram of the initial state of the system stack.

A push operation needs to adjust the stack pointer, and then copy the data to the stack. Pentium assembly language code to push the contents of register EAX on the stack is

```
sub    ESP, 4
mov    [ESP], EAX
```

A pop operation copies the data from the stack, and then adjusts the stack pointer to point to the empty location at the top of the stack. A code fragment to pop the top doubleword from the stack into register EAX is

```
mov     EAX, [ESP]
add     ESP, 4
```

Pushing and popping data from the system stack is such a common operation that the Pentium instruction set includes instructions to push and pop data. An example of the `push` instruction to place the contents of register EAX on the stack is

```
push    EAX
```

The instruction first adjusts the stack pointer register, ESP, to allocate the space. It then copies the data from the register to the allocated space. An example of the `pop` instruction to pop the top doubleword from the stack into register EAX is

```
pop     EAX
```

This instruction copies the data at the top of the stack to the register, and then deallocates the space by adjusting the stack pointer register, ESP.

Using the Stack for Return Addresses

One common use of the system stack is saving return addresses. A return address can be pushed onto the stack once a procedure has been called, and it can be popped off just before the return. Figure 11.3 contains the fragments of a Pentium procedure that implements the call and return, showing the save of the return address on the stack. Since procedure calls are such a frequent occurrence, the Pentium architecture includes a single instruction, `call`, both to save a return address (on the stack) and to transfer control to a procedure. A return instruction, `ret`, is also included in the Pentium's instruction set. It pops the return address off the stack, and then branches to that return address. Figure 11.4

```
.code
               .
               .
               .
               lea     EAX, ret_addr
               jmp     proc1
ret_addr:              ; code here that would be
                       ; executed following the return
               .
               .
               done
proc1:         push    EAX
                       ; procedure's code goes here
               .
               .
               .
               pop     EAX
               jmp     [EAX]
```

Figure 11.3 Code fragment to show saving and restoring of return address.

```
.code
                .
                .
                .
                call   proc1
                ; code here that would be executed
                ; following the return
                .
                .
                .
                done
proc1:                ; procedure's code goes here
                .
                .
                .
                ret
```

Figure 11.4 Procedure call and return instruction usage.

Instruction	Operands	Notes
push	r/m	
pop	reg	
call	r/m	push return address and jump to effective address
ret	immed	pop return address and adjust ESP by immed bytes

Figure 11.5 Pentium stack and procedure call instructions.

presents the same example as in Figure 11.3, but using the `call` and `ret` instructions. Their use reduces the necessary amount of code but has the same effect. These Pentium instructions are detailed in Figure 11.5.

An example containing a code fragment that uses the `call` and `ret` instructions to keep track of the flow of control is given in Figure 11.6. The function calculates $base^{exponent}$. Variable `base` is kept in memory. The code assumes that a value for the exponent is placed in register ECX before the function is called. The implementation given in Figure 11.6 uses global variables instead of parameters. This is done in order to give an example of using the system stack for saving return addresses, while ignoring the issue of parameter passing.

The procedure is **recursive**. Recursive procedure calls are a special case of nested procedure calls. An example of recursion is when a procedure directly calls itself. Because of the recursion, it is necessary that return addresses be saved on the stack so that they are not overwritten and lost. As part of the `call` instruction, the return address is saved on the stack. The return address is obtained by popping it off the stack as part of the `ret` instruction.

```
.data
base    dd      10

.code
                .
                .
                ; ECX contains the exponent
                call    powerfcn
                .
                .
                .
                done

powerfcn:       mov     EAX, 1
                cmp     ECX, 0          ; base case
                jz      returnpt
                dec     ECX
                call    powerfcn        ; recursive call
                imul    EAX, base
returnpt:       ret
```

Figure 11.6 Pentium code fragment to calculate base ^{exponent}.

A procedure that does not call any other procedures is known as a **leaf procedure**. It does not need to store its return address onto the stack. The use of `call` and `ret` hides the implicit saving and restoring of the return address.

11.3 ACTIVATION RECORDS

A compiler's role is to generate correct assembly language for high-level language code. The code generated must correctly implement the high level language rules. The rules include those of **scope**. Rules of scope generally refer to which variables, memory locations, and other procedures a currently invoked procedure has access to. For example, the scope of a local variable declared within a C function is only within that procedure. This implies that variables of the same name declared within different functions are not related, and they may be assigned different values at the same time.

When a procedure is invoked, a new **environment** is created. In this newly created environment, new local variables are defined, while the values of the previous environment must be preserved. Variables for holding intermediate values during a computation like expression evaluation may also be needed. Like return addresses, these local variables are dynamic data whose values must be preserved over the lifetime of the procedure, but not beyond its termination. At the termination of the procedure, the current environment disappears and the previous environment must be restored.

At procedure invocation, memory space must be allocated for holding the information associated with the new environment. This space is used not only for a return address, but also for preserving the values from other registers, and as a place to keep parameters. The allocated space is a single block of memory, known as an **activation record** or **stack frame**. In general, an activation record consists of all the information that corresponds to

```
main()
{
      A();
}

A()
{
      B();
      C();
}

B()
{
      D();
}

C()
{}

D()
{
      E();
}

E()
{}
```

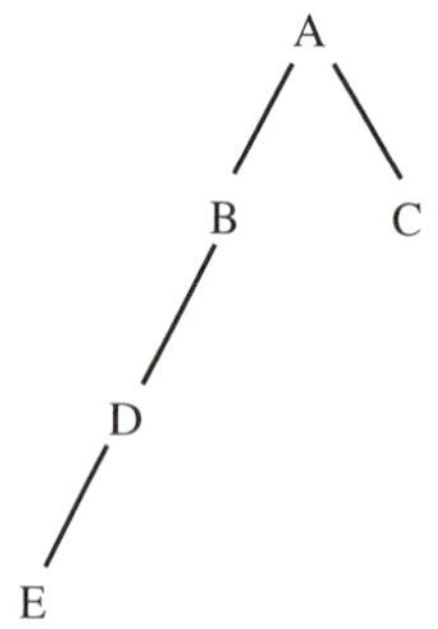

Figure 11.7 Example code block and call tree.

the state of a procedure. It contains enough information about a procedure for nested procedure calls to be handled correctly. An activation record is pushed onto the stack by allocating space for it. The stack pointer is adjusted to allocate space on the stack. When returning from a procedure, the activation record associated with its invocation is popped from the stack. Figure 11.7 shows skeletons of C code and its associated call tree for an example. The tree shows the nesting of procedure calls, and the root of the tree is shown as procedure A.

The stack pointer must be adjusted by the size of the activation record. This size varies for different procedures. The adjustment of the stack pointer allocates space for the activation record. When the procedure returns to the calling program, the activation record is popped off the stack. The stack pointer must be adjusted by the same amount, leaving the stack the same size it was prior to the invocation of the procedure. A compiler generating the code to implement this chooses a size for an activation record. Many compilers calculate and allocate the exact amount of memory space for an activation record. Other compilers use a default size for all activation records. The default size is too large for most procedures, and therefore some of the space within the activation record will go unused.

Figure 11.8 follows the state of the stack for the code given in Figure 11.7. The state of the stack is shown immediately following each new procedure invocation. The letters represent the activation record for the procedures.

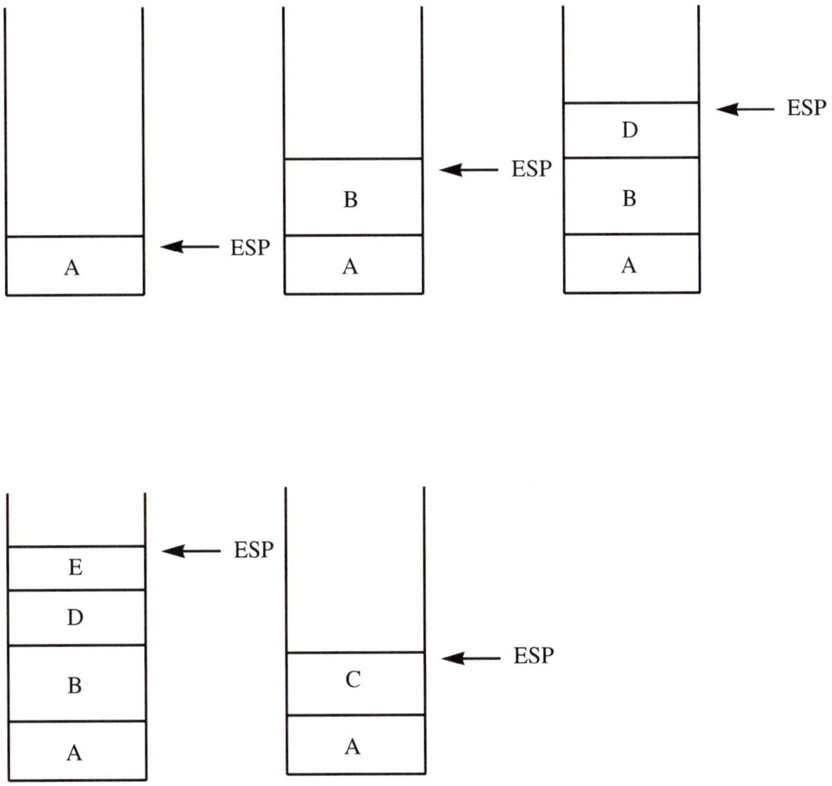

Figure 11.8 Stack immediately following each new procedure invocation.

Skeleton Pentium code for this example is given below. The size of an activation record for leaf functions is arbitrarily set to be four doublewords. Nonleaf procedures are assigned an activation record size of six doublewords. This code shows the allocation and deallocation of the activation records. The saving and restoring of return addresses within the stack frame is accomplished by the `call` and `ret` instructions. This return address is considered part of the frame for the procedure. The first doubleword within the frame is the return address. For a non-leaf procedure, the amount of space allocated for the remainder of the frame is one doubleword fewer than the size of the frame, since the `call` instruction allocates (and uses) space for the return address.

```
; main()
        call A
        .
        .
        .
        done

A:      sub ESP, 20 ; allocate frame for A
        ; return address is at [ESP+20] in A's frame
```

```
        call B
        call C
        add ESP, 20 ; deallocate A's frame
        ret

B:      sub ESP, 20 ; allocate frame for B
        ; return address is at [ESP+20] in B's frame
        call D
        add ESP, 20 ; deallocate B's frame
        ret

C:      sub ESP, 12 ; allocate frame for C
        ; unnecessary copy of C's return address is at [ESP+12]
        add ESP, 12 ; deallocate C's frame
        ret

D:      sub ESP, 20 ; allocate frame for D
        ; return address is at [ESP+20] in D's frame
        call E
        add ESP, 20 ; deallocate D's frame
        ret

E:      sub ESP, 12 ; allocate frame for E
        ; unnecessary copy of E's return address is at [ESP+12]
        add ESP, 12 ; deallocate E's frame
        ret
```

One item of interest that this example does not show is a saving and restoring of the return address from `main()`. The operating system could view the execution of a program as a procedure call. Given this view, the main program would have its return address saved as the program is entered (using `call`), and the return address would be restored as the program exits with `ret`. Then the operating system is free to execute other programs.

The example given so far presumes that the stack pointer is freely moved to accommodate the allocation and deallocation of activation records. A more traditional (and usually more efficient) implementation maintains a second pointer into the stack called a **frame pointer**. The frame pointer always points to the start of the currently invoked procedure's activation record. The stack pointer is used always to point to the top of the stack. On the Pentium, this is the full location at the top of the stack. Then, within a procedure, the stack pointer may be used for pushing and popping temporary values used in expression evaluation, without affecting the access to values within the current activation record. All accesses within the activation record are accomplished using offsets from the frame pointer. A register is often dedicated to be a frame pointer.

The following Pentium code fragment shows the implementation of procedure B assuming the use of a frame pointer. Register EBP is the frame pointer.

```
B:   push EBP          ; save caller's frame pointer
     mov EBP, ESP      ; set frame pointer to B's activation record
     sub ESP, 16       ; allocate remainder of B's activation record
```

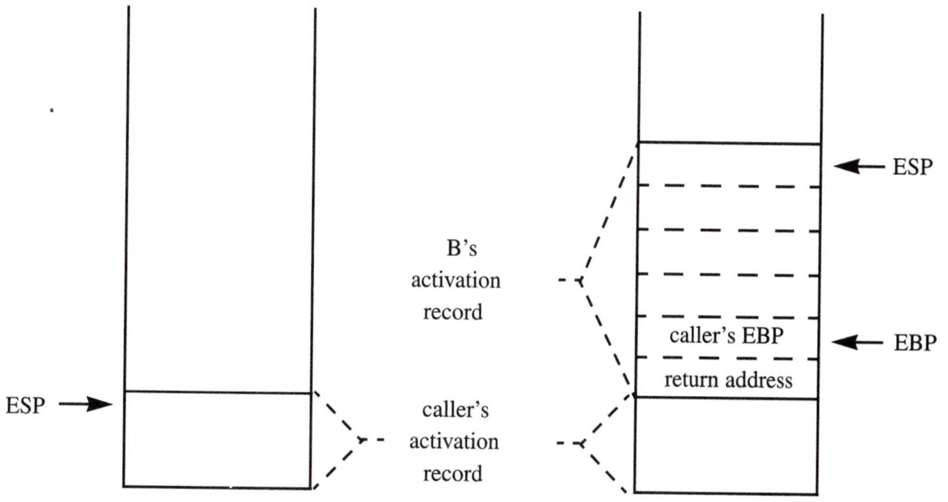

Figure 11.9 Stack contents before and after invocation of procedure B.

```
; procedure B's body here

mov ESP, EBP      ; deallocate B's activation record
pop EBP           ; restore caller's frame pointer
ret
```

There are several policy issues set in this example. One is that the allocation of the remainder of the activation record for procedure B is done within B itself. This is beneficial to a compiler, because it means that the code of the caller does not need knowledge of the size of the activation record of the procedure it calls. Another point in this code is that the deallocation of both temporary values pushed onto the stack and (most of) the current activation record is a matter of setting the stack pointer to the current value of the frame pointer. Figure 11.9 contains diagrams of the stack before and after the invocation of procedure B. After procedure B returns, the state of the stack is the same as it was before procedure B was called.

11.4 PARAMETER PASSING

The passing of parameters to a function or procedure is implemented in three parts. The first part has the calling program placing the parameters in a fixed location. The second part is the use of the parameters. The called procedure retrieves the parameters from the fixed location and uses them. The third part of the implementation has to do with what happens to the parameters after the procedure is done. For **call by value** parameters, the parameters are no longer needed once the procedure is done; so the fixed location where

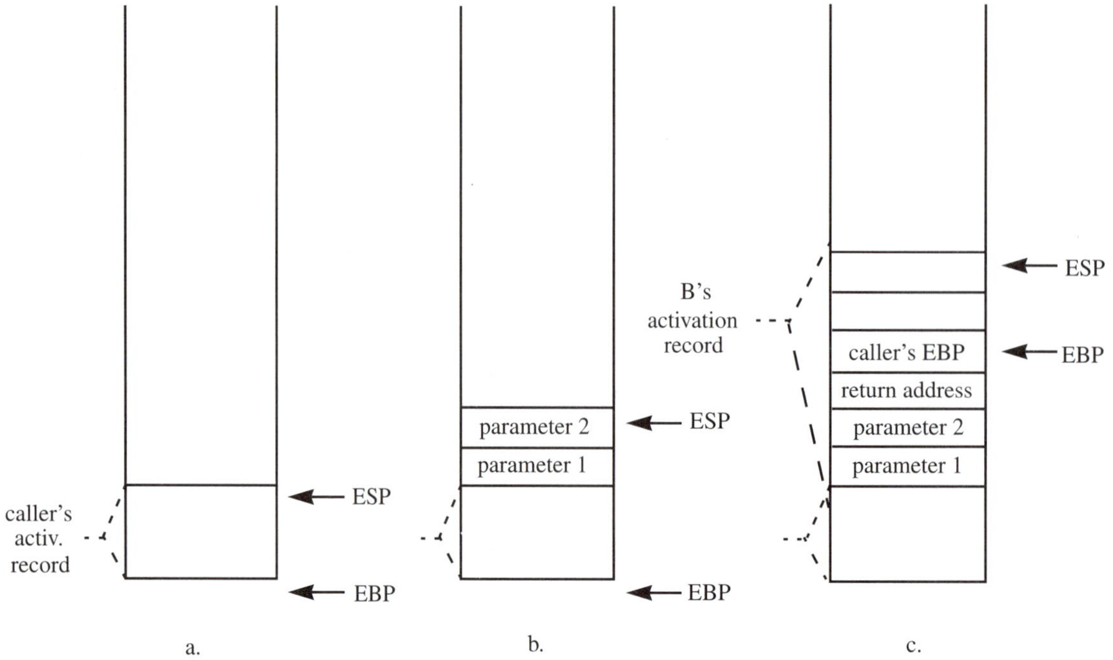

Figure 11.10 Stack state during parameter setup.

the parameters have been placed can be overwritten with other data. For **call by reference** parameters, new values assigned to the parameters within the procedure will need to be copied from the fixed location back to the variable.

Setting up parameters to pass to a function or procedure is straightforward using space within the activation record for the procedure. A compiler will calculate the correct amount of memory space needed to hold all parameters to a procedure. Memory space for the parameters is allocated, and then the calling program can place parameters into the activation record.

The parameters will be placed onto the stack between the calling program's and called procedure's activation record. They will be included as part of the called procedure's activation record. Figure 11.10 shows the state of the stack through the setup of parameters. The initial state of the stack has the caller's activation record and frame pointer as shown in Figure 11.10a. To set up the procedure call, two parameters are pushed onto the stack, to give the state of the stack in Figure 11.10b. Then control is passed to procedure B (using `call`). Procedure B allocates space for the remainder of its activation record, and then sets it up as in Figure 11.10c. The code fragment given in Figure 11.11 shows the setup of parameters on the stack, the call, and the return. The code to restore the state of the stack to that of the caller is the same as before, but adds an operand to the `ret` instruction. An immediate as an operand in the `ret` instruction gives the number of bytes that are to be popped off the stack (and discarded) after the return address is popped off the stack. This form of the `ret` instruction allows the called procedure to completely remove its own activation record. An alternative

```
.code
        .
        .
        push p1
        push p2
        call B
        .
        .
        .
        done

B:      push   EBP           ; save caller's frame pointer
        mov    EBP, ESP      ; set frame pointer to B's activation record
        sub    ESP, 8        ; allocate remainder of B's activation record

        ; procedure B's body here

        mov    ESP, EBP      ; deallocate B's activation record
        pop    EBP           ; restore caller's frame pointer
        ret    8             ; after popping return address, deallocate
                             ; 8 bytes to remove B's parameters
```

Figure 11.11 Parameters passed on the stack; parameters removed by called procedure.

method that accomplishes the same thing is given in Figure 11.12. The responsibility for removal of parameters is taken by the calling program. It is the implementation of a compiler for a high-level language that will decide whether the calling program or called procedure removes parameters from the stack.

Within the procedure, access to the parameters is accomplished by the use of a base displacement addressing mode or by copying the values from their location within the activation record to a register. For this same example, the first parameter could be copied to register EAX using the Pentium instruction

```
mov EAX, [EBP+12]
```

Alternatively, the first parameter for this example could be copied to register EAX with

```
mov EAX, [ESP+20]
```

This alternative eliminates the need for a frame pointer (EBP). It is less commonly used, since the displacement to the first parameter from the stack pointer (ESP) may change within the procedure. A compiler generating code that accesses parameters is simplified by using a fixed displacement from EBP rather than a variable displacement from ESP.

An alternative method for passing parameters is to pass values directly in registers. It can be more efficient than using the stack, because there may be fewer memory accesses. Instructions are not spent pushing parameters on the stack and then copying the parameters back into registers during the procedure's execution. Like return addresses, procedure

```
.code
        .
        .
        push   p1
        push   p2
        call   B
        add    ESP, 8          ; remove B's parameters
        .
        .
        .
        done

B:      push   EBP             ; save caller's frame pointer
        mov    EBP, ESP        ; set frame pointer to B's activation record
        sub    ESP, 8          ; allocate remainder of B's activation record

        ; procedure B's body here

        mov    ESP, EBP        ; deallocate B's activation record
        pop    EBP             ; restore caller's frame pointer
        ret
```

Figure 11.12 Parameters passed on the stack; parameters removed by called program

parameters are dynamic data; so they can only be passed in registers to procedures that do not themselves use those same registers for parameter passing to a nested procedure call. In general, passing parameters in registers alone will not work for programs that contain nested procedure calls.

The code in Figure 11.13 uses the same example of procedure B as given in Figure 11.12, modified only in that the two parameters are passed in registers EDX and ECX instead of on the stack. Space for the parameters is still allocated within the activation record in this example. When parameters are passed in registers, both a procedure and its nested procedure call will want their parameters in the same registers. In order to avoid losing the procedure's parameters, the procedure's parameters are saved in the procedure's activation record before placing the nested procedure call's parameters in the registers. The procedure's parameters are restored after the return from the nested procedure.

Although passing parameters in registers can be simple and quick, the Pentium architecture suffers from the problem that there are too few registers. Passing parameters in registers requires enough registers to hold the parameters.

Returning a result from a function is similar in many ways to passing a parameter. The difference is that the information is being passed the reverse direction—from the called procedure to the calling program. In addition, the time during which the value must be preserved is very short. The value must be preserved only over the interval from when the result is generated until control is returned to the calling program. It is simple and expedient to return the value within a register. The common practice on the Pentium architecture is to pass a return value in register EAX. The system stack could be used for this purpose. Space for the function return value could be allocated on the stack just before any parameters are pushed onto

```
.code
        .
        .
        mov    EDX, p1
        mov    ECX, p2
        call   B
        .
        .
        .
        done

B:      push   EBP           ; save caller's frame pointer
        mov    EBP, ESP      ; set frame pointer to B's activation record
        sub    ESP, 16       ; allocate remainder of B's activation record

        ; procedure B's body here

        mov    ESP, EBP      ; deallocate B's activation record
        pop    EBP           ; restore caller's frame pointer
        ret
```

Figure 11.13 Passing parameters in registers.

the stack. The function places the return value into the allocated space. Then the calling program retrieves the value from the stack.

11.5 SAVING REGISTERS

A procedure often needs to use many registers for local variables, copies of parameters, and temporary calculations. The state of the registers is part of the current environment, however; so the values in the registers set by the calling program should be left intact. Therefore, any register that is part of the environment of the calling program cannot be used by a newly called procedure unless its value can first be preserved and then be restored upon return to the calling program. Once again, use of activation records provides a convenient solution. Register values can be saved by the called procedure within its activation record. Then the registers can be reused by the procedure. Before returning, the registers are restored to their original values. The activation record is therefore defined to include space for any registers that might need to be saved. This method of clearing out registers for the procedure's use is called **callee save**. It is said that register values are preserved across procedure calls, because the register values of the calling program are not changed by a called procedure.

An alternative to callee saved registers is **caller saved** register values. These register values are said to *not* be preserved across procedure calls. The calling program saves any values that it does not want the called procedure to overwrite. Before a procedure is called, any registers whose values should not be modified by the procedure to be called are first saved in the caller's activation record. After the procedure returns, the register values can be restored by retrieving them from the activation record.

Both caller saved and callee saved schemes are used in practice. It is up to the programmer to choose one, although many systems adopt a fixed convention to improve interoperability of procedures written in different environments. The calling program and the called procedure must have the same understanding about what registers are being saved, and when.

11.6 A PENTIUM PROGRAM THAT USES PROCEDURES

The following Pentium code contains a modular program that calculates the greatest common divisor of two positive integers. The user is prompted for two integers. The program then calculates the greatest common divisor, and prints out the result. This Pentium program uses a recursive function to calculate the greatest common divisor.

```
title gcd program
; This program prints out the greatest common divisor
; of 2 user-entered positive integers.
.486
.model flat, stdcall
.stack 1000h
INCLUDE Pmacros.inc

.data
newline       dd     0ah     ; newline character
space         dd     020h    ; space character
tab           dd     09h            ; tab character
m             dd     ?              ; integer for calculating gcd(m,n)
n             dd     ?
base          dd     10
prompt        db     'Enter positive integer:', 0
msg1          db     'The greatest common divisor is ', 0
msg2          db     'Error in input. Quitting.', 0




.code
main:
        lea          EDX, prompt
        put_str      EDX
        lea          EAX, m
        push         EAX
        call         get_int        ; get first user integer (m)
        cmp          EAX, -1
        je           error
```

```
        lea         EDX, prompt
        put_str     EDX
        lea         EAX, n
        push        EAX
        call        get_int        ; get second user integer (n)
        cmp         EAX, -1
        je          error

        push        m
        push        n
        call        gcd            ; find gcd(m,n)

        lea         EDX, msg1
        put_str     EDX
        push        EAX
        call        print_int      ; print gcd(m,n)
        done

error:
        lea         EAX, msg2
        put_str     EAX
        done

; get_int function
;       Reads in user entered characters, skipping white space,
;       until an integer is found.
; Return value:     EAX = 0 if no error in getting an integer.
;                   EAX = -1 if error encountered in user input.
; Parameters: address of integer variable
get_int:
        push        EBP
        mov         EBP, ESP

        mov         ECX,0          ; calculated int is in ECX
process_ch:
        get_ch                     ; character returned in EAX (AL)
        cmp         EAX, space     ; skip white space characters
        je          process_ch
        cmp         EAX, newline
        je          process_ch
        cmp         EAX, tab
        je          process_ch


get_loop:
        cmp         EAX, 48
        jl          not_a_digit
        cmp         EAX, 57
        jg          not_a_digit    ; if dropped through to here,
                                   ; have a good digit
        sub         EAX, 48
```

```
        imul        ECX, 10
        add         ECX, EAX
        get_ch
        jmp         get_loop

try_another:
        get_ch
not_a_digit:
        cmp         EAX, space
        je          try_another
        cmp         EAX, newline; newline marks end of the integer
        je          done_line
        cmp         EAX, tab
        je          try_another  ; if fallen through to here,
                                 ; have a bad character
        jmp         bad_int

done_line:
        mov         EAX, 0       ; return value, integer is good
get_int_rtn:
        mov         EBX, [EBP+8] ; get address of integer
        mov         [EBX], ECX   ; store integer
        mov         ESP, EBP
        pop         EBP
        ret         4

bad_int:
        get_ch                   ; clear out remainder of input line
        cmp         EAX, newline
        jne         bad_int

        mov         EAX, -1      ; return value, integer is bad
        mov         ECX, 0
        jmp         get_int_rtn
; end of get_int function


; gcd function
; Calculates the greatest common divisor of 2 positive integers.
;       Defined recursively by
;               gcd(m,n)     = m,                 if n=0
;                            = gcd(n, m mod n),   if n>0
; Return value: EAX = greatest common divisor
; Parameters: 2 positive integers
gcd:
        push        EBP
        mov         EBP, ESP

        cmp         DWORD PTR [EBP+8], 0
        jg          n_greater    ; if n>0, return m (base case)
        mov         EAX, [EBP+12]
        jmp         gcd_rtn
```

```
n_greater:
        push        [EBP+8]       ; first parameter to gcd
        mov         EAX, [EBP+12]; calculate m mod n
        mov         EBX, [EBP+8]
        mov         EDX, 0        ; divisor is EDX:EAX
        div         EBX           ; remainder is in EDX
        push        EDX           ; second parameter to gcd
        call        gcd

gcd_rtn:
        mov         ESP, EBP
        pop         EBP
        ret         8
; end of gcd function

; print_int procedure
;       Prints out a positive integer. Pushes each digit onto the stack,
;       and then pops them back off in reverse order to print out.
; Parameter: the integer to print out
print_int:
        push        EBP
        mov         EBP, ESP
        mov         ECX, base
        mov         EBX, ESP      ; to remember how many digits
                                  ; pushed on stack
        mov         EAX, [EBP+8]  ; get the integer
        cmp         EAX, 0        ; special case if integer is 0
        jne         more_digits
        push        0
        jmp         more_chars

more_digits:
        mov         EDX, 0
        idiv        ECX           ; does EDX:EAX / ECX, EAX = quotient
        push        EDX           ; EDX = remainder
        cmp         EAX, 0
        jg          more_digits

more_chars:
        pop         EAX
        add         EAX, 48
        put_ch      EAX
        cmp         ESP, EBX
        jne         more_chars
        put_ch      newline
        mov         ESP, EBP
        pop         EBP
        ret         4
; end of print_int procedure

end
```

SUMMARY

Procedures have both advantages and disadvantages when it comes to assembly language programming. The disadvantage is that extra code is needed to deal with parameter passing, register saving and restoring, and stack accesses. Yet procedures also have advantages. They facilitate modular code, and they are easy to use in high-level languages. Fortunately, compilers provide the benefit of generating assembly code automatically.

PROBLEMS

1. What is the point of having procedures in a high-level language? Is there a point to having a procedure mechanism in assembly language?

2. When is the use of a stack necessary in implementing procedure call and return mechanisms?

3. What would go wrong with a program that was written with the instruction

   ```
   jmp procedure
   ```

   used for procedure calls instead of

   ```
   call procedure
   ```

   without first saving a return address?

4. How is a nested procedure call different from a recursive procedure call? Are the returns different?

5. Write Pentium code for a procedure called `switch` that takes two (integer) parameters and swaps them. Write the code that implements a procedure call and the procedure. Pass the parameters on the stack.

6. Write Pentium code for a procedure called `switch` that takes two (integer) parameters and swaps them. Write the code that implements a procedure call and the procedure. Pass the parameters in registers EAX and EDX.

7. Write a Pentium function that reads a single line of characters entered by the user into an array, and then returns as the function value the address of the array.

8. Write Pentium code for a procedure that initializes each element of a 50-element array of integers. Initialize each element to -1. The one parameter passed to this procedure will be the base address of the array, and it will be passed on the stack.

9. Write Pentium code for a function that returns a count of the number of non-NULL characters in an array of 80 characters. The one parameter passed to this function will be the base address of the array, and it will be passed on the stack.

10. Write a Pentium function that sums the elements of an array. The function receives as parameters the base address of an array of integers and the number of elements in the array.

11. Write a Pentium function that implements the factorial function recursively. Factorial is recursively defined by

```
factorial(0) = 1

factorial(x) = x * factorial(x-1)
```

12. Write a modular Pentium program to calculate the integer X, where

$$X = \sum_{i=1}^{n} i$$

The user enters an integer value for n.

13. Write a modular Pentium program that prints out a user-entered integer in base 3, base 5, and base 8 (octal).

14. As an alternative to passing parameters on the stack or in registers, space for parameters to a procedure could be allocated in memory. Show declarations, the call, and a skeleton of a procedure that uses this method of parameter passing. When does this method of parameter passing fail?

CHAPTER
12

THE ASSEMBLY PROCESS

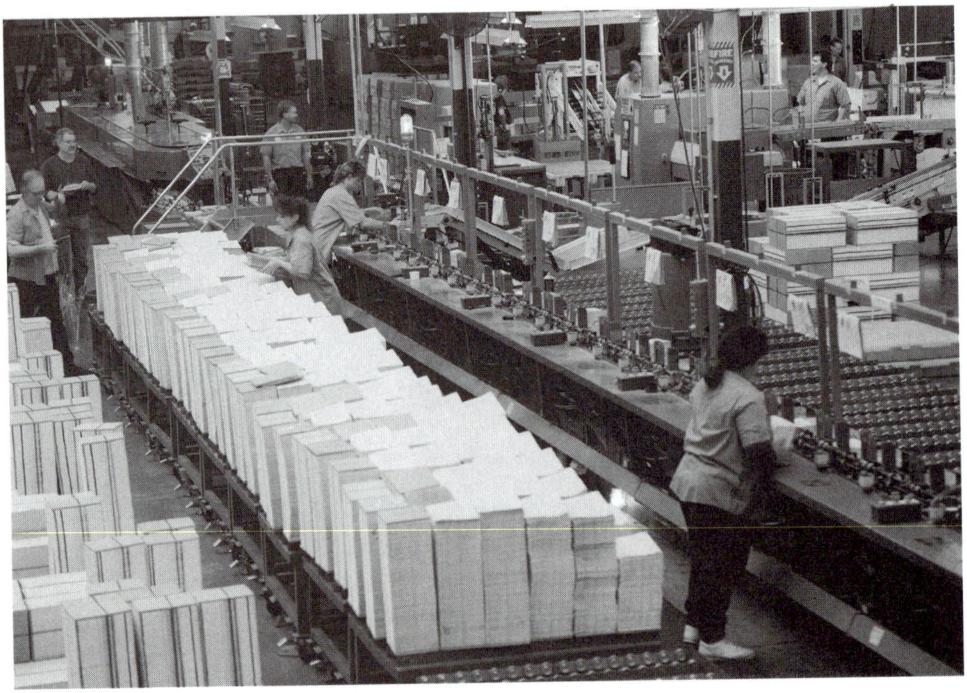

This chapter discusses the process of translating Pentium assembly language code into the code that can be understood and executed by a Pentium processor. This translation is called **assembly**, and the program that does assembly is an **assembler**. The chapter begins by describing what an assembler must do. It provides a lengthy example that goes through the entire assembly process. The subject of linking and loading is then discussed.

12.1 WHERE ASSEMBLERS FIT IN, AND WHAT ASSEMBLERS DO

The assembly process starts out with assembly language source code. The source code consists of directives, data specifications, and instructions. A processor understands and executes **machine code**. The code portion is a sequence of binary bits that form instructions. The job of reducing the program from assembly language to machine code is mechanical (deterministic), but repetitive and tedious.

The first step in getting from source code to machine code is one that is now most often done before assembly even begins. It is often the case that a sequence of instructions is repeated several times within a program. An example of a sequence of instructions might be the operation that sends a single character to the display. A mechanism that lets the programmer define sequences of instructions, and associate these instructions with a key word or phrase, is called a **macro**. Macros allow the programmer to define a level of abstraction. The assembler provides the convenience of macros by substituting the key word with the sequence of instructions. The macro that does the `put_ch` code is given in Figure 12.1. When a Pentium program has this macro defined, and the code contains the symbol `put_ch`, it is a macro call, and the macro's defined code is substituted instead. A macro language specifies rules for the substitution of text. This example shows a macro procedure, with a required parameter to the procedure given the variable name `thechar`. A more modern approach uses a **preprocessor** program to scan through the source code, substituting the key word or phrase of a macro with the expanded code sequence. Other functionality such as including source files and setting conditional text (for example, the `ifdef` in C) is also placed into the preprocessor.

A current trend in the assemblers associated with newer architectures is to increase their functionality. Traditionally, the assembly language of a processor was what an assembly language programmer used to write programs. This is what Pentium assembly

```
EXTERN putchar:NEAR

put_ch        MACRO         thechar: REQ
       push          eax          ;; save registers
       push          ebx
       push          ecx
       push          edx
       push          thechar
       call          putchar      ;; standard C function
       add           esp, 4       ;; pop thechar from stack
       pop           edx          ;; restore registers
       pop           ecx
       pop           ebx
       pop           eax
ENDM
```

Figure 12.1 The `put_ch` macro.

language is. There is a one-to-one correspondence between instructions in an assembly language source program and encoded instructions in the machine code. The complexity of an assembler is not greatly increased by having it take on a bit of what was once only a compiler's role. The assembler can translate more abstract instructions understood by the assembler into the assembly language instructions given by the instruction set.

The assembler's job is to produce a mapping of what the initial state of the memory should be plus some other information in order to be able to place a program in memory and execute it. This includes both the data sections and the code sections, although all or part of the data sections may be initialized during the execution of the program. The assembler places all this information in a file for later use by a link and load program. The linker and loader takes the information produced by assembly and initializes memory so that the program can be executed.

An assembler has two major tasks. It must translate assembly language code into machine code, and it must assign addresses for all symbolic labels. To accomplish its tasks, the assembler scans through the source code program to be assembled from beginning to end. On a line-by-line basis, the assembler encounters directives, data declarations, and instructions. The assembler deals appropriately with each line, generating the mapping of memory that will represent the initial state for the program when executed.

12.2 MACHINE CODE FORMAT AND CODE GENERATION

An assembler mechanically translates assembly language to machine code. It must produce a complete image of what the initial contents of memory must be for the program to run. A computer can execute an instruction in the form of machine code; it does not understand the character strings that form assembly language instructions. Besides translating the instructions to machine code, it is the assembler's responsibility to assign addresses. As the assembler reads source code, it can do both the translation of instructions and address assignment.

The Pentium assembly language contains unusual features not found in other more recently designed architectures. Its machine code instructions are of variable length, an extra byte is utilized to specify addressing modes for some operands, and there are repeat prefixes. Presented here is a subset of the Pentium instruction set and their machine code. This chapter is intended to explain how assemblers work and what they do. For a complete specification of the machine code generated, see the *Pentium Processor Family Developer's Manual, Volume 3: Architecture and Programming Manual.*

The assembler's initial image of memory contains assumptions about how memory space is utilized. In practice, the regions of memory containing instructions and data are usually separate. This is easily facilitated in the Pentium architecture when the segmented memory model is used, since the code is allocated to a different segment than the data. Instructions are usually stored beginning at location 0x0000 0000 independent of the assumed memory model. Figure 12.2 diagrams one possibility for memory allocation of the various parts of a running program. Each program is allocated space for its data, its instructions, and its stack.

As the assembler scans through the source code, it keeps track of the memory image that it is producing through the use of its own internal data structures. One of these data

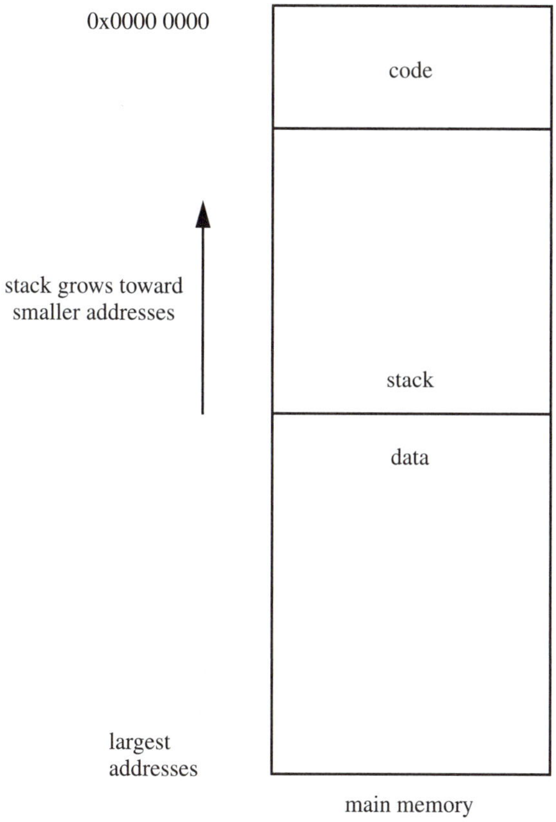

Figure 12.2 Allocation of memory (simplified) for the Pentium architecture.

structures is the **symbol table**. This table lists the labels (symbols) together with the addresses assigned to each label by the assembler. There will also be data structures describing the assembler's view of the data section and the code section.

An Example Program

To illustrate the assembly process, this section shows the generation of machine code for a simple program. The program adds up the squares of the first 20 positive integers. It leaves the result in a variable.

The assembler receives as input assembly language source code. By starting with a C program, and using the compiler's output of an assembly language listing, a realistic example is formed. Figure 12.3 shows the simple C program for summing the squares of the first 20 positive integers. The assembler would receive as input a Pentium version of the program, like the one shown in Figure 12.4. It is a slightly modified version of the assembly language generated by a C compiler. The directives have been modified, comments have been added, and the labels have been changed. The code is exactly the same as that generated by a compiler. It is easy to understand the code when it is broken up into three parts. The first part of the code consists of the six instructions that begin at label `main`. The compiler considers that any program will be called by the operating system as a function (or procedure). It therefore contains a prologue that sets up a stack frame as the first thing in a program. The last part of the code is the function's epilogue. It consists of

```
/* C program to sum squares of the first 20 positive integers. */

main()

#define NUMINTEGERS 20

{
        int squares;
        int counter;

        counter = 1;
        squares = 0;
        while ( counter <= NUMINTEGERS ) {
                squares = squares + (counter * counter);
                counter = counter + 1;
        }
}
```

Figure 12.3 C program to sum the squares of the first 20 positive integers.

the instructions from label `LABEL2` to the end of the program. The epilogue restores register values and deallocates the stack frame. The portion of code from `LABEL1` to `LABEL2` implements the functionality of the C program given in Figure 12.3. Space for the two variables local to the program are allocated space on the stack. An offset from the frame pointer (EBP) is used to access the two variables. The compiler also uses the value of the C code constant `NUMINTEGERS` directly in the code as an immediate operand.

What the Assembler Does

The assembler begins the process of assembly by scanning the Pentium source code program line by line. For each line it encounters, it takes appropriate action regarding the generation of machine code and symbol table. The first line scanned in the example starts with `title`. The assembler really has no use for the title in terms of generating machine code; so it reads and throws away all remaining characters on the line.

The second line of the source code starts with the ';' character. The assembler recognizes this character as the start of a comment. Assembly language comments generate no machine code. As the ';' character is encountered, the assembler skips over all remaining characters on the line. At the beginning of the next line, it continues scanning.

The next nonblank line is the line with the string `.486`. A string beginning with a period, like `.486`, indicates an **assembler directive**, also called a **pseudo-opcode** or **pseudoinstruction**. Directives are a way of providing information for the assembler. Directives are not instructions to be executed when the program is run, and the assembler does not generate machine code as a result of a directive. This particular directive identifies for the assembler exactly which member of the Intel family of architectures to generate code for. Since there are differences in the instruction sets offered by the processors within the x86 family, the assembler must ensure that the correct machine code is generated. For example, if the code were to be generated for 80286, the assembler must flag as an error any operand that specified the 32-bit form of a register, such as

```
title       sumsquares
; Pentium program to sum squares of the first 20 positive integers

.486
.model flat, stdcall

_squares = -8
_counter = -4

.code
main:
       push         ebp                      ; set up stack frame, pointers
       mov          ebp, esp
       sub          esp, 8
       push         ebx
       push         esi
       push         edi

       mov          DWORD PTR _counter[ebp], 1
       mov          DWORD PTR _squares[ebp], 0
LABEL1:
       cmp          DWORD PTR _counter[ebp], 20
       jg           LABEL2
       mov          eax, DWORD PTR _counter[ebp]
       imul         eax, DWORD PTR _counter[ebp]
       add          DWORD PTR _squares[ebp], eax
       inc          DWORD PTR _counter[ebp]
       jmp          LABEL1
LABEL2:
       pop          edi                    ; remove stack frame
       pop          esi
       pop          ebx
       leave
       ret          0
end
```

Figure 12.4 Pentium program to sum the squares of the first 20 integers.

```
add    EAX, 1
```

The 80286 has only 16-bit forms of the registers, not 32-bit forms.

The `.model` directive specifies two pieces of information for the assembler. The word `flat` tells the assembler to use the flat memory model instead of the segmented memory model. The word `stdcall` tells the assembler to use a standardized naming convention for symbols and to use a standardized calling convention for procedure/function calls.

This program contains no data section. The small number of needed variables are kept on the stack. If present, a `.data` directive identifies a section within the source code that contains declarations. The `.data` directive tells the assembler that what follows are not instructions, but declarations of data associated with the program. This information is needed by the assembler in order that it assign addresses in the correct section of memory. It allocates space in the data section as appropriate for each declaration.

As an example, if the assembler reads the line

```
flag          dd     -1
```

it picks out pieces of the line, called **tokens.** The tokens are strings or numerical values that are separated by spaces or other punctuation marks, such as a colon. The first token read on the line is the symbol (label) `flag`. An address must be assigned to all symbols; so the assembler assigns the first available memory location for this symbol. If this line of the source file comes after a `.data` directive, the assembler knows to assign the first available location within the data section. Remember that the assembler is a program. As such, it can keep track of various addresses easily, since they are variables within the program. Both the symbol and its assigned address are placed in the symbol table. After dealing with the symbol, the next token read by the assembler will be the directive `dd`. This directive tells the assembler to allocate one doubleword (four bytes) of data section space at the location assigned to the symbol `flag`. The third (required) token will specify an initial value for the doubleword allocated. The assembler sets the bits in the memory image it is forming. In this example, an initial value of negative one (-1) is specified; so the assembler places the 32-bit two's complement representation of the integer negative one into the doubleword at the location it assigned for the symbol `flag` in its data structure representing the data section.

There are two lines in the source code that specify values to be used as immediates. This specification of `_counter` and `_squares` uses macro processing to specify offsets from the frame pointer where the variables are kept. The immediates are used in the code generation.

After this is the line that contains the `.code` directive. This directive tells the assembler that the lines that follow will contain instructions. Subsequent addresses assigned and machine code generated will be allocated within the code section of the memory image. As the tokens comprising an instruction are encountered, the assembler produces machine code for each instruction. The assembler assigns an address to the instruction. The first instruction is placed at the beginning of the text section. Subsequent instructions are assigned to consecutive addresses, and the memory image of the code section is filled in accordingly.

The first token read after the `.code` directive is the label `main`. The assembler identifies `main` as a label because it ends with a colon. As with all newly encountered symbols, the assembler must assign an address. The address assigned for the symbol `main` will be 0x00000000. This is the location of the next address available for code. Since the first instruction has not yet been assembled, it is also the first address possible. For each entry in the symbol table, there must be a label and its assigned address. Each time the assembler sees a symbol as it works its way through the source code, it checks the symbol table to see if the symbol is there. If not, then a new entry is put into the table.

The first time a symbol is encountered, it may be either as an operand in an instruction, or as a label. If it is as a label, the next available address is assigned to the label. If it is as an operand, then an address for the symbol may not yet have been assigned. Therefore, the machine code that depends on the address assignment cannot be completely generated at that instant. Completion of the machine code must wait until the label is assigned an address. A common and simple solution to this problem is to have the assembler make two passes over the source code. The first pass enters symbols into the table as they are encountered. It also enters addresses as they are assigned by keeping track of the amount of space required for each declaration and instruction even though the machine code for the instruction itself is not generated. By the end of the first pass, all symbols will be entered in the table and have been assigned addresses. The second pass uses the symbol table to complete the generation of machine code.

A two-pass assembler is less efficient than a one-pass assembler. The one-pass assembler keeps a list of locations in machine code that have not yet been completed due to lack of addresses for symbols. As addresses are assigned, the assembler uses them to complete the machine code in the list. At the end of the first pass, all symbols have been assigned addresses, and therefore all the machine code will be completed.

Machine Code from Instructions

The generation of the machine code is the task that remains. After assembling and loading the program, the computer will fetch and execute the machine code instructions. The computer must interpret the bits of the instruction fetched, determining precisely what operation is to be performed. It must also be able to determine what operands to use, where to put the result, and what instruction to fetch next. To accomplish this task, the machine instructions are broken into fields. All instructions contain an opcode field. This field contains information about the operation to be performed, and it implies the number of operands that will follow.

The opcode field also contains information about the addressing modes of the operands in the Intel family of architectures. For the Pentium architecture, the opcode field is either 8 or 16 bits. What Intel has done with many instructions is to reduce the overall size of the instruction by encoding addressing mode information in the opcode. In this way, a unique opcode also describes an operand. An alternative machine code instruction encoding (not used by this architecture) would be to assign a single opcode for an instruction, and then assign further bits in the instruction to describe the operand. This would require a larger number of bits for the instruction's encoding. As the x86 architecture was defined at a point in time when main memory space was significantly smaller than it is today, the usage of smaller instructions was a positive design decision. As memory space has become much more plentiful, it has become more important to implement machine code instructions of a fixed size.

Following the label `main` is the first instruction within the program:

```
push   ebp
```

From the table given in Appendix C, the opcode for this instruction is written as 50h + *rd* . The value given for *rd* listed in a table in Appendix C modifies the opcode based on the register given as an operand. The operand, register EBP, is assigned the value 5. Therefore, the opcode for this instruction is 55h. Since the opcode for this instruction completely describes the single operand, this one byte is the machine code for the instruction. The assembler places this bit pattern at the first available location in the memory image it is creating. This machine code will be placed at location 0x0000 0000. The assembler also updates its internal pointer to the next available location for an instruction to 0x00000001, the next byte in memory.

After assembly, linking, and loading are done, the program will be executed. The first byte of memory where an instruction is located is fetched and decoded. The decoding of the instruction reveals the intended operation involved, the single operand, and that this `push` instruction is encoded in a single byte. During execution of the instruction, the processor will update its program counter (called an instruction pointer by Intel). It adds the value one to the program counter, since the size of the instruction executed is one byte. The assembler must assign to the next sequentially available address, 0x0000 0001, to the second instruction in the code, or the fetch and execute cycle will not work.

After completing the assembly of the first instruction within the code, the assembler continues scanning on the second line. There it encounters another instruction:

```
mov    ebp, esp
```

The opcode for this instruction where both operands use a register addressing mode is 0x8b. Like many Pentium instructions, this one-byte opcode is followed by a second byte that encodes the addressing mode information needed for both operands. The standard form of this byte is called a ModR/M byte, and it is given in Figure 12.5. Operand specification on this architecture may incorporate the addressing mode for an operand into the opcode, resulting in a one-byte instruction, or there may be either one or two bytes following the opcode that describe the addressing mode of the operands. If an immediate operand is specified, or if there is an address required by the addressing mode, then this immediate value or address is placed after the addressing mode information within the instruction.

Intel calls the second byte of addressing mode information a SIB byte. It has three fields as shown in Figure 12.6. Only a few addressing modes require a SIB byte following a ModR/M byte to give addressing mode information. Values for the fields are given in a table in Appendix C.

To form the machine code for the instruction

```
mov    ebp, esp
```

the first step is to find the appropriate opcode. There are two possible choices for opcode, 0x8b or 0x89. Opcode 0x8b is chosen by the compiler. Both operands using register mode

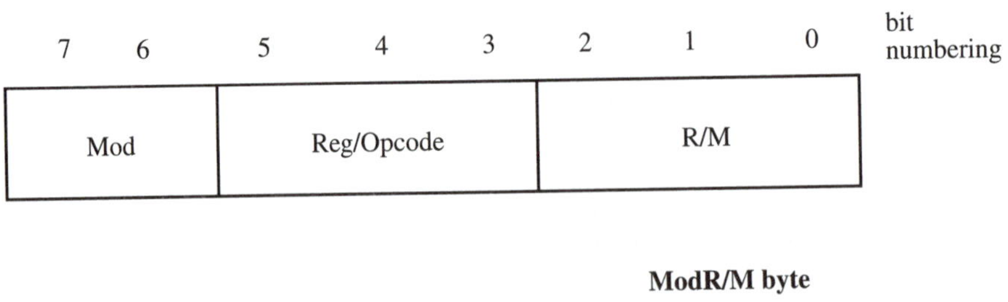

Figure 12.5 The ModR/M addressing mode byte.

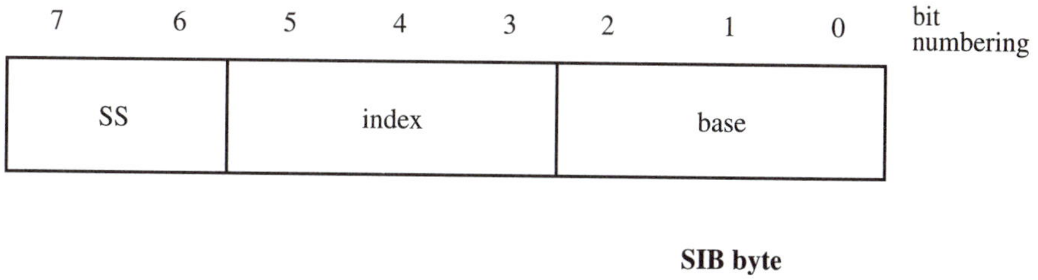

Figure 12.6 The SIB addressing mode byte.

allow this choice of opcodes. Using the information in the table, a ModR/M byte is needed to describe the addressing mode of the second operand (source operand). The first operand's (destination operand) register is designated by the Register/Opcode field of the ModR/M byte as 101 (register EBP). The Mod and R/M fields are found in a separate table accessed by the addressing mode of the source operand. Since the source operand is register mode, the Mod field is 11, and the R/M field is 100. The machine code for the entire instruction is the two-byte sequence 0x8b ec.

The assembler continues is this manner, assigning each subsequent instruction to the next available address, and generating the machine code for each instruction.

The generation of machine code is straightforward until the second `mov` instruction at address 0x0000 0009:

```
mov    dword ptr _counter[ebp], 1
```

It provides a second example for describing addressing mode information. The opcode chosen for this `mov` instruction is 0xc7, since the source operand uses an immediate addressing mode. From the table, this instruction will require a ModR/M byte for addressing mode information. The instruction (c7 /0) also specifies that the Register/Opcode field of the ModR/M byte contains the value 000. The Mod and R/M fields are as given in the table for a base displacement addressing mode. The displacement is -4, the value given for the symbol `_counter`. This value can be encoded into eight bits; so the addressing mode will be disp8[ebp]. Mod field bits for this addressing mode are 01, and R/M field bits for this addressing mode are 101. The 8-bit immediate encoding for the value -4 follows the ModR/M byte. The 32-bit immediate for the value one follows this byte in the machine code. The machine code for the entire instruction is 0xc7 45 fc 01 00 00 00, and its generation is described in Figure 12.7. Note that immediate values (and addresses) in the machine code are always given least significant byte first.

Figure 12.8 contains a partial translation of the program into machine code. There are two instructions that have not been completely specified. Completion of these instructions requires addresses. The assembler must use the addresses in the symbol table to complete the calculations.

A completed symbol table for the code is given in Figure 12.9. An assembly language requires a label as an operand to specify the target address of a control instruction. In the machine code for the instruction, however, the target address is expressed not as an

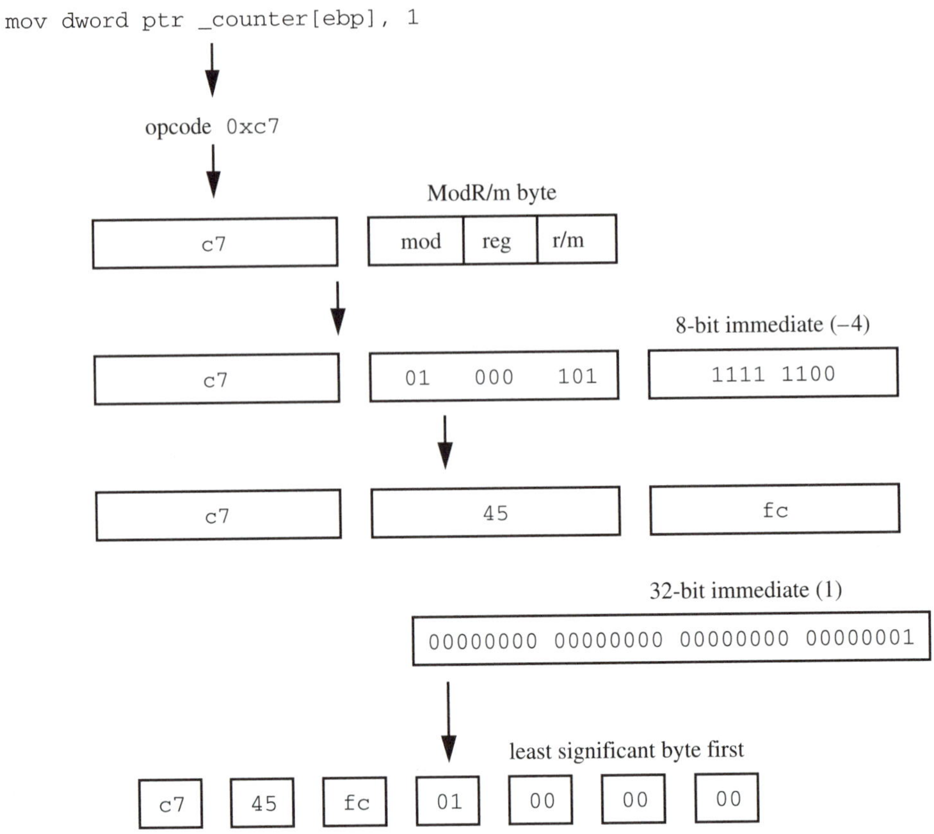

Figure 12.7 Machine code generation for `mov dword ptr_counter[ebp], 1.`

absolute address, but rather as a displacement, or offset, from the address of the control instruction. That is, the addressing mode is PC-relative.

The machine code specifies the offset from the current PC (program counter). During execution, if the jump or branch is to be taken, the offset is added to the value in the PC. The result is then placed back in the PC, and the next instruction can be fetched. It is the assembler's job to calculate the necessary offset given the addresses defined in the symbol table. The formula used in calculating the offset for control instructions is

offset = target address – address of instruction following control instruction

This offset is defined in terms of bytes. It is given as a 32-bit two's complement value. A two's complement value is used because the offset may be positive or negative. If the target address appears later in the code than the control instruction, then the offset will be positive. If the target address is earlier in the code than the control instruction, then the offset will be negative.

The offset is given in terms of the address of the instruction *following* the control instruction. It might be more intuitive to the assembly language programmer if the offset calculation used the difference between the target address and the address of the control instruction itself. The complexity of the calculation is the same for the assembler either

Pentium Assembly Language	Address (in hexadecimal)	Machine Code (in hexadecimal)
`main:` `push ebp`	0x0000 0000	55
`mov ebp, esp`	0x0000 0001	8b ec
`sub esp, 8`	0x0000 0003	83 ec 08
`push ebx`	0x0000 0006	53
`push esi`	0x0000 0007	56
`push edi`	0x0000 0008	57
`mov DWORD PTR _counter[ebp], 1`	0x0000 0009	c7 45 fc 01 00 00 00
`mov DWORD PTR _squares[ebp], 0`	0x0000 0010	c7 45 f8 00 00 00 00
`LABEL 1:` `cmp DWORD PTR _counter[ebp], 20`	0x0000 0017	83 7d fc 14
`jg LABEL2`	0x0000 001b	0f 8f ?? ?? ?? ??
`mov eax, DWORD PTR _counter[ebp]`	0x0000 0021	8b 45 fc
`imul eax, DWORD PTR _counter[ebp]`	0x0000 0024	0f af 45 fc
`add DWORD PTR _squares[ebp], eax`	0x0000 0028	01 45 f8
`inc DWORD PTR _counter[ebp]`	0x0000 002b	ff 45 fc
`jmp LABEL1`	0x0000 002e	e9 ?? ?? ?? ??
`LABEL2:` `pop edi`	0x0000 0033	5f
`pop esi`	0x0000 0034	5e
`pop ebx`	0x0000 0035	5b
`leave`	0x0000 0036	c9
`ret 0`	0x0000 0037	c3

Figure 12.8 Machine code for the program that sums the squares of the first twenty integers.

Symbol	Address (in hexadecimal)
`main`	0x0000 0000
`LABEL1`	0x0000 0017
`LABEL2`	0x0000 0033

Figure 12.9 Symbol table for the program that sums the squares of the first twenty integers.

way, and the hardware can be designed to work faster if the address of the instruction following the control instruction is used. The size (number of bytes) of the control instruction is easily calculated. The reason for using the address of the instruction following the control instruction in the calculation is given by the way the instruction fetch and execute cycle works. The step that updates the PC is most often implemented so that it occurs in parallel with the execution of the instruction. Therefore, at the time the offset is to be added to the PC, the PC has already been updated to point at the instruction that follows the control instruction. The assembler is written to ensure that the offset it calculates takes this into account.

For the `jg` instruction, the assembler will calculate the offset to be

$$\begin{aligned} \text{offset} &= \text{address } \texttt{LABEL2} - \text{address of instruction after } \texttt{jg} \\ &= \text{0x00000033} - \text{0x00000021} \\ &= \text{0x00000012} \end{aligned}$$

The assembler will therefore place the 32-bit two's complement value

0000 0000 0000 0000 0000 0000 0001 0010

directly after the `jg` opcode to complete the machine code for the instruction.

Calculation of the offset to be placed after the opcode in the `jmp` instruction is the same as the calculation for the `jg` instruction.

$$\begin{aligned} \text{offset} &= \text{address } \texttt{LABEL1} - \text{address of instruction after } \texttt{jmp} \\ &= \text{0x00000017} - \text{0x00000033} \\ &= \text{0xffffffe4} \end{aligned}$$

Like most architectures, the Pentium has a way of placing an **absolute address** in the machine code, instead of an offset. An absolute address may be the target address of a control instruction. At execution time, the address is taken from the instruction and placed in the program counter. This form of addressing is not used for control instructions in the Pentium when the flat memory model is used. It only appears for control instructions when the segmented model is used. The Pentium does place an absolute address in the machine code for a `lea` instruction.

The completed machine code for the example program is given in Figure 12.10.

Pentium Assembly Language	Address (in hexadecimal)	Machine Code (in hexadecimal)
`main:` `push ebp`	0x0000 0000	55
`mov ebp, esp`	0x0000 0001	8b ec
`sub esp, 8`	0x0000 0003	83 ec 08
`push ebx`	0x0000 0006	53
`push esi`	0x0000 0007	56
`push edi`	0x0000 0008	57
`mov DWORD PTR _counter[ebp], 1`	0x0000 0009	c7 45 fc 01 00 00 00
`mov DWORD PTR _squares[ebp], 0`	0x0000 0010	c7 45 f8 00 00 00 00
`LABEL 1:` `cmp DWORD PTR _counter[ebp], 20`	0x0000 0017	83 7d fc 14
`jg LABEL2`	0x0000 001b	0f 8f 12 00 00 00
`mov eax, DWORD PTR _counter[ebp]`	0x0000 0021	8b 45 fc
`imul eax, DWORD PTR _counter[ebp]`	0x0000 0024	0f af 45 fc
`add DWORD PTR _squares[ebp], eax`	0x0000 0028	01 45 f8
`inc DWORD PTR _counter[ebp]`	0x0000 002b	ff 45 fc
`jmp LABEL1`	0x0000 002e	e9 e4 ff ff ff
`LABEL2:` `pop edi`	0x0000 0033	5f
`pop esi`	0x0000 0034	5e
`pop ebx`	0x0000 0035	5b
`leave`	0x0000 0036	c9
`ret 0`	0x0000 0037	c3

Figure 12.10 Completed machine code for the example program.

12.3 LINKING AND LOADING

The assembler generates machine code. The machine code alone is not enough to be able to execute a program. Before execution, the machine code must be loaded into memory. The question that needs to be answered is where in memory will the code be put? The obvious answer is that the code must be placed in memory at precisely the locations specified by the assembler. The code will not work correctly otherwise.

Real situations arise in which it is not feasible to assemble an entire program. Situations also exist in which it is not possible to place assembled machine code at the location assigned by the assembler. Consider the case where a large program is being developed by more than one programmer. Each programmer works separately on a different module, and each module is assembled separately from the others. When the program is ready to be executed as a whole, it needs to be loaded into memory. Yet the separate assembly will result in the problem that all modules are specified to occupy the same memory space. Figure 12.11 depicts small portions of two separately assembled modules, both requiring placement in the same memory space.

There are also situations in which a symbol is defined within one module and referenced by code in another module. A common example of this is a procedure call where the procedure is defined within a separate module. The assembler cannot complete the machine code for the procedure call instruction because it does not have the target address.

The solution to these difficulties comes just before program execution. **Linking** and **loading** a program positions the various segments of machine code and data, and it handles all unresolved references. The assembler generates as much of the machine code as it can, and it identifies all locations within the code that cannot be completed. Linking and loading resolves any references that cross module boundaries, and places the various modules in memory in order to execute the program. All addresses or references that depend on addresses within the code must then be fixed, since the modules will be placed in memory at locations that differ from those assumed by the assembler. The program that does linking and loading goes by different names in different systems. It may be called a linking loader or a load and go program.

Address	Assembly Language		Machine Code (in hexadecimal)
	Module 1		
0x0000 0000	`push`	`ebp`	55
0x0000 0001	`mov`	`ebp, esp`	8b ec
0x0000 0003	`sub`	`esp, 8`	83 ec 08
0x0000 0006			
	Module 2		
0x0000 0000	`mov`	`-4[ebp], 0`	c7 45 fc 00 00 00 00
0x0000 0007	`add`	`eax, ecx`	03 c1
0x0000 0009			

Figure 12.11 Separately assembled modules requiring the same memory space.

When the program is to be loaded into memory and executed, the linker and loader defines where the code and data for each module are to be placed within memory. This fixes the starting address (base address) of each module. Any location within a module can be expressed relative to the module's starting address. To place the modules, the assembler calculates and provides the number of bytes required for a module to the linking and loading program. The amount of memory space required by each module is needed to ensure that the correct amount of space is set aside for each module, and that parts of modules do not overlap.

To facilitate later linking and loading, the assembler also needs to identify each part of the memory image it creates that may need to be fixed in the linking and loading step. The identification can come in the form of two tables. One of the tables identifies all code and data that rely on address definitions. Examples of this within the Pentium architecture are control instructions and other instructions that contain an absolute address, like the `lea` instruction.

The second table generated by the assembler contains any address assignments that are permitted to be used outside the module. All high-level languages have a way to express the exporting of symbols. A C language example of a variable defined elsewhere is

```
main()
{
        extern int count;

        count = 0;
        return 0;
}
```

The definition of the variable `count` may be in a separate module as

```
int count;
```

The tables generated by the assembler are given to the linker and loader program. They give enough information to find the bytes of memory to be fixed and know how to fix them. Enough information to find the bytes to be fixed consists of the base address of the segment, an offset from the base address of the segment, and an identification of what needs to be fixed.

An example contrived to show what happens during linking and loading is given in Figure 12.12. Small portions of a program that is spread across two modules are shown. The figure shown contains the information produced by the assembler. Note that the assembler is assumed to start both data and code sections at address 0x0000 0000. All addresses assigned are then offsets from the starting address of a segment. It is further assumed that Module 1 and Module 2 are separately assembled. Byte offsets are needed to identify the starting address of code to be fixed.

Module 1 has no symbols to be exported; so there is no table showing exports. Module 2 has a symbol for export. The label `sort` is assigned by the assembler at an offset of 0xabc0 from the Module 2 code base address. Module 2 shows no code that would need to be fixed; so no table is shown.

Module 1 does contain a jump (`call`) to a location outside the module's boundaries. Therefore, the linker and loader program will search other modules' export tables to find a

MODULE 1

Offset	Contents	Memory image (in hexadecimal)
0x0000 0000	`array dd 100 dup(0)`	
0x0000 0000	`lea eax, array`	8d 05 ?? ?? ?? ??
0x0000 0008	`call sort`	e8 ?? ?? ?? ??
	. . .	

starting byte (within module) to be changed	type	address needed
2 (code)	absolute address	base of module's data + 0
9 (code)	jump target	external symbol: sort

MODULE 2

Offset	Contents	Memory image (in hexadecimal)
	. . .	
0x0000 abc0	`sort: add ecx, 20`	81 09 14 00 00 00
0x0000 abc6	`jmp done_sort`	e9 35 0f 00 00
	. . .	
0x0000 bb00	`done_sort:` `ret`	c3

symbol for export	address
sort	base of module's code + 0xabc0

Figure 12.12 Memory image and tables generated by assembler for partial code example.

relative address for the label `sort`. The Module 1 table will be completed as shown in Figure 12.13.

Loading the program into memory for execution entails placing each module's memory image in memory and fixing the relative addresses within the modules. For this example, there are three segments to be positioned in memory: the data section for Module 1, the code section for Module 1, and the code section for Module 2. Assume that these segments are placed in memory as given in Figure 12.14. Note that the various segments have no implied order in memory. The linker and loader program is free to place the segments in any order at any available location in memory. It cannot split a segment among free blocks of memory, but it can reorder the segments. Once the memory image is copied into the assigned positions in memory, the linking loading program works its way through the tables, fixing the addresses within the image. After fixing the image, memory contents will be as given in Figure 12.15. Once loaded in memory, the program is now ready to be exe-

Starting Byte (within module) to Be Changed	Type	Address Needed
2 (code)	`lea` instruction	base of module's data + 0
9 (code)	jump target	base of module 2's code + 0xabc0

Figure 12.13 Module 1 table after completion.

Segment	Base Address Assigned
Module 1 data	0x0044 0000
Module 2 code	0x0088 0000
Module 1 code	0x00a0 0000

Figure 12.14 Segment locations in memory.

Address	Contents	Assembly Code Represented
	. . .	
0x0044 0000		`array dd 100 dup(0)`
	. . .	
0x0088 abc0	81 09 14 00 00 00	`sort: add ecx, 20`
0x0088 abc6	e9 35 0f 00 00	`jmp done_sort`
	. . .	
0x0088 bb00	c3	`done_sort: ret`
	. . .	
0x00a0 0000	8d 05 00 00 44 00	`lea eax, array`
0x00a0 0008	e8 c0 ab 88 00	`call sort`

Figure 12.15 Contents of memory after loading.

cuted. The PC is loaded with the address of the first instruction to be executed. This starts the program running.

The efficiency of linking and loading is critical to a computer system. A moderately large program may have more than 5000 modules to be linked and loaded. Database programs are an example of this. Whenever the program is to be run, it must be linked and loaded before execution begins. So linking and loading must be fast. To facilitate this, data structures for holding the memory image and tables, and algorithms for placing the code and fixing it, must be carefully chosen.

SUMMARY

An assembler's task is to create a memory image for a program, plus enough information for later linking and loading. This requires an assembler to translate assembly language source code into machine code and assign addresses. The job is tedious, but straightforward. More modern assembly languages allow programmers to write source code that does not match the instruction set offered by the architecture. Such abstraction requires the assembler to synthesize more abstract code out of the instructions available.

PROBLEMS

1. Hand assemble the following Pentium code. Start instructions at address 0x0000 4400.

```
push   ecx
inc    eax
dec    esp
pop    edx
```

2. Hand assemble the following Pentium code. Start instructions at address 0x0008 0400.

```
add    eax, 26
push   eax
pop    ebx
```

3. Hand assemble the following Pentium code. Start instructions at address 0x0000 aa00. Assume that label `label1` is assigned address 0x0010 ffe4.

```
add    ebx, ecx
sub    eax, 15
mov    dword ptr label1, eax
```

4. Hand assemble the following Pentium code. Start instructions at address 0x00ab cd00.

```
                 and    dword ptr [eax], 0a0a0b0bh
                 jge    j_label
j_label:         mov    4[esp], -1
```

5. Hand assemble the following Pentium code. Start instructions at address 0x0008 8800. Start data at address 0x0004 4400.

```
.data
count            dd 0

.code
loop:            inc    count
                 mov    eax, dword ptr count
                 inc    eax
                 cmp    eax, 100
                 jz     loop
```

6. Hand assemble the following Pentium instruction.

```
add    12[ecx + eax*4], edx
```

7. Hand assemble the following Pentium code. Start instructions at address 0x0008 8300.

```
label1:       jle    label2
              mov    4[esp], 24
              not    -4[ebp + 4*eax]
              sub    ecx, eax
              jz     label1
label2:
```

8. Disassemble the following Pentium machine code. Make up label names as needed. The code starts at address 0x0040 0000. Each line of the table is a separate instruction.

Address (in hexadecimal)	**Contents (in hexadecimal)**
0x0040 0000	55
0x0040 0001	81 c4 04 00 00 00
0x0040 0007	48
0x0040 0008	81 0b cd 00 ab 00

9. Disassemble the following Pentium machine code starting at address 0x0000 0000.

   0x2d 09 00 00 00 23 c8 89 44 24 04

10. Write Pentium code that checks for overflow in the case of the multiplication.

```
imul  ecx
```

    Overflow for this problem is where the result will not fit into 32 bits.

11. Explain how it is possible for the `add`, `and`, `or`, `sub`, and `xor` instructions all to have the same one-byte opcode, 0x81.

CHAPTER

13

INPUT AND OUTPUT

Computers are only useful if they can accept input from, and provide output to, the outside world. These operations, referred to collectively as I/O (input/output), have been presented as the result of simple statements. The commands provide abstractions for complex operations that have been conveniently ignored up to this point. This chapter explores the important aspects of this vital part of the computer system.

Input and output devices vary enormously in their purpose, function, cost, and speed. Traditionally, most I/O devices have had a mechanical component to them, and this resulted in the notion that I/O devices are generally slow to respond relative to the time to execute an instruction. The existence of many varieties of I/O devices makes characterization difficult. Few specific statements can be made that apply to all I/O devices. It is possible to identify three general categories of I/O devices, according to their function. Figure 13.1 categorizes some I/O devices.

User Interface Devices	Mass Storage Devices	Outside Communication
keyboard printer mouse video display scanner video camera	disk magnetic tape drive CD ROM drive	networks and gateways modem

Figure 13.1 I/O device categorization.

Input	Input and Output	Output
keyboard mouse scanner CD ROM drive	disk magnetic tape drive network modem	video display printer

Figure 13.2 Alternative I/O device categorization.

Within the category of user interface devices, traditional output devices physically change the world around them, and traditional input devices detect when a physical change has occurred. These are the classic communication paths that allow computers to interact with their surroundings. They vary enormously in every respect (such as speed, format of data, and intended use), except input devices supply data to the computer, and output devices accept data from the computer. Common examples of such input devices are keyboards and mice. Common examples of such output devices are video displays and printers.

Typical examples of mass storage devices are disks and magnetic tape drives. Disks can be either rigid or flexible. This class of devices holds large quantities of data, and these devices act in most ways more like the memory than like I/O devices. However, most such devices are slow when compared to the speed of main memory. For that reason, their behavior has traditionally been controlled in a manner similar to other I/O devices.

Increasingly, computers are hooked together by networks, in order to communicate with other computers. This comes under the category of outside communication. Some computers are a few inches away, and others are on the other side of the world (or beyond). The connections to networks that facilitate communication between computers often exhibit long delays relative to instruction execution speeds, and so networks can be treated as if they were conventional I/O devices.

An alternative classification of I/O devices is based on whether they do input, output, or both input and output. Figure 13.2 lists some I/O devices based on this categorization. For the most part, the variety of critical characteristics within each of these categories is greater than the variety between categories. It is convenient to lump all the I/O devices together for the purpose of interactions between processor and I/O device. However, there are some important differences between devices. Many user interface devices deal with relatively small amounts of data, and at relatively slow speed. Human-activated input devices generally do not generate more than a few dozen characters of data per second.

Many output devices are limited to a few thousand characters per second, although some go much higher. It is common that the computer is expected to respond to a single input character. Both extended memory devices and networks tend to transfer larger blocks of data, ranging from hundreds or thousands to millions of characters.

13.1 TYPICAL I/O DEVICES

All I/O devices tend to be unpredictable in their behavior. Mechanical devices are limited by their physical properties, which means that they generally do not provide or accept data at the rate that the processor would like to receive or supply it. It might be too fast, or it might be too slow, but the rate is dictated by the mechanical characteristics of the device. Output devices can only accept a limited amount of data, and then they must have a way of refusing more data until they are ready to receive more. Input devices may be arbitrarily slow. A keyboard will not produce any data at all until a user presses a key. An input device must have a way of telling the processor when it is ready to supply data. It is generally necessary, therefore, that the processor accommodate itself to the I/O device rather than the other way around. The computer must accept data when the input device has it available, and provide data only when the output device is ready to accept it.

The Keyboard

The ASCII keyboard is a simple input device. It has a very low data rate. The fastest typist cannot type as many as 100 characters per second. The keyboard detects when a key is touched. It reacts by sending a designated sequence of ASCII characters to the processor. For most keys, the keyboard sends a single ASCII character. The characters are said to be **mapped** to the keys. A table describes what character or sequence of characters gets sent to the computer for each key.

Some keys are treated differently, and pressing them does not result directly in the transmission of any data. Instead, these keys have the effect of changing the mapping of the other keys, and therefore changing the designated sequence of characters to be sent when another key is pressed. These keys, such as the SHIFT and CONTROL keys, have an effect only as long as they are held down. For example, the key designated as 'A' sends the ASCII character '`a`' (0x61) when it is typed. If the SHIFT key is down when the 'A' key is pressed, the ASCII character '`A`' (0x41) is sent to the computer. If the CONTROL key is down when the 'A' is pressed, the ASCII character 'soh' (0x01), sometimes designated control-A, or ^A, is sent to the computer. In addition to the SHIFT and CONTROL keys, computer keyboards often have several special keys that modify the effect of other keys. These keys may be referred to as the **alternate** key, the **meta** key, and so on. Each such key effectively doubles the number of possible designated sequences that can be sent to the computer.

Mappings of characters vary from keyboard to keyboard. For example, holding down both the SHIFT and CONTROL keys may send one character to the processor, a sequence of characters, or nothing at all; there is no standard behavior. Many combinations of special keys may simply send nothing. Some keys are programmed to send a sequence of characters to the computer when they are typed. The function keys are an example of this.

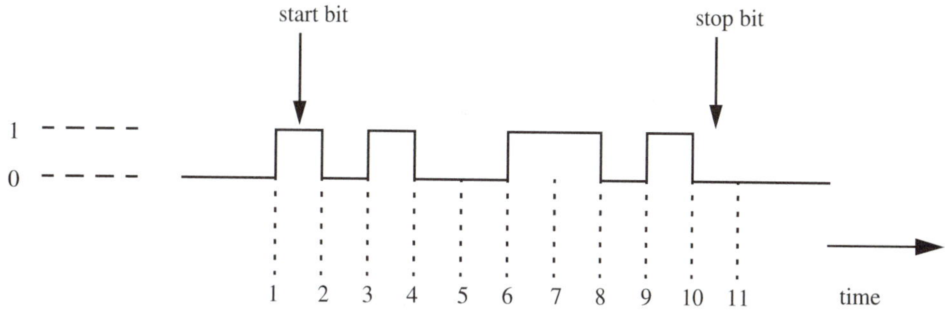

Figure 13.3 Serial signal to send the character 'M.'

Some keyboards simply notify the computer each time a key is pressed and each time a key is released. With the notification of these **events**, it is possible for the processor to remember which keys have been pressed, and change the mapping of different keys just as if the keyboard were to do it. This allows simplification of the keyboard. The keyboard always sends the same character, but it complicates the processor. The processor must remember which keys are pressed at all times.

The bits of an ASCII character are usually sent to the processor through a single wire, with the individual bits of the ASCII character sent serially. The rate at which these individual bits are sent is referred to as the **baud rate**, and it is given in units of bits per second. While a variety of transfer rates is possible, the processor must know approximately the rate at which the input device is sending the bits in order to recognize the data when they arrive. Since the keyboard has nothing to send most of the time, it must have a way of indicating to the computer when it has a character to send. It sends an extra bit at the beginning of each word, the **start bit**, to indicate that it is not sending the NULL character. It also must send an extra bit (or two) at the end of each character, the **stop bit**, to indicate that it is finished. The computer uses the stop bit(s) to detect the difference between a subsequent character being sent and nothing being sent. Figure 13.3 diagrams the 8-bit ASCII character 'M' sent serially down a wire. Each bit is sent by asserting its value for a fixed time period. Following the start bit, the binary sequence 01001101 is sent, most significant bit first.

A Display

A video display is a common output device. Displays can take a variety of forms, very simple to complex. A **glass teletype** is a device that imitates a typewriter, or teletypewriter. When a typewriter prints a sequence of characters, the position of each character is well defined. The platen moves to the left (or the print head moves to the right) so that each character is printed immediately to the right of the previous character. When the carriage return lever is activated, the platen moves the paper up one line, and aligns the print head with the left side of the page. Many typewriters are capable of backing up one space or skipping forward to a designated column. Teletypewriters have no capability to back up beyond the beginning of the current line.

An **ASCII terminal** consists of a keyboard and a display that transmit ASCII characters. A terminal is therefore both an input device and an output device. Like the display of a teletypewriter, the current line of text is visible at the bottom, and the position where the next character will appear is shown by a **cursor**, usually indicated by underlining the space, inverting the color of the display for that space, or causing the character to blink. When a carriage return is signaled, all the text on the screen is shifted up by one line, simulating the moving of the paper in a typewriter, and the cursor is moved back to the beginning of the bottom line. This action of shifting all the lines up by one line is known as **scrolling**. The cursor never leaves the bottom line in this simple display.

Each time a printable ASCII character is sent to the display of the terminal, it reacts by displaying the character in the position where the cursor was, and moving the cursor to the right, one position. When other, nonprinting ASCII characters are sent, the display reacts in a predictable way. For example, when the ASCII character 'cr' (0x0d) is received, the terminal moves the cursor to the beginning of the current line and does not scroll. When the ASCII character 'nl' (0x0a) is received, scrolling is initiated, but the cursor position is not moved. When these two characters are received in either order, the effect is one of moving the cursor to the beginning of the next line.

A more complex display allows the cursor to move around on the screen. Other nonprinting ASCII characters may be interpreted as instructions to move the cursor in different ways. For example, a character or sequence of characters means "move the cursor up one position." Another character, usually either 'bs' (0x08) or 'del' (0x7f), moves the cursor to the left one position. Still another character moves the cursor to the upper lefthand corner of the screen (a position called HOME), and so on. If the cursor is on the bottom line when an 'nl' character is received, then scrolling is initiated, and the cursor moves down one line. Often a sequence of characters is defined to move the cursor to an arbitrary position on the screen, although there is no standard for this operation. (The real problem, unfortunately, is that there are *many* standards.) A position must be conveyed in such a command, and this requires several characters' worth of data. It is convenient if all the ASCII characters can be used to convey positional information; so the typical protocol is to send a single, special character [for example, 'esc' (0x1b)] followed by a sequence of characters indicating the position. Of course, these must be understood not to be printable ASCII characters; so the use of the 'esc' character indicates "special character sequence to follow."

Terminals with many enhancements are generally referred to as smart terminals. Among the features of a smart terminal are the ability to clear the entire screen, clear the rest of the line from the current cursor position, highlight or underline characters, and special kinds of scrolling, such as reverse scrolling, or partial scrolling. Partial scrolling may be used, for example, to create a blank line in the middle of the screen by scrolling the top half only.

A smart terminal is actually a specialized piece of hardware that is controlled by a simple computer. This **controller** is responsible for receiving the characters from the processor and updating the screen appropriately. More complex displays are capable of manipulating individual dots on the screen, known as **pixels**, rather than simply printing the ASCII characters at predetermined points on the screen. Such displays are known as **bit-mapped** displays. Usually such a display has a more complicated interface to the processor, because the additional flexibility of the display requires more sophisticated communication to use it effectively.

The display and keyboard of a terminal are usually not directly connected, although they appear to be. The processor reacts to most keyboard events by capturing them and sending the appropriate character or sequence of characters to the display. In the typical case of a printable character, the computer simply sends to the display the same ASCII character received from the keyboard. This behavior is known as **echo**. When certain characters are typed, something different must happen. For example, when the 'cr' character is received from the keyboard, the computer must send to the display both the character 'cr' and the character 'nl.' Another example is what the computer must do when the backspace character is received. Usually sending the character 'bs' to the terminal simply moves the cursor back one space, leaving the cursor at a location still displaying the character in that location. If it is desired to clear the last character printed, most terminals must be sent a three-character sequence of a backspace character ('bs') followed by a space character, followed by another backspace character.

A Rigid Disk—An Extended Memory Device

A rigid disk or hard disk is an I/O device whose function is to increase the capacity of the memory system. The device differs from main memory in that a large **block** of memory is written in a short period of time. The data are blocked because the time required for reading or writing is so long, taking tens of thousands of times longer than reading or writing a word in main memory. It is also blocked because the disk does not inherently associate an address with the data stored; the identifying information must be stored along with the data.

Appropriate methods for reading and writing to a disk are based on the physical characteristics of the disk. Figure 13.4 shows some of these physical characteristics. A disk is made up of one or more **platters**. Each platter is physically similar to a compact disk. It has two sides, where each side is called a **surface** and the platters rotate at a fixed speed. There is a read/write arm for each surface, where each arm may have one or more read/write heads. The platters are all physically connected to a **spindle**, and they all rotate together around the axis of the spindle. All the platters are generally sealed as a unit, to keep out any elements of dust and dirt that could ruin the high-quality magnetic surface of the disk.

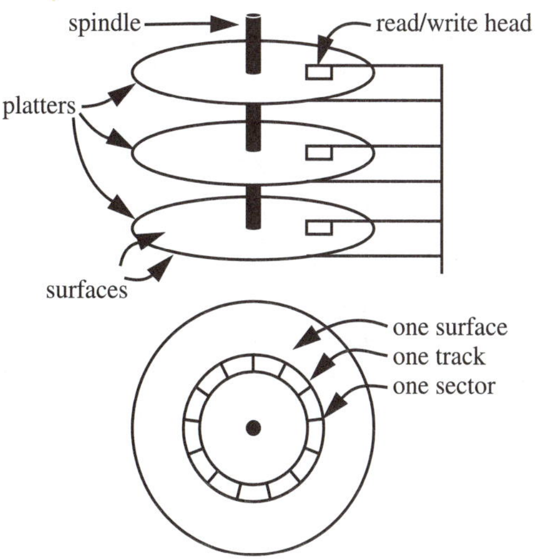

Figure 13.4 A hard disk.

The data on a platter are organized into **tracks**. Each track is a concentric circle. Taking all the tracks in the same concentric location on all the platters forms a **cylinder**. Within each track, the data are broken into **sectors**.

The disk must be first informed of the position where the data are to be read or written. This is in the form of an address. The read/write arm **seeks** the proper position (a cylinder), then informs the computer that it is ready to receive or transmit data.

After seeking, the disk must rotate until the correct sector is positioned under the read/write head, and reading or writing must occur at the appropriate moment. The disk must be supplied with a sequence of bytes when it is being asked to store information. These bytes must be supplied at the rate at which the device can accept them. If they are supplied too quickly, the device will lose them. If they are supplied too slowly, the device will have nothing to write as the sector rotates past the read/write head. Conversely, when the device is reading, it will supply data to the processor at its own pace. The processor must take the words when they are ready, or they are lost.

Thus the computer interacts repeatedly with the disk, first giving it instructions about from where the data should come or go, then providing it with the data to be written, or accepting the data that it provides. The rate at which a disk accepts or receives data is generally faster than other input or output devices, ranging as high as millions of bytes per second. Flexible (floppy) disks generally transfer data at a lower rate.

A Network Interface

It is difficult to characterize the communication of a computer through a network. Often the computer sends or receives blocks of data, as opposed to single bits. Some networks are capable of very high transfer rates, while others are quite slow. Transfers are often highly unpredictable, failing to respond at all for long periods, then quite suddenly providing large bursts of activity. The physical characteristics of any network may be described by the maximum number of bits per second that can be transferred, its **bandwidth**.

Networks are designed to handle certain kinds of transfers effectively. A **local area network** (LAN) is designed to facilitate communication among computers all located physically close to each other, generally less than one kilometer. A network better suited to transferring data among computers located far from each other is a **wide area network**. Like other I/O devices, a combination of hardware and software implements the functionality of a network.

13.2 THE PROCESSOR–I/O INTERFACE

At its most basic level, a processor must be able to send and receive bits from I/O devices. Some computers have special instructions to allow them to communicate with I/O devices. Consider a very simple computer system, as shown in Figure 13.5. It contains a processor, main memory, and two I/O devices comprising a simple terminal: a keyboard and display. When the program running on the processor needs to output a character, it executes an I/O instruction. Assembly language for such an instruction might take the form

```
output char
```

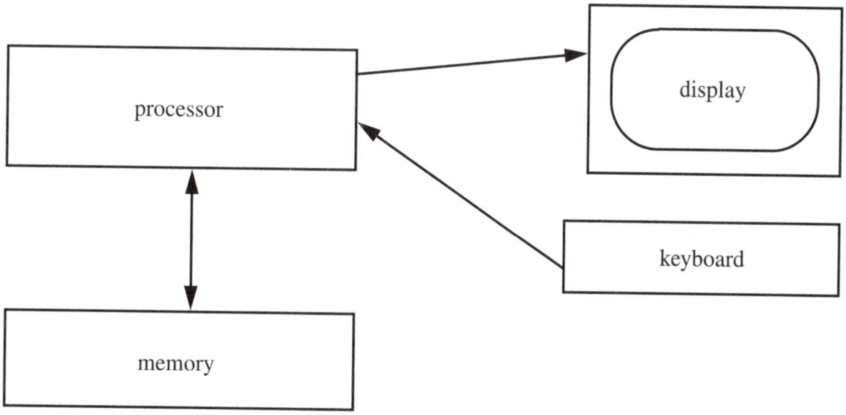

Figure 13.5 A very simple computer system.

where `char` is a byte containing the ASCII character to be displayed. The execution of this instruction causes signals to be sent down a wire connecting the display to the processor. At the display, the bits are decoded, and the ASCII character is placed on the screen.

Assembly language to get a character of input from the keyboard might take the form

```
input char
```

where the ASCII character code for the key pressed on the keyboard is placed into the byte variable `char`.

A difficulty with this simple setup arises. The processor (executing a program) can generate `output` instructions faster than the display can place the characters on the screen. The processor will be able to execute an `output` instruction every few nanoseconds (1 nanosecond = 10^{-9} seconds). A simple display cannot dispose of characters at that rate. The same sort of difficulty arises in conjunction with the keyboard. The rate that the user types is much slower than the rate that the processor can execute `input` instructions. The keyboard will have a place to keep the ASCII character typed by the user. When an `input` instruction is executed, this ASCII character is provided by the keyboard to the processor. There is no way for the processor to know when, and which, character was typed relative to the execution of the `input` instruction. If no new character was typed since the previous `input` instruction was executed, the processor may receive a character more than once.

The solution to this problem introduces the concept of device **status**. A device provides an indication of whether it is **ready** or **busy**. A ready device is ready and able to do what the processor wants it to do. A busy device is not able to do what the processor wants it to do. The keyboard becomes ready when it has a character to transmit. The keyboard becomes busy (not ready) as soon as it has sent a character to the processor, and remains busy until another character is typed. The display is ready when it is able to accept another character. The display becomes busy as a result of receiving a character to display. When it finishes displaying the character and is ready to receive another one, it changes its status to ready. Implementation of a status indication is as simple as allocating a single bit for the processor to look at before it executes input or output instructions. For some I/O devices, there may be other kinds of status information as well, such as the fact that an error occurred.

Input/Output Programming

Some computers have special instructions to allow them to communicate with I/O devices. One of the cleanest and simplest ways to communicate with an I/O device, however, is to design the hardware so that a region of the memory is not really memory at all, but rather a collection of communication channels to I/O devices. This is known as **memory-mapped I/O**. This approach allows a processor to communicate with I/O devices without separate I/O instructions. A memory access to a memory-mapped location provides a means of performing I/O. Most modern architectures provide support for memory-mapped I/O. The important concept here is that communication with an input or output device does not require an expansion of the instruction set. Note, however, that hardware is necessary to support this illusion; memory accesses to a memory-mapped I/O address must be intercepted and treated by hardware as an I/O operation.

Memory-mapped I/O implies that the hardware will be configured such that the memory needed for the status and characters is not physically located in the memory. Two locations are needed for each device, one for the status and the other for the data. Figure 13.6 diagrams this configuration. The memory location for the display's data is called `Display_Data`, and it is not in memory at all. It is physically located in the display, or more likely, in hardware called a **controller**. When the processor stores to location `Display_Data`, data are sent to a display device and the character so written appears on the display. Likewise, if the hardware is configured so that the memory location `Keyboard_Data` is not memory, but rather a communication channel to a keyboard, a load from that location would result in the data generated as a result of a keyboard event being sent to the processor. Thus the primary instruction in the code to do input is

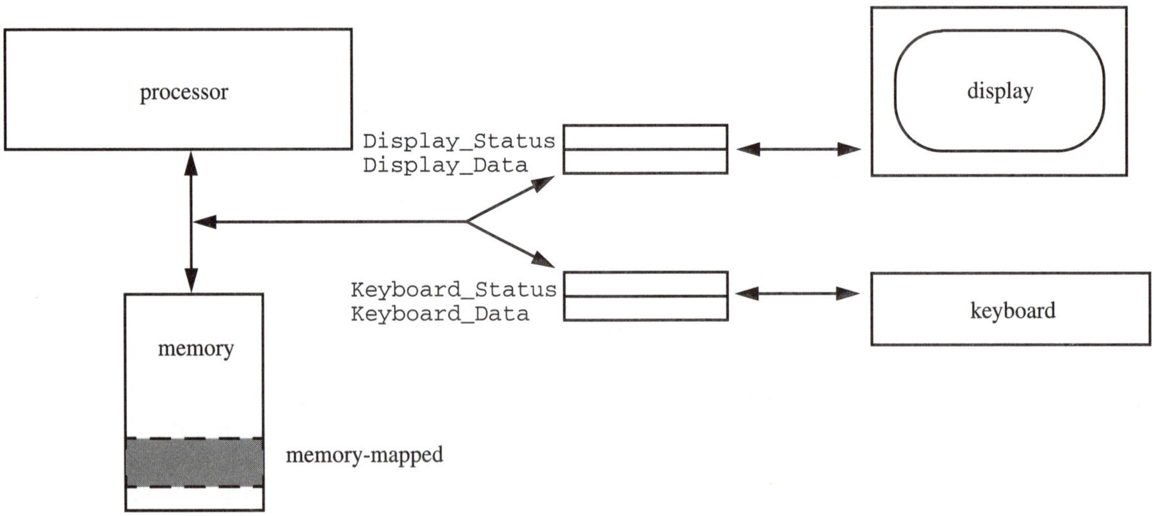

Figure 13.6 A very simple computer system showing memory-mapped I/O.

```
mov    EAX, dword ptr Keyboard_Data
```

and the primary instruction in the code to do output is

```
mov    dword ptr Display_Data, EAX
```

The code to do I/O functions must take into account the status of the device. Suppose that the status is implemented as a 32-bit register within a controller. The most significant bit of this status register is a bit that indicates if the device is ready. Further define the bit such that a 1 indicates the device is ready, and 0 indicates that the device is busy. Then executing the code

```
keyboard_wait:
       test   Keyboard_Status, 80000000h
       jz     keyboard_wait
       mov    EAX, dword ptr Keyboard_Data
```

implements an input function that waits until a key has been typed on the keyboard, and then gets a copy of the ASCII character in the least significant byte of register EAX. If no new character has been typed when this code is executed, then the status will indicate that the device is busy. This code will stay within the small loop (called a **spin wait loop** or **busy wait loop**), continually testing for a change in the keyboard's status. When a key is typed, the controller gets the ASCII character code in `Keyboard_Data`, and then changes the most significant bit of the status to indicate that the keyboard is ready. Within the loop, the result of the `test` instruction changes; so the loop is exited. The `mov` instruction then receives the character and places it into register EAX. The controller also must reset the status of the keyboard to indicate it is busy as the memory-mapped location `Keyboard_Data` is accessed. This will assure that the processor does not receive the same character twice.

A spin wait loop for an output device is strikingly similar to that for an input device:

```
display_wait:
       test   Display_Status, 80000000h
       jz     display_wait
       mov    dword ptr Display_Data, EAX
```

The two-instruction loop for the display continually checks the status of the display. When the display becomes ready, the `Display_Status` indicates this, and the loop is exited. The character is then sent to the display. Sending a character to the memory-mapped location `Display_Data` also causes the controller to change the display's status to busy.

Protection Issues

The spin wait loops used together with memory-mapped I/O provide a clean solution for doing input and output on the very simple computer system. However, there are likely no computer systems with only a processor, memory, and two simple I/O devices. The simple system is too simple to be realistic. A computer system is expected to handle a variety and greater number of I/O devices. Computer systems today are also expected to provide a **multiprogrammed** environment. In such an environment, the operating system is given responsibility for having more than one program running concurrently on a single processor. The operating system runs one program at a time, but provides the illusion of having multiple programs running at once. It does this by running only part of a program at one time. The operating system keeps track of where the program left off, in order to be able to continue its execution at a later time.

When the processor can be programmed to handle each byte that arrives from the input device, and every byte to be sent to an output device, this is known as **programmed I/O**. For a multiprogrammed system, there are two properties of I/O devices that make the solution using spin wait loops problematic. First, I/O devices are typically much slower than the processor, often by orders of magnitude. This means that a program is tied up for long periods in a spin wait loop waiting for devices to become ready when the processor could be making progress on another program. Second, input devices might have data ready while the processor is currently executing another program.

A third difficulty of having programs do their own I/O directly is a problem of synchronizing the usage of I/O devices. Suppose that two programs are to be executed on a simple computer system. The system has one printer, and both programs send output to the printer. Without further synchronization, the printer output of the two programs is likely to be interspersed.

A solution to all these difficulties is to place the responsibility of synchronizing access to I/O devices in the operating system. The operating system keeps track of what I/O device is accessible to each program, and ensures that programs do not interfere with each other. The operating system provides a method for programs to request I/O transfers. The spin wait loops presented may be used, but only within the operating system. This may be accomplished by having some I/O instructions that only the operating system is allowed to execute, or by restricting access to the memory-mapped locations to the operating system.

Asynchronous I/O Programming

Consider the problem of writing a string of 50 characters to a display. Each character may require, say, 1 millisecond to transmit to the display device (a moderately fast rate). If the processor can execute 10 million instructions per second, in 50 milliseconds it could execute approximately half a million instructions. Except for the spin-waiting instructions, the necessary number of instructions executed to write the 50 characters is probably under 500; so roughly 99.9% of the time is wasted in the spin wait loop executing unproductive instructions. If this happens often, the processor's computing power is being wasted. Consider how this power might be better used.

Separate the check for a ready device from the sending of a character to the device. This method involves two steps to accomplish the printing of the string. One step copies the string into a predefined location (a queue). This is procedure `printstring`. The second step is another procedure, `putnextchar`, which checks to see if the output device is busy. If the device is busy, it simply returns. If the device is not busy, it checks to make sure that there is a character in the queue waiting to be displayed, and it sends the character to the output device. It updates its pointers and returns. When `printstring` returns, only a single character at most will have been printed, but it returns quickly.

```
.data
putqueue    db   256
tp_put      dd   0              ; tail pointer
hp_put      dd   0              ; head pointer

.code
putnextchar:
      test        Display_Status, 80000000h
      jz          putret                  ; return if display not ready
      cmp         hp_put, tp_put
      je          putret                  ; return if queue empty
      inc         hp_put                  ; advance head pointer
      and         hp_put, 000000ffh       ; modulo queue size
      mov         EAX, hp_put
      mov         BL, byte ptr putqueue[EAX] ; get character to print
      mov         Display_Data, EBX       ; send character to display
putret:
      ret
```

Figure 13.7 Pentium code for procedure `putnextchar`.

The operating system must periodically call `putnextchar`. Each time it is called, a character will be sent if the device is ready. If the queue is empty, then there are no more characters to send, and the procedure returns. If a second string is to be displayed before the first has been completely sent, the second string can be carefully placed in the queue, concatenating the second string to the first, taking care to assure that there is contiguous memory space to hold the combined string. In cases where the queue is full, the procedure could spin wait, calling `putnextchar` constantly, until enough characters had printed so that space in the queue is available to copy the string. A sample coding for `putnextchar` is given in Figure 13.7.

An analogous scheme is possible for separating the check for keyboard input from the passing of a character to a program. The operating system periodically checks if a character is ready and waiting at the keyboard. This procedure is called `getnextchar`, and it behaves the same as `putnextchar`, returning without doing anything if the device is busy, indicating that no character is available. If a character is available, then it is read and placed into a queue of characters. Procedure `getachar`, is called by the user's program to request a character from this queue. If the queue is empty, then `getachar` spin waits, calling `getnextchar` until a character is available. A sample coding for `getnextchar` is contained in Figure 13.8.

This asynchronous solution allows more efficient usage of the processor while the I/O devices are busy, even if a large number of characters must be input or output. However, it has several drawbacks. First, there will be a period after an output device has become ready until the next call to `putnextchar`. During that time, the I/O device could be in use, but it is not. Thus characters are not being transmitted to the I/O device as fast as the I/O device can handle them. Second, the operating system must call `putnextchar` periodically, or the queue will never get printed. Failure to call `putnextchar` for an extended period results in degraded performance, but correct results. For an input device

```
.data
getqueue      db     256
tp_get        dd     0              ; tail pointer
hp_get        dd     0              ; head pointer

.code
getnextchar:
       test         Keyboard_Status, 80000000h
       jz           getret                       ; return if keyboard not ready
       inc          tp_get                       ; advance tail pointer
       and          tp_get, 000000ffh            ; modulo queue size
       cmp          hp_get, tp_get
       je           getret                       ; return if queue empty
       mov          EAX, tp_get
       mov          EBX, Keyboard_Data           ; get character
       mov          byte ptr getqueue[EAX], BL ; place in queue
getret:
       ret
```

Figure 13.8 Pentium code for procedure `getnextchar`.

like the keyboard, the operating system must call `getnextchar` often enough that it will not miss input characters. Such a failure gives incorrect results; if a second character is typed before the first one is read, the first will be lost.

13.3 DIRECT MEMORY ACCESS (DMA)

While user interface devices often transmit a small number of characters, both mass storage devices and network interfaces are designed to transfer larger blocks of data. For example, a text file may be stored on disk, and the file is to be copied into main memory. What is needed in this case is that the entire file be copied sequentially into memory. The transfer of such a file using programmed I/O would tie up the processor for an extended period of time. If the goal is low cost of hardware, using the processor in this way is perhaps acceptable. The large time required, and the ease with which it can be avoided, make attractive an addition that allows the processor to continue with other work.

The controller attached to a mass storage device, such as a disk, can be made more complex. It is then given the responsibility of making block transfers between main memory and the disk without requiring the use of the processor. The controller is actually a simple computer. It runs a program that does **direct memory access** (DMA). A diagram of such a system is given in Figure 13.9.

The processor sets up a transfer by giving commands to the controller. The processor tells the controller the details of a block transfer that needs to be done. The direction of transfer, size of transfer, and starting addresses in main memory and the disk are specified. The controller then does the transfer independent of the processor. The processor can run other programs while the transfer is in progress.

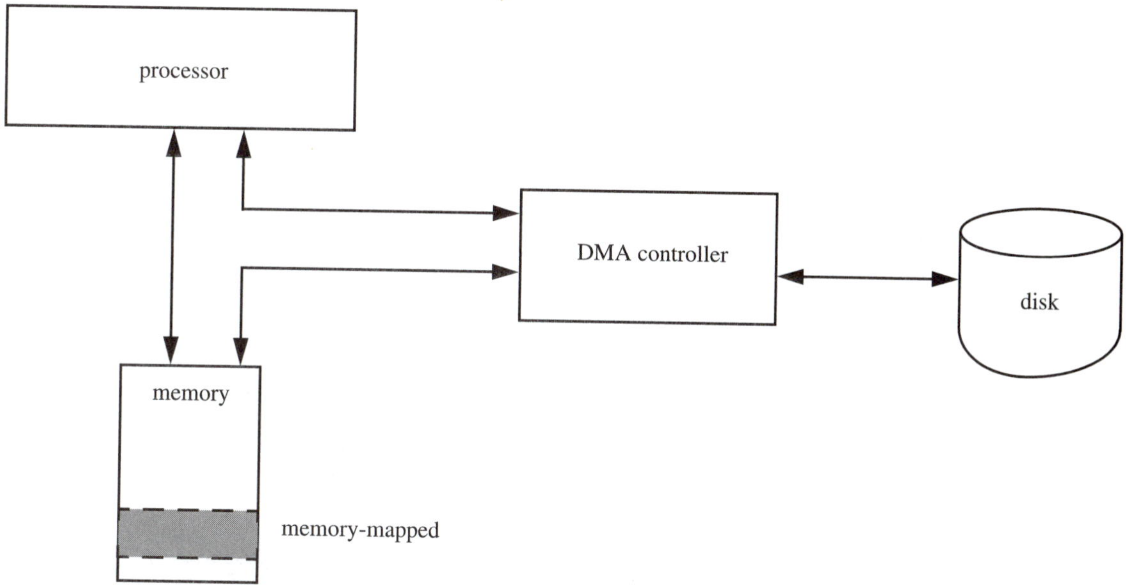

Figure 13.9 I/O using DMA.

SUMMARY

Computers are not isolated devices, and they are only useful if they can communicate. Communication can be with humans, with storage and other devices, or with other computers. Memory-mapped I/O allows an economy of instructions since no special instructions are needed to interact with an I/O device. The device can be treated as if it were memory, supplying and accepting data when it is addressed.

The key difficulty lies in synchronizing the transfer of information, since I/O devices are not synchronized to the internal speed of the processor, and the processor must accommodate the I/O device, whatever its idiosyncrasies. Testing the status of an I/O device allows the processor to determine if an input device is ready to transmit a character, or if an output device is ready to receive one. A status indication permits the processor to test the I/O device, supplying or receiving data at a rate acceptable to the device. While this solution is inadequate for high-performance systems, the method is simple, permitting a variety of I/O capabilities at modest cost. Accommodating the I/O device makes efficient use of the computer difficult because the devices may be demanding, providing or accepting data only infrequently, and at difficult-to-predict rates.

Direct memory access (DMA) provides a solution that deals with higher-speed devices. It allows the processor to execute programs while I/O transfers are taking place.

This chapter explored the use of special procedures to deal with I/O devices by queuing the data to be input or output and periodically checking to see if the I/O device was ready for service. This is only a partial solution because it is difficult to program a processor so that it checks at the right frequency. Chapter 14 explores a better solution, allowing the I/O device to interrupt the processor, demanding attention when the I/O device is ready for service.

PROBLEMS

1. Why is spin waiting a bad idea for input/output programming?

2. What would happen on a computer system that used a spin wait loop to print a character if a printer jammed?

3. Is asynchronous I/O a better solution than spin waiting for very fast I/O devices?

4. Does an assembly language programmer have any control over what type of I/O implementations are offered?

5. A processor sends characters down a wire to a simple output device. If the transmission of bits requires one start bit and two stop bits, with each bit requiring 2 microseconds to send, what is the baud rate?

6. A disk spins at 4800 revolutions per minute (RPM), transfers data at 4 Mbytes per second, and has a maximum seek time of 20 milliseconds. How long does it take to transfer a 1 Kbyte block residing on one sector?

7. Why should I/O functionality be handled by the operating system, instead of allowing the applications to handle it directly?

8. The processor sends commands to a DMA controller to set up a DMA transfer. How can this be accomplished?

CHAPTER
14
INTERRUPTS AND EXCEPTION HANDLING

A processor executes the instructions of a program in a well-defined, sequential order. Individual instructions take varying lengths of time to complete. An executing program generally has no concept of time other than the notion of "now." Each instruction is executed as quickly as possible, but there is no concept of deadlines or rate of execution. When an I/O device is ready to be serviced, the processor is expected to respond. But from the standpoint of the program, it is the I/O device that makes a request, and the processor can only ask the question "has the request occurred yet?"

I/O events are examples of external events that interact with a program. The processor accommodates external events by the process of **synchronization**. There are generally two categories of events that require the program to synchronize: events resulting from I/O and events resulting from the execution of another program. The previous chapter demonstrated one method for synchronizing events. The operating system performs some kind of test that succeeds or fails, depending on whether the anticipated event has occurred. It might spin wait on the event, repeatedly testing until it occurs. Alternatively the operating system might attempt to do other things, occasionally testing (polling) for the event occurrence.

Both spin waiting and checking periodically are problematic. Spin waiting wastes computing power whenever the processor must wait for an event. Moreover, some awaited events may never occur, or take an arbitrarily long time to occur; so the processor may get stuck waiting for one event and miss other events. Polling has the problem that the operating system must check periodically. Even if it is known approximately when the next event is likely to occur, it is difficult to schedule the check at the right time. Checking too soon means wasting time testing. Waiting too long to check means the I/O device must wait, an eventuality that can have serious repercussions. An efficient solution that guarantees correct operation is required.

One solution is to create a system with a separate processor dedicated to detecting and handling external events. In such a system, one processor could continuously test for such events and service them, while the other executed the program. To be fully general, each I/O device would require its own processor, since one computer trying to service multiple I/O devices might still face the original problem of responding to requests from one device while it is busy servicing another. If the servicing of requests from I/O devices can be handled quickly, however, a single processor might handle all the I/O devices testing each device serially for requests.

The use of a separate processor for handling external events transforms the problem of synchronizing with I/O devices into one of synchronizing with another processor. There must be a way for the processor servicing an I/O request to communicate with the processor executing the program. There are several possibilities, but the example from Chapter 13 suggests an obvious way: through a data structure stored in memory. In the previous chapter, the routines `getnextchar` and `putnextchar` were used together with `getachar` and `printstring` to overlap use of the processor. A separate I/O processor could execute the routines `getnextchar` and `putnextchar`, reacting immediately whenever an I/O device indicated that it was ready for service. Meanwhile the regular processor could execute `getachar` or `printstring` at appropriate points, whenever it wished to read a character or write one, respectively.

Such a method is not without problems. Care must be taken to assure that the two programs interact correctly. For example, suppose the I/O processor is executing the code for `getnextchar` and reads a character from the keyboard. After it determines that there is a character to be read, it changes `tp_get`, then reads the character from the keyboard, and only then actually writes the character into the memory location indicated by the variable `tp_get`. If the regular processor executes `getachar` concurrently and should happen to read `tp_get` immediately after it is modified, it might read the memory location indicated by `tp_get` before the I/O processor had written the new value into the memory, thus incorrectly reading the next character that should be supplied by `getnextchar`. Such a problem is known as a synchronization failure. To avoid such problems, communicating programs must guarantee that they update a data structure completely before the other program observes any of the changes. This requirement is referred to as an **atomic update** of the data structure.

14.1 THE MECHANISM

The notion of separate processors executing concurrently is an appealing concept, but providing multiple processors is expensive. An alternative mechanism has evolved over the years that accomplishes the same goal in a less costly way, by allowing a single processor effectively to execute more than a single program at a time.

This mechanism permits the processor to respond to an external stimulus, such as an I/O request, and interrupt the execution of a program. A combination of hardware and software transfers control to a different program, which can save the current state of the interrupted program. The request is serviced, and then the state of the interrupted program is restored. When control is returned to the interrupted program, it continues execution. It picks up where it left off, fetching and executing the first instruction that was not executed previously, and it continues as if nothing had happened. To the program, it appears as if nothing happened, except that some time has been lost. The mechanism is referred to as an **exception**. One class of exceptions is an **interrupt**. The relative timing of exception handling is given in Figure 14.1. The occurrence of an exception appears to the program as if a procedure call has been inserted, with no parameters being passed, and no results returned. Because an interrupt might occur after any instruction in the program, it is sometimes characterized as an **asynchronous procedure call**.

A combination of hardware and software is necessary to deal with exceptions. The hardware chooses the appropriate time to interrupt the program, and transfers program control to a program known as an **exception handler** written explicitly for the purpose of dealing with exceptions. The exception handler determines what event has just occurred to cause the exception, and decides what should be done about it. The exception handler might handle an I/O request immediately if no waiting is required, or it might transfer control to a program that will handle the request. The important point is that, when initially invoked by the interrupt mechanism, the exception handler must preserve the state of the program that was previously executing so that execution of the interrupted program may

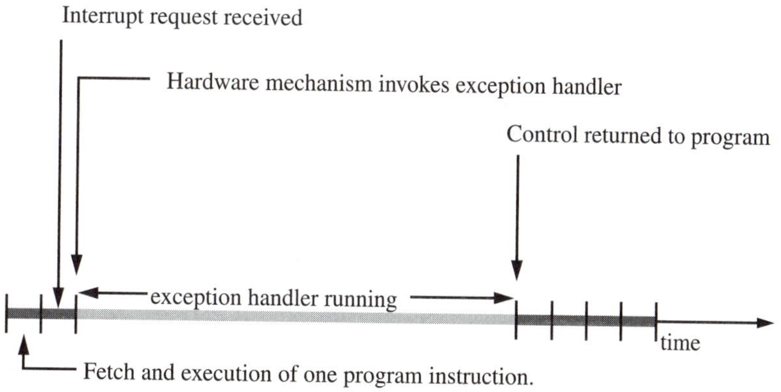

Figure 14.1 Relative timing of exception handling.

be continued at a later time. Like returning from a procedure call, the interrupted program continues execution with the next sequential instruction. Except for the lost time, and whatever explicit effects the exception handler might have had, the program appears to run continuously. Since a program has only a rudimentary notion of time to begin with, the loss of time is generally tolerable if it is not excessive. A few milliseconds is considered tolerable.

Since the code for the exception handler might be executed at any time, there can be no explicit preparation for it or direct use of its results as there is with a conventional procedure call. In other words, the exception handler cannot have parameters, nor can it return a value. The procedures `getnextchar` and `putnextchar` have no arguments, and they return no value. They communicate with a user-level program through variables accessed by `getachar` and `printstring`, which are called explicitly by the program. These restrictions must be taken into account when the computer is designed to assure that the computer can handle exceptions correctly and efficiently.

An additional constraint on the code of the exception handler concerns the use of registers. The exception handler must be written carefully to assure that register values being used by the interrupted program are not affected. Notice this is the same problem encountered with a procedure call except that the exception handler must do all the work, since it can be invoked at any time. Before returning control to the program, the exception handler must restore the registers to their original state.

The interrupt mechanism is more generally useful than just for handling I/O requests. There are a variety of reasons why it is desirable to interrupt the execution of a program. In addition to an I/O device demanding service, the operating system may reassert control of the processor by interrupting the execution of a program that is currently running. To provide this capability, the hardware generally provides a timer that will delay for a scheduled time, then send an interrupt request, returning control to the operating system. The duration of the delay is controllable by the operating system. In some computer systems, a timer or clock causes an interrupt to occur at fixed intervals.

Another use for the exception mechanism is to take care of extraordinary conditions that occur during the normal execution of a program. For example, when an arithmetic instruction results in overflow, it is important that this fact be recognized so that the program can deal with the error, or at least be terminated with an appropriate error message. It is inefficient if a program must itself explicitly test for overflow every time it performs an arithmetic operation. This situation can be handled cleanly by generating an exception. In this case, the exception is referred to as a **trap**, because it is a direct result of the execution of the program, not an external event. Notice that a trap is a synchronous event; if the same program is executed again using the same input data, a trap will occur again at the same place in the program.

Another reason for invoking the exception handler is if the program attempts to do something that is not permitted or not defined. For example, attempting to access a memory location outside the legal range will be designed to cause an exception, as will an instruction containing an undefined opcode. Yet another way the exception handler might be invoked is as the result of a request from the program. Some of the computer's capabilities are not available to a user program. For example, I/O devices cannot be read directly by a user-level program. When the program wishes to read from the keyboard, it must request the service from the operating system. Such a request can be made by explicitly invoking an exception.

An exception is either a trap or an interrupt. Synchronous exceptions, resulting directly from the execution of the program, are called traps. Asynchronous exceptions are called interrupts. Intel uses the term exception to describe traps.

14.2 THE ROLE OF THE OPERATING SYSTEM

The **operating system** is a program that allocates and controls the use of all system resources: the processor, the main memory, and all I/O devices. The operating system coordinates the I/O by interrupting running user-level programs to handle asynchronous I/O requests. In addition, the operating system can be written to allow multiple, independent programs to share computer resources while running concurrently. This is known as **multiprogramming**. The operating system avoids wasted processor time by recognizing when one program cannot proceed and switching control of the processor to a different program. An example of a program that cannot proceed is one that is waiting for keyboard input, when no key has been pressed. Instead of spin waiting for a key to be pressed, the operating system can run a different program. The operating system can service requests from external devices by interrupting the currently running program when a device demands service. It can control the use of the processor by deciding which program should be run next, and it can interrupt long-running programs periodically to allow other programs to run.

A **process**, or **task**, consists of a program to be executed, together with information about the state of execution of the program. Normally this means all the memory and all the registers of the processor, both general purpose and control registers (like the program counter). This must also include the condition codes. An operating system can control multiple processes running concurrently by using interrupts to allocate the processor to different processes periodically, giving each process some portion of the computing time. For each process that is not currently executing, the operating system must have memory allocated where it can store all the critical information about the state of the process, including the registers.

When a program executes an instruction intended to get a character from the keyboard, for example, and no character has been typed on the keyboard, the program cannot proceed until the character is typed. The instruction is blocked, and does not complete until a character can be returned to the program. For a user-level program, the conventional way this is handled is by invoking the operating system to fetch the character. If no character is available, then the operating system remembers that the process is waiting for the I/O device to provide a character, but allocates the processor to a different process until the character is received. The process is said to be **blocked** until the operating system returns control to the blocked process once a character becomes available.

An operating system may have a single exception handler, used for all programs and all kinds of interrupts, or an operating system may use pointers to multiple exception handlers. The critical code used by the operating system to decide what code should be executed next is called the **kernel**.

When multiple processes are running concurrently on a computer, the operating system must be able to control the system resources, allocating them according to a designated policy, and making sure that individual processes do not interfere with each other. The operating system must be able to protect itself from programs that attempt to defeat its policies, either accidentally or maliciously. For example, it must not be possible for user-level programs to modify, or even execute portions of, the exception handler. Allowing this would make it possible for a user-level program to bypass the operating system to accomplish its own objectives. The operating system must have privileges associated with it that normal user programs do not have. Privileges reserved for the operating system generally include access to all I/O devices, certain regions of memory, some special-purpose registers, and often special instructions.

14.3 THE PENTIUM EXCEPTION MECHANISM

The exception handling mechanism on the Pentium is much like the exception handling mechanism within other architectures. There is a combination of hardware and software that works together to accomplish its task. The hardware mechanism is invoked first eventually to allow the software that handles the exception (the exception handler) to run.

The hardware portion of exception handling hardware first detects an exception either on input pins or from within the processor's circuitry. Detection of a request comes as a **vector**, a value that classifies the type of the exception. Figure 14.2 gives a sample of some of the vectors for the Pentium. The vectors and type of exceptions are set by Intel. The vector is used as an index into an array that contains information about the location and handling of each exception. This array is called an Interrupt Descriptor Table (IDT), as given in Figure 14.3, and each element of the table is an 8-byte descriptor that Intel calls a **gate**. This table is located in memory. A control register in the processor, called the IDTR (Interrupt Descriptor Table Register), contains the base address of the table and a limit used to check that the vector does not attempt to access a descriptor not kept in the table. The table could contain as many as 256 entries. In implementation, the table may contain less than 256 if not all the maskable interrupts are used.

Vector	Exception
0	divide by zero
2	nonmaskable interrupt
3	breakpoint
4	overflow
6	invalid opcode
7	device not available
13	general protection
16	floating point error
18	machine check
32-255	maskable interrupts

Figure 14.2 Vector numbers and descriptions.

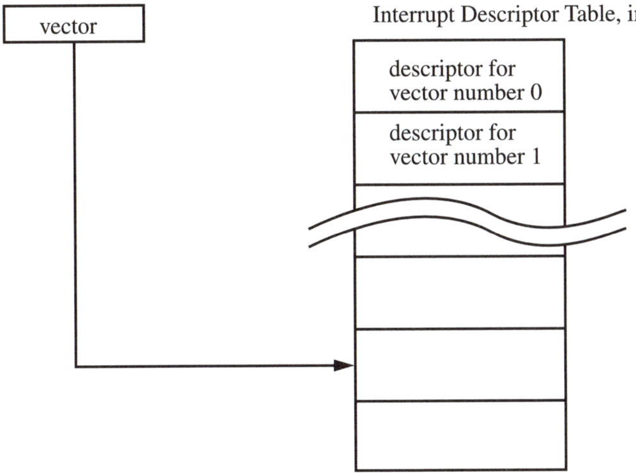

Figure 14.3 The Interrupt Descriptor Table.

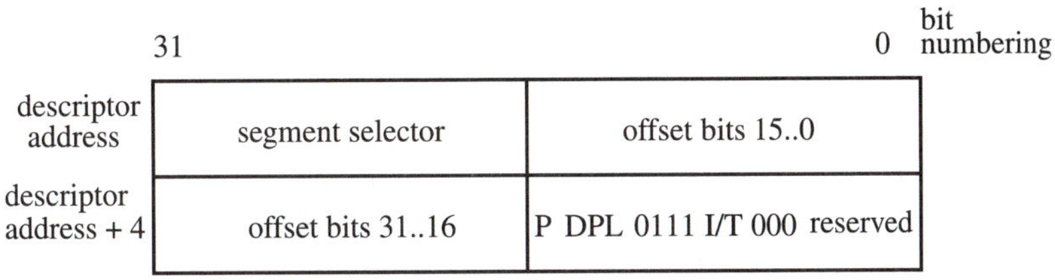

Figure 14.4 Contents of an interrupt or trap gate.

Figure 14.4 diagrams a single descriptor from the IDT. The hardware accesses the descriptor; it contains the information necessary to access the code that will handle the exception. The segment selector field accesses an entry in a table that contains the base address (starting address) of a segment of memory that contains the exception handler. The offset fields within the descriptor provide an offset from the base address of the segment to the starting address of the exception handler. The starting address of the exception handler is placed in the PC (Intel's Instruction Pointer) to execute it. The descriptor also contains other bits that give the processor information about how the exception handler may run.

The five least significant bits of the descriptor are reserved for use by Intel. Their contents are not defined for the programmer, and the programmer may not use the bits. Later architectures within the family may use these reserved bits for other purposes. The bit labeled I/T is a single bit that distinguishes whether the exception is an interrupt or a trap. It is 0 for an interrupt, and it is 1 for a trap. The bit labeled P identifies whether the segment containing the exception handler is currently resident in main memory or not.

State information from the interrupted program needs to be saved. The most convenient place to save the information is on a stack. Like other architectures, the Pentium supports multiple stacks, used for different purposes. There is a stack used exclusively when an exception is being handled. This stack is separate from the stack used by user-level programs. It is defined to function the same way as the user-level stack already described. The

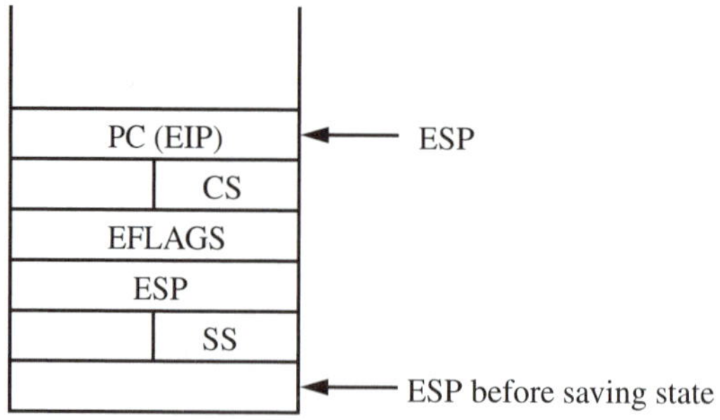

Figure 14.5 Exception handling stack after saving state.

stack grows from larger addresses toward smaller addresses, and the stack pointer is register ESP. Register ESP points to the data currently at the top of the stack.

Register ESP can only point to one stack at a time. Before changing the value in ESP to point to a different stack, the current value of ESP must be saved. This difficulty is present on many architectures, and it is solved in a variety of ways. Each way requires that the processor have at least one temporary location for saving the value of the stack pointer register before it is overwritten to point to a different stack. The Pentium architecture uses a table that contains the necessary information (including stack pointers) about each of the stacks.

Since an exception occurs due to something outside the control of the running user-level program, the state information saved on the stack must include everything the user-level program might need to continue its execution. The state therefore includes the PC (Instruction Pointer, EIP), EFLAGS register, current stack pointer (ESP), and the segment pointers CS and SS. The hardware pushes these values on the stack used for exception handling in the order given in Figure 14.5.

When all the state information is saved, new values for registers (like ESP) have been set, and the address of the exception handler is in the PC, the exception handler can be executed. It does whatever is necessary. If an interrupt was generated by an output device like a display, the exception handler for the display is executed. The handler is likely to check the status of the device. If the interrupt occurred due to the display becoming ready to accept another character, the handler makes note that the device is currently ready. An implementation that queues characters to be sent to the display will also check if the queue contains a character to send. If it does, then the handler will immediately send a character, causing the display to become busy again. The handler will also update the queue data structure and its pointers.

If the exception handler contains code that requires the use of a register, then the handler must save the register's values before overwriting it with a new value. The value will likely be saved on the stack (used by exception handlers).

After an interrupt has been handled, the processor should again run the program that was interrupted. It must appear to the interrupted program as if nothing happened, that is, no interrupt occurred. As the interrupt handler is code, the code must do something to cause the hardware to restore the interrupted program's state and restart the interrupted program executing again. The activation of the hardware on the Pentium is the instruction `iret`. The `iret` instruction restores the saved state by popping values off the stack (used by exception handlers) back into their appropriate places. The PC (EIP) will contain the address of the next instruction to be fetched within the user-level program. The EFLAGS register will be restored to the value it had just before the exception was taken. The stack pointer (ESP) will be restored to point again to the top of the user-level program's stack.

The handling of a trap differs from the handling of an interrupt in only small ways. One difference is likely to be the return location after the exception has been handled. As an example, consider the trap caused due to the detection of an attempt to divide by zero. The execution of a divide instruction in a user-level program causes a trap. The mechanism triggered for getting to the exception handler that deals with this condition is exactly the same as for an interrupt. However, it is likely that the exception handler cannot resolve the problem other than to issue an error message and cause the program's execution to terminate. The state information saved on the stack may be useful in issuing an error message that identifies the instruction that caused the trap. The return point within the user-level program is no longer useful. Instead, the piece of code to be executed after the divide by zero exception handler completes will be the portion of the operating system kernel that schedules program execution.

14.4 ADVANCED ISSUES IN EXCEPTION HANDLING

In order for the operating system to be able to control the system in a secure way, it must be able not only to take control away from other processes, but to control access to I/O devices. The operating system also must be able to assure that its own code and data are protected from programs that might, accidentally or maliciously, try to corrupt them.

Privilege and Protection

In the Pentium, these goals are accomplished by restricting the memory available to the program. This is a commonly used method of operating system protection. If a program tries to access the memory outside its own allocated space, an addressing error exception occurs, resulting in a trap to an exception handler as described above. It also protects the operating system code and data by making specific instructions available only to operating system code.

The Pentium architecture protects memory access through the use of privilege levels. Access to portions of memory as well as the execution of certain instructions are restricted according to a privilege level. The Pentium implements 4 privilege levels, numbered 0–3, with 0 being the highest privilege level, and 3 being the lowest, or most restricted, privilege level.

At each memory access and instruction execution, the privilege level associated with the currently executing program is compared with the privilege level required to access the memory location or execute the instruction. The **current privilege level** (CPL) is the privilege level of the program currently in execution. Its value (0–3) is stored in the code segment descriptor. The descriptors for program code and data are similar to the interrupt gates (descriptors) described. The privilege level required to access a memory location is the **descriptor privilege level** (DPL). The DPL is located in the descriptor for the memory segment. A comparison of the CPL with the DPL is done in the case of a data access. If the CPL is not the same or higher (corresponding to a lower privilege level value) than the DPL, a trap is generated, indicating that a memory access was attempted without the proper privilege level. For example, if the CPL is 3 (the lowest privilege level), and the DPL in the descriptor for the memory access is less than 3, a trap is generated. In this manner, data and code that must be protected are given a higher privilege level (a lower value than 3).

The CPL may be changed when control is transferred to code that uses a different code segment descriptor. One relevant example of this is when an interrupt is taken. The current code segment descriptor is saved (on the stack used by exception handlers). A new CPL is contained in the new code segment descriptor for the exception handler.

There is a stack associated with each privilege level, giving four stacks implemented for the Pentium. At a specific privilege level, all stack accesses are implied to go to the stack of that privilege level. This is facilitated by a set of control registers that contain the location and a stack pointer for each stack.

An operating system would be implemented with its code and data having a privilege level of 0 (the highest privilege). User-level code is most often an application of some sort, and applications would be implemented at privilege level 3 (the lowest level). The privilege levels in between are used for programs that require more protection than applications, but less protection than the operating system. An example would be the code within a device driver, a program that handles the intricate details of an I/O device.

Aside from restricting memory access, many computers have a small set of instructions that may only be executed by programs with a high privilege level. These are generally instructions that operate on data critical to the working of the operating system. If a user-level program were allowed to execute a privileged instruction, then that user-level program would have the ability to corrupt the operating system. An example of this on the Pentium is the instruction that loads the IDTR. Any program allowed to modify this control register could write its own value into the register, changing the pointer to the base address of the interrupt descriptor table. The result would be that a new and possibly malicious set of exception handlers would be referenced on interrupts. This would effectively allow any program to subvert the operating system by substituting its own code for the operating system's code. Privileged instructions are implemented on the Pentium by checking the CPL upon decode of each instruction. The manufacturer sets the privilege level required for each instruction when the processor is designed. If the CPL is not high enough for that required by an instruction, a trap is generated.

Priorities and Reentrant Exception Handlers

An interrupt request is an asynchronous event; the stimulus causing it may occur at any time. Further than that, it is possible for more than one interrupt request to occur at one time. A processor does not control the timing of interrupt requests. On the way to running an exception handler, the hardware must save the state of the processor before it can begin handling the interrupt. If the hardware detects a second interrupt request, and is interrupted a second time before it has a chance to save state information, then part of the state information will be lost. Once lost, the processor will not be able to recover the state information, and may never be able to return control to the program that was originally interrupted. To assure correct execution of the exception handler, a **nonreentrant** exception handler can be written. Such a handler prohibits further interruptions until the exception handler has completed its operation and returned control to the program. This may be impossible or undesirable, since some exceptions may take a long time to service. Also, the processor may wish to wait in the kernel for an interrupt, for example, if the computer literally has nothing to do.

On the Pentium, a nonreentrant handler is facilitated by the architectural definition. As part of the hardware mechanism that invokes an exception handler, interrupts are disabled. Within the EFLAGS register, bit number 9 is the Interrupt Enable flag (IF). If its value is 0, then all maskable interrupts are disabled. If its value is 1, then all maskable interrupts are enabled. The hardware disables interrupts by clearing the IF bit in the EFLAGS register after saving the original state of the register on the stack used by exception handlers. This essentially disables interrupts on the way towards invoking an exception handler. Disabling interrupts simply means deferring their handling and ignoring them temporarily, not eliminating them. Interrupts must not be disabled indefinitely, but can be safely ignored momentarily. After the interrupt is handled, the exception handler executes the `iret` instruction. The `iret` instruction causes the hardware to restore the previous contents of the EFLAGS register. Presuming interrupts were enabled (as they must have been, to allow an interrupt to be taken), restoring the EFLAGS register returns the processor to that state. At that point in time when interrupts are enabled, and an interrupt is pending, it is treated by the hardware as if a request just occurred, and the exception handler is immediately invoked.

A **reentrant** exception handler is one that can itself be interrupted. To facilitate this, the processor must be able to execute uninterrupted long enough to be able to save away the information just created regarding the reason for the interrupt, and the state of the processor immediately before the interrupt occurred. Since an exception handler is invoked with (maskable) interrupts disabled, the processor may save away any needed state information first thing during the exception handler. The handler then reenables interrupts using the privileged instruction `sti`. The `sti` instruction sets the IF; this allows interrupts to be taken. There is also a privileged instruction, `cli`, that clears IF, disabling (maskable) interrupts.

Some exception conditions are important to handle more promptly than others. For example, if a processor detects some sort of internal error condition (like an electronic component gone bad), the processor will probably want to halt the execution of all programs immediately. If execution continued, erroneous results could be generated, causing all sorts of problems. On the other hand, when an output device becomes ready to accept more data, the interrupt should be handled soon for performance reasons, but is not critical. If an internal error were detected at the same time as an output device became ready, the more important (internal error condition) should be handled first. By assigning priority levels to the various types of traps and interrupts, determining which is most important becomes easy. The mechanism that checks for pending requests also checks priority levels before handling an interrupt. Only an interrupt of a higher priority level will interrupt a currently running program. The higher the priority, the more important the exception is to handle promptly. On the Pentium, interrupts are detected and prioritized in a piece of hardware called the Programmable Interrupt Controller (PIC). The PIC also holds pending interrupts when multiple requests must be handled.

SUMMARY

Computers must deal with asynchronous, external devices as well as inconvenient or unexpected events within a program. In addition, the operating system has a need to reassert control over recalcitrant processes that would not give up use of the processor voluntarily. The exception mechanism provides a way to interrupt normal program execution to handle special circumstances when they arise, allowing the operating system to reassert control as well as to handle external, asynchronous events in a timely manner. While sometimes difficult to understand and tricky to program, interrupts are an important aspect of a computer system. They are seldom made visible at the user interface. The Pentium architecture has been used to provide an example of how interrupts can be implemented. The definition of exceptions lies at the edge of the architectural definition of a computer system, and different implementations of a computer, or different computer systems based on the same architecture, often have different rules regarding the way exceptions occur and how they are dealt with. This chapter has attempted to present the basic concepts. Many subtle aspects have been ignored for the sake of simplicity.

Asynchronous operations, in general, introduce a new degree of complexity in programming because they violate the simple, sequential execution order previously present in the execution of a program. The fact that a program can execute in different ways even when supplied with the same data makes the program much harder to understand, and much harder to debug. The handling of I/O operations and interrupts introduces many of the difficulties that must be addressed in any kind of parallel computing.

PROBLEMS

1. How is a trap different from an interrupt?

2. Why should an exception handler have a higher privilege level than user-level code?

3. Assign priorities to the following exception conditions from most important to least important. Justify the ordering.

   a. Clock

   b. character output, from a user-level program

   c. arithmetic overflow

4. Execution of a simple exception handler can generally be accomplished in a few microseconds. User-interface I/O devices interrupt typically less than once per millisecond. What is the likelihood that the exception handler will be executing when another interrupt occurs? Can you think of any reason that a trap handler is likely to see multiple interrupts pending concurrently?

5. What should happen if overflow occurs during the execution of an arithmetic instruction that is within an interrupt handler?

6. What would be the effect if an exception handler returned control to a user-level program without reenabling interrupts?

7. Is it possible for the exception handler to return control to a user program without restoring its privilege level? What would be the effect if this were to happen?

8. If a reentrant exception handler did not disable interrupts as it prepared to return control to the interrupted program, and was in the process of restoring the registers to their previous values when another interrupt occurred, could the registers still be restored correctly after the second interrupt was handled? What could go wrong?

9. It requires an extremely brief time for an exception handler to be invoked and save the state. If a reentrant handler enabled interrupts before saving state information, what could go wrong? How often might this happen?

10. On a particular computer system, if a user types 256 characters consecutively without typing a newline or return character, the computer stops echoing the characters and responds to each additional character typed by echoing the bell character (^G). Give a plausible explanation for the cause of this behavior.

11. Write the Pentium exception handler to deal with the vector 0; attempt to divide by zero. What should the handler do? Where should the handler return once it is finished?

CHAPTER
15 FEATURES FOR ARCHITECTURAL PERFORMANCE

The simplest computer would have only one way to perform a given operation. Computers are made to achieve higher performance by identifying functions that are required frequently, and providing more efficient ways to achieve those capabilities. Often this results in new instructions, or additional capabilities within an instruction. Adding such capabilities to a computer creates some redundancy, meaning that some functions can be accomplished in more than one way. The programmer, or compiler, is therefore faced with choices. Choosing the best can be difficult, since the best solution may vary. It can be the way that attains the quickest solution, the one that costs the least, the one that is the easiest to understand, the one that is the easiest to debug, or the one that is the easiest to modify.

The definition of a new computer architecture requires a deliberate choice of instructions together with a careful attention to extra architectural features. The interplay of these extra features can make or break the performance of a computer. Those features of a computer that are visible to the programmer are considered part of the architecture. The most common features that enhance performance are the use of parallelism and memory hierarchies. These features are not visible to the programmer, but are part of the implementation of the architecture. This chapter discusses these features.

15.1 MINIMAL INSTRUCTION SETS AND CHOICES

The instruction set of a modern computer offers many choices in how to implement an algorithm. Various cases have been presented in this book where two different code sequences achieved similar or identical results. Many control instructions could be eliminated entirely from an instruction set, since their inverse test condition also exists. Code can always be restructured to reverse the sense of the test. Immediate operands are simply short ways of supplying constants, avoiding their explicit storage as part of the data section in a program. But going further, multiplication and division can be synthesized from additions and subtractions. Floating point instructions do not add additional functionality, but the performance gain for programs dealing with floating point variables is immense. Even the addition instruction could be eliminated. In the Pentium architecture, the instruction

```
add EAX, EDX
```

could be replaced with

```
neg EDX
sub EAX, EDX
```

A computer could be specified with a very small number of instructions. In the extreme case, a single arithmetic instruction (subtract) and a single conditional control instruction would form a sufficient instruction set. Any additional instructions provide the computer with no additional functionality, although they reduce the size of the program, as well as making writing and debugging significantly easier. The result of richer instruction sets is that the programmer is given a choice in coding a particular algorithm.

Complicating the choice further is the fact that not all instructions require the same length of time to execute. Some instructions take much longer than others to complete, and some take a varying amount of time depending on the context.

Measures of Cost

When creating an assembly language program, several possible criteria might be applied in selecting the appropriate instruction sequence when a choice is possible. The most obvious choice would be the sequence of instructions that executes the fastest. It would be natural to expect that the shorter a program, the faster it executes. It is not uncommon to find cases where shorter programs actually execute more slowly than longer ones. There are other criteria to consider, as well, when trying to make the best choice. If a compiler is generating the code, then an important consideration might be the time required to compile the program. If the compile time is substantially lengthened by the selection of the fastest code sequence, the code of choice might be the one that is easiest to generate. Simple code sequences often have the advantage that a compiler may apply other kinds of optimizations, such as making a particularly effective use of registers. Another criterion might include the ease in understanding the code, for debugging and later for modifying it. Still another might be the concern about compatibility with other computers—some architectures have instructions that are included only in the more expensive implementations, or are implemented in software on the low-end models.

Space versus Time Tradeoffs

A tradeoff seen over and over again in the field of computer science is the interplay between space and time. Within this tradeoff, space refers to memory. The effect of this tradeoff on algorithms is that the more data space that is used, the faster code runs. For program code, it would be expected that eliminating an instruction from a program would make the program run faster. Substituting a single instruction in place of two others reduces the size of the program, but it will not necessarily speed up the program. This is because some instructions take longer to execute than others. How, then, can the programmer hope to choose the fastest code sequence?

By design, high-speed computers tend towards instruction sets of elemental instructions that can be executed, or at least initiated, in approximately the same time. Very often in these instruction sets there is only a single, or at least a clearly best, code sequence. In such architectures, reducing the number of instructions in the code usually results in an increase in speed. In many cases, the speed of the execution cannot be predicted exactly because of another feature of modern, high-performance architectures. They exploit a variety of techniques intended to handle most operations very quickly, but sometimes these same operations take quite a bit longer. Because of these techniques, performance is not predictable. Thus the architecture relies on probability to achieve its performance; the execution of a particular instruction will usually be very fast, but under some circumstances it may take longer to complete.

The VAX architecture provides an example of the space versus time tradeoff. On this successful computer architecture, two unique instruction sequences might have exactly the same effect, but their execution times might differ. This variation made instruction selection difficult. Experience in writing VAX assembly language code eased the situation, since the selection of a code sequence was largely heuristic. Many compilers were designed to select the code sequence that minimized the size of the program. This often resulted in slower program execution than an alternative code sequence. A smaller amount of memory space for code resulted in a program that took more time to execute.

15.2 INSTRUCTION LEVEL PARALLELISM

The execution of a single instruction involves a sequence of steps, and each step requires time to complete. An instruction must be fetched from memory, decoded, the operands loaded, an operation performed, and the result must be stored. The PC also must be updated to identify the next instruction to execute. A programmer expects that the instructions within a program will be executed in the order specified. This expected model of program execution

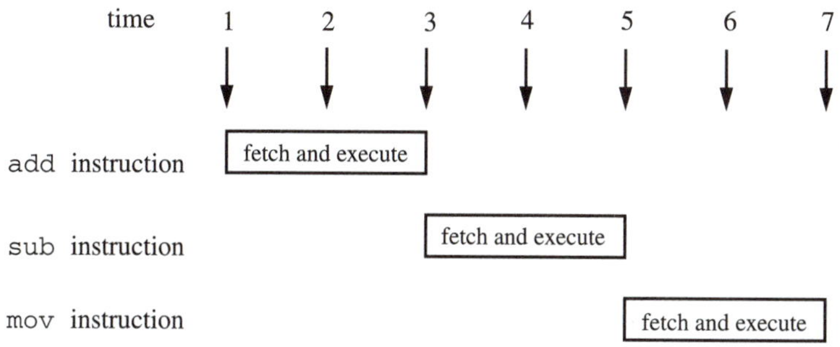

Figure 15.1 Relative timing of a processor without pipelining.

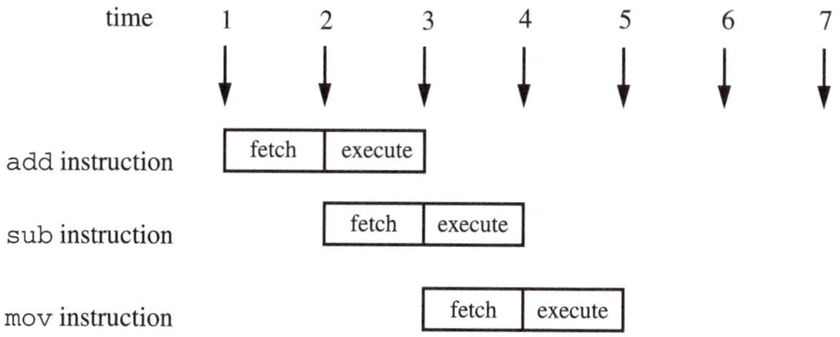

Figure 15.2 Relative timing of a two-stage pipeline.

is **sequential**. One instruction follows the next. A first instruction completes its execution before a second instruction is fetched.

Making programs execute faster requires hardware that works faster. As technology improves, the hardware does run faster. But improving performance beyond just waiting for technological changes requires innovation. **Parallelism** offers hope for gains in performance. Parallelism takes sequential steps and executes one or more of them at the same time. At the level of a single processor executing instructions, parallelism can be introduced by implementing a hardware design technique called **pipelining**. Without violating the programmer's model that the instructions in a program are executed sequentially, pipelining overlaps the operations within instructions, beginning one or more additional instructions before the first has completed. The program results and variables are the same executed on a processor with pipelining as on a processor without pipelining.

For purposes of comparison, the relative timing of instruction fetch and execution for a processor without pipelining is given in Figure 15.1. The earliest implementations of pipelining separated the instruction fetch and execute cycle into two parts. Each of these parts is called a stage. One stage fetches instructions and updates the PC. The other stage executes all the other steps needed (decode, operand load, and so on) to complete the instruction's execution. While the execution of a first instruction is taking place, a second instruction is being fetched. Timing for this pipeline is shown in Figure 15.2. The latency of each instruction execution is shown as the same both with and without pipelining. This is a realistic assumption. However, the **throughput** of instruction execution doubles for this two-stage pipeline. Throughput gives the rate of instruction completion.

The amount of hardware used to implement pipelining does not double for this two-stage pipeline. By separating the hardware into stages, it is more heavily utilized. There is still just one part of the hardware that does instruction fetch, but it is used during each time

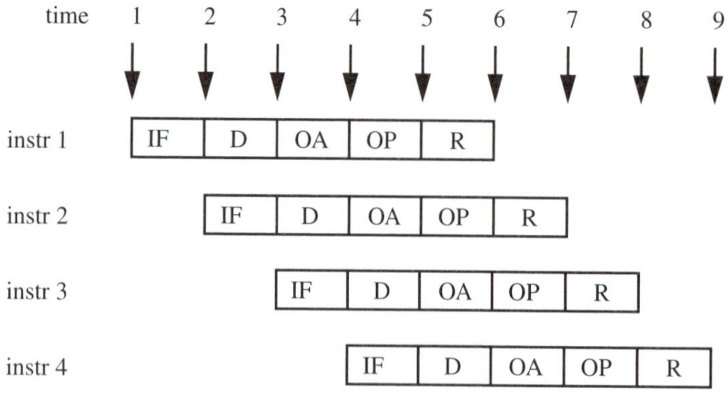

Figure 15.3 Relative timing of a five-stage pipeline.

abbreviations for pipeline stages:

IF -- instruction fetch and PC update
D -- decode
OA -- operand access
OP -- arithmetic operation
R -- store results

period to fetch a new instruction. In a sequential implementation, the fetch hardware is used (to fetch an instruction), and then it sits idle until the current instruction completes its execution.

In high-performance computers, pipelines most often contain more than two stages. One possible breakdown for the stages of a pipeline is the same steps as outlined in the instruction fetch and execute cycle.

Stage 1. Instruction fetch and PC update
Stage 2. Decode
Stage 3. Operand access
Stage 4. Arithmetic operation
Stage 5. Storage of result

A five-stage pipeline implies that up to five instructions can be somewhere in their execution at the same time. Figure 15.3 illustrates the relative timing of this five-stage pipeline.

The throughput of a machine that implements pipelining can be greater than one that does not. As long as instructions are continually fetched and sent through the pipeline, the performance gains are large. Performance goes down, however, if **holes** (also called **bubbles** or **stalls**) are ever introduced into the pipeline. Holes are places where a stage is not working on an instruction, and they are caused by dependencies.

Dependencies

Many instructions create a result value that is used in some way by a future instruction. The time to compute this result can be overlapped with the fetching of a subsequent instruction, and even with its execution if the subsequent instruction does not need the result. A **dependency** between two instructions is created whenever a result from one instruction is required for the execution of the other. The most common dependencies occur when an arithmetic or data movement instruction places its result in a register and a subsequent instruction reads the updated value from the register. Such an occurrence is known as a **data dependency**. When a data dependency exists, the execution of the dependent instruction may not be initiated until the result of the previous instruction is available, causing a hole in the pipeline. On some computers the execution of an instruction that uses operands not generated in the previous instruction can be initiated before the previous instruction has generated its result. Thus the order in which instructions are specified may affect the time necessary to complete the execution.

An example of a code sequence with no data dependencies can be seen in the following:

```
add    EAX, EDX
mov    EBX, int_data
```

An example of a data dependency can be seen in the code sequence:

```
add    EAX, EDX
mov    int_data, [EAX]
```

The result of the `add` instruction must be placed into register EAX before it can be used by the `mov` instruction. For a two-stage pipeline, there is no performance degradation due to a pipeline hole with this code sequence. In the five-stage pipeline, however, there will be holes in the pipeline. Figure 15.4 shows a diagram of the pipeline with the holes that appear for this example. The operand access for the `mov` instruction (getting EAX) may not occur until the last pipeline stage of the `add` instruction completes. It is the last stage that places the result of the addition into register EAX. Note that any instructions fetched after the dependent instruction will also contain holes due to the unavailability of the hardware in the pipeline.

Control instructions cause **control dependencies**. Within a control instruction, the PC may get overwritten with the address of the instruction to fetch next in the last stage of the pipeline. In a pipelined execution, one or more instructions may have already been fetched and partially executed by the time which instruction to fetch after the control instruction has been determined. The wrong instructions may have been fetched and partially executed. If so, the processor must have a way to undo things done by the wrongly fetched and partially executed instructions. An alternative correct operation would require that a hole be introduced into the pipeline until the address of the next instruction to be fetched were known. A processor fetches a **stream of instructions**, starting with the target address

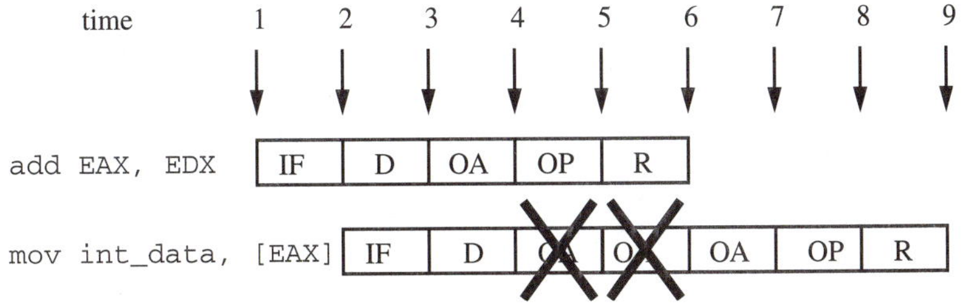

Figure 15.4 Data dependency in the five-stage pipeline.

of a control instruction, and continuing with consecutive instructions until another control instruction aborts the sequence and initiates a new one.

Reducing the Effects of Control Dependencies

When a control instruction might modify the PC other than simply to increment the PC, the situation is worse than simply not being able to execute the next instruction. Since the instruction is not even identified, it cannot even be fetched. Control instructions make prediction difficult for two reasons: They affect the PC other than a simple increment, and they may have more than one possible successor instruction. Thus control instructions are inherently difficult to overlap with other instructions. Even if the fact that the instruction may affect the PC is detected early, and even if it is correctly determined which of the successor instructions will be executed, it is very difficult to fetch the successor instruction without additional delay.

Consider the sequence of events that must be performed in the execution of a conditional control instruction:

1. The conditional branch instruction is fetched, and the PC is incremented.
2. The instruction is decoded.
3. The test condition is identified.
4. The test is performed.
5. If the test is successful, the new value for the PC is computed.

If instructions are being fetched in advance, the next instruction can only be identified after the test has been executed and the new value of the PC computed.

A great deal of effort has been expended over many years in attempting to speed up the execution of control instructions, and many different solutions have been tried. One technique that has been identified is to separate the effort into multiple instructions, making it possible under some circumstances to insert instructions between the parts. There are three distinct operations that must be performed, and they can in theory each be performed in separate instructions, or in any combination.

1. An instruction that performs the test might set a flag or indicate by some mechanism whether the test succeeded. Of course, testing the flag is a test in itself, but a simple one that can be performed very quickly. Because the test takes time, it may make sense to insert other instructions after the test instruction before the results of the test are utilized.
2. After the test condition has proven successful, the target address must be calculated, and instructions beginning at the new address can be fetched. Again, other instructions can conceivably be inserted at the end of the current instruction stream, after the branch target address has been determined but before the new instruction stream has been fetched.
3. After the first instruction of the new instruction stream has been fetched, the transfer to the new instruction stream takes place.

Minimizing the effect of control dependencies in a program depends on minimizing the time lost due to the process. Adding extra instructions means that additional instructions must be decoded and executed, but trying to perform too much in a single instruction may mean unnecessary delay while memory operations are pending, missing the opportunity to overlap other operations.

Control instructions can cause inordinate delay in fetching and executing instructions because they limit the processor's ability to fetch instructions ahead of time. While unconditional control instructions introduce some delay because of the time needed to begin fetching the new instruction stream, conditional control instructions are inherently worse because of the uncertainty regarding the outcome of the test. If it were possible to predict the outcome reliably, the control dependency would be much easier to handle. It could be treated like an unconditional control instruction, which can begin fetching the new stream as soon as the branch address can be computed, or better yet, continuing execution down the same stream. Many techniques have been evaluated to assist the hardware in guessing which way a branch decision might go, because even guessing correctly most of the time results in performance gains.

One branch prediction technique is commonly used. One **static prediction** technique always predicts that a branch will not be taken. Performance is not degraded at all in the case of a control instruction that is not taken. The new instruction stream is already in the pipeline, and it continues. By careful design of the pipeline stages, the last stage will be the only one that changes processor state other than the PC update implicit in every instruction. For such a design, a taken control instruction causes the final pipeline stage of any incorrectly partially fetched and executed instructions to abort. These incorrect instructions continue down the pipeline, but they never complete. Performance in this case of incorrect prediction reduces to that of sequential execution. Performance of code running on a machine that uses this branch prediction technique may be further enhanced by its compilers. The compiler often has a choice of assembly language implementations for any high-level language statement. By giving the compiler knowledge of the architectural implementation, it may be able to structure the code such that a control instruction not taken is the common case. For example, consider the case of a loop to be executed many times as given in Figure 15.5. This short C code fragment will execute the loop one million times. At the top of the loop, there is a test of variables `a` and `b`. The Pentium assembly language code generated for this code fragment could be as in Figure 15.6 or 15.7. Performance of the code on an implementation that used pipelining with static branch prediction is better in Figure 15.6 than in Figure 15.7. In Figure 15.6, the `je` instruction does not take the jump the first one million times through the loop. For static branch prediction, this means that there will be no holes introduced into the pipeline, and therefore no performance degradation. Only the last time through the loop will the jump be taken. This last time will cause performance to be reduced to that of a sequential implementation. A compiler can analyze the structure of the loop enough to

```
a = 0;
b = 1000000;
while ( a != b) {
        a++;
}
```

Figure 15.5 C program fragment.

```
          mov   ECX, 0
          mov   EAX, 1000000
loop_top: comp  ECX, EAX
          je    loop_done
          inc   ECX
          j     loop_top
loop_done:
```

Figure 15.6 One assembly language implementation for C program fragment.

```
           mov   ECX, 0
           mov   EAX, 1000000
loop_top:  comp  EAX, ECX
           jne   increment
           j     loop_done
increment: inc   ECX
           j     loop_top
loop_done:
```

Figure 15.7 A second assembly language implementation for C program fragment.

determine that it will be executed many times. It then uses that knowledge to generate the assembly language code as in Figure 15.6.

A static branch prediction that always predicts that a jump or branch will be taken is called **squashing**. The address of the instruction following the jump or branch is saved in case the prediction is incorrect. The target of a taken jump or branch is fetched, and it is sent down the pipeline, but before any results are written or stored, a decision is made whether the instruction partially executed should have been. If it should not have been executed, then the saved address is used to fetch the next instruction. Any instructions that are at some point within the pipeline must be backed out. The effect must be as though they had never even been fetched. If the prediction is correct, then performance is as if there were no control dependencies.

Dynamic prediction goes further than static prediction. It adds hardware to keep track of control instructions that have already been executed. When a control instruction is executed for the first time, the hardware makes a static prediction. It then logs information about which way the control instruction went (taken or not taken). Subsequent execution of the same instruction causes the hardware to predict that the control instruction will go the same way as its previous execution. Dynamic prediction will result in higher performance than static prediction for most applications. Consider again the implementation of the C loop given in Figure 15.5. Like many loops, the assembly language code generated will have two control instructions, one at the top of the loop and one at the end of the loop. For the assembly language implementation in the figure, the jump at the top of the loop is not taken each time except for the last time through the loop. The jump at the end of the loop is always taken. Therefore, static prediction will always be wrong for one of these control instructions, each time through the loop. A dynamic prediction is likely to predict incorrectly for one of the jumps the first time through the loop. But for the remainder of the loop iterations, it will predict correctly for both jumps. The performance improvement is gained at the cost of extra hardware to log predictions.

A recently popular technique for minimizing the effect of control dependencies is to limit tests to those that can be performed very quickly, and separating the changing of the

PC from the test by delaying the point at which the control operation takes effect. In other words, a control instruction performs a test and, if the test is successful, modifies the PC. The modification does not take effect on the very next instruction. Rather, one or more (normally a fixed number) instructions is executed after the branch *whether the branch is to be taken or not*. Only after executing the succeeding instructions does the effect of the control instruction take place and execution of the new instruction stream initiated. This technique is known as a **delayed branch**. The assembly language generated for such an implementation does not change. The assembler is given the task of reordering the instructions within an instruction stream to take advantage of the delayed branch. The delayed branch means that the following instruction is actually executed before the PC is modified.

A sophisticated assembler is capable of analyzing the dependencies of instructions and identifying instructions that do not affect the branch test. Such instructions are candidates for reordering, and the code sequence can often be reordered without affecting the logical program behavior by moving another instruction to be executed after the branch. If no instruction can be found to move to the space after the control instruction, then the assembler must place a **no op** after the control instruction. No op is the mnemonic often given to an instruction that does nothing. The performance is the same for placing a no op into the instruction stream as for putting a hole into the pipeline.

15.3 MEMORY HIERARCHIES

One of the slowest operations performed on a computer is a memory access. Three properties of memory are desired: capacity, cost, and speed. It is possible to build fast memory, but it can be quite costly. The larger the memory (capacity), the slower it becomes due to time to decode addresses. A design has not yet been found that gives a very large, very fast memory for a low cost.

Memory access patterns are extremely complex, but they are far from random. In fact, the vast majority of all memory accesses are aimed at a small fraction of the memory. The patterns of memory access exhibit the property of **locality**. There are two kinds of locality, **spatial** and **temporal**. Spatial locality is the property that given a memory reference to a specific location, other physically close locations are likely to be referenced. Programs tend to exhibit high spatial locality for instruction fetches. In the absence of control instructions, when one location is accessed for an instruction fetch, a second instruction fetch is at a location adjacent to the first. References to certain data structures also exhibit a high degree of spatial locality. For example, system stack access will exhibit spatial locality. The references to data in the stack are physically close, often adjacent. Temporal locality is the property that given a memory reference to a specific location, that location is likely to be accessed again soon. Instruction fetches to the instructions within a loop tend to exhibit a high degree of temporal locality. The iterations of a loop fetch the same instructions many times. For relatively short loops, the same instruction is fetched many times in a short amount of time.

Since designers do not have the very large, very fast, very inexpensive memories that they want, the best approach found is to introduce a **memory hierarchy**. It is possible to exploit the locality of memory references by taking a layered approach to memory, providing a very small, very fast memory backed up by a somewhat larger, somewhat slower second-level memory, backed up by a still larger, still slower, third-level memory. The number of levels can be carried farther than this. By controlling which variables are stored in which level of the memory hierarchy, it is possible to satisfy a remarkably large portion of the memory requests by accessing only the top levels of the hierarchy.

In some cases this hierarchy is explicitly made visible to the programmer. Registers may be considered the first level in the hierarchy. The fastest access is to registers, yet there are relatively few of them. In other cases, the management of the memory is done either by hardware or software mechanisms, or a combination of the two.

Cache Memory

Perhaps the most widely used technique beyond registers to exploit a relatively small, high-speed memory is the use of a **cache**. A cache memory is inserted between the main memory of the computer and the processor, as shown in Figure 15.8. The cache memory is very fast relative to the speed of the main memory. Part of what makes it fast is its physical proximity to the processor. Requests to the cache do not need to travel a long distance. The cache stores a redundant portion of the main memory. Memory requests go from the processor directly to the cache (not main memory). If the cache has a copy of the requested data, the cache is said to **hit**, and it returns the data quickly to the processor. If the cache does not have the requested data, the cache **misses**, and the requested data are forwarded to main memory. Any data fetched from main memory are both placed in the cache and supplied to the processor.

If a memory access hits in the cache, the access time is very small. It will be the time to initiate one or possibly two regular instructions. But if the access misses in the cache, the access time is much larger since the cache access must be followed by an access to main memory. If time is measured in clock ticks, the following formula gives the average memory access time (AMAT) for a memory access as a function of the **miss ratio**. Miss ratio is the ratio of requests that miss to the total number of requests:

$$\text{AMAT} = T_{cache} + (M \times T_{main\ memory})$$

In this formula, T_{cache} is the number of clock ticks to access the cache, $T_{main\ memory}$ is the number of clock ticks to access main memory, and M is the miss ratio. For example, if it takes one clock tick to access the cache, 10 clock ticks to access main memory, and the miss ratio for a specific program is 0.05, then the AMAT for the program is

$$\text{AMAT} = 1 + (0.05 \times 10) = 1.5$$

The average is 1.5 ticks, but memory accesses will always take either 1 clock tick or 11 clock ticks. The miss ratio varies for each different program. Each has its own memory

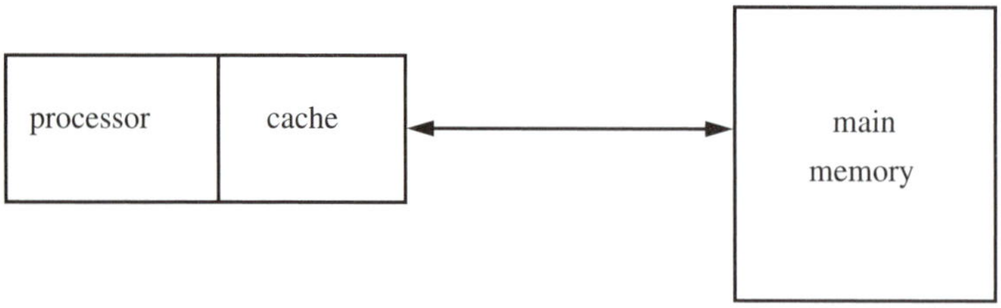

Figure 15.8 Location of a cache within a computer.

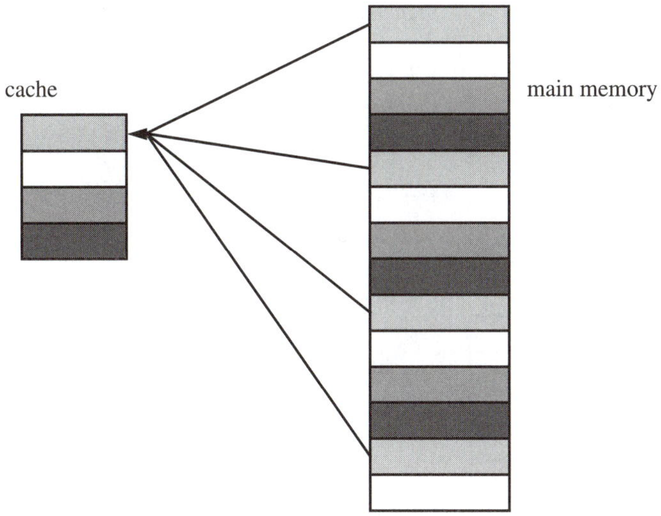

Figure 15.9 Mapping of main memory blocks to cache blocks.

access patterns, and these patterns together with the design and implementation of the cache determine which data are in the cache. This makes it difficult to predict performance.

Implementations of caches vary widely from architecture to architecture. Yet all caches share certain details. A cache is always smaller than main memory. It is used to keep copies of **blocks** of data from main memory, and the size of a block is implementation dependent. Main memory can also be divided into blocks. Then each block maps to a specific **line** of the cache, as shown in Figure 15.9. The figure shows a cache with only four lines. This is much too small a number of lines to be realistic.

Given that only one of many main memory blocks can be in a cache block, there needs to be a method for distinguishing which main memory block is currently in the cache. The information that distinguishes among main memory blocks is a **tag**. The tag is ordinarily a portion of an address, usually its most significant bits. Figure 15.10 shows a simplified diagram of a cache. Each data block has a tag, and there is one block per line in the diagram. A cache with one block per line is called a **direct mapped** cache. Also required is a way to determine if a cache block is empty, as all blocks will be when power is cycled or just before a program starts its execution. A single bit for each block, called a **valid bit**, tells if the cache block contains nothing or a block from main memory.

As a program begins its execution, it will be generating memory requests. The first memory access will miss in the cache, since the valid bit for each block indicates that the block is empty. The processor generates that first memory access, probably for an instruction fetch. The cache responds by using the address to identify in which line of the cache the block would reside. The valid bit for that block is checked, and the tag portion of the address is checked to see if it matches the tag for the cache block. If the valid bit is not set or if the tag does not match, then there is a cache miss. The request is forwarded to main memory. Main memory responds by sending not just the word of memory requested, but by sending the entire block surrounding the word. The requested word is then given to the processor. At the same time, the entire block of data is copied into its location in the cache, its valid bit is set to indicate the block is valid, and the tag portion of the address is saved in the tag field for the block. A subsequent request for a word within this block results in a cache hit.

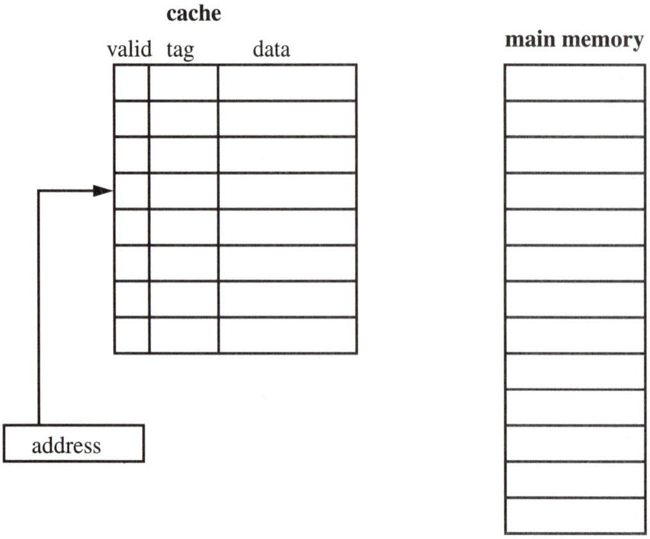

Figure 15.10 Simplified cache block diagram.

The size of a data block has an effect on the miss ratio for most programs. The design and implementation of a cache must fix the block size. Computer architects consider a large range of block sizes. As block size is increased from one word to multiple words (usually a power of two), the miss ratio will decrease for most programs. This is due to spatial locality. A miss to one word causes a block to be loaded into the cache. References that show spatial locality are likely to access other words within the same block. These references will hit in the cache. Increasing the block size only increases performance up to a point. The point is different for different programs, since the access patterns vary from program to program. As block size increases, so does the amount of time it takes to place the block in the cache (on a miss). For block sizes that are too large, data within the block will never be accessed. It wastes time to bring data that will never be accessed into the cache.

All memory accesses are either reads or writes. For reads, the cache works as discussed. Writes present more challenges for cache designers. The cache contains copies of data held in main memory. A write to a word within a cache block must also be written to the block in main memory. The timing of the write affects both performance and the complexity of the cache hardware. In general, performance is worse if all writes to data within the cache are written to main memory at the same time. The implementation of this policy is called **write through**. The performance for all memory accesses that are writes reduces to a computer system that does not have a cache. An alternative that requires more hardware is called **write back**. In a write back policy, writing cache blocks to memory is done only when necessary. This means increased performance, or lower average memory access time, for those cases where the same cache block is written more than once. Where a write through cache policy would generate two memory accesses to write a single piece of data twice, the write back cache policy only generates one. The data are copied back to the main memory block only when the program is complete or when the cache block is to be overwritten with another block. The implementation of the write back policy requires an extra bit in the cache associated with each block. The bit identifies whether the data block has been modified, and must at some point be written back to main memory.

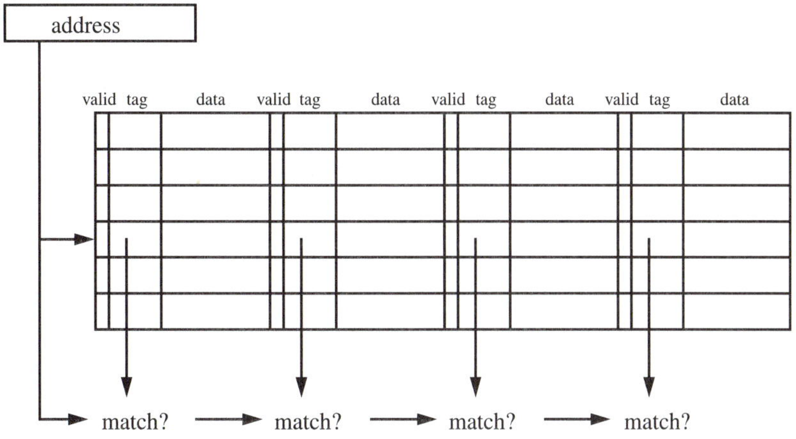

Figure 15.11 A four-way set associative cache.

Another way to decrease the miss ratio while keeping the same amount of data storage is to place more than one block per line of the cache. This changes the associativity of the cache. The direct mapped cache presented is actually a set associative cache, with a set size of one. By increasing the set size, there are more locations per line for cache blocks. A diagram of a four-way set associative cache is given in Figure 15.11. A block from main memory maps to a specific line. Within that line, it can be placed into any one of the four block frames on the line. For a cache access, bits within the address are used to determine the line for the block. The tag of each block must be checked to see if it matches the tag portion of the address. In addition, the valid bit for each block must be checked. There is a cache hit if a tag matches and that block's valid bit is set. On a cache miss, the block received from main memory may be placed in any empty cache block on the line. If there are no available empty blocks, then the cache's replacement policy is brought into action. One of the blocks on the line must be thrown out of the cache to make room for the new block. More hardware can be introduced to each line of the cache to help determine which block will be replaced.

Increasing the Number of Caches

Increasing the number of levels in the memory hierarchy has been shown to increase performance by further reducing the average memory access time. A second level of cache included in a memory system is becoming more common, as diagrammed in Figure 15.12. The smallest, fastest cache is closest to the processor. It is called a level 1, or L1, cache. A larger, somewhat slower cache is placed between the L1 cache and memory. This is a level 2, or L2, cache. All memory accesses begin by going to the L1 cache. L1 cache hits do not require further memory access. L1 cache misses forward requests to the L2 cache. A hit in the L2 cache returns the block of data requested. A miss in the L2 cache requires a main memory access. The block is returned from main memory, and it is placed in the L2 cache. The L2 cache then gives the required block to the L1 cache, satisfying the original request.

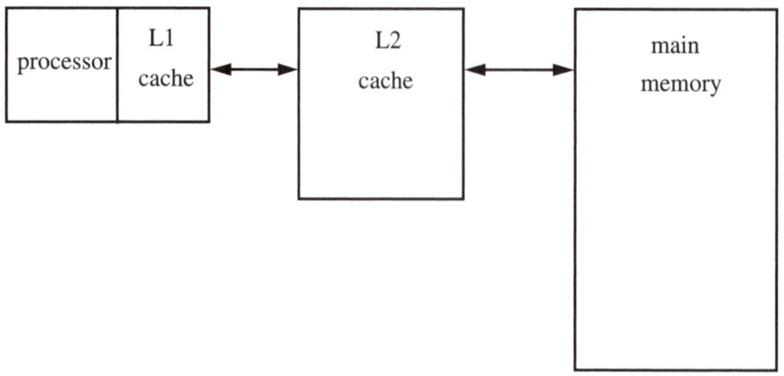

Figure 15.12 Memory hierarchy with two levels of caches.

Effective Use of Registers

A cache is invisible to the assembly language programmer. Whether an operand is found in the cache or must be fetched from memory affects the speed of execution, but not the functional behavior of the program. The programmer does have control over which variables are stored in registers, however, making it possible to guarantee that the most important ones will always be accessible. Conceptually, registers are bound to variables, but the binding time can be very limited. A variable is **live** if it will be read before it is written again. A single register can be bound to multiple variables as long as the variables are not live simultaneously. Of course, when a variable can no longer be allocated to a register but is still live, it must be allocated space in memory. The space allocated is typically on the stack. The register is **spilled**, written out to that location for temporary storage until it can be reallocated to a register. Making the most effective use of the registers is a challenging problem for the compiler writer, and it is a topic of ongoing research.

Register allocation can be more effective than depending on the cache memory, because it is possible for the programmer (or compiler) to exercise prescience to determine which variables will be accessed the soonest by looking ahead in the code execution. Registers do not necessarily perform better than cache memory, however, because cache block replacement algorithms can take advantage of the dynamic behavior of programs, something that cannot be done at the time the program is being assembled due to the limited knowledge about control instruction outcomes.

Cache Access Prediction

Just as a compiler may have information that allows it to predict the outcome of branches, it also may be able to provide information that allows the hardware to recognize, in advance, when a word of memory, not present in the cache, is about to be accessed. While the cache is invisible to the program in the sense that a cache hit or miss only affects the speed of the execution, many modern computers give the processor a way to provide a hint to the hardware that a future memory reference is likely. This information may be provided in the form of an instruction, which explicitly informs the cache of a (probably) pending read or write operation. If possible, the cache responds by prefetching the cache block containing the address. The cache hardware can do what it wants with the operation, including ignoring it completely, but a well-designed processor can enhance performance by taking advantage of such hints. Incorrect hints do not cause incorrect behavior, but they may degrade performance. A prefetch may cause a valid block to be thrown out of the cache. That thrown out block may be accessed again, causing a cache miss. For an incorrect prefetch of a block, not only is time wasted in copying the block from memory, but if the thrown out block is accessed, it also causes a miss, resulting in more wasted time.

SUMMARY

The performance of computer architectures can be enhanced by the design and implementation of various features. Pipelining is a design technique that overlaps some of the operations needed to fetch and execute instructions. When there are no (or very few) holes introduced into the pipeline, the throughput of a computer can be much faster than one that implements the same functionality without pipelining. Various branching techniques attempt to reduce pipeline holes caused by branch and jump instructions. The implementation of a hierarchical memory improves the average time for a memory access. Its implementation increases performance by taking advantage of the spatial and temporal locality exhibited by programs.

PROBLEMS

1. Show how to build a logical left shift (by 1 bit) function out of the minimal instruction set containing only a subtract and a branch if equal instruction.

2. What is the absolute minimum number of instructions necessary for a computer if I/O is included? Design such a minimal instruction set.

3. An addition instruction can be synthesized by two subtraction instructions. However, it is not possible to synthesize a subtraction instruction from any number of addition instructions. What is the property of subtraction that makes the instruction inherently more powerful than addition?

4. Produce two pieces of Pentium code. One piece is to be shorter, but takes longer to execute than the second piece.

5. Identify a scenario where the compile time of a program would be an important measure of cost.

6. Give an expression to describe the latency of instruction execution on an architecture where each instruction takes the same amount of time to execute.

7. Give an expression that describes the throughput of instruction execution for a pipelined machine.

8. The Pentium code

```
add    EAX, ECX
mov    [EAX], 300
```

has a data dependency. Identify what the dependency is and what effect it would have on a pipelined processor.

9. What is the relationship between the number of pipeline stages and the number of conditional branch instructions in a program?

10. **Hit ratio** is the ratio of number of cache hits to the total number of cache accesses. Give an expression for the hit ratio in terms of miss ratio.

11. Main memory accesses on a specific computer system take 20 clock cycles. The system is upgraded to include a cache that takes 4 clock cycles for memory accesses. A benchmark is executed on the system both before and after adding the cache. The benchmark has a miss ratio of 0.08. What speedup does the system show for the benchmark?

12. A computer system uses 32-bit addresses. It has a direct-mapped cache with 16-byte blocks and 1K lines. Draw a diagram of this cache, showing how an address is used to access the cache. How many total bytes of data are in the cache?

13. Give an expression for AMAT for a computer system with L1 and L2 caches.

CHAPTER

16

ARCHITECTURE IN PERSPECTIVE

Over the past thirty years, rapidly evolving technologies in both hardware and software have driven the design of new computers, but never more than today. Rapid advances on many technological fronts have produced a state of near-continuous revolution in computer design and use. Hardware costs have continuously dropped concurrently with the development of ever-more-powerful computers, resulting in a constantly expanding range of applications for computers. Today home computers costing in the range of $2,000 are more powerful than the most powerful computers built before the mid-1970s.

Needless to say, the design of computers has seen the coming and going of many ideas. What is truly remarkable is how little has changed since the early von Neumann computer architecture appeared in the 1950s. While the techniques have evolved and become more sophisticated, the basic machine has changed very little. Early computers had load and store instructions, program counters, and registers. They grappled with the representation of integers and floating point numbers, arriving at solutions not greatly different from those used today. They had far less memory—hundreds of words instead of millions—and they were far slower, taking milliseconds instead of nanoseconds to complete operations. Nevertheless, most of the concepts present in a modern computer architecture had emerged by the early 1960s. The variety and combinations of ideas implemented in various computers since that time are enormous, but in many ways, the computers today are more similar to early computers than to more recent ones.

Hardware and design costs both interact with, and conflict with, architectural performance. Computer designs fall into all parts of the spectrum of possibilities. At different stages in the evolution, the technology has favored certain styles of architecture. At all times there has been a difference in approach taken between the low-end and high-performance computers. The low-end computers have been focused primarily on minimizing costs, while the high-performance computers were more freely able to pursue alternative techniques that, while expensive, could be relied on to achieve higher performance. As technology advanced, many of the ideas that first appeared in high-performance computers have gradually appeared in lower-cost models, eventually becoming commonplace. Examples of such techniques include general register files, hardware multiplication and division, pipelining, and cache memory.

Many ideas have appeared in different architectures over the years, often reappearing years later in a slightly modified form. There is always a tendency to think of the currently popular architectures as the final, or at least the best, architectures yet invented. This is a dangerous trap, for many of the ideas currently in favor will almost certainly disappear in the coming years as technology continues to change the relative costs, once again favoring techniques that have fallen out of favor, or never been tried. Thus a study of alternative architectures is useful even though many of the features that make them noteworthy are currently thought to be old-fashioned. Successful architectures last a long time—the most popular architectures of the 1970s and 1980s still have large markets, though their market share is shrinking. Many of the characteristics of successful architectures from the past are likely to show up in future products, combined in novel ways with concepts present in currently popular architectures and possibly even some completely new ideas. Thus it is important to be familiar with techniques that have been useful in the past, even if some of them are currently out of favor.

This chapter discusses several successful architectures that contain characteristics and features different from the Pentium architecture. In the single-chip processor category are the Motorola 68000, the SPARC, the MIPS RISC, and the Alpha architectures. The Cray 1 is an important architecture because it demonstrates features that are favored when performance is the overriding concern. It was designed for high performance, particularly in the area of scientific computation. It might be argued that the Cray 1 is the quintessential RISC, although its design substantially predates the use of the term.

16.1 WHAT'S ALL THIS ABOUT RISC?

Throughout the history of computing, the fastest computers have generally been load/store architectures. From very early days, designers recognized that faster instruction execution could be obtained by exploiting instruction overlap (pipelining) and memory reference locality. These considerations led naturally to the use of registers for intermediate storage.

Computers that were designed for high performance, rather than low cost, have long assumed this computing model. The MIPS RISC architecture is one excellent modern example of such load/store architectures.

Until the 1980s, only very expensive, high-end computers were designed with pipelining in mind. Many computers were designed with a primary goal of minimizing cost. Such computers often resulted in different architectures than the high-end architectures. The formula for success is complicated, and there are many examples of highly successful computer architectures that are clearly inferior to other, less successful ones. Nevertheless, the compelling requirement of compatibility has meant that the successful architectures tend to have future computers based on them. This results in common architectures with aspects that are not necessarily effective, but because of their success they are widely employed and occasionally imitated.

Historically, both memory and processors were far more expensive than they are today. Both have become far less expensive over the past twenty years, although memory has decreased in price more rapidly than processors have. In the past decade the emphasis in processor design has been primarily in making them faster, while the emphasis on memory has been to reduce the cost by increasing capacity. The improvements in speed of memory systems have not kept pace with that of processors. The use of cache memory and other techniques helps to mitigate this speed differential, so that today, large memory systems are commonplace. Until recently, however, making the best use of the memory was a primary concern, sometimes leading to innovative, complex processors.

If memory is expensive, then the less expensive computers must use a small amount of memory. A smaller amount of memory means that there is a large benefit in reducing the size of a program. During the 1960s and 1970s, memory was at a premium. Therefore, much effort was expended on minimizing the size of individual instructions and on minimizing the number of instructions necessary to implement a program. Studies showed that certain sequences of instructions occurred frequently. New instructions were created and placed in instruction sets to replace an entire sequence of instructions. For example, a loop variable is often decremented, followed by a branch operation if the result is positive. New architectures therefore introduced a single instruction to decrement a variable and branch conditionally based on the result. Another example of a frequent sequence of instructions is the loading or storing of multiple registers. A single instruction could be designed to accomplish this task.

This and other motivations led to the development of instructions of great complexity. In many ways, an instruction came to be more like a procedure than a simple operation. Just as a procedure has parameters, the new complex instructions might include numerous operands. The sequence of operations to perform the function could be stored in one place for each instruction. If such instructions were used frequently, memory could be saved for the same reason that procedures save space. Finding instructions that are used frequently, however, implies that the instructions must be fairly general purpose. More and more, the operand specifiers took on the flavor of parameters for a procedure. Powerful single instructions were defined, occasionally requiring four or more parameters. As an example, the IBM System/370 architecture has a single instruction that copies a character string of arbitrary length from any location in memory to any other location in memory, while translating characters according to a table stored in memory.

This complexity within an instruction was accommodated by the concurrent introduction of **microprogramming**. Figure 16.1 shows a simplified block diagram of the

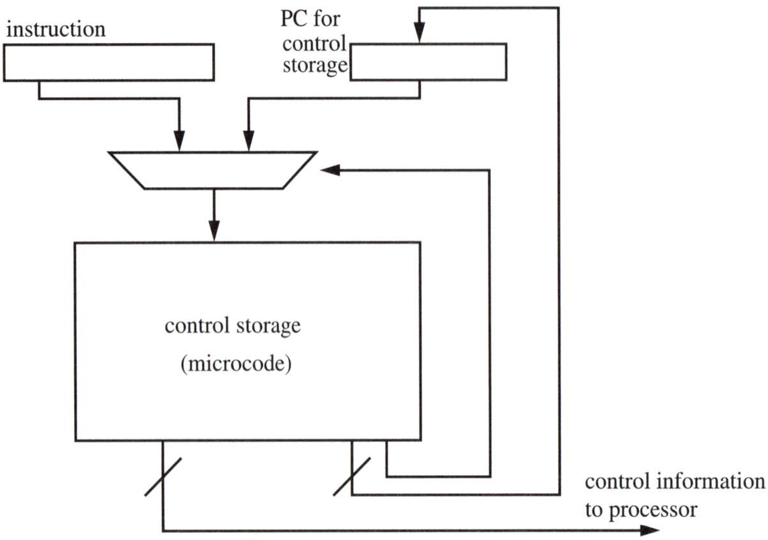

Figure 16.1 Simplified block diagram of hardware to implement microprogramming.

hardware within a microprogrammed computer. In a microprogrammed computer, each instruction is essentially a procedure call, with the code for the procedure being fetched from a special memory, called **control storage**. The control storage is not directly accessible to the program or programmer, but rather is accessed by the hardware in interpreting each instruction. The control storage outputs bits that direct the rest of the hardware within the processor. In the simplified block diagram, a single bit can be used to decide if the next address to access within the control store will come from a newly fetched instruction or from a separately maintained address. This address is essentially a program counter specifically for fetching instructions within the control store. An instruction could be arbitrarily complex, with several microinstructions comprising the steps required to complete the functionality of a single instruction. The added hardware cost for microprogramming is primarily the addition of a small amount of control storage. The savings in memory accrue in the same way they do for a conventional procedure call. Although a procedure may be invoked from many different places, the code is stored only once. An instruction that is invoked frequently saves the most memory if it accomplishes many things. The control storage can also be optimized to make the most efficient use of its memory, because of the fact that it is not modified.

The zenith of the trend toward complex instructions perhaps occurred with the Digital Equipment Corporation VAX computers. Among other things, a single instruction was provided to perform all the operations associated with a procedure call, including storing an arbitrary subset of the registers on the stack, adjusting the stack pointer and frame pointer, saving the return address, and jumping to the procedure. An equally complex instruction was provided for returning. It restored registers from the stack, adjusted the stack and frame pointers, and returned to the correct location.

A major effort to increase the functionality of instructions centered around the method of specifying the operands of an instruction. Many computers were provided with the capability to specify that operands would come either from a register or from memory, eliminating the need for load and store instructions. Allowing a large variety of addressing modes for any instruction increased the functionality of instructions. For example, many machines had an **auto-increment addressing mode**, which has the side effect of incrementing the value in a register used in the computation of the address of the operand. Thus the entire process of computing the address of an operand and modifying the address could be rolled into the single instruction that accesses the variable.

The trend was toward more complex instructions, and by the late 1970s, instructions had become remarkably complex. The VAX architecture has more than 200 instructions, dozens of distinct addressing modes, and instructions with as many as six operands. The instructions were so powerful that a program written in C required only about as many assembly language instructions as there were lines in the program. Because of careful encoding of information in the instruction, the memory space required to store the code was very small—perhaps half the size needed to store an equivalent program written for a load/store architecture. Unfortunately, such code density comes at a cost; the instructions are much more difficult to decode, and the pipelining becomes difficult. Because of this, high-performance implementations of such architectures are inherently difficult.

An architecture such as the VAX is today sometimes called a **complex instruction set computer**, or **CISC**. Although many examples of such architectures are present today, very few new CISC architectures have been introduced since the mid-1980s. An argument can be made that CISC architectures have only survived as general-purpose computers because of the importance of compatibility with previously successful computers.

Modern load/store architectures that have elemental instructions, with few addressing modes, are often referred to as **reduced instruction set computers**, or **RISC** computers. While the term RISC is primarily useful as a marketing concept, a dramatic change in direction in new architectures occurred in the mid-1980s. This trend was intimately tied to the constraints of single-chip processors, and it coincided with the introduction of pipelining in these processors and a much greater reliance on sophisticated compilers to achieve high performance. A strict definition of a RISC is open to debate.

16.2 THE SINGLE-CHIP CONSTRAINT

From the early 1960s, when the first integrated circuits were fabricated, increasingly more complex circuits have become reality. At first only a few gates could be manufactured on a single **integrated circuit**, or **chip**, but steady progress allowed more and more gates until, by the early 1970s, it was possible to fabricate a single chip that contained the entire processor of a simple computer. The earliest processors were not very elegant computers, because they had to struggle with severe constraints in order to fit onto a single chip at all. They had extremely small words, and they were quite slow. The first single-chip computer had a word width of only four bits. Initially they were successful primarily for low-end, inexpensive applications. The chips came to be known as **microprocessors**. They gradually achieved enormous success, and they greatly expanded the applications for computers of all kinds. The term "single-chip" computer is often used to describe a microprocessor, although that designation is slightly deceptive. A system typically comprised a microprocessor along with dozens of other chips, including memory chips and other chips to support the microprocessor chip.

The advantages of a single-chip computer are significant. Not only is manufacturing cost greatly reduced, but internal delays within a chip are much lower than the delays experienced when signals must cross chip boundaries. As circuit speeds have increased in the past few years, performance has increasingly been limited by speed-of-light delays. The only known solution for decreasing these delays is to put the components closer together.

By the late 1970s, the microprocessor was firmly established as a low-end computing engine, with limited capabilities but at a very low cost. The 1980s saw a major upheaval as technology continued to advance, making possible more complex circuits and therefore more powerful single-chip processors. Today, the capabilities of single-chip processors have grown enormously, challenging the most powerful computers in the world in many applications. **Massively parallel computers** are systems composed of many single-chip computers. Such systems are currently available, and they are a great hope to provide advances in supercomputing.

16.3 THE MOTOROLA 68000 FAMILY

In the late 1970s, the Motorola Corporation introduced a series of single-chip processors that are significant because of their success and longevity. The individual models in the family have similar architectures. Newer models generally have much higher performance and greater capabilities. The line of architectures started with the 68000 and progressed through the 68010 to the 68020, and beyond.

The Motorola 68000 architectures have condition code bits like the Pentium architecture. Instructions can specify 8-, 16-, or 32-bit operands. The architecture specifies 32-bit registers, although early implementations did not generally support 32-bit operations. Motorola uses the term **word** to identify a 16-bit quantity, and the term **long word** when referring to a 32-bit quantity. The 68000 family contains two register files, and each of the register files has its own intended use. Figure 16.2 contains a diagram of the register files. One of the files comprises the A registers. They are generally used to hold addresses. Of these registers, only A7 is not general purpose; it is dedicated as a stack pointer. The other file comprises the D registers. They generally contain data other than addresses. The distinction between addresses and other data is not always clear. Dividing 16 registers into two groups of eight has the advantage that a register within a register file can be designated with only three bits instead of four. Which register file is to be used is specified implicitly by other parts of the instruction. There are no load or store instructions, since any instruction can get its operands out of memory and store its result into memory. There is a general purpose move instruction that will copy an operand from anywhere to anywhere.

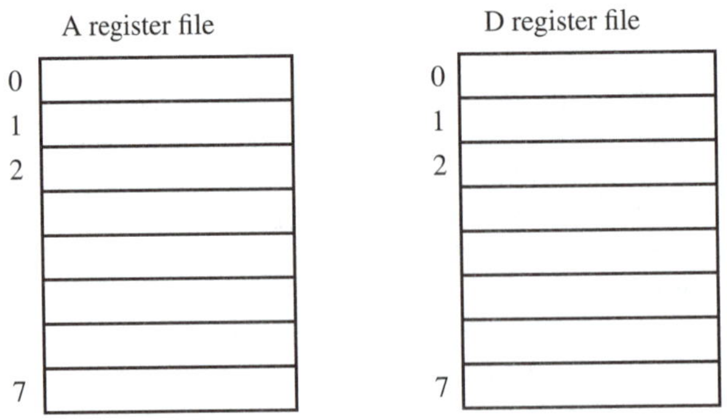

Figure 16.2 The Motorola 68000 register files.

Making efficient use of the bits designated to hold instructions was an important design criterion when the 68000 was first designed. Therefore, a two-address instruction set is specified as opposed to a three-address instruction set, and the encoding of bits within instructions is highly efficient. Instructions are nominally 16 bits in length, but instructions can contain additional 16-bit words, in some cases as many as four. The first word, known as the "Operation Word," comes in one of 18 different formats. Opcode size varies from instruction to instruction. At least two of the bits are opcode, and for some instructions, all 16 bits are opcode. An example of this is the `RESET` instruction. It consists of the 16-bit opcode 0x4e70.

To understand instruction decoding and the addressing modes of the 68000, consider the add instruction, `ADD`. The instruction format is given in Figure 16.3.

`ADD` is a two-address instruction. A source and destination are specified, and the destination serves to specify both the second source operand and the destination. Two address specifications are included: a register and another operand. The operand may be derived in a variety of ways. The **Op-Mode** field indicates whether the Register specification or the Effective Address is to be used to store the result. It determines whether the Register field specifies the source or the destination. The Op-Mode field also gives information about the size of data on which the instruction is to be performed. The size of all operands may be 1, 2, or 4 bytes. The table given in Figure 16.4 shows bit encoding for the Op-Mode field.

An addressing mode specifies an effective address. The Effective Address field can specify an operand's whereabouts in more than one way. The field is split into two subfields, called **Mode** and **Register**. The Mode subfield indicates how to interpret the Register subfield in order to derive the address. In many cases, the three bits of the register subfield specify a register within one of the register files. Figure 16.5 shows how some addressing modes are encoded.

Two variants of the Address Register Indirect addressing mode are notable. The Address Register Indirect with Postincrement mode has the side effect of incrementing the content of the A register specified in the Register subfield *after* it has been used to compute the effective address, as shown in Figure 16.6. The size of the increment is the length of the operands, in bytes. The Address Register Indirect with Predecrement mode has the side

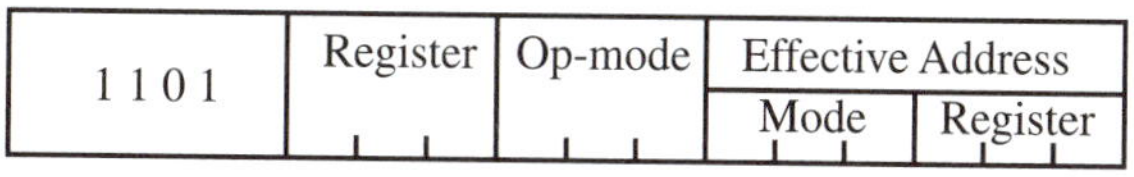

Figure 16.3 Motorola 68000 `ADD` instruction format.

Op-Mode	Operand Size	Destination Field
000	byte	Register
011	word	Register
010	long word	Register
100	byte	Effective Address
101	word	Effective Address
110	long word	Effective Address

Figure 16.4 Op-Mode field bit encoding.

Mode	Addressing Mode	Register
000	data register direct	D register number
001	address register direct	A register number
010	address register indirect	A register number
101	address register indirect with postincrement	A register number
110	address register indirect with predecrement	A register number
011	address register indirect with displacement	A register number
100	address register indirect with index	A register number
111	absolute short	000
111	absolute long	001
111	program counter with displacement	010
111	program counter with index	011
111	immediate	100

Figure 16.5 Motorola 68000 addressing mode encoding.

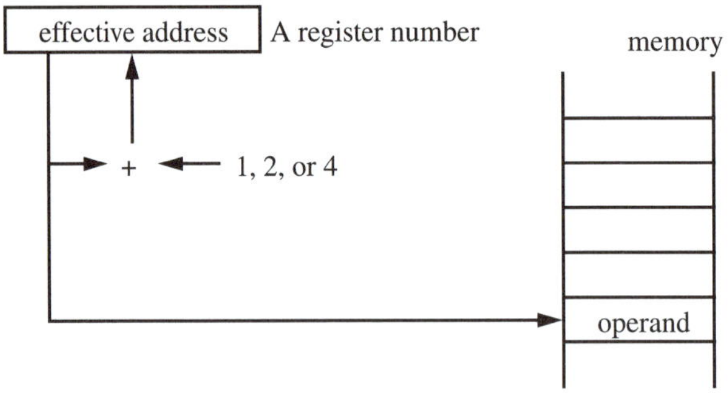

Figure 16.6 Address Register Indirect with Postincrement addressing mode.

effect of decrementing the content of the A register specified in the register subfield *before* it has been used to compute the effective address. These addressing modes permit the modification of an address without requiring a separate instruction. It is possible to access a character from a string and update the register containing the address of the character in a single instruction. The side effect of these addressing modes corresponds to the C language operations `i++` and `--i`. They are particularly well suited for manipulating a stack, making it possible to execute a push or pop operation in a single instruction.

Not all possible addressing modes are permitted with all instructions in the Motorola 68000. There is enough redundancy in the instruction set and allowed addressing modes such that the restrictions are not a problem. Virtually the same operation can be achieved with either a different instruction, or with the same instruction and a different addressing mode. As an example, consider the case where both operands are taken from data registers and the result is to go into one of them. It would appear either that the Data Register Direct mode could be used with the Effective Address as the destination, or that the Register could be designated as the destination. In fact, only the latter is permitted. The reason is simply a matter of cost. It would be nice to have all modes implemented, since that would make generating programs easier. But there is a cost for each addressing mode implemented. The 68000 designers decided that it was not cost-effective to provide redundant capabilities simply for generality.

The two-address format requires more instructions in some situations than the more general, three-address format typical of load/store architectures. Nevertheless, the rich set of addressing modes gives the 68000 family great power and permits small, dense programs. Register-to-register instructions require only 16 bits. The `MOVE` instruction serves the purpose both of load and store, as well as moving operands between registers (including between register files), and placing immediate operands into registers or memory.

The use of two register files reduces the size of instructions by reducing the number of bits necessary to specify a register. There is a cost associated with this. The mode field has more addressing modes for the A registers than for the D registers. In addition, the instruction itself must implicitly indicate which register file is designated by the Register field. Additional instructions (in the instruction set) are required in some cases. For example, there is an `ADDA` instruction that differs from the `ADD` instruction primarily in that the destination is always an A register. Unless every instruction must be replicated, adding an additional opcode costs less than adding an extra bit to specify a register.

A comparison between the Motorola 68000 instruction set and the Intel 8086 instruction set is appropriate. The two single-chip processors were competitors for the same microprocessor market. Their technological constraints were similar, since they were designed during the same period of time. Both were limited by the number of transistors that could be placed on a single chip. Both were also constrained by the number of external connections (pins) to the chip. And both were designed at a point in time where the amount of main memory in a computer system would be considerably less than in today's computer systems. The limits on main memory were due to its physical size and the cost of the memory.

Since memory space was at a premium, both the Motorola 68000 and the Intel 8086 were designed with two-address instruction sets. The encoding of information within machine code instructions was very tight, leading to few bits required for each instruction. The most commonly used instructions also required the fewest bits.

Both architectures also provide for similar choices in the programmer's selection of addressing modes. Giving the programmer such a wide variety of choices in addressing modes should have the effect of further reducing the size of the machine code for a program. It is a design decision consistent with the goals set for these microprocessors.

Another relevant comparison is in the number and size of registers in each architecture. The Motorola 68000 has both more and a larger number of bits per register than the Intel 8086. A larger number of registers can lead to better performance for code that efficiently uses the registers. When the Motorola 68000 first came out, the compiler technology was not as well developed as it is today. Therefore, the registers might not have been well utilized for code produced by a compiler. Today's compilers will likely use any available register. As the later versions of the Intel architectures were designed, Intel added a few more registers and increased the size of their registers to 32 bits. The effect of not having enough registers is reduced by the wide variety of addressing modes available.

16.4 THE CRAY-1

The Cray-1 supercomputer was designed by Seymour Cray in the mid-1970s. Now obsolete, it was a very successful computer because it performed a wide range of numerical applications at extremely high speed. Having been designed in an era when few computers were designed for raw speed, it has served as an example for many modern computers.

All aspects of the Cray-1 were designed with speed of computation in mind. The instruction set was chosen so that the clock speed could be extremely high, yet one instruction could be initiated on nearly every clock cycle. The machine is a load/store architecture, and it has a three-address instruction set. In addition, the hardware that performs arithmetic and logical operations is specialized to perform specific tasks quickly. A specialized piece of hardware can most often be designed to be faster than one that performs many operations. These **functional units** are used individually, meaning that the functional units can operate on different pieces of data concurrently.

Register Files

The Cray-1 processor is capable of issuing instructions that consume operands at an extremely high rate, and the memory system is capable of supplying operands at a very high rate. However, the **latency** of memory, the time required to load a single operand from memory, is long relative to the high speed of the processor. The Cray-1 tolerates this long latency by providing a very large number of registers and providing for the concurrent loading of many registers. The Cray-1 has nearly 5000 bytes of register storage. Such a large number of registers would result in very large register specification fields within an instruction, if a single register file were used. Thus multiple register files are used, each with its own intended usage. One of the five register files, the S-file, includes eight **scalar** registers for holding 64-bit operands. A second file, the A-file, includes eight 24-bit registers intended for addresses. A third register file, the V-file, includes the eight 64-element vector registers.

Each of these register files consists of only eight registers. Therefore, only three bits are needed to specify each register operand. This allows the Cray-1 to have 16-bit arithmetic and logical instructions. Load and store instructions are 32 bits.

In the time needed to load an operand from memory, the Cray-1 can initiate many other instructions, including additional memory operations. This pipelining introduces the possibility of data dependencies. To ensure correct operation, the hardware must keep track of registers that are scheduled to be modified but have not yet received their data. One example of when a register is scheduled to be modified but has not received data is at the initiation of a load instruction. Another example is when an arithmetic instruction is initiated, and the result is scheduled to be written to a register. The processor continues to initiate instructions until it encounters an instruction that needs to reference a register that does not yet contain the data necessary. The processor then waits until the data arrive.

Having a large numbers of registers enhances performance for two reasons. First, because the processor is so fast, there is a correspondingly large benefit in keeping frequently referenced variables in registers. The larger the number of registers, the fewer variables that will need to be stored in memory due to insufficient register space. Second, because many instructions may be concurrently in execution, a large number of registers helps to avoid register conflicts due to data dependencies. Instead of a cache (which misses some of the time), the Cray-1 provides a set of secondary registers for intermediate storage. These secondary registers are used for temporary storage. Data can be moved between memory and the registers or between the secondary registers and the primary registers. Operands saved in the secondary registers can be accessed much more quickly than

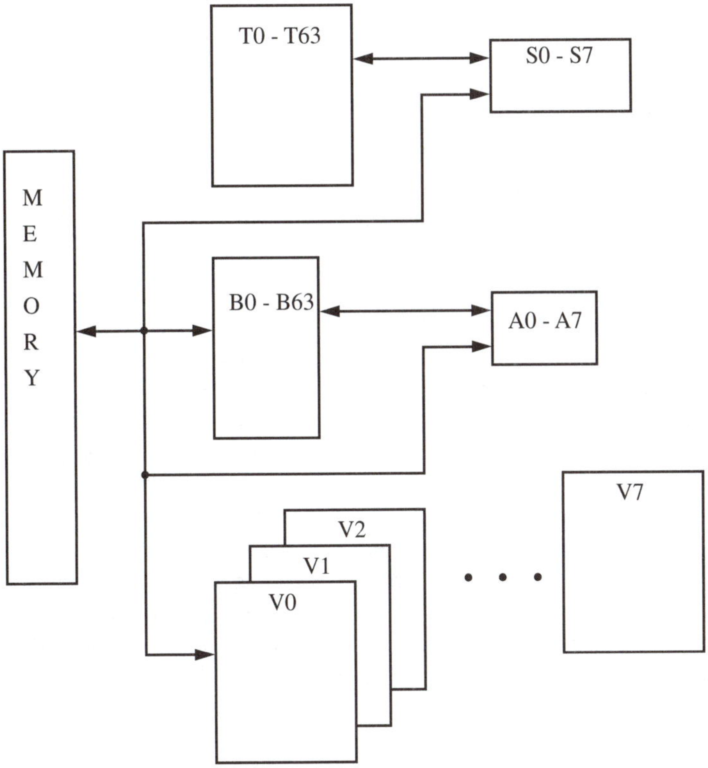

Figure 16.7 The Cray-1 register files.

those operands stored in main memory. Arithmetic and logical operations may use operands only from the primary A- and S-files. The secondary register files consist of 64 registers, requiring six bits for specification. There are two sets of secondary registers. The B-file connects to the A-file, and the T-file connects to the S-file, as shown in Figure 16.7. A single instruction is provided that can load a block of data from memory into a portion of either the B or the T registers. Notice that the B and T registers serve much the same function of a cache memory, saving frequently used variables for rapid access. The primary difference with this technique is that the programmer is explicitly responsible for the management of the B and T registers. In a cache memory, the hardware makes decisions of what variables to keep in fast storage based on usage.

The explicit overlapping of the execution of instructions makes programming the Cray-1 somewhat tricky. Execution speed can be greatly enhanced by anticipating when operands will be needed and initiating needed load operations in advance of their use as operands. Thus changing the order of certain instructions within a program can have a huge impact on the speed of execution without changing its functionality.

Vector Instructions and Registers

One of the most important innovations of the Cray-1 was the ability to operate on vector quantities with single instructions. A vector is a one-dimensional array of data. A vector operation involves applying an operation pairwise on the individual elements of two vectors.

For example, if A, B, and C are vectors each consisting of 64 elements, the high-level language C code to add the elements of A to the elements of B and store the results into C is

```
for (i = 0; i < 64; i++)
        A[i] = B[i] + C[i];
```

The additions for this entire loop can be performed on the Cray-1 by a single instruction. The addition is applied pairwise to the elements of the vector. Figure 16.8 diagrams this addition.

A **vector register** is capable of holding a vector of up to 64 elements, where each element is a 64-bit quantity. Thus a single vector register consists of 512 bytes of memory. Instructions are included to provide for the loading or storing of the many elements of a vector register by issuing a single instruction. The individual elements of the vector are initially stored in memory. The elements needed as a vector may be stored in contiguous locations in memory, as a one-dimensional array would be, or they may be scattered throughout a portion of memory with regular separations. An example of this would be the elements of a row in a two-dimensional array that is stored in column major order. A vector load instruction is capable of gathering up elements by loading beginning at an arbitrary address and separated by a fixed amount, known as the **stride**. As an example, consider a 10 by 16 two-dimensional array, stored in column major order. For a two-dimensional array, the individual elements of the first column of the array can be loaded into vector register 3 with the Cray-1 assembly language instruction

```
V3,A0,1
```

where register A0 contains the address of the first element of the array. A special register, called VL, maintains the number of elements within a vector register to be worked on. It would need to be previously set to contain the number of elements to be fetched, 10 for this example. Alternatively, to load the first row of the array into a vector register, VL

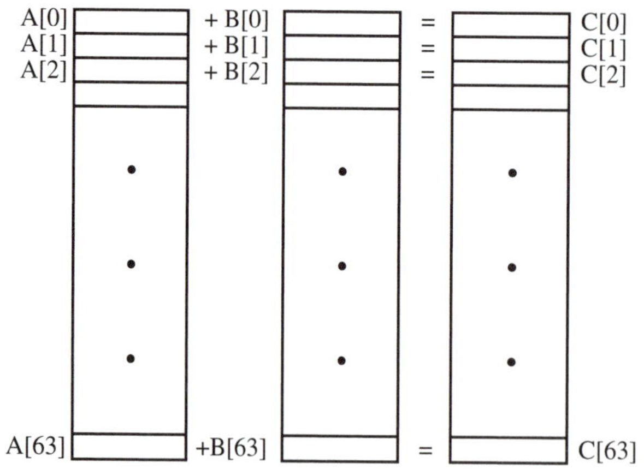

Figure 16.8 Vector addition example.

should be set to 16. If the elements of the first row of the array were to be loaded into vector register 4, the following instruction could be used:

```
V4,A0,A1
```

Register A0 contains the address of the first element of the array, and register A1 must contain the value 10, the stride of column elements. Note that there are block load and block store instructions, not only for the vector registers on the Cray-1, but also for the B- and T-register files.

The high-level programming languages taught in introductory programming courses do not have the syntax to specify vector operations. Therefore, the compiler written to produce code for the Cray-1, or any architecture with vector registers and instructions, would need to do an analysis of the code to determine where and when the vector registers and instructions might be used. There are versions of FORTRAN and other high-level programming languages that have been extended to include syntax for vector operations. This makes it possible to write programs that can be compiled to include instructions that operate on vector quantities. In many ways, the use of vectors is a natural extension to the programming language. Vector operations are generally performed using a for loop (called a DO loop in FORTRAN) to operate pairwise on elements within vectors. The compiler attempting to vectorize such a program for a language that is not extended to include vector operations has the task of recognizing when the programmer has serialized an inherently parallel operation. It must then recreate the original vector operation.

Although the Intel 8086 and the Cray-1 were designed during approximately the same period in time, they have vastly different architectures. Their design goals placed these two architectures at opposite ends of the spectrum. Where the Intel 8086 was stretching the limits of the circuitry that could be placed on a single chip, the Cray-1 utilized more circuitry wherever the addition of the circuitry would cause a performance increase. This can be seen as another example of the space versus time trade off as applied to computer architecture. The Intel 8086 used less physical space for circuitry at the expense of a loss in performance. It would take more time to execute code. The Cray-1 used much more physical space for circuitry in order to gain performance. Code executed faster, and it therefore required less time.

16.5 MIPS RISC

The MIPS RISC architecture was introduced in the 1980s. The MIPS project was researched at Stanford University under the leadership of Professor John Hennessy. Out of this project grew MIPS, Inc., and the MIPS RISC architecture. The R2000 was implemented as a single chip processor. It might be considered a chip set, since the hardware to do floating point arithmetic resided on a separate chip.

The MIPS RISC is a load/store architecture. Explicit load and store instructions are the only instructions that do memory accesses to get data. The three-address instruction set assembles into fixed-size 32-bit machine code instructions. The architecture is byte addressable, and integers are 32 bits. Conditional control instructions base their decisions not on condition codes, but on comparisons of the contents of registers.

bit numbers	31 26	25 21	20 16	15 0
	op code	register	register	offset

Figure 16.9 Control instruction format in MIPS RISC architecture.

The instruction set is small, as is the case for most of the architectures classified as RISC architectures. Six bits within the instruction are opcode. Instruction decode is simplified by placing specific fields within instructions always in the same location. For example, the control instructions (called branches in the MIPS RISC architecture) that contain an offset from the current instruction location are always encoded as in Figure 16.9. The most significant six bits are opcode. The next most significant bits designate registers, and the least significant 16 bits specify the offset.

The addressing mode for every operand is fixed, and it is implied by the instruction. A load instruction requires two operands. The first operand is register mode. The register specified is the destination for the data loaded from memory. The second operand uses base displacement addressing mode. This requires a register (the base) and a displacement. The MIPS architecture utilizes a 16-bit immediate to hold the displacement. An effective address is calculated by adding the contents of the (base) register to the immediate field (displacement). Note that having the addressing modes of the operands implied by the instruction, the length of the instruction can be reduced. No bits within the instruction need be used for specifying the addressing mode. This also facilitates a reduction in the number of machine code instruction formats and fixed-size instructions. Note that the machine code format given for control instructions in Figure 16.9 will be the same one used for load and store instructions. Fixed-size instructions also tend to reduce the control hardware (circuitry) required to fetch instructions. This can have the further effect of reducing the amount of time required to fetch instructions.

There are 32 32-bit registers. They are not all general purpose. For example, register 0 always contains the constant 0. Many modern architectures designate a register to contain the value 0. Doing so helps to reduce the size of the instruction set. Clearing a register is a common operation. Copying a value from one register to another is also a common operation. Yet by designating a register value to contain the constant 0, these two instructions can be eliminated. In the MIPS RISC instruction set, clearing a register can be accomplished with the instruction

```
add $8, $0, $0
```

where a '$' character placed before a number designates a register. Adding 0 to 0, and placing the resulting 0 sum in a register is the same as clearing the register. Copying a value from one register to another can also be accomplished with the `add` instruction:

```
add $12, $16, $0
```

The value 0 plus the contents of a register sums to the same contents of that register. The sum is then placed into another register, resulting in a register-to-register copy.

Other special-purpose registers include the designation of two registers that are only to be used by the operating system. This facilitates the operating system's task of saving state information within the kernel. Another register is set aside for use exclusively as a stack pointer. And a register is used implicitly to save the return address in a `jal` (jump and link) instruction. This instruction saves the address of the instruction following the `jal` instruction in register 31, and then transfers control to the target of the jump. This instruction facilitates procedure calls.

The MIPS RISC architecture also exhibits a trend seen in recent assembly languages. As compiler technology has improved, it has become easy for a small amount of compiler functionality to be placed within the assembler. The assembly language recognized by the assembler can differ from the assembly language instructions implemented by the architecture. The assembler is given the task of translating instructions offered in the assembly language, but not implemented as part of the architecture, into instructions that are implemented by the architecture. As an example, the MIPS RISC instruction

```
move $5, $9
```

does a register-to-register copy. This instruction is allowed in the assembly language, and is translated by the assembler into the instruction

```
add $5, $9, $0
```

Other more complex instructions translate from one assembly language instruction into multiple machine language instructions. This is different from the traditional assembly language, as in the Pentium architecture, where assembly language instructions mapped one-to-one with machine language instructions. The ability for the programmer to expand the instruction set to include more convenient instructions has always been available in the form of programmer-specified **macros**. The programmer is required to define and specify the macro, giving its translation into instructions known by the architecture. In the MIPS RISC architecture, macros are not supported. Instead, the assembly language is already specified to include those instructions thought to be convenient.

The MIPS RISC architecture uses a delayed branch to improve pipeline performance in the case of control dependencies. There is a reduction in holes within the pipeline for those cases where an instruction can be found to fill the delay slot. There is no performance improvement for the case where an instruction cannot be found to move into the delay slot.

A comparison between the Pentium architecture and the MIPS RISC architecture highlights the evolution of architectural design philosophies. A fundamental difference between the two architectures is that the MIPS RISC is a load/store architecture, and the Pentium is not. Over time, the newer architectures have all been load/store architectures. With a load/store architecture, it is possible to have a three-address instruction set, while keeping a fixed-size instruction and limiting the number of memory accesses required for each instruction. These features facilitate the pipelined implementation of an architecture.

The complex and large instruction set of the Pentium exists because of the previous processors within its architectural family. Pentium maintains compatibility with earlier versions. The earliest versions of the architecture were designed to reduce memory requirements. Memory is not a restricting factor now; so current new designs emphasize fixed-size instructions, and many fewer addressing modes in order to simplify circuitry.

16.6 SPARC

The Scalable Processor ARChitecture (SPARC) was developed in the late 1980s by Sun Microsystems, Inc. SPARC was developed at roughly the same time as the MIPS RISC architecture, and has many similarities to MIPS RISC. The SPARC architecture is a load/store architecture, and it has three-address instructions. A delayed branch with squashing is used for control instructions. The control instructions depend on condition code bits for making branch decisions. Integers are 32 bits, and all machine code instructions are 32 bits and of fixed size. The architecture is implemented as a single-chip processor.

Register Windows

Although there many minor differences between the MIPS RISC architecture and the SPARC architecture, perhaps the most important difference is the use of registers in SPARC. The SPARC architecture has a set of eight global registers that are accessible in the same way that the general registers are accessible in the MIPS RISC architecture. In addition, SPARC has a large set of registers from which only a subset can be accessed at any time.

SPARC is designed with the intention of supporting procedure call and return efficiently. In addition to eight global registers, SPARC has a large register file. The exact number of registers in the file varies from implementation to implementation, but because of the way the registers are accessed, the exact number is not important. At any time, 24 of those registers can be accessed. Those 24, plus the eight global registers, are designated as a **register window**. The 24 registers are the top of the stack. Programs use a register window in a way similar to an activation record.

At any time, instructions can access the registers in the current register window. Operands can be specified among these 32 registers in a manner similar to the MIPS RISC architecture, and the 32 registers can be loaded and stored in a manner similar to the MIPS RISC. Note, however, that there is no way to access data not in the current register window. Most of the registers are not accessible at any one time, and are only being saved for the time when their window again becomes the one at the top of the stack.

The 24 nonglobal registers in a register window can be split into three equal groups of eight registers. The first group comprises registers containing data shared with the procedure that called the current procedure. These eight, called INS, contain information passed to the procedure, and will include the parameters to the procedure. The second group are registers holding variables that are private to the currently invoked procedure. Examples of these are local variables, and these eight are called LOCALS. The third group of registers are those containing data shared with a procedure that will be called or has just returned from being called. These are the OUTS. The parameters to a procedure are placed in the OUTS, and function results can be returned in these shared registers.

When a procedure is invoked, the set of registers accessible is changed, and a new set of 24 registers is made available. These include the eight registers available from the previous register window, eight more dedicated registers, and another eight to be shared with a future procedure to be invoked. Figure 16.10 identifies three register windows corresponding to three levels of procedure calls. The OUTS from one procedure become the INS to

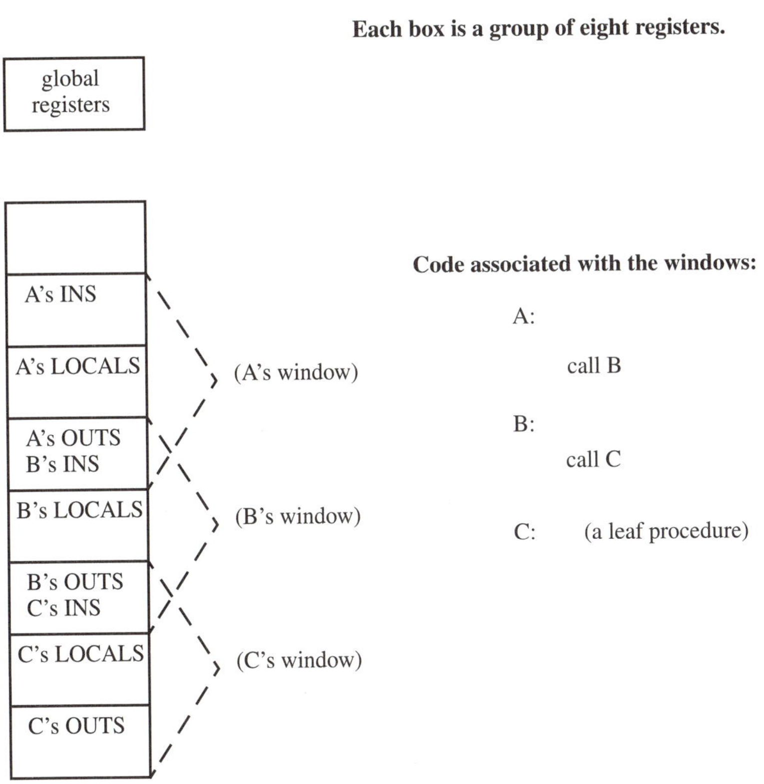

Figure 16.10 SPARC register windows.

the newly invoked procedure. Note that the OUTS allocated for use by a leaf procedure will go unused.

The number of register windows available is implementation dependent, with anything from 2 to 32 windows allowed. The windows are thought of as circular, so that there is no limit to the size of the stack. If all the windows have been allocated and a new procedure is called, a software mechanism is invoked to save the registers to memory, freeing them for current use. These registers can be reloaded by a similar mechanism when windows are popped off the stack.

The key ideas of the SPARC architecture originally emerged from the RISC architecture, developed at the University of California, Berkeley, under the leadership of Professor David Patterson.

16.7 ALPHA

The Alpha architecture was developed starting in 1988 at Digital Equipment Corporation. It is also implemented as a single-chip processor. The philosophy behind the architectural design is to fix what are seen as the problems with other architectures, making them right in the Alpha architecture.

Like other modern designs of single-chip architectures, Alpha is a load/store architecture, with fixed-size 32-bit instructions. There are many similarities with both the MIPS

RISC architecture and the SPARC architecture. Alpha has a three-address instruction set, and comparisons in control instructions involve one register. There are no condition codes. There are two register files, and each has 32 64-bit registers. One register file is for integer operands, and the other register file is for floating point operands. Instructions imply in which register file an operand is located. Also like the MIPS RISC architecture, one of the integer registers always contains the value zero. The Alpha instruction set benefits from this dedicated value the same way that the MIPS RISC does.

Memory is byte-addressable; so each byte has a unique address. Yet the instruction set has no instructions to load or store byte quantities. This is done because it simplifies (speeds up) the memory management hardware's implementation.

Unlike the MIPS RISC and SPARC architectures, the Alpha architecture does not specify delayed branches to try to increase performance for control instructions. It simplifies a pipelined implementation and it simplifies the assembler not to implement a delayed branch. Other hardware implementations that do branch prediction or just fetch both instruction streams work well.

Alpha differentiates itself from the other single-chip processor architectures described by fully supporting 64-bit processing. There are 64 bits of address to access memory, and the size of integer operands on the processor are 64 bits. The other architectures described have had 32-bit operands and 32-bit address spaces. There are a small number of Alpha instructions that operate on 32-bit integers. Most work on 64-bit integers. Alpha's designers predict that the near future will bring a desire for a higher precision in integer arithmetic as well as a desire for a larger address space. The reduction in transistor size, resulting in an increased density of transistors available with today's technology, makes it possible to implement this in a single-chip processor. Note that this shift from a 32-bit processor to a 64-bit processor is similar to the shift made approximately two decades ago, when architectures went from 16-bit processing to 32-bit processing. It is likely that other newly defined architectures will also support 64-bit processing.

SUMMARY

An important trend of the past decade has been a rapid increase in processor speed. While the underlying reason for this improvement is unquestionably advances in the hardware technologies employed, there have been important advances at the hardware/software interface—the architecture. The overlapping of instructions is being extended beyond simple pipelines, with newer computers actually *initiating* multiple instructions simultaneously. So far the most successful architectures have been those that maintained the appearance to the programmer of sequential execution. Computer science is actively engaged in finding new ways of exploiting parallelism at many different levels to achieve higher performance, whether it be the overlapping of instructions or procedures, or applying multiple processors concurrently. The trend will surely continue, with many new architectures exploring extensions and variations of the current architectures. If history is any guide, however, the new architectures will be only incrementally different from previous architectures.

The architecture of computers has been steadily evolving throughout the history of computing, and there is no reason to believe that the pace of innovation is slackening. As more and more capabilities appear in the underlying technologies, and as architects strive to exploit that technology to the full, there will undoubtedly be new developments at the hardware/software interface. It is likely that future innovations will not be completely new, but rather variations of schemes previously considered. Historically, many ideas have been proposed, or even implemented on certain machines, but failed to gain wide acceptance until the technology matured enough to make their implementation cost-effective. The continuing rapid advances in semiconductor technology virtually guarantee that this trend will continue.

The most significant trend in the past decade has been to expose the details of the hardware more and more to the programmer, allowing the exploitation of that knowledge to achieve very high performance. Many such examples have been explicitly chosen because of the knowledge that programmers generally do not write programs at this level, and that most assembly language code is in fact produced by compilers. It is reasonable to expect that this trend will continue, with increasing interaction between the hardware and the compiler, making the job more and more difficult for those unfortunate programmers who find it necessary to write programs at this level.

PROBLEMS

1. What defines a computer's architecture?

2. What architectural features correspond to a RISC architecture? A CISC architecture?

3. A computer designed for a special application may have very special instructions that are explicitly designed for that application. Carrying this to an extreme, it is possible to build a computer that has only a single instruction: `do_it`. Identify an application where such an instruction might be appropriate.

4. Why are single-chip processors important?

5. Why would the Motorola 68000 architecture have two register files of eight registers each instead of one register file of 16 registers?

6. Write a high-level language program fragment that could utilize the Motorola 68000 autoincrement addressing mode when compiled.

7. Why might the B and T registers of the Cray-1 computer be preferable to a cache memory? What is the disadvantage of this "explicit cache"?

8. Write a high-level language program fragment that would benefit from being compiled to use the Cray-1 vector registers.

9. Compare the Pentium architecture to the M68000 architecture. What features are the same? What features are different?

10. Compare the Pentium architecture to the MIPS RISC architecture. What features are the same? What features are different?

11. Write a high-level language program fragment that is likely to require fewer assembly language instructions on the SPARC architecture than on the MIPS RISC architecture, once compiled. Does the high-level language program fragment identify a situation that is likely to occur frequently in high-level language code?

CHAPTER
17

MEMORY MANAGEMENT AND VIRTUAL MEMORY

Barton P. Miller

The earliest computers ran only a single program at a time. When a program was loaded into memory to run, it was loaded into a fixed, known address (the same for every program) and the code and data of the program had to fit into the available memory. Computers that could only load one program into memory at a time were called **uniprogrammed** systems. Of course, modern computers appear to execute many programs at one time. A personal computer or workstation is probably such a **multiprogrammed** system, with its mailer, Web browser, clock, shell, and network services (like remote file access) all ready to run in memory at the same time.

This chapter contributed by Barton P. Miller, University of Wisconsin, Madison.

Multiprogramming brings up three critical issues:

1. Protection: With multiple programs in running in memory at the same time, one program should not be able to crash another program or the operating system. In assembly language programming (and many high-level languages such as C or C++), memory addresses are directly manipulated, and it is easy to make mistakes so that a program writes into a random part of memory. Modern computers use their memory management hardware to protect against this problem.
2. Space: Even with the large memories of current computers, it is often impossible to fit many programs entirely into memory at the same time. In addition, the new operating systems can require 10 megabytes (or more!) of memory. Modern memory management hardware allows the operating system to bring into memory only those pieces of a program that are needed at the moment. The parts not currently required are kept on disk. The programmer is given the illusion of having much more memory (RAM) than is actually installed, although with some loss of performance.
3. Relocation: In the early uniprogrammed systems, the starting address of the program was known by the programmer (or the linker). This information is crucial, so that control instructions such as branches, jumps, and calls can point to the right place. In a multiprogrammed system, the programmer never knows where the program will end up. The program could be modified each time it is loaded from disk, fixing up all branch and call instructions. This technique is called **relocation**, and it was used in early computer systems. Relocation has two big disadvantages. First, it is expensive in terms of the amount of time required to do the relocation, and it must be done every time a program is to be loaded into memory. Second, once a program is loaded, it cannot be moved, either to other places in memory, or back and forth to and from the disk.

This chapter introduces some of the kinds of hardware that have been used for memory management. The acronym **MMU** stands for **memory management unit**, and it is a generic term for the hardware used for memory management. As computers get faster and memories get larger, the technology in this area continues to change. The material in this chapter provides the basics for understanding these new memory management architectures.

17.1 BASIC CONCEPT AND TERMS

The description of some basic terms facilitates the understanding of memory management and virtual memory.

- **Physical Memory**: The physical memory, or RAM (random access memory), is the amount of memory actually installed in a computer. The size of the physical memory is based on the size and number of RAM chips installed. The CPU fetches instructions and loads data from this memory.
- **Virtual Memory**: Virtual memory is the memory that the operating system allows a program to believe that it has. With appropriate memory management hardware and by allocating a part of a disk, the operating system can run programs that are larger than will fit into the physical memory. The operating system allocates space on the

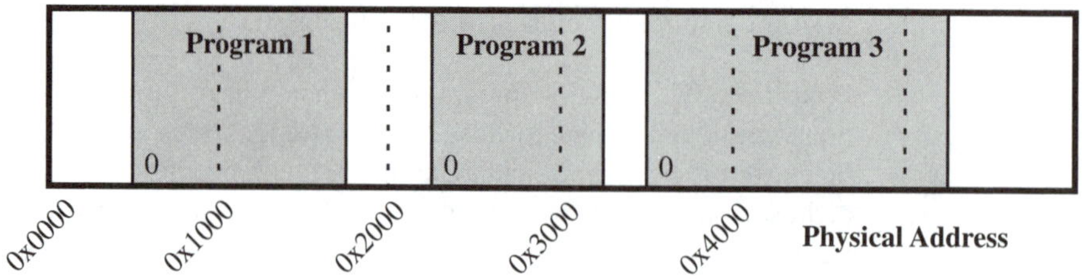

Figure 17.1 Three programs in memory, each thinking that it starts at (virtual) address 0.

disk to store the parts of the programs that currently do not fit into memory. This area on the disk is usually called **swap space** or **backing store**. The operating system transfers pieces of programs to and from memory as needed.

- **Physical Address:** A physical address is a memory location in the physical memory. A specific address refers to a physical place, a specific place in the RAM of the computer.
- **Virtual Address:** In modern computers, each program is linked to start at address 0 (or some other fixed, low address). All addresses generated by an executing program are specified relative to this 0 starting point. Each program has the illusion that it has the entire memory to itself. These 0-based addresses are **virtual addresses**.
- **Address Translation:** Even though a program generates virtual addresses in instructions, the operating system places parts of programs in various places within the physical memory. Figure 17.1 presents an example that shows three programs in memory. Each starts at a different physical address, but each thinks it starts at (virtual) address 0. Each time a program references memory, the MMU translates the virtual address to a physical address. It is the job of the operating system to tell the MMU where the pieces of the programs reside within physical memory.
- **Address and Address Space Sizes:** Memory addresses are typically unsigned integer values. An address that is n bits wide can address up to 2^n locations in memory, with addresses from 0 to 2^n-1. An **address space** is the set of virtual addresses that a program may access.

There are many variations in memory management and virtual memory design, and many details on real systems that make the designs more complex. This chapter provides a foundation for understanding many of the important designs, but there is much more to learn after this. Some topics not discussed include translation lookaside buffers (TLBs or address caches), inverted page tables, operating system kernel virtual memory, and virtual memory scheduling (replacement) policies.

The following sections describe various kinds of memory management hardware, starting with early, simple ones, building up to more contemporary designs. The operation of a virtual memory system is a careful cooperation between the MMU and the operating system. The operating system decides where in memory to place programs and loads this information into the MMU.

17.2 BASE AND BOUNDS

An early form of memory management hardware, and one of the simplest, is called **base and bounds**. This scheme allows multiple programs to be placed into memory, each with its own address space, each thinking that it starts at address 0, and each restricted to accessing only its own memory locations. This scheme is was used on the Cray 1 supercomputer.

In the base and bounds scheme, a program must be loaded completely into a contiguous piece of physical memory. Only two values are needed in the MMU to describe the location of the program: A base address specifies the starting physical address of the program, and the bounds specifies the size of the program. Note that the bounds specifies the largest *virtual* address in the program (this can be tricky to picture, so take a minute to think about it).

Figure 17.2 illustrates the simple hardware for a base and bounds MMU. The virtual address is the address generated by the program. This virtual address goes into the MMU to be translated to a physical address. Two things happen at the same time:

1. The virtual address is added to the base address to produce the physical address. The physical address is then used to access the appropriate location in physical memory.
2. The virtual address is compared to the bounds to see if the program tried to use an address beyond the end of its allocated space. If the address is a good one (less than the bounds), then all is well. If the address is too large, a memory fault is generated in the form of a trap, causing the operating system take over and (most likely) terminate the offending program.

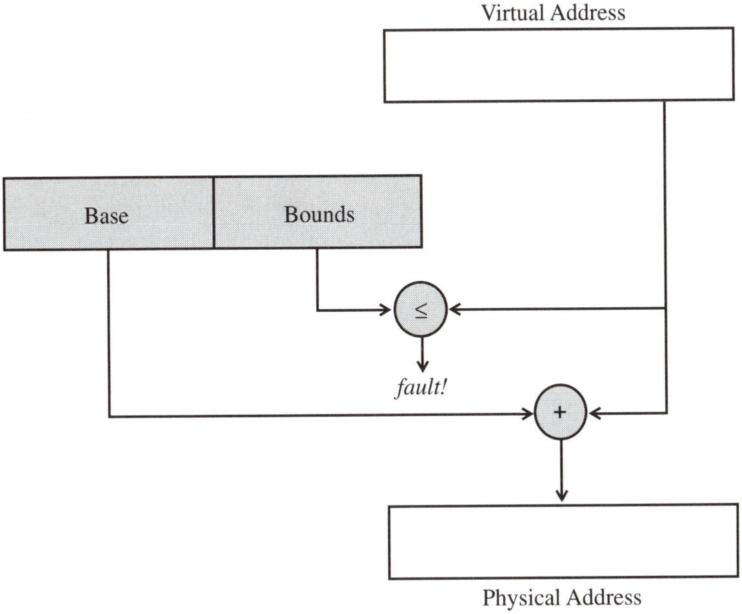

Figure 17.2 Base and bounds memory hardware.

Note that the MMU does not have to check for an address that is too small (less than 0). Since addresses are unsigned numbers, it is not possible to specify a negative address.

The MMU only holds one set of base and bounds registers, so the hardware describes the address space for only one program at a time. Each time the operating system switches between programs (called a **context switch**), it reloads the base and bounds registers with the values for the program that is to run next.

Both the virtual address space and the physical address space for base and bounds virtual memory are required to be one contiguous piece. When a program is placed in memory, it requires a contiguous piece of physical memory.

The base and bounds scheme has the advantage that it is extremely simple to build. It has several disadvantages. First, it requires an entire program to be loaded completely into memory for execution. If there is not enough unallocated space in the physical memory, entire programs must be moved to the disk to free up physical memory space. Second, it is difficult for more than one program to share parts of memory, such as might be done for a shared library or data. Third, the program's code, data, and stack must be placed into the memory allocated for the program. The space required for the data and stack is likely to grow as the program executes. It is difficult to have more than one part of a contiguous piece of memory grow.

17.3 SEGMENTATION

A program can be split up into several logical pieces. There are several ways of splitting a program. One example of a logical split is a code piece, static data piece, dynamic (heap) data piece, and a stack piece. This way of splitting a program is commonly used on many systems. Another way of splitting up a program is to place the code for each separately compiled file in its own piece, and then have additional pieces for the static data, dynamic data, and stack. Each of these logical pieces of a program is called a **segment**.

In a computer that has memory management hardware to support segmentation, a program is split into several logical pieces. The size of the piece is determined by the space needed to store the piece. If the code for a program takes 35,224 bytes of memory, then the code segment size will be set to 35,224. The MMU stores the base and bounds for each segment of a program. This information is kept in a table that is usually called the Segment Table (ST). There is one segment table for each running program. Each entry in the ST describes one segment for a program; it is called a Segment Table Entry (STE). Each STE has a bounds field so that the segment allocated in physical memory needs to be only as big as necessary. The maximum size of a segment is determined by the number of bits in the bounds field. In the example in Figure 17.3, a segment could have up to 2^{24} bytes (16 megabytes).

A common design places the ST for a running program in the operating system's memory. When the operating system switches from running one program to running another, it must communicate with the MMU, identifying the ST for the next program. The operating system points to the current ST by loading the physical address of this table into the Segment Table Base Register (STBR). The operating system also loads the Segment Table Size Register (STSR) in the MMU to identify how many entries are allocated in the ST. If a program has only three segments, a bigger table is unnecessary; the STSR is loaded with the value 3.

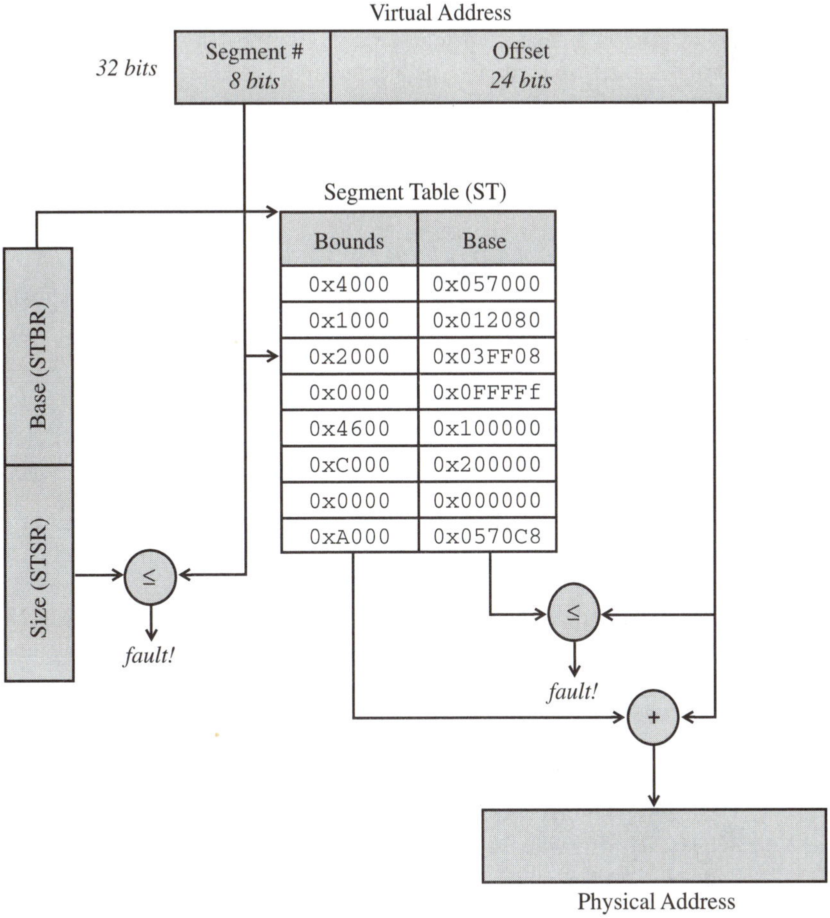

Figure 17.3 Segmentation memory hardware.

Each running program is permitted to access only its own segments. If two (or more) programs want to share some memory, a separate segment can be created and allocated for this segment. The STE for each running program that is sharing the segment will point to the same piece of memory.

The next question is how does the MMU select which segment to access? The most common scheme uses some of the bits of the virtual address to select the segment number. Note that this is different from the one built into the Intel 8086 processor and its successors; the x86 scheme is described in the next section. Looking at the example in Figure 17.3, the virtual address is 32 bits wide. The address is split into two pieces: The most significant 8 bits are a segment number, and the least significant 24 bits are an offset into the segment. As an example, the code is in segment 0, the static data in segment 1, the dynamic data in segment 2, the stack in segment 3, and a shared library in segment 4. The most significant 8 bits of the address provide a means of describing the location of the STE within the ST.

When a program references memory, the segment number bits are used to index into the current ST to select the appropriate STE. This entry contains the physical base address for the segment in memory. The base address is added to the offset in the virtual address to produce the final physical address. There are two places where a trap may occur due to incorrect operation. This trap is called a **segmentation fault**. First, if the segment is too big, when it is compared to the STSR a fault is generated. Second, the offset is compared to the bounds for the appropriate segment (in the STE) to see if the offset is attempting to access past the end of the segment. This second check is the same as for the simple base and bounds memory management.

In a segmentation system, when the compiler and linker finish with a program, they have split it into segments. The information about the number and size of the segments is stored in the file containing the executable (binary) version of the program. When the operating system loads a program into memory, it reads this information to figure out how much memory to allocate for the program and how to set the ST entries for the program.

Each segment is a logically contiguous piece of memory (contiguous in virtual memory) and must be allocated contiguously in physical memory. A segment can be loaded anywhere in physical memory as long it is completely present. Part of a segment may not be loaded. Segments for a program do not have to be adjacent to each other in physical memory or even all loaded at the same time.

As time goes on, segments are created and destroyed. Since each segment is sized according to its need, the size of a new segment will likely not match the size of other segments. Further, the sizes of the free gaps in physical memory may not match well with the new segments. Eventually, physical memory may end up with many small fragments of unallocated space, none of which is big enough to fit a new segment. This situation of having the memory fragmented into many small pieces is called **external fragmentation**. When this situation occurs, the operating system can stop all the programs that are running and compact the memory. Unfortunately, this can be quite slow.

Something to think about: A segmentation scheme with zero bits of segment number in the virtual address has $2^0 = 1$ segment. This scheme is base and bounds.

17.4 SEGMENTATION ON THE PENTIUM

The Intel 8086 processor was the 16-bit successor the popular 8-bit Intel 8080. The 8080 had 16-bit addresses and the 8086 was still based on 16 bits. 16 bits allows only 64 Kbytes to be addressed. To allow the new 8086 to address more than 64 Kbytes, the address space was divided into four segments, one for the code, data, stack, and "extra" data. Each segment could be a maximum of 64K in size; so a program could now address (that is, its virtual address space was now) 256 Kbytes of memory. Before the segment base address was added to the virtual address, it was shifted left 4 bits (multiplied by 16). In effect, the 8086 segment base registers were 20 bits long, with the low-order 4 bits always 0.

The base addresses for the four segments were stored in registers (CS, DS, SS, and ES) rather than in a table in memory. The four segment base registers, taken together, form the segment table for the 8086.

In subsequent versions of the x86 architecture, the number and size of segments grew, and bounds entries (registers) for each segment were added. Intel calls these bounds **limits.**

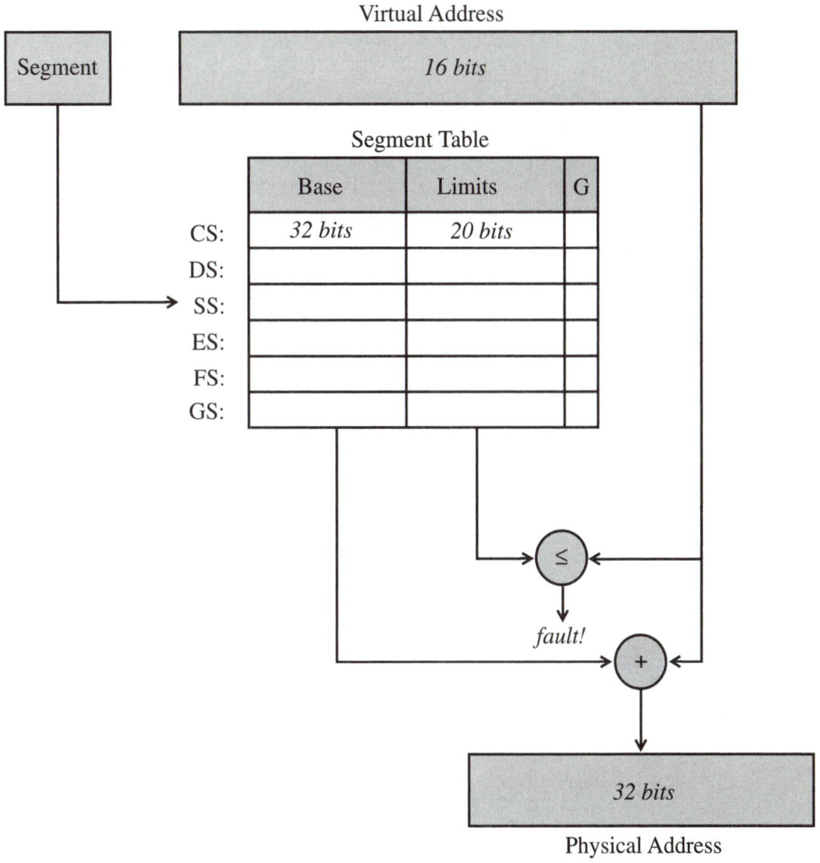

Figure 17.4 Pentium segmentation memory hardware.

In the Pentium design (see Figure 17.4), there are now six segments, with the base field being 32 bits wide and the limit (bounds) field being 20 bits wide. For each segment, there is also a bit flag, called the granularity (G) bit. When the G bit is set to 0, the limit registers specify the size of the segment in bytes; so the maximum segment size is 2^{20} (1 megabyte). When the G bit is set to 1, the limit registers specify the size of the segment in 4K (2^{12}) byte chunks; so the maximum segment size is 2^{32} (4 gigabytes).

The Pentium does not specify a segment number in the virtual address. Instead, the processor decides which segment to use based on what kind of access it is making. If the processor is fetching an instruction, it selects segment CS; if it is accessing a variable in memory, it selects DS; if the access is to the stack, it selects segment SS. Once a segment is selected, the proper entry in the ST is used and the address calculation works exactly the same as for standard segmentation.

A program can override the default segment by putting a modifier byte in front of an instruction. For example, a logical `and` instruction that would default to using data from the data segment:

```
and    eax, [ebx]
```

To change the data reference in this instruction to use ES instead, the code becomes

```
and    eax, es:[ebx]
```

The assembler uses a segment override prefix with the instruction.

In this book, and the associated programming assignments, the Pentium segments have not been used. Most modern systems use what is called a **flat** address space. All segment registers are loaded with the same base address, and the result is that it appears programs have a simple, 32-bit virtual address. The virtual address translation is then handled by MMU hardware, providing more conventional segmentation or paging (described in the next section).

17.5 PAGING

While segmentation is a handy way to break up an address space, it has the problem that segments are of variable size. While compilers and programmers may like being able to size segments to match code, data, or whatever, allocation of variable-sized memory (or anything) is more complex than allocation of fixed-size pieces. An alternative memory management strategy is to split a program's address space into fixed-size pieces, called **pages**.

In a memory management system that supports pages, the system designers pick a page size for all programs. There are some computers that allow multiple page sizes, but these systems are rare, and operating system designers have not yet figured out good ways to use them. Page sizes vary from 512 bytes to 64 Kbytes, with the most common sizes in the 1 to 8 Kbyte range. Earlier chapters viewed physical memory as a very large array of bytes, where allocation is in multiples of bytes. In a page-based system, physical memory is now treated as an array of pages, where allocation of memory is in units of pages. Physical memory is only allocated in page-size units and on page boundaries. The locations for pages in physical memory are **page frames**. The example from Figure 17.1 is shown in Figure 17.5 for a page-based system.

A program's virtual address space is split into pages, and these pages can be located in the page frames. Notice from Figure 17.5 that a program's pages can be scattered about memory. When more physical memory is needed, allocation of a frame is all that is

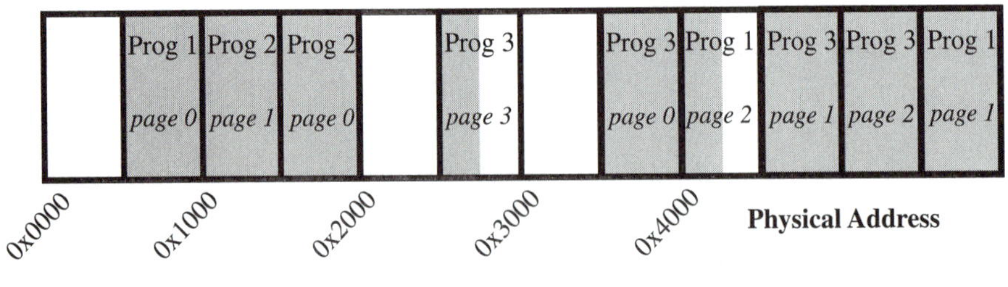

Figure 17.5 Three programs in memory, starting on page boundaries and allocated in units of pages.

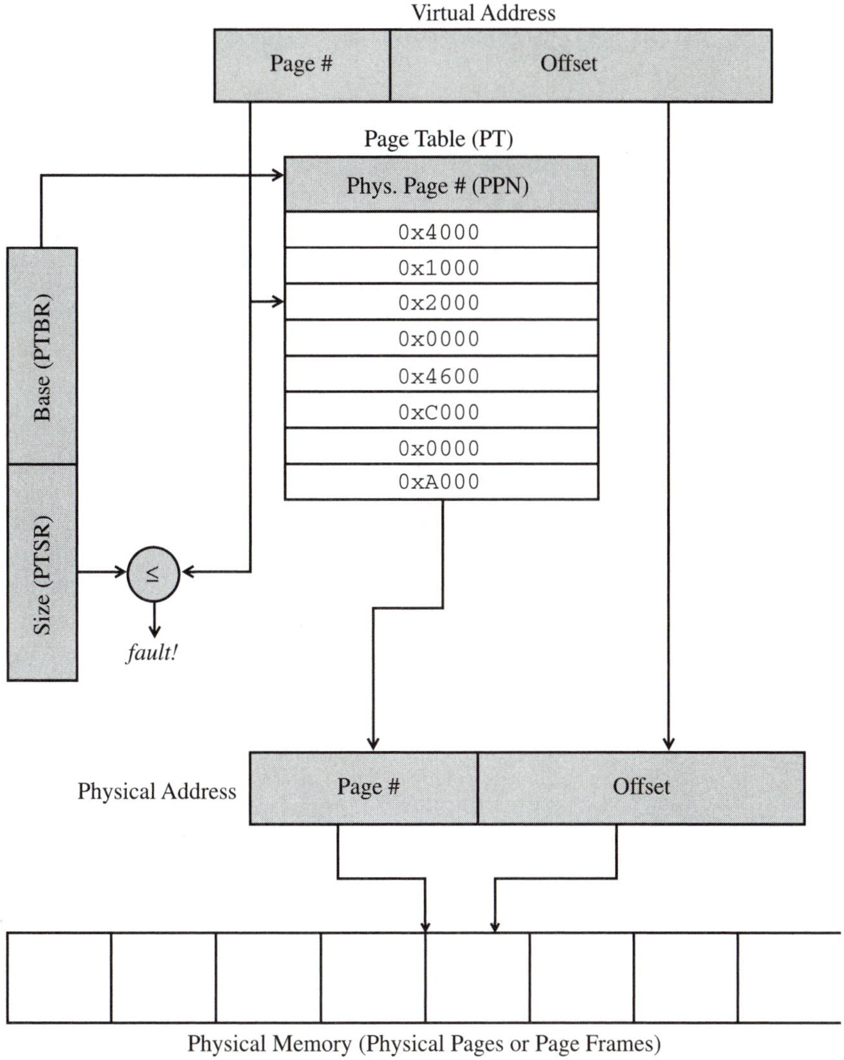

Figure 17.6 Paging memory hardware.

needed. The data structures needed to track allocation of the page frames are simple: as easy as an array of bits, one for each frame.

Figure 17.6 diagrams the use of paging for address translation. As with segmentation, some of the most significant bits in the virtual address are used to index into a Page Table (PT). The Page Table Entry (PTE) contains the physical page frame number of the frame containing the virtual address. Note that since page frames all start on page boundaries and page frame sizes are always powers of two, the complete physical address of the frame does not need to be stored. For example, in a system with 4 Kbyte pages, page frame 0 has address 0x00000000, frame 1 has address 0x00001000, frame 2 has 0x00002000. In this example, the least significant 12 bits are always zero; so they do not need to be stored in a PTE.

After lookup in the PT gives a page frame number, it is concatenated with the offset from the virtual address to form the physical address. This is simpler than segmentation (compare Figure 17.3 to Figure 17.6), since segmentation requires an addition of the segment base and the offset.

As with paging, each running program can access only its own pages. If two or more programs want to share some memory, a page can be allocated and the PTE for each program that is sharing the page will point to the same page frame.

Pages are a handy mechanism for virtual memory. The fixed-size pieces can be easily transferred between disk and memory. If all the page frames (in physical memory) are currently allocated and a program needs one more, any frame may be chosen. The contents of the chosen page frame are transferred to disk to free the necessary space. Since all pages are the same size, a virtual page can be placed in any frame.

There is a subtle distinction between the use of segments and pages. Segments are usually an architectural feature that the programmer and compiler/linker know about. Each segment has a particular meaning. Information is placed into a segment based on its use. If the number of segment number bits in a virtual address were changed, the programmer or compiler/linker might not understand and programs could execute incorrectly. With paging, the programmer is typically unaware of the page size or where the page boundaries fall. Pages are simply a hardware and operating system mechanism to facilitate flexibility in memory allocation. Another way to think about it is that for page allocation, the next page is only allocated when the previous one is completely full. With segments, they are allocated to whatever size makes sense, allocating a new one when there is a new type of object.

Since all pages are fixed size, paging systems do not have external fragment like that found in segmentation systems. But, since space is allocated for each program in multiples of the page size, there can potentially be wasted space in the last page of each program. On the average, a waste of 1/2 page would be expected for each program. This wasted space inside the last page is called **internal fragmentation**.

One problem with paging is that the size of the page tables can get quite large. A 32-bit virtual address and a 4K byte page size (requiring 12 bits of offset) leaves 20 bits for the page number. Twenty bits of page number can require a page table with up to 2^{20} (more than a million) entries. If code starts at the beginning of the virtual address space and, as is commonly done, the stack is at the high end of the address space, the full 2^{20} entries must be allocated. The page tables would be too large, and would consume an excessive amount of physical memory. Two schemes that address this problem appear in the next two sections. The first scheme combines segmentation and paging, and the second scheme splits the page table into two levels, like a tree data structure.

17.6 PAGING AND SEGMENTATION

Segmentation provides logical sizing and grouping of parts of a program's address space, but dealing with variable-sized pieces of memory is awkward. Paging provides a convenient and simple scheme for managing a program's virtual memory using fixed-sized pieces. To get the best of both schemes, systems have been developed that provide architecturally visible segments that are allocated in page size units. This scheme is sometimes called **paged segmentation**.

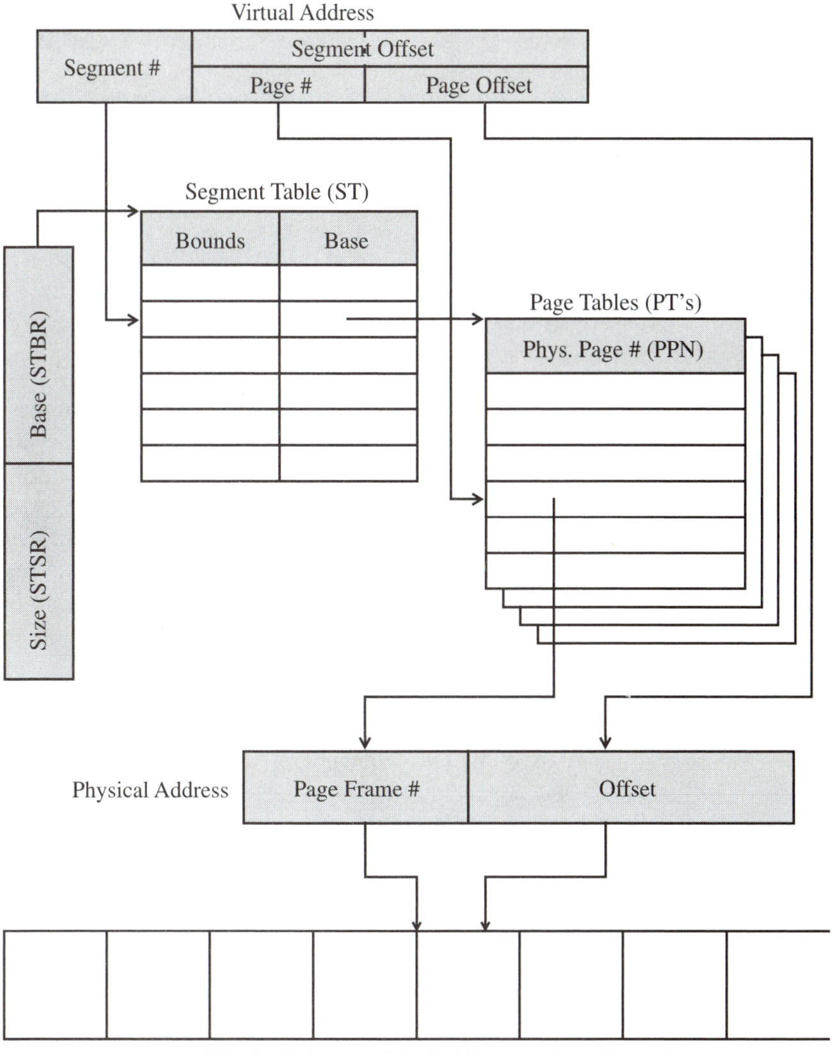

Figure 17.7 Segmentation and paging memory hardware. Bounds checking is not shown.

Figure 17.7 diagrams the address translation required in paged segmentation. As in regular segmentation, the virtual address is logically split into two pieces: segment number and offset within the segment. The segment number is used to index into the segment table. The base field of STE does not point to the physical address of the segment (as it did in regular segmentation). Instead, the STE base field points to the starting address of the page table for this segment. Since segments are allocated as pages, the segment offset field is further divided into a page number and offset within the page. The page number is used to index into the selected page table, producing the physical page number. As with the regular paging scheme, the physical page number and page offset are concatenated to form the physical address.

The STBR points to the starting address of a program's ST. The segment number is compared to the STSR to make sure that the reference is to a valid segment within the segment table. Each STE also has a bounds field. When the page number is used to index into the appropriate page table, it is compared to the bounds field for that segment's page table. This comparison ensures that the memory reference is not beyond the end of the segment. Note that the length of a segment is now counted in number of pages, not number of bytes.

In paged segmentation, there is one segment table per running program. For each running program, there is also one page table per segment.

17.7 MULTILEVEL PAGING

The page-based memory management scheme has the advantage that the address space and physical memory are divided into fixed-size pieces that are easy to manage. Unfortunately, this scheme can also result in huge page tables. For paged segmentation, the address space is divided into segments, and then paging is used for each segment. That scheme required that the programmer and compiler/linker be aware that the address space is segmented. To address the large page table problem without introducing segments, the page table can be split into two (or more) levels, as shown in Figure 17.8. This is a common scheme on many current systems, such as the Sun SPARC. Multilevel page tables can sometime have three or four levels.

The multilevel page table looks, in many ways, similar to the paged segmentation in Figure 17.7. Note that the page number field is divided into two parts. In the first part, the most significant bits of the page number are used to index into the first-level page table. The first-level page table points to a list of second-level page tables. In the second part of the page number, the least significant bits are used to index into the selected second-level page table. The first-level page table is relatively small. The second-level page tables are only allocated for allocated parts of the virtual address space.

17.8 PAGE AND SEGMENT ATTRIBUTES

For all the memory management schemes that have been described in this chapter, there is additional information that can be included in each PTE or STE. This information is used to control access to a page or segment. It records how a page or segment was actually accessed. This information appears as extra bits in the PTE or STE.

Typical access controls on a page or segment include read (R), write (W), and execute (X) permissions. In other words, to be able to read the page or segment, the R bit in the PTE or STE must be set; to be able to write to that page or segment, the W bit must be set, and to be able execute instructions from that page or segment, the X bit must be set. Some systems have separate R/W/X bits in each PTE or STE for user programs (UR, UW, UX) and for the operating system (SR, SW, SX).

Physical Page #	R	W	X	mod	ref

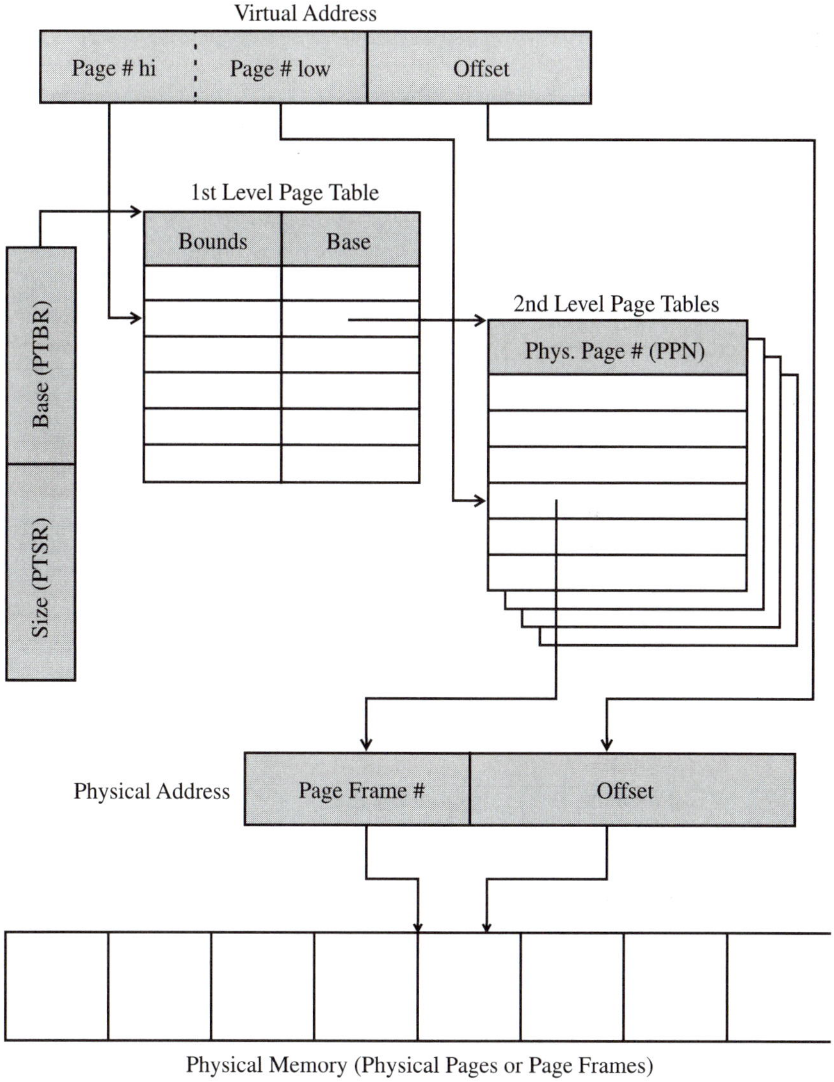

Figure 17.8 Multilevel paging memory hardware. Bounds checking is not shown, but takes place on references to both first- and second-level page tables.

Table entries can also record information about how a segment or page has been accessed. A common case is the **reference** bit (also called the **use** bit). If there is a reference bit in the PTE or STE, then each time a memory location in the page or segment is accessed, the bit is set. Another common case is the **modify** bit (also called the **dirty** bit). This bit is set each time a memory location in the segment or page is written. These bits are used by the operating system to decide which pages or segments to keep in physical memory and which to throw out when more space is needed.

SUMMARY

Virtual memory provides an abstraction for a program's simple notion of an address space. A combination of hardware and software provides this illusion. The physical memory can be a different size than the virtual memory assumes. Except for the base and bounds memory management, an executing program does not need to be entirely resident in the physical memory. The operating system can place portions of programs into the physical memory, keeping the remainder on a disk. The need for relocation of code is eliminated with virtual memory. Access to programs and data can be controlled by the operating system. Access can be restrictive or open, allowing sharing of code or data among programs.

PROBLEMS

1. What is the difference between a uniprogrammed system and a multiprogrammed system?
2. Can a program's virtual address space be smaller than physical memory in a computer system? Explain.
3. Can a program's virtual address space be larger than physical memory in a computer system? Explain.
4. What is relocation? On a uniprogrammed system, when is relocation done?
5. On a system with base and bounds memory management, what happens if the physical memory size is smaller than a program requires?
6. In a base and bounds memory management system, the base and bounds are kept in registers. When would the operating system modify these registers?
7. What does the operating system need to do to set up the execution of a program on a system with base and bounds memory management?
8. On a system with base and bounds memory management, why is it a better idea that the bounds be a virtual address instead of a physical address?
9. On a system with base and bounds memory management, should the base and bounds be kept in physical memory or in registers within the processor? Explain.
10. On a system with segmentation-based memory management, should the segment table base register and segment table size register be kept in physical memory or in registers within the processor? Explain.
11. Will a system with segmentation-based memory management be capable of having segments from more than one program be resident in physical memory at one time? Explain.
12. Consider a memory management scheme that uses paging. If virtual addresses are 32 bits and page frames are 4 Kbytes, what is the maximum number of virtual pages a program could have?

13. Consider a memory management scheme that uses paging. If virtual addresses are 32 bits, and pages are 8 Kbytes, how many bits within the virtual address are used to form an offset within a page?

14. What does the operating system need to do to set up the execution of a program on a system with paging for its memory management?

15. Compare the diagrams in Figures 17.7 and 17.8. Describe the difference between paged segmentation and multilevel paging.

APPENDIX

A

RESERVED WORDS

FROM SASM INSTRUCTIONS

at_my_code	fpadd	la	put_ch
bez	fpdiv	land	put_fp
bgez	fpmul	llsh	put_i
bgz	fpsub	lnot	put_str
blez	get_ch	lor	rash
blz	iadd	lxor	rlsh
bnz	idivi	m	rrot
br	imult	move	
compare	ineg	moveb	
compareb	irem	movesx	
done	isub	movezx	

FROM PENTIUM INSTRUCTION NAMES

aaa	bts	cwd	fchs	fiadd
aad	cbw	cwde	fclex	ficom
aam	cdq	daa	fcom	ficomp
aas	clc	das	fcomp	fidiv
adc	cld	dec	fcompp	fidivr
add	cli	div	fcos	fild
and	clts	enter	fdecstp	fimul
arpl	cmc	esc	fdisi	fincstp
bound	cmp	f2xm1	fdiv	finit
bsf	cmps	fabs	fdivp	fist
bsr	cmpsb	fadd	fdivr	fistp
bswap	cmpsd	faddp	fdivrp	fisub
bt	cmpsw	fbld	feni	fisubr
btr	cmpxchg	fbstp	ffree	fld

fld1	fstp	jnae	loopw	ror
fldcw	fstsw	jnb	loopz	sahf
fldenv	fsub	jnbe	loopzd	sal
fldenvd	fsubp	jnc	loopzw	sar
fldenvw	fsubr	jne	lsl	sbb
fldl2e	fsubrp	jng	lss	scas
fldl2t	ftst	jnge	ltr	scasb
fldlg2	fucom	jnl	mov	scasd
fldln2	fucomp	jnle	movs	scasw
fldpi	fucompp	jno	movsb	seta
fldz	fwait	jnp	movsd	setae
fmul	fxam	jns	movsw	setb
fmulp	fxch	jnz	movsx	setbe
fnclex	fxtract	jo	movzx	setc
fndisi	fyl2x	jp	mul	sete
fneni	fyl2xp1	jpe	neg	setg
fninit	hlt	jpo	nop	setge
fnop	idiv	js	not	setl
fnsave	imul	jz	or	setle
fnsaved	in	lahf	out	setna
fnsavew	inc	lar	outs	setnae
fnstcw	ins	lds	outsb	setnb
fnstenv	insb	lea	outsd	setnbe
fnstenvd	insd	leave	outsw	setnc
fnstenvw	insw	les	pop	setne
fnstsw	int	lfs	popa	setng
fpatan	into	lgs	popad	setnge
fprem	invd	lgdt	pop	setnl
fprem1	invlpg	lidt	popf	setnle
fptan	iret	lldt	push	setno
frndint	iretd	lmsw	pusha	setnp
frstor	iretdf	lock	pushad	setns
frstord	iretf	lods	pushd	setnz
frstorw	ja	lodsb	pushf	seto
fsave	jae	lodsd	pushfd	setp
fsaved	jb	lodsw	pushw	setpe
fsavew	jbe	loop	rcl	setpo
fscale	jc	loopd	rcr	sets
fsetpm	jcxz	loope	rep	setz
fsin	je	looped	repe	sgdt
fsincos	jecxz	loopew	repne	shl
fsqrt	jg	loopne	repnz	shld
fst	jge	loopned	repz	shr
fstcw	jl	loopnew	ret	shrd
fstenv	jle	loopnz	retf	sidt
fstenvd	jmp	loopnzd	retn	sldt
fstenvw	jna	loopnzw	rol	smsw

stc	stosb	sub	wait	xlat
std	stosd	test	wbinvd	xlatb
sti	stosw	verr	xadd	xor
stos	str	verw	xchg	

FROM MACRO EXPANSION, OPERATORS AND DIRECTIVES

Reserved words not listed are those that start with the characters '@', '.', or containing the character '?'.

addr	elseifnb	ifb	near16	struc
alias	elseifndef	ifdef	offset	struct
assume	end	ifdif	opattr	substr
basic	endif	ifdifi	option	subtitle
byte	endm	ife	org	subttl
c	endp	ifidn	page	sword
catstr	ends	ifidni	pascal	syscall
comm	eq	ifnb	popcontext	tbyte
comment	equ	ifndef	proc	textequ
db	even	include	proto	this
dd	exitm	includelib	ptr	title
doseg	extern	instr	public	type
dq	externdef	invoke	purge	typedef
dt	extrn	irp	pushcontext	union
dup	far	irpc	qword	vararg
dw	far16	label	real4	while
dword	for	le	real10	width
echo	forc	length	record	word
else	fortran	lengthof	repeat	
elseif	fword	local	rept	
elseif1	ge	low	sbyte	
elseif2	goto	lowword	sdword	
elseifb	group	lroffset	seg	
elseifdef	gt	lt	segment	
elseifdif	high	macro	short	
elseifdifi	highword	mask	size	
elseife	if	name	sizeof	
elseifidn	if1	ne	sizestr	
elseifidni	if2	near	stdcall	

FROM REGISTER NAMES

AH	CS	DX	SI
AL	CX	EAX	SP
AX	DH	EBP	SS
BH	DI	EBX	ST
BL	DL	ECX	TR3
BP	DR0	EDI	TR4
BX	DR1	EDX	TR5
CH	DR2	ES	TR6
CL	DR3	ESI	TR7
CR0	DR6	ESP	
CR2	DR7	FS	
CR3	DS	GS	

APPENDIX

B

SASM

SASM Instruction		Operation or Equivalent C Statement	Notes
`la`	`x, y`	`x = &y;`	
`move`	`x, y`	`x = y;`	
`moveb`	`x, y`	`x = y;`	both `x` and `y` are characters
`movesx`	`x, y`	8-bit `y` is sign extended to 32 bits and placed in variable `x`	
`movezx`	`x, y`	8-bit `y` is zero extended to 32 bits and placed in variable `x`	
`ineg`	`x`	`x = -x;`	sets condition codes
`iadd`	`x, y`	`x = x + y;`	sets condition codes
`isub`	`x, y`	`x = x - y;`	sets condition codes
`imult`	`x, y`	`x = x * y;`	
`idivi`	`x, y`	`x = x / y;`	
`irem`	`x, y`	`x = x % y;`	
`land`	`x, y`	`x = x & y;`	bitwise logical and
`lnot`	`x`	`x = ~x;`	bitwise logical not
`lor`	`x, y`	`x = x | y;`	bitwise logical or
`lxor`	`x, y`	`x = x ^ y;`	bitwise logical xor
`llsh`	`x, y`	logical left shift of `y` by 1 place; result is placed into `x`	`x` and `y` are 32-bit variables
`rash`	`x, y`	arithmetic right shift of `y` by 1 place; result is placed into `x`	`x` and `y` are 32-bit variables
`rlsh`	`x, y`	logical right shift of `y` by 1 place; result is placed into `x`	`x` and `y` are 32-bit variables
`rrot`	`x, y`	rotate right of `y` by 1 place; result is placed into `x`	`x` and `y` are 32-bit variables

SASM Instruction		Operation or Equivalent C Statement	Notes
`compare`	`x, y`		does the operation (`x - y`) to set condition codes
`compareb`	`x, y`		does the operation (`x - y`) to set condition codes; `x` and `y` are 8-bit variables
`br`	`label`	unconditional branch	goto label
`bgz`	`label`	branch if greater than 0	if ZF=SF=0, goto label
`bgez`	`label`	branch if greater than or equal to 0	if ZF=0 or SF=0, goto label
`blz`	`label`	branch if less than 0	if SF=1, goto label
`blez`	`label`	branch if less than or equal to 0	if SF=1 or ZF=1, goto label
`bez`	`label`	branch if equal to 0	if ZF=1, goto label
`bnz`	`label`	branch if not equal to 0	if ZF=0, goto label
`get_ch`	`x`	get single character in `x`	
`put_ch`	`x`	print single character in `x`	
`put_fp`	`x`	print floating point value in `x`	
`put_i`	`x`	print integer value in `x`	
`put_str`	`label`	print null terminated string starting at `label`	
`fpadd`	`x, y`	`x = x + y;`	`x` and `y` are IEEE single-precision floating point representations
`fpsub`	`x, y`	`x = x - y;`	
`fpmul`	`x, y`	`x = x * y;`	
`fpdiv`	`x, y`	`x = x / y;`	

APPENDIX C

MACHINE LANGUAGE SPECIFICATION

The following table describes the machine code for a subset of Pentium instructions. The tables that follow further specify the abbreviations used in this table and addressing modes.

Mnemonic	Pentium Machine Language	
	Operands	**Machine Language Encoding**
add	reg, r/m	03 /r
	r/m, reg	01 /r
	r/m, immed	81 /0 id
cmp	reg, r/m	3b /r
	r/m, reg	39 /r
	r/m, immed	81 /7 id
	r/m8, immed8	80 /7 ib
	r/m, immed8	83 /7 ib
dec	reg	48 + rd
	r/m	ff /1
div	r/m	f7 /6
idiv	r/m	f7 /7
imul	r/m	f7 /5
	reg, r/m	0f af /4
	reg, r/m, immed	69 /r id
inc	reg	40 + rd
	r/m	ff /0
mul	eax, r/m	f7 /4
neg	r/m	f7 /3
sub	reg, r/m	2b /r
	r/m, reg	29 /r
	r/m, immed	81 /5 id
and	reg, r/m	23 /r
	r/m, reg	21 /r
	r/m, immed	81 /4 id
not	r/m	f7 /2
or	reg, r/m	0b /r
	r/m, reg	09 /r
	r/m, immed	81 /1 id

Mnemonic	Pentium Machine Language	
	Operands	**Machine Language Encoding**
test	r/m, reg	85 /r
	r/m, immed	f7 /0 id
xor	reg, r/m	33 /r
	r/m, reg	31 /r
	r/m, immed	31 /6 id
rol	r/m, 1	d1 /0
	r/m, immed8	c1 /0 ib
ror	r/m, 1	d1 /1
	r/m, immed8	c1 /1 ib
sal	r/m, 1	d1 /4
	r/m, immed8	c1 /4 ib
sar	r/m, 1	d1 /7
	r/m, immed8	c1 /7 ib
shl	r/m, 1	d1 /4
	r/m, immed8	c1 /4 ib
shr	r/m, 1	d1 /5
	r/m, immed8	c1 /5 ib
lea	reg, m	8d /r
mov	reg, r/m	8b /r
	r/m, reg	89 /r
	r/m, immed	c7 /0 id
	reg, immed	b8 + rd id
movsx	reg, r/m8	0f be /r
movzx	reg, r/m8	0f b6 /r
pop	reg	58 + rd
	reg	50 + rd
push	r/m	ff /6
	immed	68 id
fadd	ST, ST(i)	d8 c0 + i
	ST(i), ST	dc c0 + i
	m32	d8 /0
	m64	dc /0
faddp	ST(i), ST	de c0 + i
fchs		d9 e0
fcom	ST(i)	d8 d0 + i
	m32	d8 /2
	m64	dc /2
fdiv	ST, ST(i)	d8 f0 + i
	ST(i), ST	dc f8 + i
	m32	d8 /6
	m64	dc /6
fdivp	ST(i), ST	de f8 + i
fdivr	ST, ST(i)	d8 f8 + i
	ST(i), ST	dc f0 + i
	m32	d8 /7
	m64	dc /7
fdivrp	ST(i), ST	de f0 + i
finit		9b db e3
fld	ST(i)	d9 c0 + i
	m32	d9 /0
	m64	dd /0

Mnemonic	Operands	Pentium Machine Language Machine Language Encoding
fldz		d9 ee
fmul	ST, ST(i)	d8 c8 + i
	ST(i), ST	dc c8 + i
	m32	d8 /1
	m64	dc /1
fmulp	ST(i), ST	de c8 + i
frndint		d9 fc
fst	ST(i)	dd d0 + i
	m32	d9 /2
	m64	dd /2
fstp	ST(i)	dd d8 + i
	m32	d9 /3
	m64	dd /3
fstsw	AX	9b df e0
fsub	ST, ST(i)	d8 e0 + i
	ST(i), ST	dc e8 + i
	m32	d8 /4
	m64	dc /4
fsubp	ST(i), ST	de e8 + i
fsubr	ST, ST(i)	d8 e8 + i
	ST(i), ST	dc e0 + i
	m32	d8 /5
	m64	dc /5
ftst		d9 e4
fxam		d9 e5
je / jz	rel32	0f 84 *cd*
jg / jnle	rel32	0f 8f *cd*
jge / jnl	rel32	0f 8d *cd*
jl / jnge	rel32	0f 8c *cd*
jle / jng	rel32	0f 8e *cd*
jmp	rel32	e9 *cd*
	r/m	ff /4
jne / jnz	rel32	0f 85 *cd*
jns	rel32	0f 89 *cd*
jo	rel32	0f 80 *cd*
js	rel32	0f 88 *cd*
call	rel32	e8 *cd*
	r/m	ff /2
ret	immed	c2 iw
cli		fa
sti		fb

Abbreviation	Explanation	
r/m	a doubleword register or memory operand, addressing mode given by ModR/M byte	
r/m8	one of the 8-bit registers	
reg	one of the 32-bit registers	
immed	32-bit immediate operand	
immed8	8-bit immediate operand	
rel32	32-bit offset	
/r	the ModR/M byte contains both a register operand and an r/m operand	
/0	Reg field of ModR/M byte is 000	
/1	Reg field of ModR/M byte is 001	
/2	Reg field of ModR/M byte is 010	
/3	Reg field of ModR/M byte is 011	
/4	Reg field of ModR/M byte is 100	
/5	Reg field of ModR/M byte is 101	
/6	Reg field of ModR/M byte is 110	
/7	Reg field of ModR/M byte is 111	
+ rd	register	amount added
	EAX	0
	ECX	1
	EDX	2
	EBX	3
	ESP	4
	EBP	5
	ESI	6
	EDI	7
id	32-bit immediate	
iw	16-bit immediate	
ib	8-bit immediate	
+ i	i given by operand in ST(i)	
cd	32-bit code offset	
ST	top element of FPU register stack	
ST(i)	FPU register stack element, i away from ST	

ModR/M Byte Specification			
Addressing Mode	**Mod**	**R/M**	**Notes**
[EAX]	00	000	
[ECX]		001	
[EDX]		010	
[EBX]		011	
[?][?]		100	requires SIB byte, following ModR/M byte
disp32		101	32-bit displacement follows, to be added to the index
[ESI]		110	
[EDI]		111	
disp8[EAX]	01	000	8-bit displacement follows, to be sign extended and added to the index
disp8[ECX]		001	8-bit displacement follows, to be sign extended and added to the index
disp8[EDX]		010	8-bit displacement follows, to be sign extended and added to the index
disp8[EBX]		011	8-bit displacement follows, to be sign extended and added to the index
disp8[?][?]		100	8-bit displacement follows SIB byte, to be sign extended and added to the index
disp8[EBP]		101	8-bit displacement follows, to be sign extended and added to the index
disp8[ESI]		110	8-bit displacement follows, to be sign extended and added to the index
disp8[EDI]		111	8-bit displacement follows, to be sign extended and added to the index
disp32[EAX]	10	000	32-bit displacement follows
disp32[ECX]		001	32-bit displacement follows
disp32[EDX]		010	32-bit displacement follows
disp32[EBX]		011	32-bit displacement follows
disp32[?][?]		100	32-bit displacement follows SIB byte, to be added to the index
disp32[EBP]		101	32-bit displacement follows
disp32[ESI]		110	32-bit displacement follows
disp32[EDI]		111	32-bit displacement follows
EAX/AX/AL	11	000	
ECX/CX/CL		001	
EDX/DX/DL		010	
EBX/BX/BL		011	
ESP/SP/AH		100	
EBP/BP/CH		101	
ESI/SI/DH		110	
EDI/DI/BH		111	

ModR/M Byte Specification								
Reg/Opcode Field								
r8 (/r) r32 (/r)	AL EAX 000	CL ECX 001	DL EDX 010	BL EBX 011	AH ESP 100	CH EBP 101	DH ESI 110	BH EDI 111

SIB Byte	
Base Register	**Base Field**
eax	000
ecx	001
edx	010
ebx	011
esp	100
? or ebp	101
esi	110
edi	111

SIB Byte		
Scaled Index	**SS**	**Index**
[EAX]	00	000
[ECX]		001
[EDX]		010
[EBX]		011
none		100
[EBP]		101
[ESI]		110
[EDI]		111
[EAX * 2]	01	000
[ECX * 2]		001
[EDX * 2]		010
[EBX * 2]		011
none		100
[EBP * 2]		101
[ESI * 2]		110
[EDI * 2]		111
[EAX * 4]	10	000
[ECX * 4]		001
[EDX * 4]		010
[EBX * 4]		011
none		100
[EBP * 4]		101
[ESI * 4]		110
[EDI * 4]		111
[EAX * 8]	11	000
[ECX * 8]		001
[EDX * 8]		010
[EBX * 8]		011
none		100
[EBP * 8]		101
[ESI * 8]		110
[EDI * 8]		111

INDEX

D

I

J

K

L

M

Q

R